national
STATISTICS

Social Trends

No. 37

2007 edition

Editors: Abigail Self

Linda Zealey

Office for National Statistics

palgrave
macmillan

First published 2007 by
PALGRAVE MACMILLAN
Houndmills, Basingstoke, Hampshire RG21 6XS and 175 Fifth Avenue, New York, NY 10010, USA
Companies and representatives throughout the world.

PALGRAVE MACMILLAN is the global academic imprint of the Palgrave Macmillan division of St. Martin's Press, LLC and of Palgrave Macmillan Ltd. Macmillan® is a registered trademark in the United States, United Kingdom and other countries. Palgrave is a registered trademark in the European Union and other countries.

ISBN 978-1-4039-9394-6
ISSN 0306-7742

This book is printed on paper suitable for recycling and made from fully managed and sustained forest sources. Logging, pulping and manufacturing processes are expected to conform to the environmental regulations of the country of origin.
A catalogue record for this book is available from the British Library.

10 9 8 7 6 5 4 3 2 1
16 15 14 13 12 11 10 09 08 07

Printed and bound in Great Britain by
Hobbs the Printers Ltd,
Totton, Hampshire.

A National Statistics publication

National Statistics are produced to high professional standards set out in the National Statistics Code of Practice. They are produced free from political influence.

About the Office for National Statistics

The Office for National Statistics (ONS) is the government agency responsible for compiling, analysing and disseminating economic, social and demographic statistics about the United Kingdom. It also administers the statutory registration of births, marriages and deaths in England and Wales.

The Director of ONS is also the National Statistician and the Registrar General for England and Wales.

Contact points

For enquiries about this publication, contact the Editor.

Tel: 020 7533 5778
E-mail: social.trends@ons.gsi.gov.uk

For general enquiries, contact the National Statistics Customer Contact Centre.

Tel: 0845 601 3034 (minicom: 01633 812399)
E-mail: info@statistics.gsi.gov.uk
Fax: 01633 652747
Post: Room 1015, Government Buildings,
        Cardiff Road, Newport NP10 8XG

You can also find National Statistics on the Internet at:
www.statistics.gov.uk

Publication orders

To order a copy of *Social Trends* or any other Palgrave Macmillan publication call 01256 302611 or order online at:
www.palgrave.com/ons

Contents

List of figures and tables

Numbers in brackets refer to similar items appearing in *Social Trends 36*

3: Education and training

6: Expenditure

Page

9: Crime and justice

10: Housing

11: Environment

Page

13: Lifestyles and social participation

List of contributors

Authors:	Simon Burtenshaw
	Jenny Church
	Aleks Collingwood Bakeo
	Steve Howell
	Ian Macrory
	Nazma Nessa
	Kwabena Owusu-Agyemang
	Chris Randall
	Matthew Richardson
Production manager:	Mario Alemanno
Production team:	Lola Akinrodoye
	Julie Crowley
	Usuf Islam
	Shiva Satkunam
	Steve Whyman

Acknowledgements

The Editors would like to thank all their colleagues in contributing Departments and other organisations for their generous support and helpful comments, without which this edition of *Social Trends* would not have been possible. Thanks also go to the following for their help in the production process:

Data:	Core Table Unit
Design and artwork:	Michelle Franco
	Andy Leach
Publishing management:	Phil Lewin
Index	ONS Library and Information Service
Maps:	Jeremy Brocklehurst
	Alistair Dent
	Deborah Rhodes
Reviewers:	Paul Allin
	Jenny Church
	Francis Jones
	Nina Mill
Photographer:	Dean Beevor

Introduction

This is the 37th edition of *Social Trends* – one of the flagship publications from the Office for National Statistics (ONS). *Social Trends* draws together statistics from a wide range of government departments and other organisations to paint a broad picture of our society today, and how it has been changing.

Social Trends is aimed at a wide audience: policy makers in the public and private sectors; service providers; people in local government; journalists and other commentators; academics and students; schools; and the general public.

This year several changes have been made to *Social Trends*. The number of charts and tables has been rebalanced across the chapters to provide more even coverage for each topic and the article which previously accompanied the themed chapters has been removed. The changes are part of an ongoing programme to ensure *Social Trends* continues to meet the needs of its users whilst also delivering value for money. The editorial team welcomes views on these changes and suggestions on how *Social Trends* could be improved. Please write to the Editor at the address shown below with your comments.

New material and sources

To preserve topicality, over half of the tables and figures in the 13 chapters of *Social Trends 37* are new compared with the previous edition. These draw on the most up-to-date available data. Items which provide updates to those included in *Social Trends 36* are referenced in the list of figures and tables.

In all chapters the source of the data is given below each figure and table, and where this is a survey the name of the survey is also included. A list of contact telephone numbers, including the contact number for each chapter author and a list of useful website addresses, can be found on pages 183 to 189. A list of further reading is also given, beginning on page 190. Regional and other sub-national breakdowns of much of the information in *Social Trends* can be found in the ONS publication *Regional Trends*.

Definitions and terms

Symbols and conventions used in this publication can be found on page 200 and the Appendix gives definitions and general background information, particularly on administrative and legal structures and frameworks. Anyone seeking to understand the figures and tables in detail will find it helpful to read the corresponding entries in the Appendix. An index to this edition starts on page 220.

Availability on electronic media

Social Trends 37 is available electronically on the National Statistics website, www.statistics.gov.uk/socialtrends. The full report is available as an interactive PDF where excel spreadsheets containing the data used in the publication can be accessed and downloaded by clicking on the relevant chart or table. There are also links from the web version of *Social Trends* to topic-based summaries, which contain a key chart and short interpretative commentary.

Contact

Abigail Self

Office for National Statistics
Social Economic Micro Analysis and Reporting Division
Room: 2.164
Government Buildings
Cardiff Road
Newport
Gwent
NP10 8XG

Email: social.trends@ons.gov.uk

Population

- There were 60.2 million people living in the UK in 2005, more than ever before. (Table 1.1)

- In 2005, 16 per cent of the UK population were aged 65 and over, a rise from 13 per cent in 1971. Over the same period, the proportion of under-16s fell, from 25 per cent to 19 per cent. (Page 3)

- There were more females than males living in the UK in 2005 – 30.7 million compared with 29.5 million, although on average 105 boys are born each year for every 100 girls. (Table 1.2)

- The Total Fertility Rate was 1.79 children per woman in the UK in 2005, having increased for four consecutive years from a record low of 1.63 children per woman in 2001. (Page 6)

- In 2005, Scotland gained 14,500 people from net migration within the UK, and Wales gained 5,900 people. England experienced a net loss of 19,900 people and Northern Ireland, a net loss of 500 people. (Table 1.11)

- The UK received 30,800 applications for asylum (including dependants) in 2005, a fall of around one-quarter compared with 2004. (Page 10)

Chapter 1

Information on the size and structure of the population is essential to understanding many aspects of society such as the labour market and household composition. The number of births and deaths, and the number of people entering and leaving the country all affect the size, sex and age structure, and the geography of the population. Changes in demographic patterns influence social structures and have implications for both public policy and commercial decisions. Such decisions include those on the provision of health, education, transport, social services as well as those for new products and the location of retail outlets.

Population profile

The population of the UK has grown steadily since 1971 to reach 60.2 million in 2005 (Table 1.1), an increase of 4.3 million people. During this period the populations of England, Wales and Northern Ireland all grew but the population of Scotland declined by 0.1 million people.

Table 1.1

Population[1]

United Kingdom
Millions

	1971	1981	1991	2001	2005	2011	2021
United Kingdom	55.9	56.4	57.4	59.1	60.2	61.9	64.7
England	46.4	46.8	47.9	49.5	50.4	52.0	54.6
Wales	2.7	2.8	2.9	2.9	3.0	3.0	3.2
Scotland	5.2	5.2	5.1	5.1	5.1	5.1	5.1
Northern Ireland	1.5	1.5	1.6	1.7	1.7	1.8	1.8

1 Mid-year estimates for 1971 to 2005; 2004-based projections for 2011 and 2021. See Appendix, Part 1: Population estimates and projections.

Source: Office for National Statistics; Government Actuary's Department; General Register Office for Scotland; Northern Ireland Statistics and Research Agency

Table 1.2

Population:[1] by sex and age

United Kingdom
Thousands

	Under 16	16–24	25–34	35–44	45–54	55–64	65–74	75 and over	All ages
Males									
1971	7,318	3,730	3,530	3,271	3,354	3,123	1,999	842	27,167
1981	6,439	4,114	4,036	3,409	3,121	2,967	2,264	1,063	27,412
1991	5,976	3,800	4,432	3,950	3,287	2,835	2,272	1,358	27,909
2001	6,077	3,284	4,215	4,382	3,856	3,090	2,308	1,621	28,832
2005	5,946	3,613	3,933	4,579	3,817	3,448	2,389	1,754	29,479
2011	5,744	3,768	4,074	4,293	4,301	3,598	2,652	2,008	30,438
2021	5,821	3,436	4,487	4,133	4,201	4,042	3,158	2,664	31,943
Females									
1971	6,938	3,626	3,441	3,241	3,482	3,465	2,765	1,802	28,761
1981	6,104	3,966	3,975	3,365	3,148	3,240	2,931	2,218	28,946
1991	5,709	3,691	4,466	3,968	3,296	2,971	2,795	2,634	29,530
2001	5,786	3,220	4,260	4,465	3,920	3,186	2,640	2,805	30,281
2005	5,652	3,470	3,964	4,667	3,896	3,577	2,659	2,846	30,730
2011	5,487	3,563	4,050	4,358	4,412	3,755	2,898	2,931	31,454
2021	5,578	3,257	4,347	4,146	4,295	4,244	3,452	3,465	32,784

1 Mid-year estimates for 1971 to 2005; 2004-based projections for 2011 and 2021. See Appendix, Part 1: Population estimates and projections.

Source: Office for National Statistics; Government Actuary's Department; General Register Office for Scotland; Northern Ireland Statistics and Research Agency

The 2004-based population projections suggest that the UK population will exceed 65 million in 2023, 67 million by 2031 and will continue rising slowly to 2074, the end of the current projection period. The projected rise between 2004 and 2031 represents an increase of 7.2 million people. Fifty-seven per cent of this increase is projected to be net migration and 43 per cent is attributable to net natural change (the difference between births and deaths). However the components of the population increase are not independent of each other. Some births are to migrants therefore an even greater proportion of population change will be attributable to migration than to natural change.

Projected trends differ for England, Wales, Scotland and Northern Ireland. Between 2004 and 2031 the population in England is predicted to increase by 13 per cent to 56.8 million and by 10 per cent to 3.3 million in Wales. Beyond 2031 both populations are projected to continue growing: very slowly in Wales but at a steady pace in England. The population of Scotland is expected to increase by around 50,000 (1 per cent) until 2019, and then start to fall again, while the Northern Ireland population is projected to reach a peak of 1.86 million (9 per cent increase) by the early 2030s and then start to decline.

Despite differences in demographic changes across the UK, the population of England, Wales, Scotland and Northern Ireland as proportions of the UK population varied little between 1971 and 2005. In 2005 England represented approximately 84 per cent of the population, Scotland 8 per cent, Wales 5 per cent and Northern Ireland 3 per cent. Similar proportions are shown in the projections to 2031.

In the UK in 2005, there were more females than males – 30.7 million and 29.5 million respectively (Table 1.2). However, more boys than girls have been born each year since 1922 (the first year for which UK figures are available). In 2005, 370,000 boys were born compared with under 353,000 girls. In the same year, there were between 14,000 and 25,000 more males than females at each age from birth through to age 20. Between the ages of 20 and 30, the number of young men relative to young women decreased. This is partly because there are different levels of migration among males and females in the 15 to 24 age group. Higher death rates from accidents and suicide among young men compared to young women have also contributed to the fall in the number of young men in their 20s, although the number of deaths at these ages was low.

The population of the UK is ageing. Over the last 35 years, there has been a decline in the younger population and an increase in the number of those aged 65 and over. In 1971, 25 per cent of the population (14.3 million) were aged under 16 compared with 13 per cent of the population (7.4 million) who were aged 65 and over. By 2005 the proportion of people aged under 16

had fallen to 19 per cent of the population (11.6 million), a decline of 2.7 million people. In comparison the proportion of those aged 65 and over had risen to 16 per cent of the population (9.6 million), an increase of 2.2 million people. Projections indicate that by 2014, the number of people aged 65 and over are expected to exceed those aged under 16 for the first time. This trend is expected to continue and by 2031, 17 per cent of the population are projected to be aged under 16 and 23 per cent aged 65 and over. Between 2004 and 2005, the number of people aged 85 and over increased by 64,000 (6 per cent) to reach a record 1.2 million, and made up almost 2 per cent of the population.

Past trends in births, deaths and migration have led to an ageing UK population. This is illustrated by the population pyramids for Great Britain for 1821 (when age was first collected in the Census) and 2005 (Figure 1.3). In 1821 the population pyramid shows a sharp decline in population with age and was much larger at the bottom than at the top, whereas the 2005 pyramid

Figure 1.3

Population: by sex and age, 1821 and 2005

Great Britain

Millions

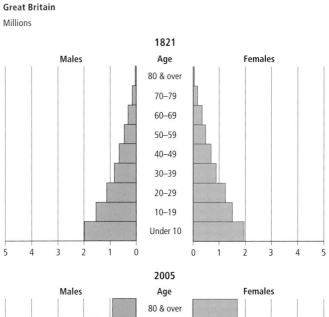

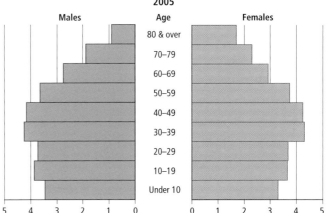

Source: Office for National Statistics; General Register Office for Scotland

shows a more gradual decline with increases within the 30 to 39 and 40 to 49 age groups. These differences are mainly as a result of changes in both survival rates and fertility rates between the two years compared. As a proportion of all ages, in 1821 there were more children under 10 than in 2005, which illustrates a higher fertility rate. However poor survival rates resulted in the population decreasing at each ten-year age band with few surviving to the older ages. By 2005 proportionally far fewer children were born than in 1821, which combined with better survival rates and higher net in-migration meant that the largest age groups in 2005 were not the youngest, but the young adult population and those in their 30s and 40s.

The ageing of the population can be attributed to a number of factors. These include decreasing fertility rates that began towards the end of the 19th century and a fall in infant mortality rates from the early 20th century, which increased the number of people surviving to adulthood. During the last three decades of the 20th century, population ageing was also attributed to falling mortality rates at older ages.

An ageing population is a characteristic common to many of the 25 member states that form the European Union (EU-25). In 2005 Italy had the largest percentage of people aged 65 and over (19.5 per cent), followed by Germany (18.6 per cent) and Greece (18.1 per cent) (Table 1.4). Ireland had the lowest proportion, at 11.2 per cent. In the UK, 16.0 per cent of the population were aged 65 and over, just under the EU-25 average of 16.7 per cent. For children aged under 15, the UK had a higher than average proportion: 18.1 per cent compared with the EU-25 average of 16.2 per cent. This was similar to the Netherlands (18.5 per cent), Malta and Sweden (both 17.6 per cent). The country with the largest proportion of people aged under 15 was Ireland at 20.7 per cent – nearly twice the proportion of people aged 65 and over. In 2005, 16 of the EU-25 member states had larger populations aged under 15 than populations aged 65 and over.

Historically the population of Great Britain has predominantly consisted of people from a White British ethnic background. The pattern of migration, particularly to England since the 1950s, has produced a number of distinct ethnic minority groups within the general population. The 2001 Census provides the most comprehensive breakdown of the population of Great Britain by ethnicity. It shows that in 2001 the majority of the population (88.2 per cent) were White British (see classification of ethnic groups box on page 5). The remaining 11.8 per cent of the population (6.7 million people) belonged to other ethnic groups.

Table **1.4**

Population: by age, EU comparison, 2005

Percentages

	Under 15	15–64	65 and over	All people (=100%) (thousands)		Under 15	15–64	65 and over	All people (=100%) (thousands)
Austria	16.1	67.9	16.0	8,207	Luxembourg	18.7	67.0	14.3	455
Belgium	17.2	65.6	17.2	10,446	Malta	17.6	69.0	13.3	403
Cyprus	19.2	68.9	11.9	749	Netherlands	18.5	67.5	14.0	16,306
Czech Republic	14.9	71.0	14.0	10,221	Poland	16.7	70.1	13.1	38,174
Denmark	18.8	66.2	15.0	5,411	Portugal	15.6	67.3	17.0	10,529
Estonia[1]	15.4	68.0	16.5	1,348	Slovakia	17.1	71.3	11.6	5,385
Finland	17.5	66.7	15.9	5,237	Slovenia	14.4	70.3	15.3	1,998
France	18.7	65.1	16.2	62,371	Spain	14.5	68.7	16.8	43,038
Germany	14.5	66.9	18.6	82,501	Sweden	17.6	65.2	17.2	9,011
Greece	14.4	67.5	18.1	11,083	United Kingdom	18.1	65.9	16.0	60,060
Hungary	15.6	68.7	15.6	10,098	EU-25	16.2	67.1	16.7	461,331
Ireland	20.7	68.1	11.2	4,109					
Italy	14.1	66.4	19.5	58,462					
Latvia	14.8	68.7	16.5	2,306					
Lithuania	17.1	67.8	15.1	3,425					

1 'All people' includes data for individuals where age was not defined.

Source: Eurostat; Office for National Statistics; Statistics Estonia

Classification of ethnic groups

Membership of an ethnic group is something that is subjectively meaningful to the person concerned. Ethnic group questions are designed to ask people which group they see themselves belonging to. This means the information collected is not based on objective, quantifiable information like age or sex.

There are two levels to the National Statistics classification of ethnic groups. Level 1 has five main ethnic groups: White, Mixed, Asian or Asian British, Black or Black British, Chinese or other ethnic group. Level 2, the preferred approach, provides a broader breakdown than level 1 and is used in this chapter (see Appendix, Part 1: Classification of ethnic groups).

Of these, the largest was the Other White group (2.5 per cent), followed by Indians (1.8 per cent), Pakistanis (1.3 per cent), White Irish (1.2 per cent), those of Mixed ethnic backgrounds (1.2 per cent), Black Caribbeans (1.0 per cent), Black Africans (0.8 per cent) and Bangladeshis (0.5 per cent). The remaining ethnic minority groups each accounted for less than 0.5 per cent of the population of Great Britain.

Most ethnic minority groups in Great Britain have a younger age structure than the White British population (Figure 1.5).

Figure **1.5**

Population: by ethnic group[1] and age, 2001

Great Britain
Percentages

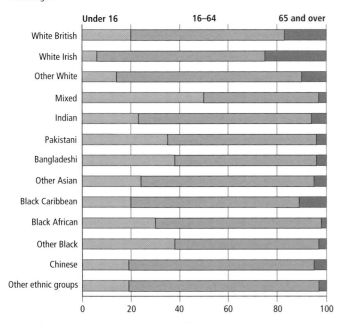

1 See Appendix, Part 1: Classification of ethnic groups.

Source: Census 2001, Office for National Statistics; Census 2001, General Register Office for Scotland

In 2001 the Mixed population had the youngest profile, with 50 per cent aged under 16. Most of these (79 per cent) were born in the UK and are the children of inter-ethnic partnerships, predominantly between first or second generation migrants and White British people. The Bangladeshi, Other Black and Pakistani groups also had young age structures; 38 per cent of both the Bangladeshi and the Other Black group were aged under 16, as were 35 per cent of Pakistanis. This was almost double the proportion of the White British population, where one in five (20 per cent) were under the age of 16. The age structures reflect past immigration and fertility patterns. Migration waves early in the 20th century included economic migrants from Ireland, the Caribbean and India, followed by migrants from Pakistan and Bangladesh. Migration from Africa and China increased in the 1980s. The migration patterns of the early 20th century are partly responsible for the White Irish group having the oldest age structure, with 25 per cent aged 65 and over. The second largest proportion of people aged 65 and over were the White British (17 per cent), followed by Black Caribbeans (11 per cent), Other White (10 per cent), South Asians (3 to 7 per cent) and Africans (2 per cent).

Population change

The rate of population change over time depends upon two interrelated factors; the net natural change and the net effect of people migrating to and from the country. In the 1950s and 1960s natural change was the main factor in population growth in the UK. From the 1980s onwards, net migration had a growing influence, rising from an average of 5,000 net in-migrants a year between 1981 and 1991, to an average 68,000 net in-migrants a year between 1991 and 2001 (Table 1.6 overleaf). Between 2001 and 2005 net migration accounted for 66 per cent of the overall population change resulting in an annual average increase of 182,000 people, compared with an increase of 92,000 people through natural change. This contrasts with the 1950s when net natural change accounted for 98 per cent of population change and net migration for only 2 per cent. In the 1960s and 1970s more people left the country than arrived. This net out-migration was more than compensated for by natural increases and so the total population still increased. Between 2005 and 2021 it is projected that natural change and net migration will account for similar amounts of the overall population change. Between 2005 and 2011 natural change is projected to lead to an annual average increase of 121,000 people compared with 160,000 people through net migration. Between 2011 and 2021 the annual average increase from natural change is predicted to be 139,000 compared with 145,000 through net migration.

Table **1.6**

Population change[1,2]

United Kingdom

Thousands

	Population at start of period	Annual averages				
		Live births	Deaths	Net natural change	Net migration & other	Overall change
1951–1961	50,287	839	593	246	6	252
1961–1971	52,807	962	638	324	-12	312
1971–1981	55,928	736	666	69	-27	43
1981–1991	56,357	757	655	103	5	108
1991–2001	57,439	731	631	100	68	167
2001–2005	59,113	692	600	92	182	274
2005–2011	60,209	702	581	121	160	281
2011–2021	61,892	716	578	139	145	284

1 Mid-year estimates for 1951–1961 to 2001–2005; 2004-based projections for 2005–2011 and 2011–2021. The start population for 2005–2011 is the mid-year estimate for 2005. The annual average for 'net migration and other' for 2005–2011 includes an adjustment to reconcile the transition from estimates to projected population data.
2 See Appendix, Part 1: Population estimates and projections.

Source: Office for National Statistics; Government Actuary's Department; General Register Office for Scotland; Northern Ireland Statistics and Research Agency

In 2005 there were nearly 723,000 live births in the UK, an increase of 7,000 compared with 2004 (Figure 1.7). This was 34 per cent fewer births than in 1901 and 20 per cent fewer than 1971. The two World Wars had a major impact on the number of births. During the First World War there was a fall in the number of births followed by a post war baby boom, with births peaking at 1.1 million in 1920. The number of births then fell to 0.7 million in 1933 and remained low until the end of the Second World War when there was a second post war baby boom with births peaking at 1.0 million in 1947. The number of births then returned to pre-Second World War levels, until a more sustained period of increased fertility and third baby boom occurred in the 1960s, also peaking at 1.0 million in 1964. As the larger cohorts of women born at this time entered their child-bearing years in the late 1980s and early 1990s, there was another increase in births, peaking at 0.8 million in 1990. Numbers of births then fell during the 1990s mainly due to falling fertility rates among younger women and a smaller cohort of women born in the late 1970s reaching peak child-bearing years. Projections to 2041 suggest that the number of births will remain relatively stable ranging from 695,000 to 724,000 each year.

In 2005 the Total Fertility Rate (TFR) in the UK was 1.79 children per woman, a rise from 1.77 in 2004 and the fourth consecutive annual increase since the record low of 1.63 in 2001. It is too early to predict whether this is the start of a sustained rise.

Figure **1.7**

Live births[1,2]

United Kingdom

Millions

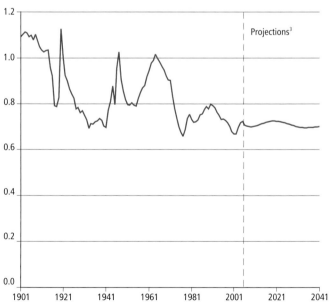

1 Babies showing signs of life at birth.
2 Data for 1901 to 1921 exclude Ireland, which was constitutionally a part of the UK during this period. Data from 1981 exclude the non-residents of Northern Ireland.
3 2004-based projections for 2006 to 2041.

Source: Office for National Statistics; Government Actuary's Department; General Register Office for Scotland; Northern Ireland Statistics and Research Agency

Total Fertility Rate (TFR)

The Total Fertility Rate (TFR) for a given year is the average number of children per woman a group of women would have if they experienced the age-specific fertility rates in the given year for their entire childbearing years. Changes in the number of births in part arise from changes in the population age structure. So the TFR is commonly used to look at fertility because it standardises for the changing age structure of the population.

Replacement level fertility

Replacement level fertility is the level at which a population would be exactly replacing itself in the long term, other things being equal. In developed countries this is estimated at 2.1 children per woman to take account of infant mortality and those who choose not to have children.

The previous trough in the TFR occurred in 1977, at 1.69 children per woman, after which followed a brief upturn, then a gradual decline throughout the 1980s and 1990s. The TFR peaked during the 1960s baby boom, at 2.95 children per woman. In 1973 the TFR fell below the level needed to replace the population (2.1 children per woman) and has remained so ever since. Across the UK, fertility fell below the replacement level in England and Wales in 1973 and one year later in Scotland (Figure 1.8). Fertility rates in Northern Ireland have been the highest across the UK for most of the last 40 years. In 1967 the

TFR was 3.28 in Northern Ireland compared with 2.87 in Scotland, 2.65 in England and 2.63 in Wales. Since the late 1980s this difference has substantially reduced; Northern Ireland's TFR dropped below the replacement level in 1993 and by 2005 had fallen to 1.87 children per woman. This compares with TFRs of 1.80 in England, 1.79 in Wales and 1.62 in Scotland. A key factor in the decline of Northern Ireland's TFR is the sharp fall in birth rates among women in their 20s over most of the last 40 years.

Despite the considerable population growth between 1901 and 2005, the annual number of deaths in the UK (including military deaths that occurred in the UK) has remained relatively steady over the period, at between 525,000 and 690,000. However, the death rate has fallen over time as the population has increased. Between 1971 and 2005 the death rate for all males fell by 22 per cent, while the death rate for all females fell by 10 per cent (Table 1.9 overleaf). During the same period, the infant mortality rate (number of deaths of infants aged under one year per 1,000 live births) fell by 72 per cent for both boys and girls. There were peaks in the number of deaths during both the First and Second World Wars. The peak of 690,000 in 1918 represented the highest annual number of deaths ever recorded, caused by both losses during the First World War and the influenza epidemic that followed it. Population projections suggest that the annual number of deaths will decline to a low of around 570,000 between 2010 and 2015 and will then gradually rise to reach around 740,000 in 2041. This rise will mostly result from the large cohorts born after the Second World War and in the 1960s baby boom, reaching old age.

Improved standards of living and developments in medical technology and practice help to explain the decline in death rates. Main causes of death differ by age; for example in England and Wales, the most common causes of death among people aged 15 to 44 in 2005 were injury and poisoning whereas those aged 45 to 64 were most likely to die from cancer. Circulatory diseases, such as heart disease and stroke, were the most common cause of deaths among those aged 65 and over (see Chapter 7: Health).

The steady increase in the population through both natural change and net migration (Table 1.6) means that a larger population live within the same geographic space. The measure of the number of people living in a country or region relative to its land area is known as population density. The population density across the UK varies considerably. In 2005 England had an average of 387 people per square kilometre compared with Wales (143), Northern Ireland (127) and Scotland (65).

Figure **1.8**

Total Fertility Rate[1]

United Kingdom
Children per woman

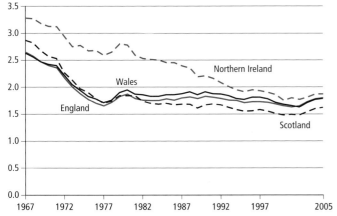

1 See Total Fertility Rate box above.

Source: Office for National Statistics, General Register Office for Scotland, Northern Ireland Statistics and Research Agency

Table **1.9**

Deaths:[1] by sex and age

United Kingdom

Death rates per 1,000 in each age group

	Under 1[2]	1–15	16–34	35–54	55–64	65–74	75 and over	All ages	All deaths (thousands)
Males									
1971	20.2	0.5	1.0	4.8	20.4	51.1	131.4	12.1	329
1981	12.7	0.4	1.0	4.0	18.1	46.4	122.2	12.0	329
1991	8.3	0.3	0.9	3.1	14.2	38.7	111.2	11.3	314
2001	6.0	0.2	0.9	2.8	10.4	28.7	96.6	10.0	288
2005	5.7	0.2	0.8	2.6	9.2	24.6	89.0	9.4	277
2011	5.2	0.1	0.7	2.7	8.9	20.3	78.7	9.0	275
2021	4.7	0.1	0.6	2.5	7.9	18.1	68.4	9.4	299
Females									
1971	15.5	0.4	0.5	3.1	10.3	26.6	96.6	11.0	317
1981	9.5	0.3	0.4	2.5	9.8	24.7	90.2	11.4	329
1991	6.3	0.2	0.4	1.9	8.4	22.3	85.0	11.2	332
2001	5.0	0.1	0.4	1.8	6.4	17.9	81.6	10.4	316
2005	4.4	0.1	0.4	1.6	5.8	15.7	78.8	9.9	305
2011	4.6	0.1	0.3	1.7	5.8	13.3	74.4	9.5	298
2021	4.3	0.1	0.3	1.6	5.0	11.9	61.9	9.0	295

1 2004-based projections for 2011 and 2021.
2 Rate per 1,000 live births.

Source: Office for National Statistics; Government Actuary's Department; General Register Office for Scotland; Northern Ireland Statistics and Research Agency

With boundary and classification changes it is difficult to trace regional population densities over time. However, it is possible to see that London had the highest concentration of people per square kilometre in the UK in both 1901 and 2005 (Map 1.10). In 2005 the London Borough of Kensington and Chelsea was the most densely populated area in the UK, with around 16,200 people per square kilometre. The most populated area outside inner London was Portsmouth, with around 4,700 people per square kilometre. The Highland council area in the north of Scotland was the least densely populated area in the UK, with 8 people per square kilometre. Belfast was the most densely populated area in Northern Ireland in both 1901 and 2005. In Wales more people per square kilometre (around 2,300) populated Cardiff in 2005, while the least densely populated area was Powys, with 25 people per square kilometre.

In 2005 England recorded net losses with around 19,900 people (Table 1.11) moving to other parts of the UK. Scotland and Wales both experienced a net inflow; around 14,500 and 5,900 people respectively whereas Northern Ireland recorded a net loss of 500 people to other parts of the UK. Within England, London experienced the largest net loss with 81,500 people moving to other parts of the UK. Other regions in England to experience a net loss of people to other areas of the country were the West Midlands (4,600) and the North West (1,000). The remaining English regions had a net inflow of people; in the South West, South East and East of England there was a greater net inflow than to Scotland or Wales. The North East had little change in its population as a result of internal migration. The majority of people leaving Scotland, Wales and Northern Ireland went to England, though there was no one place within England to which migrants moved. Census data for 2001 showed that while workers in the UK tended to move to the south to find employment, students were more likely to move north to study.

Internal migration estimates

The estimates for internal migration in this volume are based on data recorded at the NHS Central Registers (NHSCRs) in England and Scotland and at the Central Services Agency in Northern Ireland. The figures have been adjusted to take account of differences in recorded cross-border flows between England and Wales, Scotland and Northern Ireland. For more information see Appendix, Part 1: Internal migration estimates.

Map **1.10**

Population density: by area, 1901[1] and 2005[2]

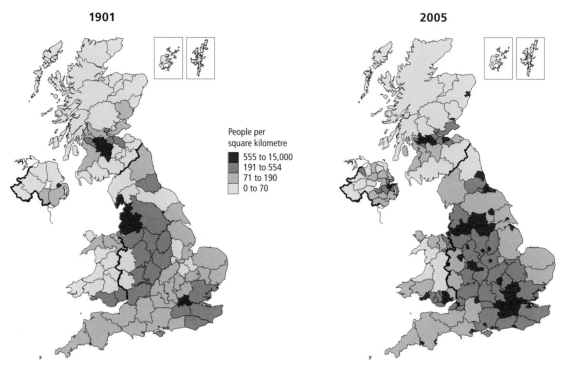

1901　　　　　**2005**

People per
square kilometre

■ 555 to 15,000
▨ 191 to 554
▧ 71 to 190
□ 0 to 70

1 Administrative boundaries for 1901 include information drawn from www.visionofbritain.org.uk and www.histpop.org.
2 Counties, unitary authorities, Inner and Outer London in England, unitary authorities in Wales, council areas in Scotland and district council areas in Northern Ireland for 2005.

Source: Census 1901, Mid-2005 population estimates, Office for National Statistics; General Register Office for Scotland; Northern Ireland Statistics and Research Agency

Table **1.11**

Inter-regional movements[1] within the United Kingdom, 2005

Thousands

	Inflow	Outflow	Balance
England	98.3	118.2	-19.9
North East	39.9	39.3	0.6
North West	102.1	103.1	-1.0
Yorkshire and the Humber	94.1	92.6	1.5
East Midlands	105.8	96.7	9.2
West Midlands	94.0	98.6	-4.6
East	138.7	123.7	15.1
London	161.2	242.8	-81.5
South East	216.5	201.0	15.5
South West	132.3	106.9	25.4
Wales	55.9	50.0	5.9
Scotland	59.2	44.7	14.5
Northern Ireland	12.2	12.7	-0.5

1 Based on patients re-registering with NHS doctors in other parts of the UK. Moves where the origin and destination lie within the same region do not appear in the table. See Appendix, Part 1: Internal migration estimates.

Source: National Health Service Central Register; General Register Office for Scotland; Northern Ireland Statistics and Research Agency

International migration

The pattern of people migrating to and from the UK changed over the 20th century. In the early part of the 20th century, more people left than entered the UK (see also Table 1.6). The balance has gradually shifted and since the early 1990s the UK has been a net receiver of migrants (Figure 1.12 overleaf). In 2005, an estimated 185,000 more people entered the UK for at least one year than left. Estimated in-migration was lower than in 2004, but was still the second highest on record. The number of people arriving to live in the UK was 565,000 in 2005, an average of over 1,500 in-migrants a day. During the same year, an estimated 380,000 people left the UK, an average of over 1,000 out-migrants a day. This was the highest recorded out-migration since the current method to estimate migration was introduced in 1991. In recent years there has been a pattern of net in-migration of foreign citizens and net out-migration of British citizens, and this has continued in 2005. Around half (198,000) of out-migrants from the UK in 2005 were British citizens. The most preferred destinations of British citizens were Australia followed by Spain and France. Of those groups migrating to the UK, 26 per cent (145,000) were citizens of the EU-25, followed by 21 per cent (121,000) from

Figure **1.12**

International migration into and out of the United Kingdom[1]

Thousands

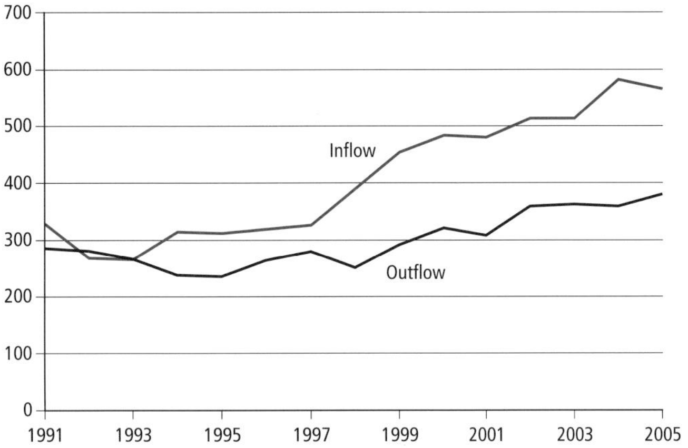

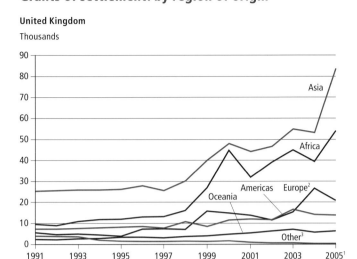

1 See Appendix, Part 1: International migration estimates.

Source: Office for National Statistics

Figure **1.13**

Grants of settlement: by region of origin[1]

United Kingdom

Thousands

1 Data for 2005 are provisional.
2 Excludes European Economic Area (EEA) for all years and Swiss nationals from 1995. All decisions on nationals from the ten countries that acceded to the European Union on 1 May 2004 are included before that date but excluded after it.
3 Includes British Overseas citizens, those whose nationality was unknown and, up to 1993, acceptances where the nationality was not separately identified; from 1994 these nationalities have been included in the relevant geographical area.

Source: Home Office

the New Commonwealth, 12 per cent (68,000) from the Old Commonwealth and 25 per cent (140,000) from other foreign countries. The International Passenger Survey estimates that more Polish citizens migrated into the UK in 2005 for at least one year than citizens of any other foreign country.

Nationals of the European Economic Area (EEA) (EU-25 plus Iceland, Liechtenstein and Norway) have the right to reside in the UK provided they are working or are able to support themselves financially. Nearly all other overseas nationals wishing to live permanently in the UK must apply to the Home Office for Indefinite Leave to Remain (or 'settlement'). The number of grants of settlement in the UK remained generally steady at around 56,000 a year throughout most of the 1990s, but from 1998 to 2005 they increased by two and a half times, from 69,300 to 179,100. Between 2004 and 2005, the overall number of grants rose by 29 per cent. Nationals of Asia received almost half of all grants (83,700 acceptances) in 2005 (Figure 1.13). Afghanistan, the Philippines and India were the Asian countries with the largest rises in the number of grants to citizens within this period. Nationals of Africa received the second largest number of acceptances, at nearly one-third of all grants followed by those from non-EEA Europe, who received one-eighth of all grants. The main reason for acceptance in 2005 was asylum (38 per cent), followed by reasons relating to employment (35 per cent), and spouses and dependants joining British citizens or persons previously granted settlement (21 per cent).

The number of people seeking asylum in the UK varies from year to year (see Appendix, Part 1: Refugees). Applications to

the UK for asylum peaked in 2002 at 103,100. In 2005 the UK received 30,800 applications for asylum, including dependants, a fall of around one-quarter compared with 2004. There were 25,710 asylum applications excluding dependants in 2005. The majority (83 per cent) of principal asylum applicants to the UK were aged under 35 years, while 15 per cent were aged between 35 and 49, and 3 per cent were aged 50 and older. The majority were also male (71 per cent).

In 2005 France received 59,200 asylum applications which was the highest amount out of all EU countries. The total number of asylum applications, including dependants, to EU-25 member states remained relatively steady between 1999 and 2002 and then declined from 2003. Despite this, almost one-quarter of EU member states recorded a rise in applications between 2004 and 2005 (6 out of 25) although the overall numbers were low. When the relative size of the individual member state's population is taken into account, the UK ranked 14th in 2005, with a rate of 0.5 asylum seekers per 1,000 population (Table 1.14). This was the same as the EU-25 average. Cyprus had the highest rate at 8.0 per 1,000 population, followed by Malta, Austria, Sweden, Luxembourg and Belgium. In comparison with the EU member states, the US received 48,800 asylum claims in 2005, 0.2 per 1,000 population.

Table **1.14**

Asylum[1] applications, including dependants: EU comparison, 2005

	Number of asylum seekers[2]	Asylum seekers per 1,000 population		Number of asylum seekers[2]	Asylum seekers per 1,000 population
Austria	22,500	2.8	Luxembourg[4]	800	1.7
Belgium[3]	18,200	1.7	Malta[4]	1,200	2.9
Cyprus[4]	7,800	8.0	Netherlands	12,300	0.8
Czech Republic[4]	4,000	0.4	Poland[4]	5,400	0.1
Denmark	2,300	0.4	Portugal[4]	100	-
Estonia[4]	-	-	Slovakia[4]	3,500	0.6
Finland	3,600	0.7	Slovenia[4]	1,600	0.8
France	59,200	1.0	Spain	5,000	0.1
Germany	28,900	0.4	Sweden	17,500	1.9
Greece[4]	9,100	0.8	United Kingdom	30,800	0.5
Hungary[4]	1,600	0.2	All applications to EU-25	249,300	0.5
Ireland	4,300	1.0			
Italy[4]	9,300	0.2			
Latvia[4]	-	-			
Lithuania[4]	100	-			

1 See Appendix, Part 1: Refugees.
2 Figures rounded to the nearest 100.
3 Figures based on Intergovernmental Consultations on Asylum, Refugees and Migration Policies in Europe, North America and Australia (IGC) data but adjusted to include an estimated number of dependants.
4 Figures based on United Nations High Commissioner for Refugees (UNHCR) data, including dependants.

Source: Home Office

International perspectives

In 2005 the world population was nearly 6.5 billion people (Table 1.15). Over 3.9 billion (60 per cent) lived in Asia, 14 per cent lived in Africa and 11 per cent lived in Europe.

The remaining 15 per cent lived in North America, Latin America and the Caribbean, and Oceania. Asia also had the highest population density, with 123 people per square kilometre. Oceania was the least densely populated with 4 people per

Table **1.15**

World demographic indicators, 2005

	Population (millions)	Population density (sq km)	Infant mortality rate[1,2]	Total Fertility Rate[2]	Life expectancy at birth (years)[2] Males	Females
Asia	3,905	123	53.7	2.47	65.4	69.2
Africa	906	30	94.2	4.97	48.2	49.9
Europe	728	32	9.2	1.40	69.6	78.0
Latin America & Caribbean	561	27	26.0	2.55	68.3	74.9
North America	331	15	6.8	1.99	74.8	80.2
Oceania	33	4	28.7	2.32	71.7	76.2
World	6,465	48	57.0	2.65	63.2	67.7

1 Per 1,000 live births.
2 Data are for 2000–05.

Source: United Nations

square kilometre. The United Nations estimate that between 2005 and 2010 the population of Africa will grow by 2.1 per cent while the population of Europe will decline by less than 1 per cent. All other areas are projected to have population growth during this period.

The Total Fertility Rate (TFR) varies widely between the different areas of the world. In Africa the TFR was 4.97 children per woman over the period 2000–05, well above its replacement level of 2.7, while in both North America and Europe, TFRs of 1.99 and 1.40 children per woman respectively, were below their replacement level of 2.1. This reflects the low infant mortality in these areas; in Europe 9.2 live babies per 1,000 died before age one between 2000–05 and in North America the rate was 6.8 live babies per 1,000. However, in Africa nearly 100 per 1,000 babies did not survive to their first birthday. Life expectancy at birth is also lower in Africa, the only area with life expectancy below the world average of 63.2 years for men and 67.7 years for women. Over the period 2000–05 life expectancy for men in Africa was 48.2 years, while in North America it was

74.8 years, a 26.6 year difference. The life expectancy for women in Africa was 49.9 years compared with 80.2 for women in North America, a difference of 30.3 years. In Europe women could expect to live 8.4 years longer than men – the largest difference of any world region.

In 2004 Total Fertility Rates were low throughout the EU-25. The lowest fertility rates are found predominantly in the ten member states that joined the EU in 2004. The lowest seven TFRs were also recorded in these states. A similar pattern also applies to infant mortality, with the highest infant mortality rates found in the ten new member states, though not necessarily the same ones with the lowest fertility rates. The UK had the highest infant mortality rate outside the ten new member states in both 2003 and 2004. Across the EU, life expectancy at birth in 2004 averaged 75.6 years for males and 81.7 for females. In the UK males were expected to live until 76.6 years, one year longer than the EU-25 male average. In contrast, women in the UK were expected to live to 81.0 years, almost one year less than the EU-25 female average (also see Figure 7.1).

Households and families

- The proportion of children living in lone-parent families in Great Britain more than tripled between 1972 and spring 2006 to 24 per cent. (Table 2.5)

- In 2005 the number of people living alone in Great Britain had more than doubled since 1971, from 3 million to 7 million. (Page 16)

- In Q2 2006, 58 per cent of men and 39 per cent of women aged 20–24 in England lived with their parents, an increase of around 8 percentage points since 1991. (Table 2.8)

- There were 15,700 civil partnerships formed in the UK between December 2005 and September 2006. Of these, 93 per cent were in England and Wales, 6 per cent were in Scotland and 1 per cent were in Northern Ireland. (Page 18)

- In 2005, 24 per cent of non-married people aged under 60 were cohabiting in Great Britain, around twice the proportion recorded in 1986. (Page 19)

- The average age for mothers at first child-birth was 27.3 years in England and Wales in 2005, more than three years older than in 1971. (Table 2.17)

Chapter 2

People live in a variety of household types over their lifetime. They may leave their parental home, form partnerships, marry and have children. They may also experience separation and divorce, lone-parenthood, and the formation of new partnerships, leading to new households and second families. Recent decades have seen marked changes in household patterns. The traditional family household of a married couple with a child or children is less common, while there has been an increase in lone-parent households. There has also been an increase in one-person households, suggesting that people are spending time living on their own before forming a relationship, after a relationship has broken down, or following the death of a spouse or partner.

Household composition

There were 24.2 million households in Great Britain in spring 2006 (Table 2.1). The trend towards smaller household sizes has contributed to the number of households increasing faster than the population and hence an increased demand for housing. The number of households in Great Britain increased by 30 per cent between 1971 and 2006. The population of Great Britain increased by 8 per cent in the same period (see Chapter 1: Population). The average household size fell over this period from 2.9 to 2.4 people. Reasons for this decrease include more lone-parent families, smaller family sizes and an increase in one-person households, although the rise in one-person households has levelled off since 1991. As a proportion of all households, one-person households increased by 9 percentage points from 18 per cent to 27 per cent, but

only by a further 2 percentage points between 1991 and 2006. Most of the increase in the proportion of one-person households since 1991 is a result of the rise in the number of people below state pension age living alone.

The proportion of households in Great Britain comprising a couple with dependent children fell from more than one-third in 1971 to less than one-quarter in 2006 (Table 2.2). The decrease was mostly among couples with one or two dependent children. Over the same period, the proportion of lone-parent households with dependent children more than doubled from 3 per cent of households in 1971, to 7 per cent of households in 2006.

There are differences in household size between the ethnic groups in Great Britain. Some ethnic groups tend to have larger families and are more likely to live in extended families. The 2001 Census showed that Indian, Pakistani and Bangladeshi households in Great Britain contained more people, on average, than households from other ethnic backgrounds (Figure 2.3).

Table 2.1

Households:[1] by size

Great Britain

Percentages

	1971	1981	1991	2001[2]	2006[2]
One person	18	22	27	29	29
Two people	32	32	34	35	36
Three people	19	17	16	16	16
Four people	17	18	16	14	13
Five people	8	7	5	5	4
Six or more people	6	4	2	2	2
All households (=100%) (millions)	18.6	20.2	22.4	23.8	24.2
Average household size (number of people)	2.9	2.7	2.5	2.4	2.4

1 See Appendix, Part 2: Multi-sourced tables, Households, and Families.
2 Data are at spring for 2001 and Q2 for 2006. See Appendix, Part 4: Labour Force Survey.

Source: Census, Labour Force Survey, Office for National Statistics

Table 2.2

Households:[1] by type of household and family

Great Britain

Percentages

	1971	1981	1991	2001[2]	2006[2]
One person					
Under state pension age	6	8	11	14	14
Over state pension age	12	14	16	15	14
One family households					
Couple[3]					
No children	27	26	28	29	28
1–2 dependent children[4]	26	25	20	19	18
3 or more dependent children[4]	9	6	5	4	4
Non-dependent children only	8	8	8	6	7
Lone parent[3]					
Dependent children[4]	3	5	6	7	7
Non-dependent children only	4	4	4	3	3
Two or more unrelated adults	4	5	3	3	3
Multi-family households	1	1	1	1	1
All households (=100%) (millions)	18.6	20.2	22.4	23.8	24.2

1 See Appendix, Part 2: Multi-sourced tables, Households, and Families.
2 Data are at Q2 each year. See Appendix, Part 4: Labour Force Survey.
3 Other individuals who were not family members may also be included.
4 May also include non-dependent children.

Source: Census, Labour Force Survey, Office for National Statistics

Figure **2.3**

Average household size: by ethnic group,[1] 2001

Great Britain

People per household

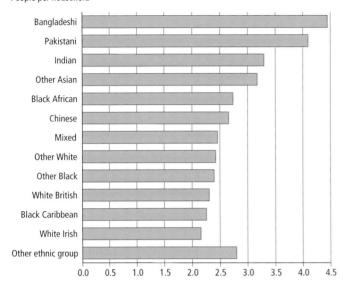

1 Of the household reference person. See Reference persons box on page 16.

Source: Census 2001, Office for National Statistics; Census 2001, General Register Office for Scotland

Bangladeshi households were largest, with an average of 4.5 people per household, followed by Pakistani households (4.1) and Indian households (3.3). White Irish households were the smallest, with an average of 2.2 people per household and Black Caribbean and White British households both had an average of 2.3 people. Variations in the age profiles of the different ethnic groups contributed to differences in household size. White British, Black Caribbean and White Irish households have an older age structure than the other ethnic groups and more than three in ten households headed by these groups were one-person households.

Table 2.2 is an analysis of households and family type, and is therefore directly relevant to housing policy and related issues. For other purposes it is necessary to understand the numbers of people in different types of households. Table 2.4 shows that more than two-thirds of people living in private households in Great Britain in spring 2006 lived in couple families. However, since 1971 the proportion of people living in the traditional family household of a couple with dependent children has fallen from more than one-half (52 per cent) to more than one-third (37 per cent) in spring 2006. Over the same period the proportion of people living in couple families with no children has increased from almost one-fifth (19 per cent) to one-quarter (25 per cent). This trend has been driven both by delayed childbearing among younger couples and an increase in the number of older couples whose children have left home.

Table **2.4**

People in households:[1] by type of household and family

Great Britain   Percentages

	1971	1981	1991	2001[2]	2006[2]
One person	*6*	*8*	*11*	*12*	*12*
One family households					
Couple					
No children	*19*	*20*	*25*	*25*	*25*
Dependent children[3]	*52*	*47*	*53*	*39*	*37*
Non-dependent children only	*10*	*10*	*12*	*9*	*8*
Lone parent[4]	*4*	*6*	*9*	*12*	*12*
Other households	*9*	*9*	*4*	*4*	*5*
All people in private households (=100%) (millions)	53.4	53.9	54.1	56.4	57.1

1 See Appendix, Part 2: Multi-sourced tables, Households, and Families.
2 Data are at spring each year. See Appendix, Part 4: Labour Force Survey.
3 May also include non-dependent children.
4 Includes those with dependent children only, non-dependent children only, and those with both dependent and non-dependent children.

Source: Census, Labour Force Survey, Office for National Statistics

One in eight people lived in a lone-parent household in spring 2006 – three times the proportion in 1971.

The proportion of dependent children within different family types has changed over the last 35 years. In April to June (Q2) 2006, 76 per cent of children lived in a family unit headed by a couple, compared with 92 per cent in 1972 (Table 2.5 overleaf). Since the early 1970s there has been a fall in the proportion of children living in families headed by a couple with three or more children, from 41 per cent in 1972 to 22 per cent in spring 2006. In contrast there was an increase in the proportion of children living in lone-parent families, from 7 per cent in 1972 to 24 per cent in Q2 2006. Lone mothers head around nine out of ten lone-parent families.

Among households with dependent children, those headed by someone from the Black ethnic group had the highest proportion of lone-parent families in Great Britain in 2001. About half of Other Black and Black Caribbean households with dependent children were headed by a lone parent (52 and 48 per cent respectively), as were more than one-third of Black African households (36 per cent). Lone-parent families were less common among Indian households (10 per cent), Bangladeshi households (12 per cent), Pakistani households (13 per cent), Chinese households (15 per cent) and White

Table 2.5

Dependent children:[1] by family type

Great Britain   Percentages

	1972	1981	1997[2]	2001[2]	2006[2]
Couple families					
1 child	16	18	17	17	18
2 children	35	41	37	37	36
3 or more children	41	29	25	24	22
Lone mother families					
1 child	2	3	6	6	7
2 children	2	4	7	8	9
3 or more children	2	3	6	6	6
Lone father families					
1 child	..	1	1	1	1
2 or more children	1	1	1	1	1
All children[3]	100	100	100	100	100

1 See Appendix, Part 2: Multi-sourced tables, Households, and Families.
2 Data are at Q2 each year. See Appendix, Part 4: Labour Force Survey.
3 Excludes cases where the dependent child is a family unit, for example, a foster child.

Source: General Household Survey, Census, Labour Force Survey, Office for National Statistics

British households with dependent children (22 per cent). Between 1991 and 2001, the proportion of lone-parent households with dependent children decreased among the Black Caribbean group (from 20 per cent to 18 per cent) and the Black African group (21 per cent to 17 per cent) (Figure 2.6). During the same period the proportion of Pakistani, Bangladeshi, Chinese and White lone-parent households with dependent children all increased between 1991 and 2001 to between 6 per cent and 9 per cent.

One of the most notable changes in household composition since 1971 has been the increase in one-person households. In 2005 there were 7 million people living alone in Great Britain compared with 3 million in 1971. This increase was most marked between 1971 and 1991 but has levelled off since 1991. In the mid-1980s and 1990s these households mainly comprised older women according to the General Household Survey. This was a reflection of there being fewer men than women in older age groups (see Chapter 1: Population) and, in particular, the tendency for women to outlive men. In 2005, 60 per cent of women aged 75 and over were living alone, much the same proportion as in 1986/87 (Figure 2.7). More recently there has been a tendency for people to live alone at younger ages. The largest increase over the past 20 years has been among those aged 25 to 44 years.

Reference persons

Though the majority of households contain one family, some households contain multiple families, while others do not contain a family at all (for example, where the household consists of one person or of non-related adults). This chapter mainly refers to the household reference person but some data are based on the family reference person. The UK Census 2001 defines family reference person and household reference person as follows:

Family reference person (FRP)

In a couple family, the FRP is chosen from the two people in the couple on the basis of their economic activity (in the priority order; full-time job, part-time job, unemployed, retired, other). If both have the same economic activity, the FRP is defined as the elder of the two, or if they are the same age, the first member of the couple listed on the form. The FRP is the lone parent in a lone-parent family.

Household reference person (HRP)

A person living alone is the HRP. If the household contains one family the HRP is the same as the FRP. If there is more than one family in the household, the HRP is chosen from among the FRPs using the same criteria for choosing the FRP. If there is no family, the HRP is chosen from the individuals using the same criteria.

Figure 2.6

Lone-parent households with dependent children:[1] by ethnic group[2]

Great Britain
Percentages

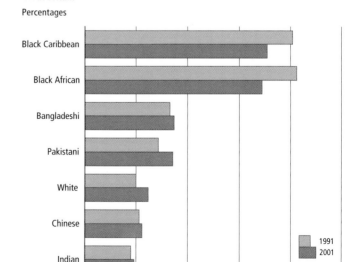

1 Living in 'one family and no others' households.
2 Of the household reference person, see Reference persons box above.

Source: Census 2001, Office for National Statistics; Census 2001, General Register Office for Scotland

Figure **2.7**

People living alone: by sex and age[1]

Great Britain

Percentages

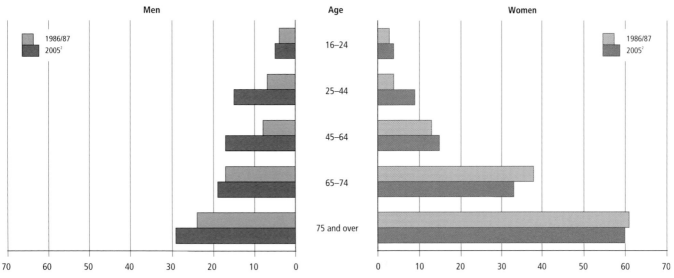

1 Data from 2001/02 onwards are weighted to compensate for nonresponse and to match known population distributions.
2 Data for 2005 includes last quarter of 2004/05 due to survey change from financial year to calendar year. See Appendix, Part 2: General Household Survey.

Source: General Household Survey (Longitudinal), Office for National Statistics

The proportion of men in this age group who lived alone more than doubled between 1986/87 and 2005 from 7 per cent to 15 per cent and the proportion of women living alone also more than doubled from 4 per cent to 9 per cent.

Another notable change in family structure and relationships has been the increase in the number of adults who live with their parents (Table 2.8). Some adults remain at home while in education or because of economic necessity, such as difficulties entering the housing market. Others choose to continue living with their parents. Young men are more likely than young women to live with their parents. In Q2 2006, 58 per cent of men aged 20 to 24 in England lived with their parents compared with 39 per cent of women in the same age group. Between 1991 and 2006 the proportion of men and women in this age group who were living with their parents increased by 8 and 7 percentage points respectively. Over the same period the proportion of women aged 30 to 34 living with their parents decreased from 5 per cent to 3 per cent while the proportion of 30 to 34-year-old men living with their parents remained at around 8 per cent.

Table **2.8**

Adults living with their parents: by sex and age[1]

England Percentages

	1991	2001[2]	2002[2]	2005[2]	2006[2]
Men					
20–24	50	57	56	57	58
25–29	19	22	19	23	22
30–34	9	8	8	8	9
Women					
20–24	32	36	37	38	39
25–29	9	11	10	11	11
30–34	5	3	2	3	3

1 See Appendix, Part 2: Multi-sourced tables, Households, and Families.
2 Data are at spring for 2001, 2002, 2005 and Q2 for 2006. See Appendix, Part 4: Labour Force Survey.

Source: Survey of English Housing, Communities and Local Government; Labour Force Survey, Office for National Statistics

Partnerships

Partnership formation patterns have changed since the early 1970s as the overall number of people marrying has decreased. Despite this, married couples are still the main type of partnership for men and women. In 2006 there were 17.1 million families in the UK and around seven in ten contained a married couple.

In 1950, there were 408,000 marriages in the UK and the number grew during the mid- to late-1960s to reach a peak of 480,000 in 1972. This growth can be attributed to the large number of babies born in the immediate post-Second World War baby boom reaching childbearing age and getting married at younger ages than in more recent years. The annual number of marriages then declined, reaching 286,000 in 2001 (Figure 2.9). From 2001 the number of marriages increased each year to 311,000 in 2004, before falling to 283,700 (provisional) in the UK in 2005.

The average age at which people get married for the first time has continued to rise. In 1971 the average age at first marriage was 25 for men and 23 for women in England and Wales. By 2005 this had increased to 32 for men and 29 for women. There has been a similar trend across Europe. Between 1970 and 2004 the average age at first marriage in the EU-25 increased from age 26 to 30 for men and age 23 to 28 for women. However, there were differences in age of first marriage between EU-25 member states. In 2004 the country with the youngest newly-weds was Lithuania, with an average age of 27 for men and 25 for women, while Sweden had the oldest, with an average age of 34 for men and 31 for women.

In England and Wales in 2005, 160,000 civil marriage ceremonies (marriages performed by a government official rather than by a clergyman) took place and accounted for more than two-thirds (65 per cent) of all marriages. This proportion was 68 per cent in 2004. More than one-third of all marriages (88,700), representing over half of all civil marriages, took place in approved premises (as opposed to places of worship or registry offices), which are licensed by local authorities under the *Marriage Act 1994* for the solemnisation of civil marriages (for example hotels or stately homes). This was a large increase from 5 per cent of all marriages in 1996 (Figure 2.10).

The *Civil Partnership Act 2004* came into effect across the UK in December 2005 (see Appendix Part 2: Civil Partnerships). The Act grants same-sex couples rights and responsibilities identical to civil marriage. Between December 2005 and September 2006, 15,700 civil partnerships were formed. Of these, 93 per cent were in England and Wales, 6 per cent were in Scotland and 1 per cent were in Northern Ireland. London and the South East were the most popular regions to register a partnership and between December 2005 and September

Figure 2.9

Marriages and divorces

United Kingdom
Thousands

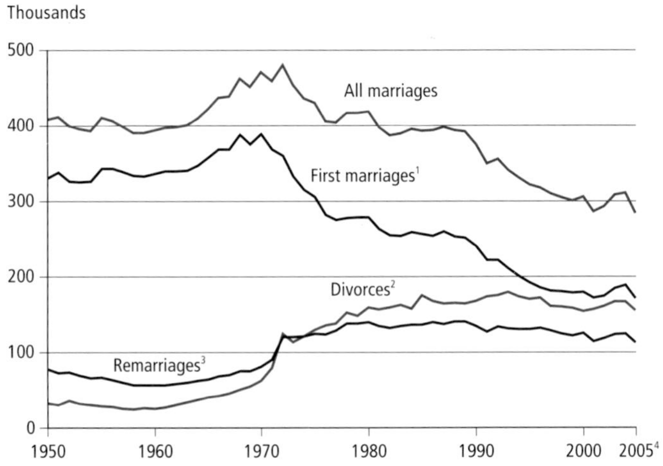

1 For both partners.
2 Includes annulments. Data for 1950 to 1970 for Great Britain only. Divorce was permitted in Northern Ireland from 1969.
3 For one or both partners.
4 Data for 2005 are provisional. Final figures are likely to be higher.

Source: Office for National Statistics; General Register Office for Scotland; Northern Ireland Statistics and Research Agency

Figure 2.10

Marriages: by type of ceremony

England & Wales
Thousands

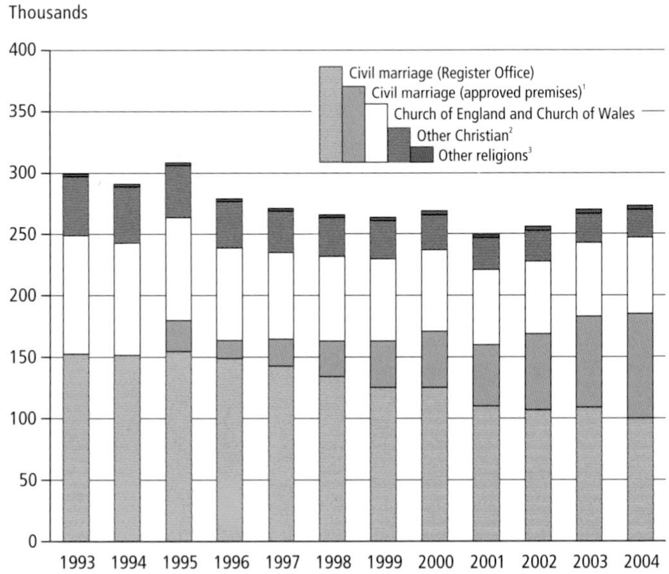

1 The *Marriage Act 1994* made provision for civil marriages to be solemnised in approved premises (with effect from 1 April 1995).
2 Includes Roman Catholic, Methodist, Congregationalist, Baptist, Calvinistic Methodist, United Reformed Church.
3 Includes Jews, Muslim, Sikh and other unattached bodies.

Source: Office for National Statistics

Table **2.11**

Age gap between males and females at marriage[1]

England & Wales		Percentages
	1963	2004
Man younger	15	26
Man 0–5 years older	64	48
Man 6 or more years older	21	26
All marriages	100	100

1 All marriages in 1963 and 2004.
Source: Office for National Statistics

Table **2.12**

Non-married people[1] cohabiting: by marital status and sex, 2005[2]

Great Britain		Percentages
	Men	Women
Single	23	28
Widowed	14	6
Divorced	36	29
Separated	22	11

1 Aged 16 to 59. Includes those who described themselves as separated but were, in a legal sense, still married.
2 Data for 2005 includes last quarter of 2004/05 due to survey change from financial year to calendar year. See Appendix, Part 2: General Household Survey.
Source: General Household Survey (Longitudinal), Office for National Statistics

2006, one in four of all partnerships registered took place in London. At the end of September 2006, more male than female civil partnerships had been formed in all four countries of the UK.

The number of divorces taking place each year in Great Britain more than doubled between the low point in 1958 (24,400) and 1968 (50,600). By 1972 the number of divorces in the UK had more than doubled again. This latter increase was partly a 'one-off' consequence of the *Divorce Reform Act 1969*, which came into effect in England and Wales in 1971. The Act introduced a single ground for divorce – irretrievable breakdown – which could be established by proving one or more certain facts including adultery; desertion; separation (with or without consent); or unreasonable behaviour. Divorce was also permitted in Northern Ireland from 1969. Although there was a slight drop in the number of divorces in the UK in 1973, the number rose again and peaked in 1993 at 180,000. The number of divorces then fell to less than 155,000 in 2000 before rising over four successive years to 167,000 in 2004. In 2005 the number of divorces fell back to 155,000.

Following divorce, people often form new relationships and may remarry. The number of remarriages, for one or both partners, increased in the UK by one-third between 1971 and 1972 to 120,000 (after the introduction of the *Divorce Reform Act 1969*) and peaked at 141,000 in 1988. Provisional figures for 2005 show there were more than 113,000 remarriages, accounting for two-fifths of all marriages.

In England and Wales, the majority of women who marry, marry men older than themselves. However, an increasing proportion of women are marrying younger men. The proportion of couples where the husband was younger than the wife increased from 15 per cent for those who married in 1963 to 26 per cent for those who married in 2004. Over the same period, the proportion of couples where the man was at most five years older than the woman fell from nearly two-thirds in 1963 to nearly one-half in 2004 (Table 2.11). There was a small increase in the proportion of marriages where the man was more than five years older than the woman: 21 per cent in 1963 compared with 26 per cent in 2004.

The proportion of people cohabiting has increased greatly since the mid-1980s. The rise in cohabitation may in part be related to people marrying later in life. The proportion of non-married men and women aged under 60 who were cohabiting in Great Britain more than doubled for men between 1986 (the earliest year for which data are available on a consistent basis) and 2005, from 11 per cent to 24 per cent; and almost doubled for women aged under 60, from 13 per cent in 1986 to 24 per cent in 2005.

Non-married cohabiting men were more usually divorced and living with a new partner whereas cohabiting women were just as likely to be divorced as single. In 2005, 36 per cent of non-married cohabiting men aged under 60 were divorced (Table 2.12) and more than one-fifth (22 per cent) were separated compared with more than one-tenth (11 per cent) of women who were separated. In Northern Ireland in 2005, non-married cohabiting men were also most likely to be divorced (31 per cent). Non-married cohabiting women were more likely to be single than divorced (16 per cent and 14 per cent respectively).

Changing patterns of cohabitation, marriage and divorce have led to considerable changes in the family environment since the early 1970s. The number of children aged under 16 in England and Wales who experienced the divorce of their parents peaked at 176,000 in 1993 (Figure 2.13 overleaf). This fell to 142,000 in 2000, and then increased each year to reach 154,000 in 2003 before starting to fall again. This number decreased to 136,000 in 2005, the second successive fall since 2003 and a decrease of 9 per cent from 2004. One-fifth of children who experienced the divorce of their parents in 2005 were under five years old and nearly two-thirds were aged ten or under.

Figure **2.13**

Children of divorced couples: by age of child

England & Wales
Thousands

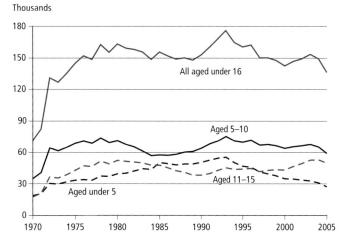

Source: Office for National Statistics

Children live in an increasing variety of family structures. Parents separating can result in lone-parent families, and new relationships can create stepfamilies. More than 10 per cent of all families with dependent children in Great Britain were stepfamilies in 2005. As children tend to stay with their mother following the break-up of a relationship, the majority of stepfamilies (86 per cent) consisted of a natural mother and stepfather, while 11 per cent consisted of a natural father and stepmother (Figure 2.14).

Figure **2.14**

Stepfamilies[1] with dependent children,[2] 2005[3]

Great Britain
Percentages

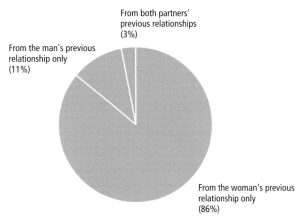

From both partners' previous relationships (3%)

From the man's previous relationship only (11%)

From the woman's previous relationship only (86%)

1 Family head aged 16 to 59.
2 Dependent children aged under 16, or aged 16 to 18 and in full-time education, in the family unit, and living in the household.
3 Data for 2005 includes last quarter of 2004/05 due to survey change from financial year to calendar year. See Appendix, Part 2: General Household Survey.

Source: General Household Survey (Longitudinal), Office for National Statistics

In the 2001 Census, 38 per cent of cohabiting couple families with dependent children were stepfamilies in the UK compared with 8 per cent of married couple families with dependent children. Married couple stepfamilies in the UK were more likely than cohabiting couple stepfamilies to have natural dependent children as well as stepchildren, 57 per cent compared with 35 per cent respectively in 2001. Stepfamilies were generally larger than non-stepfamilies, 27 per cent of stepfamilies had three or more dependent children compared with 18 per cent of non-stepfamilies in 2001. This was the case for both married and cohabiting couple stepfamilies.

Family formation

Fertility patterns influence the size of households and families, and affect the age structure of the population. The annual number of births fluctuated throughout the 20th century, but the overall trend was downward (see Chapter 1: Population). There were sharp peaks in births at the end of both World Wars and there was a more sustained boom during the 1960s. Changing fertility patterns in the UK over the last 40 years have been characterised by falling fertility rates, a rising mean age at first birth and higher levels of childlessness. Like births, the Total Fertility rate (TFR) (see Total Fertility Rate box on page 7) fluctuated throughout the 20th century, with similar peaks and an overall downward trend. The TFR fell continually from a high in the mid-1960s of 2.95 children per woman in 1964 until the mid-1970s (1.69 in 1977), resulting in a record low number of births (657,000) in 1977. Despite continued low fertility, the number of births rose in the late-1980s to 787,000 in 1988, sustained by the large generations of women born in the late 1950s and 1960s reaching their peak childbearing age (see Chapter 1: Population). More recently, both the TFR and the number of births fell during the late 1990s but increased again between 2001 and 2005.

In 2005 the TFR in the UK was 1.79 children per woman. This was the highest level since 1992 and an increase from 1.77 in 2004. These increases followed particularly low levels of fertility between 2000 and 2002, and the record low of 1.63 in 2001 (see Chapter 1: Population). The UK TFR in 2005 was higher than the average of 1.52 children per woman in the EU-25. France had the highest TFR in the EU, at 1.94 children per woman, and Poland had the lowest, at 1.24 children per woman.

The average number of children per woman is used as an indicator of family size. In the UK, family size increased from 2.07 children for women born in 1920 to a peak of 2.46 children for women born in 1934 (Figure 2.15). These women were at the peak of childbearing at around the time of the 1960s baby boom. Family size declined for subsequent generations and is projected to continue to decline to around

Figure **2.15**

Completed family size

United Kingdom

Average number of children per woman

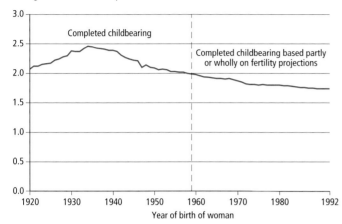

Source: Office for National Statistics; Government Actuary's Department

1.74 children for women born in the late 1980s and early 1990s. Women born in 1960 and now at the end of their childbearing years had an average 1.98 children.

Changing attitudes to family sizes, delayed entry into marriage or cohabitation, and increased female participation in education and the labour market are some of the factors that have encouraged the trend of later childbearing and smaller families. This delay before starting a family has been demonstrated by successive cohorts of women born in England and Wales since the Second World War. More than one-third (34 per cent) of women born in 1940 were childless at age 25; this increased to nearly two-thirds (64 per cent) among women aged 25 who were born in 1980. There has also been a rise in the proportion of women who were childless at age 35, from 12 per cent of those born in 1940 to 25 per cent of those born in 1970. The proportion of women reaching the end of their childbearing years (age 45) who remained childless rose from 11 per cent of women born in 1940 to 18 per cent of those born in 1960, the most recent cohort of women to have reached the end of their childbearing years.

In general, fertility rates for women aged 30 and over have increased while those for women in their 20s have declined (Table 2.16). During the 1970s, fertility rates were highest in the 20 to 24 and 25 to 29 year age groups. Throughout the 1980s and 1990s, women aged 25 to 29 had the highest fertility rates. However fertility rates at age 30 to 34 have increased steadily since the mid-1970s and by 2004 the rates for women aged 30 to 34 exceeded those of women aged 25 to 29 for the first time.

Table **2.16**

Fertility rates: by age of mother at childbirth

United Kingdom — Live births per 1,000 women

	1971	1981	1991	2001	2005
Under 20[1]	50.0	28.4	32.9	27.9	26.2
20–24	154.4	106.6	88.9	68.0	70.5
25–29	154.6	130.9	119.9	91.5	98.3
30–34	79.4	69.4	86.5	88.0	100.7
35–39	34.3	22.4	32.0	41.3	50.0
40 and over	9.2	4.7	5.3	8.6	10.6
Total Fertility Rate[2]	2.41	1.82	1.82	1.63	1.79
Total births[3] (thousands)	901.6	730.7	792.3	669.1	722.5

1 Live births per 1,000 women aged 15 to 19.
2 Number of children that would be born to a woman if current patterns of fertility persisted throughout her childbearing life. For 1981 onwards, this is based on fertility rates for each single year of age, but for 1971 it is based on the rates for each five year age group.
3 Total live births per 1,000 women aged 15 to 44.

Source: Office for National Statistics

In England and Wales the average age of mothers at childbirth increased by more than two years between 1971 and 2005, to 29.0 years (Table 2.17). Over the same period, the average age for the birth of the first child increased by more than three years to 27.3 years in 2005.

The average age of married women giving birth for the first time has increased by six years from age 24 in 1971, to age 30 in 2005. Births occurring outside marriage tend to take place at a younger age than those inside marriage. In 2005 women giving birth outside marriage were more than four years younger on average than their married counterparts.

Table **2.17**

Average age of mother:[1] by birth order[2]

England & Wales — Years

	1971	1981	1991	2001	2005
1st child	23.7	24.8	25.6	26.6	27.3
2nd child	26.4	27.3	28.2	29.2	29.6
3rd child	29.1	29.2	29.9	30.7	30.9
4th child	30.9	30.9	31.2	31.5	31.6
5th child and higher	33.6	33.8	33.5	34.4	34.6
All births	26.6	27.0	27.7	28.6	29.0

1 Age-standardised to take account of the changing population distribution of women.
2 See Appendix, Part 2: True birth order.

Source: Office for National Statistics

Although most children are born to married couples, there has been a substantial rise in the proportion of births occurring outside marriage. With the exception of the periods immediately after the two World Wars, few births occurred outside marriage during the first 60 years of the 20th century. During the 1960s and 1970s such births became more common and by 1980, 12 per cent of all births in the UK were outside marriage. By 2005 this had increased to 43 per cent (Figure 2.18). Most births outside marriage were registered by both parents rather than only one parent, indicating an increase in cohabiting parents. In 2005, 84 per cent of births outside marriage in England and Wales were jointly registered by both parents. Three in four of jointly registered births were to parents living at the same address.

The proportions of births outside marriage vary across the UK. More than one-half of all births in Wales in 2005 were outside marriage (52 per cent). This compared with 47 per cent of births in Scotland, 42 per cent in England and 36 per cent of births in Northern Ireland. Within England, the North East region had the highest proportion of births outside marriage (55 per cent), followed by the North West (49 per cent), and Yorkshire and the Humber (47 per cent). The lowest proportions of births outside marriage in England were in London and the South East (35 per cent and 38 per cent respectively).

In 2005 the UK had one of the highest levels of births outside marriage in the EU-25 (42 per cent), together with Estonia (58 per cent), Sweden (55 per cent), France (47 per cent), Denmark, Latvia and Slovenia (each 45 per cent) and Finland (41 per cent). The lowest proportion was in Cyprus at 3 per cent.

The rate of multiple births increased from 9.9 per 1,000 of all maternities in 1975 to 14.9 per 1,000 of all maternities in 2005, and 98 per cent of these multiple maternities were twins. This is likely to be a result of the increased use of IVF (in vitro fertilisation) treatment. Unlike natural conception where the chance of having a multiple birth is relatively low (1 in 80 non-IVF deliveries in the UK in 2005 were twins), assisted conception has a high chance of a multiple birth (1 in 4 IVF deliveries were twins). In 2005 twins were born at a rate of 14.7 per 1,000 maternities, while 0.2 per 1,000 maternities led to triplets, quadruplets or more (Table 2.19). Multiple-birth rates are higher for women over the age of 35. Among women aged 35 to 39 years, twins accounted for 20.7 per 1,000 maternities, and triplets for 0.4 per 1,000 maternities. In comparison, for women aged under 20, the rates were 6.5 and less than 0.1 respectively.

Despite the overall trend towards later childbearing, the teenage pregnancy rate in England and Wales has fluctuated over the last 20 years or so. After rising throughout the 1980s to a peak of 67 per 1,000 females aged 15 to 19 in 1989, it fell in the early 1990s to a low of 59 per 1,000 in 1994, before rising again between 1995 and 1998 to 65 per 1,000 females. Since then the teenage pregnancy rate has fallen to 60 per 1,000 females aged 15 to 19 in 2004. There were more than 101,260 conceptions to girls aged under-20 in 2004 (Table 2.20) and 8 per cent of these were to girls under the age of 16. Between 2003 and 2004 the under-20 conception rate for conceptions leading to maternities rose from 59.8 to 60.3 conceptions per 1,000 females aged 15 to 19. In England and Wales, the number of conceptions to girls under 14 increased from 334 in 2003 to 337 in 2004 and more than one-third of these led to maternities. Between the ages 16 and 19, the

Figure 2.18

Births outside marriage[1]

United Kingdom

Percentages

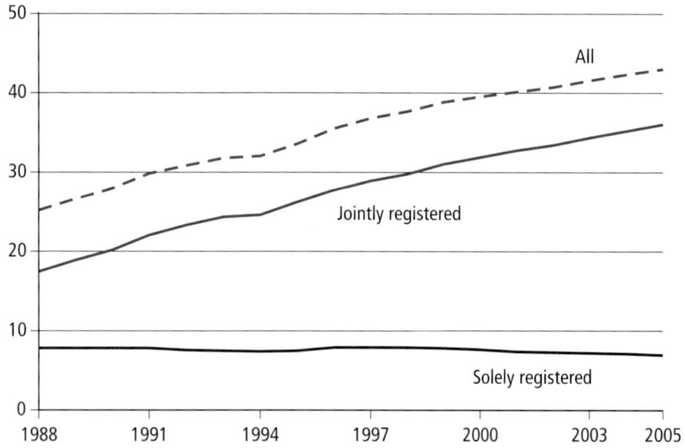

1 As a percentage of all births.

Source: Office for National Statistics; General Register Office for Scotland; Northern Ireland Statistics and Research Agency

Table 2.19

Maternities with multiple births: by age of mother at childbirth, 2005

United Kingdom Rates per 1,000 maternities

	Maternities with twins only	Maternities with triplets or more
Under 20	6.5	0.0
20–24	9.1	0.1
25–29	13.3	0.2
30–34	17.4	0.2
35–39	20.7	0.4
40 and over	22.4	0.6
All mothers	14.7	0.2

Source: Office for National Statistics; General Register Office for Scotland; Northern Ireland Statistics and Research Agency

Table **2.20**

Teenage conceptions:[1] by age at conception and outcome, 2004

England & Wales

	Conceptions (numbers)	Leading to abortions (percentages)	Rates per 1,000 females[2]		
			All conceptions	Leading to maternities	Leading to abortions
Under 14	337	62	1.0	0.4	0.6
14	1,754	63	5.2	1.9	3.3
15	5,524	55	16.5	7.4	9.1
All aged under 16	7,615	57	7.5	3.2	4.3
16	13,636	46	40.0	21.7	18.2
17	20,947	41	62.6	36.7	25.9
All aged under 18	42,198	46	41.7	22.7	19.0
18	27,373	38	82.5	51.3	31.2
19	31,691	35	94.3	61.6	32.8
All aged under 20	101,262	40	60.3	36.1	24.2

1 See Appendix, Part 2: Conceptions.
2 Rates for females aged under 14, under 16, under 18 and under 20 are based on the population of females aged 13, 13 to 15, 15 to 17 and 15 to 19 respectively.

Source: Office for National Statistics

proportion of conceptions resulting in abortions is lower than at younger ages. More than one-third of conceptions to 19-year-olds resulted in an abortion in 2004, compared with over half of conceptions to 15-year-olds.

Teenage maternity rates vary across the UK. In 2004 the under-20 maternity rate in England and Wales was 36 maternities (live births and still births) per 1,000 females aged 15 to 19, compared with Scotland with 21 maternities per 1,000 females in this age group. The maternity rate in Northern Ireland was 23 per 1,000 females aged 15 to 19.

Trends in abortion rates vary by age (Figure 2.21). Since 1969, when the *Abortion Act 1967* came into effect, abortion rates have risen overall and particularly for women aged between 16 and 34. In 2005 women aged between 20 and 24 years had the highest rate, at 32.0 per 1,000 women, whereas females aged between 13 and 15 had the lowest rate, at 3.7 per 1,000.

During the early 1990s the abortion rate among young women aged 16 to 24 fell slightly, but then rose again – as it did for all age groups – between 1995 and 1996. In 1995 the Committee on Safety of Medicines warned that several brands of the contraceptive pill carried a relatively high risk of thrombosis. This warning is believed to have contributed to the increase in abortion rates in 1996, particularly among young women as they were more likely to have been using the pill. Since the pill scare, abortion rates have not fallen back to the 1995 level but

Figure **2.21**

Abortion rates:[1] by age

England & Wales
Rates per 1,000 females

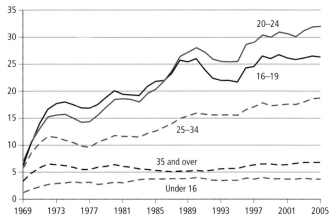

1 The rates for females aged under 16 are based on the population of females aged 13–15. The rates for women aged 35 and over are based on the population of women aged 35–44.

Source: Office for National Statistics; Department of Health

have continued to rise for all age groups except for those aged under 16, whose abortion rates have stayed roughly the same.

People may extend their families through adoption. In 2005 there were 5,600 adoptions in England and Wales. Increased use of contraception, new abortion laws and changed attitudes towards lone motherhood meant that around 16,000 fewer children were adopted in 2005 in England and Wales than in 1971 (Figure 2.22). Following the introduction of legal abortion in Great Britain in the *Abortion Act 1967* and the implementation of the *Children Act 1975* there was a rapid decline in the number of children available for adoption in England and Wales. The latter act required courts dealing with adoption applications for children of divorced parents to dismiss applications for adoption where a legal custody order was in the child's best interests. Numbers of adoptions in Scotland and Northern Ireland also decreased between 1971 and 2005, from 1,900 to 440 in Scotland and from 390 to 140 in Northern Ireland. In 2005, one-fifth of the children adopted in England and Wales were born inside marriage compared with two-fifths in 1993. Some of these adoptions may be stepchildren adoptions following the marriage of one of the natural parents.

Between 1994 and 2004 there were steady decreases in the proportion of children aged five to fourteen who were adopted, and a marked increase in the proportion adopted who were aged one to four. In 2004, 49 per cent of children adopted were aged between one and four compared with 26 per cent in 1994, and 13 per cent were aged 10 to 14 compared with 23 per cent ten years earlier.

Figure **2.22**

Adoption orders: by year of registration[1,2]

England & Wales

Thousands

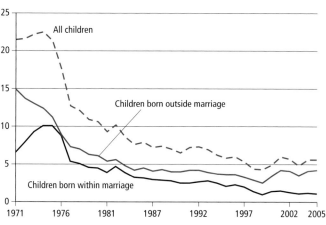

1 Year of entry into the Adopted Children Register. Data for 1990 and 2001 include cases where the child was older than 17 years.
2 Data for all children for 1985 to 1989 include cases where marital status was not stated. Where marital status for 1998 are missing they have been imputed.

Source: Office for National Statistics

Education and training

- The proportion of three and four-year-olds enrolled in all schools in the UK tripled from 21 per cent in 1970/71 to 64 per cent in 2005/06. (Figure 3.1)

- In 2005, 704,000 children were enrolled in full-day childcare settings in England compared with 539,000 in 2001. The number enrolled for part of the day has fallen, from 589,000 in 2001 to 390,000 in 2005. (Figure 3.2)

- The rate of permanent exclusion among school pupils in England has fallen by 23 per cent since 1997/98 to 12 in every 10,000 pupils of compulsory school age in 2004/05. (Page 29)

- At the end of 2005, a record 76 per cent of 16-year-olds were in full-time further education in England. (Page 29)

- In both 1996 and 2006, girls outperformed boys in teacher assessments in England, although there were improvements in the performance of both sexes at all Key Stages. (Table 3.11)

- There were 441,000 full-time teachers in mainstream schools in the UK in 2004/05, an overall fall of 10 per cent since 1981/82 despite rises since the late 1990s. (Page 38)

Chapter 3

For increasing numbers of the population, education is no longer confined to compulsory schooling. Early learning and participation in pre-school education is seen as important for building a foundation for future learning, and most people continue in full-time education beyond school-leaving age. Qualifications attained at school are increasingly supplemented by further and higher education and other training, to equip people with the skills required by a modern labour market, and to keep these skills up to date.

Early years education

Early years education aims to ensure that all children begin their compulsory education with a basic foundation in literacy and numeracy; and key skills such as listening, concentration and learning to work with others. The proportion of three and four-year-olds enrolled in all schools in the UK rose from 21 per cent in 1970/71 to 65 per cent in 2004/05, and then fell to 64 per cent in 2005/06 (Figure 3.1). This overall increase reflects both the growth in the number of places – there were over 3,300 state nursery schools in 2005/06, almost two and a half times the number in 1990/91 – and an overall fall in the number of three and four-year-olds in the population during the period 1971 to 2005. In January 2006, 35 per cent of three and four-year-olds attending early years education were enrolled in other non-school settings such as playgroups in the private and voluntary sectors, either instead of, or in addition to, their school place.

The pattern of participation in early years education varies regionally. The proportion of three and four-year-olds in maintained nursery and primary schools is generally higher in Wales and the north of England than in the south. In January 2006 around twice the proportion of three and four-year-olds attended maintained nursery and primary schools in the North East (84 per cent) and Wales (81 per cent) compared with the South East (42 per cent) and the South West of England (43 per cent). However, more children were enrolled with private and voluntary providers in the south than in other parts of the country (55 per cent in the South East and 59 per cent in the South West). It is worth noting that in England and Scotland a child may be enrolled with more than one type of provider and therefore may have been counted twice.

In 2005 the Department for Education and Skills carried out surveys of four Ofsted (Office for Standards in Education) registered childcare settings: full-day childcare, sessional childcare, out-of-school childcare, and childminders, to assess the provision of childcare in England. Full-day childcare settings are defined as facilities that provide day care for children under eight years old, for a continuous period of four hours or more in any day in non-domestic premises (for example, day nurseries). Sessional childcare settings are facilities that provide

Figure 3.1

Children under five in schools[1]

United Kingdom
Percentages

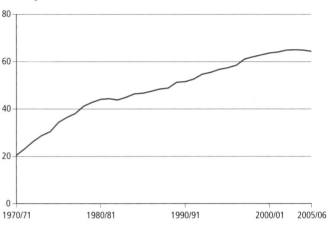

1 Pupils aged three and four at 31 December each year as a percentage of all three and four-year-olds. See Appendix, Part 3: Stages of education.

Source: Department for Education and Skills; Welsh Assembly Government; Scottish Executive; Northern Ireland Department of Education

similar day care for children under eight years old but for a session that is less than a continuous period of four hours in any day, and out-of-school childcare includes after school clubs, breakfast clubs and holiday clubs that are registered with Ofsted (see Appendix, Part 3: Stages of education).

The 2005 survey showed that there were a total of 21,800 full-day and sessional care providers in England and

Figure 3.2

Children enrolled with childcare settings: by type of setting[1]

England
Thousands

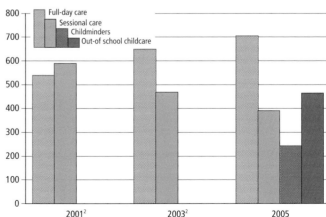

1 See Appendix, Part 3: Stages of education.
2 Data are not available for childminders and out-of-school childcare.

Source: Childcare and Early Years Providers Survey, Department for Education and Skills

that the number of full-day care providers has increased, reflecting a shift in preference away from sessional day care towards full-day care provision. The number of children enrolled in full-day childcare settings in England increased by 165,000 from 539,000 in 2001 to 704,000 in 2005, whereas the number of children enrolled in sessional care settings decreased by 199,000 to 390,000 (Figure 3.2). Over the period 2001 to 2005 the average number of children enrolled per full-day childcare provider declined from 69 in 2001 to 60 in 2005. This could be because there has been an increase in the number of full-day providers compared with a decrease in sessional providers. In 2001 there were 7,800 full-day care providers compared with 11,800 in 2005, whereas the number of sessional childcare providers fell from 14,000 to 10,000 (see also Chapter 8: Social protection).

Compulsory education

In 2005/06 there were around 34,000 schools in the UK, accommodating 9.9 million pupils (Table 3.3). Public sector schools (not including special schools) were attended by 9.1 million pupils (92 per cent), while 7 per cent of pupils attended one of the 2,500 non-maintained mainstream schools. These proportions have remained around this level since the 1970s. One per cent of pupils attended one of the 1,400 special schools in 2005/06, and there were around 480 pupil referral units (PRUs), catering for 16,000 pupils. PRUs provide suitable alternative education on a temporary basis for pupils who may not be able to attend a mainstream school. As well as pupils who have been excluded from mainstream schools and children with medical problems, PRUs may provide education for school-aged mothers and pregnant schoolgirls, school-phobics, and pupils awaiting placement in a maintained school.

Any maintained secondary school in England can apply to be designated as a specialist school. Specialist schools receive extra funding to establish curriculum centres of excellence. Although they focus on one or two chosen specialisms, these schools must still meet National Curriculum requirements and deliver a broad and balanced education to all pupils. By September 2006, 82 per cent of all secondary schools in England had become specialist schools. There were 2,610 designated specialist schools (which included 65 special schools), attended by around 2.5 million pupils in September 2006. This represents over two-thirds of all pupils in maintained secondary schools in England.

In 2005/06 the average class size in Great Britain was 25 pupils for Key Stage 1 (five to seven-year-olds) and 27 pupils for Key Stage 2 (seven to eleven-year-olds) (Table 3.4 overleaf). Key Stage 2 pupils were far more likely than Key Stage 1 pupils to be in classes of 31 or more pupils, (19 per cent compared with

2 per cent), although for both Key Stages the proportion of pupils in classes of this size has fallen since 2000/01 when 28 per cent of Key Stage 2 pupils, and 4 per cent of Key Stage 1, were in classes of 31 or more pupils. More than one in four Key Stage 2 classes in the East Midlands and the South West had 31 or more pupils in 2005/06 compared with less than one in ten classes in London, and an even smaller proportion in Northern Ireland and Wales. Northern Ireland had the smallest average number of pupils per class at both Key Stage 1 and Key Stage 2 in 2005/06. Average class size in secondary schools in England was around 22 pupils and in Wales, 21 pupils, despite secondary schools usually having more pupils than primary schools. This smaller average class size is in part because students choose different subjects in preparation for formal exams taken towards the end of their compulsory secondary schooling.

In the British Social Attitudes survey 2005, adults aged 18 and over in Great Britain were shown a selection of possible improvements to education and, regarding primary and

Table **3.3**

School pupils:[1] by type of school[2]

United Kingdom					Thousands
	1970/71	1980/81	1990/91	2000/01	2005/06
Public sector schools[3]					
Nursery[4]	50	89	105	152	151
Primary	5,902	5,171	4,955	5,298	4,975
Secondary[5]					
Comprehensive	1,313	3,730	2,925	3,340	3,453
Grammar	673	149	156	205	218
Modern	1,164	233	94	112	102
Other	403	434	298	260	214
All public sector schools	9,507	9,806	8,533	9,367	9,113
Non-maintained schools	621	619	613	626	659
All special schools	103	148	114	113	106
Pupil referral units	.	.	.	10	16
All schools	10,230	10,572	9,260	10,116	9,894

1 Headcounts.
2 See Appendix, Part 3: Stages of education, and Main categories of educational establishments.
3 Excludes maintained special schools and pupil referral units.
4 Figures for Scotland before 1998/99 only include data for Local Authority (LA) pre-schools, data thereafter include partnership pre-schools. From 2005/06, figures refer to centres providing pre-school education at an LA centre, or in partnership with the LA only. Children are counted once for each centre they are registered with.
5 Excludes sixth form colleges from 1980/81.

Source: Department for Education and Skills; Welsh Assembly Government; Scottish Executive; Northern Ireland Department of Education

Table **3.4**

Class sizes in schools:[1] by region, 2005/06

	Primary schools				Secondary schools	
	Key Stage 1[2]		Key Stage 2[2]			
	Average number in class	Percentage of classes with 31 or more pupils	Average number in class	Percentage of classes with 31 or more pupils	Average number in class	Percentage of classes with 31 or more pupils
Great Britain	25.4	2.2	26.9	18.9	..	..
England	25.7	2.3	27.3	20.7	21.5	7.7
North East	24.6	2.2	26.3	17.1	21.5	7.3
North West	25.3	2.3	27.4	24.8	21.4	8.3
Yorkshire and the Humber	25.5	3.8	27.4	23.7	21.3	7.7
East Midlands	24.8	2.8	27.3	25.8	21.6	7.4
West Midlands	25.6	2.2	27.3	19.0	21.5	8.1
East	25.5	2.7	27.4	19.6	21.6	7.9
London	27.1	1.7	27.2	8.6	21.6	5.6
South East	25.9	2.0	27.5	24.0	21.6	7.8
South West	25.4	1.7	27.3	25.7	21.7	9.5
Wales	24.4	2.3	25.0	3.5	20.6	9.3
Scotland	23.1	0.9	24.6	12.6	..	..
Northern Ireland	22.9	2.2	23.9	7.1	..	..

1 Maintained schools only. Figures relate to all classes, not just those taught by one teacher. In Northern Ireland a class is defined as a group of pupils normally under the control of one teacher.
2 Pupils in composite classes that overlap Key Stage 1 and Key Stage 2 are not included. In Scotland primary P1 to P3 is interpreted to be Key Stage 1 and P4 to P7, Key Stage 2.

Source: Department for Education and Skills; Welsh Assembly Government; Scottish Executive; Northern Ireland Department of Education

secondary education separately, were asked 'Which do you think would be the most useful one for improving the education of children in primary and secondary schools?' Reducing class sizes was seen by respondents as the best way of improving both primary (37 per cent) and secondary (26 per cent) education. Other suggested improvements to primary and secondary education favoured by respondents included: better quality teachers (16 per cent for primary level and 19 per cent for secondary); greater emphasis on developing the child's skills and interests (15 per cent and 14 per cent); and more resources for buildings, books and equipment (14 per cent and 13 per cent respectively).

Pupils with special educational needs (SEN) have either significantly greater difficulty in learning than other children of the same age, or a disability that makes it difficult for them to use normal educational facilities. When a school identifies a child with SEN it must try to meet the child's needs, in line with provisions in the SEN Code of Practice (or in Scotland, the Code of Practice on supporting children's learning). If

the initial attempts do not meet the child's needs then an education authority or board may determine the educational needs for a child with SEN, and draw up a formal statement of those needs (or from 2006 in Scotland, a Co-ordinated Support Plan) together with the action it intends to take to meet them. In 2005/06, 278,300 pupils (2.8 per cent) in the UK had these statements. This figure comprises 236,700 pupils in England, 15,800 in Wales, 13,800 in Scotland and 12,000 in Northern Ireland.

In England the number of pupils with statements of SEN increased from 194,500 in January 1994 (representing 2.5 per cent of pupils) to peak at 258,200 (3.1 per cent) in 2001. Numbers have since declined, with the total in January 2006 (236,700) representing 2.9 per cent of pupils. While the number of pupils in special schools and pupil referral units remained fairly constant in the 12 years to 2006, the number of pupils with statements of SEN in mainstream maintained schools increased – from 100,600 in 1994 to 158,000 in 2001, but has since declined by 19,000 to 139,000 in January 2006

(Figure 3.5). For more information on these data see Appendix, Part 3: Special Educational Needs data.

In 2004/05 there were 9,440 permanent exclusions of pupils from primary, secondary and special schools in England, approximately 12 in every 10,000 pupils of compulsory school age. This figure is around 4 per cent less than 2003/04 and around 23 per cent less than 1997/98, when there were 12,300 permanent exclusions of pupils in England. These pupils are excluded from the school and their name removed from the school register. They are educated at another school or through some other form of provision.

In 2004/05 the permanent exclusion rate for boys was nearly four times higher than that for girls in England. The ratio of permanent exclusion between boys and girls has remained stable over the last five years with boys representing around 80 per cent of the total number of permanent exclusions each year. This ratio was similar in Wales, where there were 465 permanent exclusions from local authority schools in 2004/05. In Scotland, there were 271 permanent exclusions in 2004/05. Nearly all exclusions in Scotland were temporary and boys accounted for 79 per cent of all exclusions.

Exclusion rates vary by ethnic group of pupils. In 2004/05, rates ranged from 2 in every 10,000 Chinese pupils being permanently excluded from schools in England, to 41 in every 10,000 pupils of mixed White and Black Caribbean origin (Figure 3.6). Black African pupils were far less likely to be permanently excluded (14 in every 10,000), than Black

Figure **3.5**

Pupils with statements of Special Educational Needs (SEN):[1] by type of school

England

Thousands

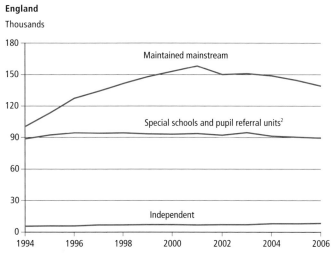

1 Data are at January each year. Estimates were made for 2001 because the SEN data were known to be incomplete. See Appendix, Part 3: Special Educational Needs data.
2 Pupil referral units did not exist before 1995.

Source: Department for Education and Skills

Figure **3.6**

Permanent exclusion rates:[1] by ethnic group, 2004/05

England

Rates per 10,000 pupils

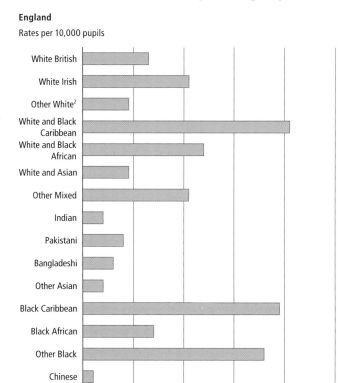

1 The number of permanent exclusions per 10,000 pupils of compulsory school age (headcount) in each ethnic group in primary, secondary and special schools (excluding dually registered pupils in special schools). Dual registration is when a pupil is registered at more than one school.
2 Excludes Travellers of Irish heritage and Gypsy/Roma.
3 Excludes unclassified pupils, pupils who were not asked to provide ethnic information, and those who refused to provide it.

Source: Department for Education and Skills

Caribbean pupils (39 in every 10,000) or those from any Other Black background (36 in every 10,000). Around 80 per cent of all permanent exclusions in 2004/05 were of White pupils.

Post-compulsory education

Following the end of compulsory education, young people aged 16 can choose whether to go on to further education. At the end of 2005, 500,000 students (76 per cent) in England who were 16 at the beginning of the academic year had gone on to full-time further education – the highest rate on record and an increase of 3 percentage points since the end of 2004. A higher proportion of females than males of this age were in full-time education (82 per cent compared with 72 per cent). Of the 16-year-olds who were not in further education (both male and female), 13 per cent were in work-based learning (for example apprenticeships), employer-funded training, or other education and training, and 11 per cent were not in education, employment or training.

Figure **3.7**

Participation of 16-year-olds in full-time education: by institution type[1]

England

Percentages

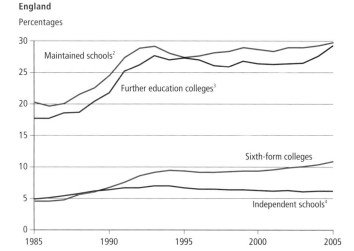

1 From 1994 there were changes in the source of further and higher education data. Participation estimates may be slightly underestimated for 16-year-olds between 1999 and 2000.
2 Includes all pupils in maintained schools and maintained special schools.
3 Includes general further education, tertiary and specialist colleges.
4 Includes all pupils in independent schools, non-maintained special schools, city technology colleges, academies and pupil referral units.

Source: Department for Education and Skills

Maintained schools and further education colleges have been the most common providers of full-time further education for 16-year-olds for the last 20 years. Between 1985 and 1993 there was a general rise in the proportion of 16-year-olds in England who were participating in full-time education in these institutions (Figure 3.7). Since then the proportions have remained fairly stable, with each type being attended by between 26 and 30 per cent of 16-year-olds between 1993 and 2005. There has also been an increase in the proportion of 16-year-olds in full-time education at sixth-form colleges, from 5 per cent in 1985 to 11 per cent in 2005.

In Wales, maintained schools and further education colleges are the main providers of full-time education for 16-year-olds. Between 1995/96 and 2004/05, 35 to 38 per cent of 16-year-olds in Wales were in full-time education in maintained schools and between 31 to 34 per cent were in full-time education in further education colleges.

In 2004/05 there were 5.0 million further education students in the UK, almost three times the number in 1970/71. There were around four times as many female further education students in 2004/05 as in 1970/71, and twice as many male students. In 1970/71 the majority (58 per cent) of further education students in the UK were men, 1 million compared with 725,000 women (Table 3.8). However, by 2004/05 the majority (59 per cent) of further education students were women, 3.0 million compared with 2.1 million men.

Table **3.8**

Students in further and higher education:[1] by type of course and sex

United Kingdom

Thousands

	Men				Women			
	1970/71	1980/81	1990/91	2004/05	1970/71	1980/81	1990/91	2004/05
Further education								
Full-time	116	154	219	532	95	196	261	551
Part-time	891	697	768	1,534	630	624	986	2,429
All further education	1,007	851	986	2,066	725	820	1,247	2,981
Higher education								
Undergraduate								
Full-time	241	277	345	549	173	196	319	680
Part-time	127	176	148	267	19	71	106	458
Postgraduate								
Full-time	33	41	50	113	10	21	34	114
Part-time	15	32	46	139	3	13	33	172
All higher education[2]	416	526	588	1,068	205	301	491	1,426

1 Home and overseas students. See Appendix, Part 3: Stages of education.
2 Figures for 2004/05 include a small number of higher education students for whom details are not available by level.

Source: Department for Education and Skills; Welsh Assembly Government; Scottish Executive; Northern Ireland Department for Employment and Learning; Higher Education Statistics Agency

Similar numbers of men and women study full time but the majority (79 per cent) of further education students studied part time in 2004/05. Women are more likely than men to study part time, 81 per cent and 74 per cent respectively of further education students. This contrasts to 1970/71 when a similar proportion of women (87 per cent) and men (88 per cent) studied part time.

There have also been substantial increases in the number of students in higher education in the UK (see Appendix, Part 3: Stages of education). In 2004/05 there were 2.5 million students in higher education compared with 0.6 million in 1970/71. During this period the proportion of female higher education students increased from 33 per cent to 57 per cent. The number of enrolments has increased for both sexes. For women, there were 1.4 million higher education enrolments in 2004/05, seven times as many as in 1970/71. For men, there were 1.1 million enrolments in 2004/05, an increase of two and a half times over the same period.

Data supplied by UK higher education institutions show the variety of courses studied by higher education students as well as the variations in subject choice by sex. When considering full-time and part-time, undergraduate and postgraduate, and home and overseas students, the most popular subjects in 2004/05 were subjects allied to medicine (for example nursing, pharmacology and physiology) and business and administrative studies (Table 3.9). Subjects within each of these subject groups were studied by 13 per cent of students. However, a higher proportion of women than men studied subjects allied to medicine, while a greater proportion of men than women studied business and administrative services. Women were also more likely than men to study subjects from the education group (11 per cent of female higher education students compared with 5 per cent of male students) (see also data on teachers on page 38). Higher proportions of men than women in higher education studied engineering and technology subjects and computer sciences. Similar proportions of men and women studied creative arts and design, historical and philosophical studies, law, and medicine and dentistry.

There has been an increase in the number of overseas domiciled students studying at UK higher education institutions in recent years, from 75,600 full-time students in 1980/81 to 240,300 in 2004/05. In 1980/81 students from Malaysia accounted for the largest proportion of the total number of overseas students, with 13,300 students (18 per cent). In 2004/05 there were 8,900 students from Malaysia, representing 4 per cent of all overseas students. The largest increase over the period has been in the number of students from China, which increased from around 200 in 1980/81 to over 45,000 in 2004/05.

Table 3.9

Students in higher education:[1] by subject[2] and sex, 2004/05

United Kingdom   Percentages

	Men	Women	All
Subjects allied to medicine	5.3	19.0	13.1
Business & administrative studies	15.4	11.3	13.1
Education	5.3	11.4	8.8
Social studies	7.6	9.2	8.5
Biological sciences	5.5	7.3	6.5
Creative arts & design	6.0	6.9	6.5
Engineering & technology	11.9	1.6	6.0
Languages	4.4	7.0	5.9
Computer science	10.2	2.4	5.7
Historical & philosophical studies	4.5	4.2	4.3
Law	3.6	3.9	3.8
Physical sciences	4.7	2.5	3.4
Medicine & dentistry	2.4	2.5	2.4
Architecture, building & planning	3.5	1.2	2.2
Mass communications & documentation	1.9	2.1	2.0
Mathematical sciences	2.0	0.9	1.4
Agriculture & related subjects	0.6	0.7	0.7
Veterinary science	0.1	0.2	0.2
Combined	5.0	5.7	5.4
All subject areas (=100%) (thousands)	979	1,308	2,288

1 Full-time and part-time, undergraduate and postgraduate, and home and overseas students. See Appendix, Part 3: Stages of education.
2 Subject data are classified using the Joint Academic Coding System. See Appendix, Part 3: Joint Academic Coding System.

Source: Department for Education and Skills; Higher Education Statistics Agency

Not everyone working towards a qualification beyond the age of 16 has worked their way continuously through the various levels of education. Over two-fifths (45 per cent) of working-age people who were studying towards a qualification in the UK in spring 2006 were aged 25 or over and around one-fifth (19 per cent) were aged 40 or over (Table 3.10 overleaf). The age distribution varies according to the qualification being studied. Adults aged 25 and over comprised 27 per cent of those studying towards a GCSE or equivalent and 19 per cent of people of working age were studying towards a GCE A level or equivalent. Sixty per cent of working-age people were taking higher education qualifications below degree level (such as a Higher National Diploma or Higher National Certificate), and 41 per cent of those studying at degree level or higher, were in this age group.

Table **3.10**

People working towards a qualification:[1] by age, 2006[2]

United Kingdom   Percentages

	Degree or equivalent or higher	Higher education[3]	GCE A level or equivalent	GCSE or equivalent	Other qualification[4]	All studying
16–19	16	20	72	67	13	35
20–24	43	21	9	6	13	21
25–29	13	13	4	4	15	10
30–39	14	22	7	9	27	16
40–49	11	17	6	9	20	12
50–59/64[5]	4	8	2	5	13	6
All aged 16–59/64[5] (=100%) (millions)	1.9	0.5	1.4	0.9	1.8	6.4

1 For those working towards more than one qualification, the highest is recorded. See Appendix, Part 3: Qualifications. Excludes those who did not answer.
2 At spring. Data are not seasonally adjusted. See Appendix, Part 4: Labour Force Survey.
3 Below degree level but including NVQ level 4.
4 Includes those who did not know the qualification they were working towards.
5 Men aged 16 to 64 and women aged 16 to 59.

Source: Labour Force Survey, Office for National Statistics

Educational attainment

Assessment at Key Stages in England and Wales is an essential component of the National Curriculum, see Appendix, Part 3: The National Curriculum. Scotland and Northern Ireland each have their own guidelines for the curriculum. In the last ten years, although the proportion of girls reaching the required standard in each of the Key Stages by teacher assessment has generally been higher than that for boys, there have been improvements in the performance of both sexes (Table 3.11). At Key Stage 1 the proportion of boys who reached the required standard in reading by teacher assessment increased by 7 percentage points between 1996 and 2006, to 80 per cent, and for writing, there was an increase of 5 percentage points to 76 per cent. For girls the proportions also increased, by 6 percentage points and 5 percentage points respectively, to 89 per cent for reading and 87 per cent for writing. In English at Key Stage 2 there were more marked improvements. Boys' performance improved by 19 percentage points and that of girls improved by 14 percentage points. There was a similar pattern of improvement for both boys and girls in mathematics and science although in all three subjects the performance against expected standards for both sexes was lower at Key Stage 2 than Key Stage 1. Similarly, although there were improvements between 1996 and 2005 for both sexes at Key Stage 3 in all three assessed subjects, the proportion who achieved the expected standard at this stage was generally lower than at Key Stage 2.

In addition to teacher assessment, pupils' performance in England is assessed by National Curriculum tests at Key Stages

Table **3.11**

Pupils reaching or exceeding expected standards through teacher assessment:[1] by Key Stage and sex

England   Percentages

	1996		2006[2]	
	Boys	Girls	Boys	Girls
Key Stage 1[3]				
English				
Reading	73	83	80	89
Writing	71	82	76	87
Mathematics	80	83	89	92
Science	83	85	88	91
Key Stage 2[4]				
English	53	68	72	82
Mathematics	58	62	78	78
Science	64	67	83	85
Key Stage 3[5]				
English	51	70	64	78
Mathematics	60	64	74	77
Science	59	61	70	73

1 See Appendix, Part 3: The National Curriculum.
2 Key Stage 3 data are for 2005.
3 Pupils achieving level 2 or above at Key Stage 1.
4 Pupils achieving level 4 or above at Key Stage 2.
5 Pupils achieving level 5 or above at Key Stage 3.

Source: Department for Education and Skills

2 and 3. These tests measure pupils' attainment against the levels set by the National Curriculum. They measure the extent to which pupils have the specific knowledge, skills and understanding which the National Curriculum expects pupils to have developed by the end of the Key Stage. There were improvements over the last ten years in tests although again, girls generally performed better than boys. For example in 1996, 50 per cent of boys and 65 per cent of girls reached the expected standard in English tests at Key Stage 2 and by 2006 these proportions had increased to 74 per cent and 85 per cent respectively. For mathematics and science the same was true although at Key Stage 2 the improvement of boys in mathematics was such that they performed better than girls in 2006, with 77 per cent achieving the expected standard compared with 75 per cent of girls.

One of the factors contributing to pupil performance is homework. The Longitudinal Study of Young People in England (LSYPE) showed that in 2004 almost all (97 per cent) pupils aged 13 or 14 in England said they were given homework and of these, more than two-thirds (68 per cent) said they were given homework on most days. The survey results show that across all three subject areas (English, mathematics and science) the average point score in Key Stage 3 tests per pupil increases as the number of evenings spent doing homework increases (Figure 3.12). Higher proportions of pupils who spend four or five evenings a week doing homework achieved the expected standards of level 5 or above at Key Stage 3 than the pupils who said they didn't spend any evenings doing homework. The average score of pupils who were given homework but didn't spend any evenings doing it was 30.2 points. Those pupils who spent some time doing homework on five evenings a week scored, on average, 37.2 points. The survey also asked about parental involvement in homework. The majority (81 per cent) of pupils said that there was someone at home who would help them with their homework and 44 per cent said that someone at home made sure they did their homework.

In 2004/05, 57 per cent of pupils in their last year of compulsory education in the UK achieved five or more GCSE grades A* to C (or equivalent), compared with 46 per cent in 1995/96. A higher proportion of girls than boys achieved these grades in 2004/05, 62 per cent compared with 52 per cent. The proportion of pupils who did not receive any graded results (for example their results were ungraded, unclassified, pending or they were absent from the examination) fell from 7 per cent to 3 per cent over the period.

There are also variations in achievement by free school meal eligibility (a measure used as an indicator of low household income, deprivation and social class) (Table 3.13). Data from England show that pupils who were not eligible for free school

Figure **3.12**

Key Stage 3 average points score:[1] by the number of evenings spent doing homework,[2] 2004

England
Average points score

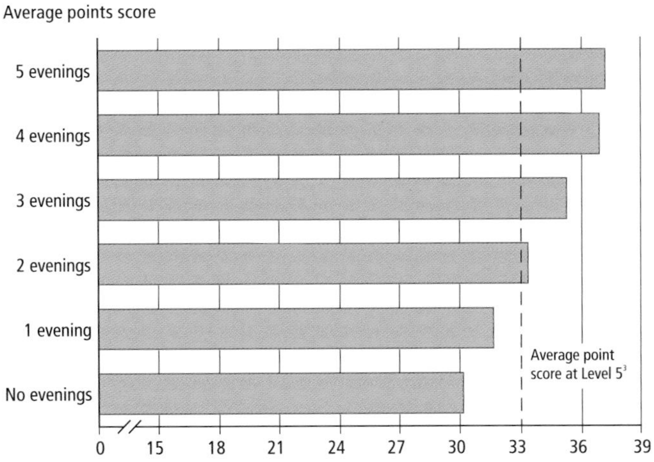

1 All pupils in receipt of homework.
2 Children aged 13 or 14 who said they spent any time doing homework were asked, 'During an average week (Monday to Friday) in term time, on how many evenings do you do any homework?'
3 Data are drawn from the average point size score of students at Key Stage 3.

Source: Longitudinal Study of Young People in England, Department for Education and Skills

Table **3.13**

GCSE or equivalent attainment: by free school meal eligibility, 2005/06

England   Percentages

	5 grades A* to C	5 grades A* to C including English and mathematics	Any passes
Boys			
Free school meals	28.3	16.6	92.5
Non-free school meals	55.8	43.2	97.4
All pupils[1]	52.2	39.7	96.8
Girls			
Free school meals	37.0	22.3	94.9
Non-free school meals	65.7	52.0	98.3
All pupils[1]	61.9	48.0	97.8
All			
Free school meals	32.6	19.5	93.7
Non-free school meals	60.7	47.5	97.8
All pupils[1]	56.9	43.8	97.3

1 Includes pupils where information was refused or not obtained.

Source: Department for Education and Skills

meals generally performed better than those who were eligible at each Key Stage, at GCSE and at post-16 level. For example, at GCSE and equivalent level, 61 per cent of pupils in England who were not eligible for free school meals achieved five or more GCSEs grade A* to C in 2005/06 compared with 33 per cent of pupils who were eligible. When English and mathematics are included in these five GCSEs the pattern is the same, although in both cases the proportions achieving grades A* to C were lower: 48 per cent of pupils who were not eligible for free school meals achieved grades A* to C compared with 20 per cent of those who were eligible.

GCE A level examinations are usually taken after two years post-GCSE study in a school sixth form, sixth-form college or further-education college, by those who stay in education full time beyond the age of 16. The proportion of young people aged 17 at the start of the academic year in England who gained two or more GCE A levels (or equivalent) increased from 25 per cent in 1993/94 to 34 per cent in 2005/06 (Figure 3.14). The proportion achieving three or more GCE A levels (or equivalent) increased from 18 per cent to 29 per cent over the same period. The proportion of students achieving at least three A grades in GCE A levels (or equivalent) increased from 1.9 per cent in 1993/94 to 3.9 per cent in 2005/06.

In 2004/05, 33 per cent of young men in England, Wales and Northern Ireland achieved two or more GCE A level (or equivalent) passes and 26 per cent achieved three or more passes. For young women these percentages were 41 per cent and 35 per cent respectively.

In 2004/05 there were around 306,000 first degrees obtained by UK and overseas domiciled students at higher education institutions in the UK. Of those first degrees, 11 per cent were graded first class with similar proportions of both men and women achieving this level. A higher proportion of women than men achieved upper second grades, 46 per cent compared with 39 per cent, while similar proportions of men and women achieved lower second class grades, 32 per cent compared with 29 per cent. Around 7 per cent of all first-degree students achieved a third class (or pass grade) and 9 per cent were unclassified.

In 2005 working-age people in Great Britain were more likely to be educated to at least degree level than to be without formal qualifications. Eighteen per cent of people held degrees or equivalent compared with 14 per cent with no qualifications. However, people were most likely to hold as their highest qualification, GCE A level or equivalent (24 per cent) or GCSE grades A* to C or equivalent level (23 per cent), compared with any other level of qualification or none at all. Differences emerged when attainment was analysed by sex. Working-age men were one and a half times more likely than working-age

Figure **3.14**

Achievement of two or more GCE A levels[1] or equivalent

England

Percentages[2]

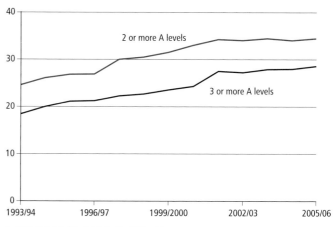

1 See Appendix, Part 3: Qualifications.
2 Young people aged 17 at the start of the academic year as a percentage of the 17-year-old population.

Source: Department for Education and Skills

women to have at least a GCE A level (or equivalent) as their highest qualification; 28 per cent of men, compared with 18 per cent of women (Table 3.15). The converse was true for those who held GCSE grades at A* to C (or equivalent) as their highest qualification: 27 per cent of women held these qualifications as their highest compared with 19 per cent of men. The sex differences became less pronounced between those educated to degree level or to another higher education qualification, those with other qualifications and those with no qualifications.

Historic social effects may have had an impact on the proportion of older working-age people with qualifications. For example, in 2005 men aged 50 to 64 were one and a half times more likely than women aged 50 to 59 to hold a degree or the equivalent. This is reflected in the higher proportion of men than women who were enrolled in higher education in the 1970s compared with more recent years (see Table 3.8). Among working-age women, those aged 50 and over were more likely than women in other age groups to hold no qualifications. Among working-age men there was a slightly different picture. Around one-fifth of working-age men aged 50 and over, and one-fifth of 16 to 19-year-olds held no qualifications; both higher proportions than men in other working-age groups.

Large differences in highest qualification levels can be found between ethnic groups. Among men in Great Britain, Chinese (34 per cent), Indian (32 per cent) and White Irish men (25 per cent) were most likely to have a degree (or equivalent

Table **3.15**

Highest qualification held:[1] by sex and age, 2005[2]

Great Britain

Percentages

	Degree or equivalent or higher	Higher education qualification[3]	GCE A level or equivalent	GCSE grades A* to C or equivalent	Other qualification	No qualification	All
Men							
16–19	-	1	27	43	9	20	100
20–24	15	6	38	23	11	8	100
25–29	29	7	23	19	13	9	100
30–39	24	8	24	20	14	10	100
40–49	21	9	28	17	13	12	100
50–64	17	9	31	11	13	19	100
All men	19	8	28	19	13	14	100
Women							
16–19	-	1	31	45	7	16	100
20–24	18	6	34	23	9	9	100
25–29	30	8	20	22	11	9	100
30–39	22	10	17	29	12	10	100
40–49	18	11	14	29	12	15	100
50–59	12	12	12	21	16	27	100
All women	17	9	18	27	12	15	100

1 Men aged 16 to 64, women aged 16 to 59.
2 January to December. See Appendix, Part 4: Annual Population Survey.
3 Below degree level.

Source: Annual Population Survey, Office for National Statistics

or higher) in 2005 while Black Caribbean (9 per cent) and Bangladeshi men (13 per cent) were least likely. A similar pattern occurred among women as those most likely to hold degrees were Chinese (31 per cent), White Irish (25 per cent) and Indian women (23 per cent), while Bangladeshi (8 per cent) and Pakistani women (10 per cent) were least likely. To some extent this reflects differences in age structure of ethnic populations, length of stay in the UK and cultural differences.

In 2004/05 the Student Income and Expenditure Survey asked students in England whether they thought financial difficulties affected their academic performance. Full-time students were more likely than part-time students to feel that their finances had some form of detrimental effect on their studies – 60 per cent of full-time students compared with 40 per cent of part-time students.

When students were asked further about how their financial situation affected their studies, there was a variety of responses with a similar pattern for both full-time and part-time students (Figure 3.16). For both full-time and part-time students, the most common effect reported was worry and stress (68 per cent

Figure **3.16**

Finance related problems cited as affecting academic performance:[1] by course type, 2004/05

England

Percentages

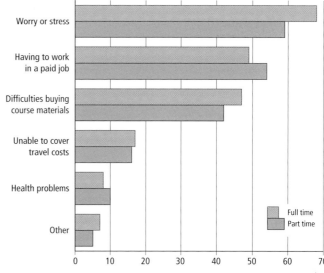

1 Students domiciled in England who felt that their finances had some effect on their academic performance. Percentages do not add up to 100 per cent as respondents could give more than one answer.

Source: Student Income and Expenditure Survey, Department for Education and Skills

of full-time students and 59 per cent of part-time students), followed by having to take on paid work (49 per cent of full-time students and 54 per cent of part-time students). See also Chapter 5: Income and wealth.

An alternative to the more traditional academic qualifications are National Vocational Qualifications (NVQs) and Scottish Vocational Qualifications (SVQs), which were introduced in 1987, and since then there has been a general increase in the take up of these qualifications. Awards are given at levels 1 to 5 with level 1 being broadly equivalent to between one and four GCSE grades A* to C and level 5 being equivalent to a higher degree (see Appendix, Part 3: Qualifications). In 2004/05 around 574,000 NVQs and SVQs were awarded in the UK compared with around 153,000 in 1991/92. Awards at level 2 have been the most common over the period with 341,000 awards, accounting for 59 per cent of awards in 2004/05. Awards at level 1 have declined over the period from 31 per cent to 10 per cent. In 1991/92, 8 per cent of all awards were at level 3 compared with 26 per cent in 2004/05. Awards at level 4 and level 5 made up 5 per cent of all awards in 2004/05.

In 2005 the British Social Attitudes survey asked adults aged 18 and over in Great Britain their opinions on various aspects of vocational qualifications. The majority of respondents (60 per cent) agreed that 'most people don't understand what vocational qualifications are' (Table 3.17). More than one-half (54 per cent) of respondents agreed with the statement 'employers don't respect vocational qualifications enough' compared with just over one-fifth (21 per cent) who disagreed. There also seemed to be a strong consensus that schools should do more to encourage young people to do vocational qualifications, 74 per cent of respondents agreed with this statement while 7 per cent disagreed. The survey also asked for attitudes regarding who should take vocational qualifications, and how vocational qualifications compared with academic qualifications. Nearly two-thirds (63 per cent) disagreed with the statement 'only people who can't do academic qualifications should do vocational ones' compared with one-fifth (20 per cent) of people who agreed with it. Nearly half of respondents disagreed with the statement 'vocational qualifications are easier than academic ones.'

Adult training and learning

Learning throughout working life is becoming increasingly necessary because of the pace of change within the labour market and the need to develop skills. There are also various education and training options available to young people who decide not to continue in full-time education, including a number of government-supported training initiatives. In England and Wales, the Work Based Learning for Young People initiative aims to ensure that all young people have access to post-compulsory education or training. Included in this initiative are apprenticeships that provide structured learning programmes for young people aged between 16 and 24, and combine work-based training with off-the-job learning. Apprenticeships offer training to NVQ level 2. Advanced Apprenticeships offer training to NVQ level 3, and are aimed at developing technical, supervisory and craft-level skills.

In 2005/06 there were 485,500 young people aged 16 to 24 on Work Based Learning schemes in England. The most common area of learning was engineering and manufacturing technologies with 92,000 young people receiving training in this. The majority (97 per cent) were men (Table 3.18). Men were also far more likely than women to be on schemes focused on construction, planning and the built environment (99 per cent). In contrast, women outnumbered men in being trained in health, public services and care (91 per cent) and business, administration and law (72 per cent).

The need for job-related training in the labour market is not exclusive to young people in Work Based Learning. In April to June 2006, 15 per cent of employees of working age in the UK had received some job-related training in the four weeks before

Table **3.17**

Attitudes to vocational qualifications,[1] 2005

Great Britain			Percentages
	Agree[2]	Neither agree nor disagree	Disagree[3]
Only people who can't do academic qualifications should do vocational ones	20	17	63
Vocational qualifications are easier than academic qualifications	29	24	47
Most people don't understand what vocational qualifications are	60	21	20
Employers don't respect vocational qualifications enough	54	24	21
Schools should do more to encourage young people to do vocational qualifications	74	19	7

1 Adults aged 18 and over were shown the above list and asked whether they agreed or disagreed with the statements. Excludes those who answered 'Don't know' or did not answer.
2 Those who said they either agreed or agreed strongly.
3 Those who said they either disagreed or disagreed strongly.

Source: British Social Attitudes Survey, National Centre for Social Research

Table **3.18**

Young people[1] in Work Based Learning:[2] by sex and area of learning, 2005/06

England   Percentages

	Men	Women	All (=100%) (thousands)
Engineering and manufacturing technologies	97	3	92.0
Retail and commercial enterprise	35	65	86.2
Business, administration and law	28	72	76.8
Construction, planning and the built environment	99	1	60.7
Health, public services and care	9	91	50.2
Information and communication technology	81	19	15.5
Leisure, travel and tourism	54	46	12.4
Agriculture, horticulture and animal care	51	49	9.6
Arts, media and publishing	91	9	1.1
Area unknown	62	38	70.8
All areas of learning[3]	58	42	485.5

1 People aged 16 to 24. Data include a small number of people aged over 24 (around 2 per cent of the total).
2 Work Based Learning for young people comprises Advanced Apprenticeships at NVQ level 3, Apprenticeships at NVQ level 2, NVQ Learning, and Entry to Employment (E2E).
3 Includes all of the areas above plus preparation for life and work, education and training, science and mathematics, history, philosophy and theology, social sciences, and languages, literature and culture.

Source: Learning and Skills Council; Department for Education and Skills

Figure **3.19**

Employees receiving job-related training:[1] by age and sex, 2006[2]

United Kingdom
Percentages

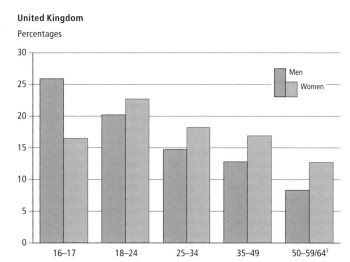

1 Employees (those in employment excluding the self-employed, unpaid family workers and those on government programmes) who received job-related training in the four weeks before interview.
2 Data are at Q2 and are not seasonally adjusted. See Appendix, Part 4: Labour Force Survey.
3 Men aged 50 to 64, women aged 50 to 59.

Source: Labour Force Survey, Office for National Statistics

they were interviewed in the Labour Force Survey: this was a similar proportion to each of the same periods since 1997. In general, greater proportions of women than men received job-related training, and the proportion was higher for younger than for older employees. Compared with other age groups, men aged 16 to 17 (26 per cent) and women aged 18 to 24 (23 per cent) were the most likely employees to have received job-related training between April and June 2006 (Figure 3.19).

In April to June 2006 the proportion of employees in the UK who received job-related training varied by occupation. Around one-quarter of employees in personal service occupations (24 per cent) and over one-fifth of employees in both professional (22 per cent) and associate professional and technical occupations (22 per cent) in the UK received job-related training in the four weeks before their Labour Force Survey interview. Employees who worked in process, plant and machine operation occupations, and elementary

occupations (such as catering assistants, bar staff and shelf fillers) were the groups least likely to have received job-related training (7 per cent and 9 per cent respectively).

In 2005/06 there were 2.9 million adults (aged 19 and over) in Learning and Skills Council-funded further education in England, which represented around four out of five of all further education learners. This was an increase of 6 per cent in the number of these adult learners compared with 1996/97 when there were 2.7 million, but a decrease of 17 per cent since 2004/05 when there were 3.5 million adult learners in further education.

In 2005/06 there were more adult learners in further education (either full-time or part-time) in the 19 to 24 age group (495,000) than in any other age group (Figure 3.20 overleaf). The number of learners generally decreased by age although in the same year there were 375,000 learners aged 35 to 39, slightly higher than those aged 30 to 34 (354,000). Women made up a higher proportion of adult learners than men in all age groups, although these proportions differed between groups. For those aged 19 to 24 (the adult age group with the lowest proportion of women learners), around 56 per cent were women. This compares with those aged 45 to 49 (the age group with the highest proportion of women) where 65 per cent of learners were women.

Figure **3.20**

Adult participation in further education:[1] by sex and age, 2005/06

England
Thousands

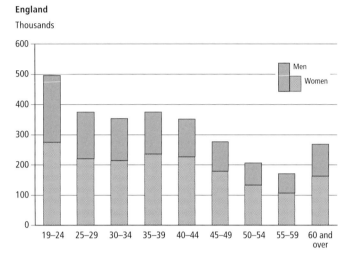

1 See Appendix, Part 3: Adult education.

Source: Learning and Skills Council; Department for Education and Skills

In 2005/06 there were 786,000 people on adult and community learning courses in England. Adult and community learning includes a wide range of community-based learning opportunities, primarily taking place through local authorities. The majority were of courses in arts, media and publishing (28 per cent); leisure, travel and tourism (18 per cent) or preparation for life and work (16 per cent). Preparation for life and work includes studies for skills that are key for personal development (for example, adult literacy, numeracy and communication) and studies for skills in preparing for working life (for example, employability and job-seeking skills).

Through the Lifelong Learning Wales Record, the Welsh Assembly Government also collects data on those aged 16 or over who are continuing learning at either further education institutions, community learning providers, or through Work Based Learning provision. In 2005/06 there were around 300,000 people aged 16 or over learning in Wales through these types of provision and of this total, 42 per cent of learners were men and 58 per cent were women. There were further variations by age. Of those aged 16 to 24, men slightly outnumbered women (52,000 compared with 51,000), however of those aged 25 or over there was a marked difference with a far higher number of women learners than men (122,000 compared with 71,400). In total around one-third (103,000) of all learners in Wales were aged 16 to 24 and around two-thirds were aged 25 or over (193,400). The most popular subjects for all learning activities were care, information technology, media, and health.

Educational resources

In the early 1980s the UK spent 5.4 per cent of gross domestic product (GDP) on education but by 1988/89 this had fallen to 4.6 per cent. The proportion then increased slightly in the early 1990s before falling back to 4.4 per cent in 1999/2000. There then followed a steady rise to 2005/06 when an estimated 5.5 per cent of GDP (amounting to £67.9 billion) was spent on education in the UK (Figure 3.21).

The number of support staff in maintained schools in England who provide additional learning resources within the classroom increased by two and a half times between 1996 and 2006, to 225,000. There was an increase in the number of support staff in all types of school, but the largest increase was in secondary schools, where the number more than tripled from 23,000 in 1996 to 71,000 in 2006. Most support staff were in primary schools, accounting for 55 per cent of all support staff in 2006. Teaching assistants providing special needs support accounted for just under one-third (31 per cent) of all teaching assistants in 2006.

The number of full-time qualified teachers in public sector mainstream schools in the UK decreased by around 52,000 to 441,000 between 1981/82 and 2004/05, although it has generally been rising since the late 1990s. The number of

Figure **3.21**

UK education spending as a proportion of gross domestic product[1,2]

United Kingdom
Percentages

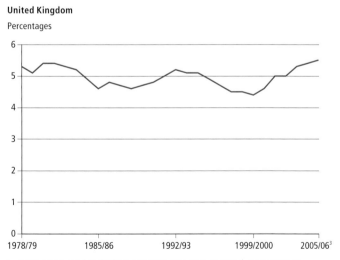

1 Data up to and including 1983/84 are on a general government expenditure basis, those from 1984/85 are on a total managed expenditure basis.
2 The effects of transfer and classification changes have been imputed prior to 1995/96.
3 Data are based on estimated outturn.

Source: HM Treasury; Department for Education and Skills

Figure **3.22**

Academic staff in higher education institutions: by sex, 2004/05

United Kingdom
Thousands

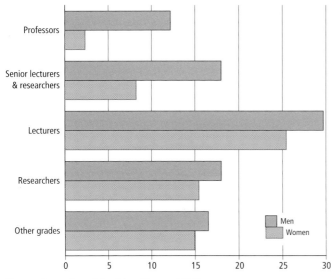

Source: Department for Education and Skills

full-time female teachers in these schools increased by 5 per cent to 308,000 over the period 1981/82 to 2004/05, while the number of male teachers fell by 33 per cent to 133,000. The majority of full-time teachers in nursery, primary and secondary schools were female. In nursery and primary schools, 85 per cent of full-time teachers were female in 2004/05, whereas in secondary schools the difference between the sexes was less marked, with females comprising 56 per cent of full-time teachers.

There are also variations in the proportions of men and women who work as academic staff in higher education institutions. In 2004/05 there were 161,000 academic staff in higher education institutions in the UK and 59 per cent were men. More than one-third (55,000) of the total academic staff were lecturers and 54 per cent of lecturers were men (Figure 3.22). The proportion of academic staff in higher education institutions who were women declined with seniority – 46 per cent of both lecturers and researchers (and 47 per cent of other grades) were women, compared with 31 per cent of senior lecturers and researchers, and 16 per cent of professors.

The increase in the use of computers as an educational resource is reflected in the decrease in the average number of pupils per computer (used mainly for teaching and learning) in maintained schools. The largest improvement in the ratio of computers to pupils was in primary schools. In 1994 there was one computer for every 23 primary school pupils compared with one for every seven pupils in 2005. In secondary schools, there was one computer for every ten pupils in 1994 compared with one for every four in 2005. Special schools had the lowest ratio in 2005: one computer for every two pupils.

The proportion of primary and secondary teachers with access to information and communication technology (ICT) resources in lessons has risen since 2002. In particular, higher numbers of teachers reported having access to dedicated subject resources as opposed to having to share. These trends reflect the patterns of increased ICT resources in schools. Around two-fifths (39 per cent) of primary level teachers had access to dedicated desktop computers for their subject in 2005. This was a rise from 2002 when 31 per cent had dedicated desktop computers. Dedicated subject laptops were available to around one-quarter (26 per cent) of primary level teachers, an increase from 6 per cent in 2002. The biggest increase was seen in access to interactive whiteboards. In 2005 nearly one-half of primary level teachers (49 per cent) had use of dedicated interactive whiteboards compared with 6 per cent in 2002. For secondary level teachers there was no change in the proportion who had access to dedicated desktop computers for their subject between 2002 and 2005 (39 per cent). However the proportions with dedicated access to laptops and interactive whiteboards increased and followed a similar pattern to that for primary teachers. In 2005, 36 per cent of secondary level teachers had dedicated access to laptops compared with 18 per cent in 2002, and 52 per cent had dedicated access to interactive whiteboards compared with 12 per cent in 2002.

Labour market

- There were 30.6 million economically active people in the UK in quarter 2 (Q2) 2006, an increase of 5.0 million since Q2 1971, whereas the number of economically inactive people increased by 2.6 million to 17.5 million. (Figure 4.1)

- In spring 2006, 15 per cent of children living in working-age households in the UK lived in households where no one was working, a fall from 19 per cent in spring 1992. (Figure 4.3)

- The UK employment rate of working-age men was 79 per cent in Q2 2006, a fall from 92 per cent in Q2 1971, while the rate for working-age women rose from 56 per cent to 70 per cent. (Figure 4.4)

- There were 5.8 million public sector workers in the UK in June 2006, 13 per cent more than in 1998 but still below the level in 1992 (5.9 million). (Figure 4.11)

- One-third of full-time working mothers in the UK used some form of flexible working pattern in spring 2005, compared with nearly one-fifth of full-time working fathers. (Table 4.13)

- The number of unemployed people in the UK increased by over 240,000 in the 12 months to Q2 2006, the first increase in four years. (Figure 4.15)

Chapter 4

Many people spend a large proportion of their lives in the labour force, and so their experience of the world of work has an important impact on their lives and attitudes. Although still large, this proportion has been falling. Young people are remaining longer in education and older people are spending more years in retirement, a contributory factor to this being the increase in life expectancy (see Chapter 7: Health). More women than ever before are in paid employment. Employment in service industries continues to increase while employment in manufacturing continues to fall.

Labour market profile

People are considered to be economically active (part of the labour force) if they are aged 16 and over and are either in work or actively looking for work. During the 35 years between Q2 1971 and Q2 2006, the number of economically active people in the UK increased by around 5.0 million to 30.6 million. Over the same period the number of economically inactive (those aged 16 and over and neither in work nor looking for work) increased by 2.6 million to 17.5 million (Figure 4.1). Since the early 1990s, there has been an increase in economic activity levels in the UK. Within the labour force, the increase in employment levels since the early 1990s has been steeper than the decrease in unemployment levels over the same period.

Working-age men and women have different patterns of economic status at most ages. In Q2 2006, the proportion of men aged 16 to 19 who worked full time was 21 per cent (Figure 4.2). Men in this age group were least likely of all working-age men to be in full-time employment. Men in their 30s and 40s were most likely to be in full-time employment (each around 85 per cent), and along with 25 to 29-year-olds were the least likely of all working-age men to be economically inactive. From the age of around 50, men begin to withdraw from full-time employment and there is an increase in both part-time employment and economic inactivity. However, after state pension age (age 65 for men and 60 for women) around one in five men aged 65 to 69 worked either full or part time.

For women the picture is different. Full-time employment was at its highest for women at ages 25 to 29 at 55 per cent, after which the proportion fell to 39 per cent of 35 to 39-year-olds. The proportion of women in full-time employment then rose to 48 per cent for 45 to 49-year-olds. Part-time employment and economic inactivity were generally more common among women of working age than among men. Ten years before state pension age, similar proportions of men and women were economically inactive (22 per cent of 55 to 59-year-old men and 23 per cent of 50 to 54-year-old women), whereas in the five years immediately before state pension age a higher

Figure **4.1**

Levels of economic activity and inactivity[1]

United Kingdom
Millions

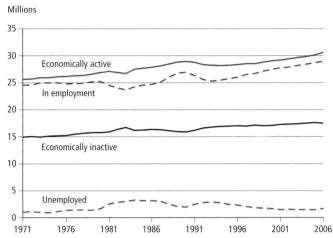

1 Data are at Q2 each year and are seasonally adjusted. People aged 16 and over. See Appendix, Part 4: Labour Force Survey.

Source: Labour Force Survey, Office for National Statistics

proportion of men than women were economically inactive (44 per cent of 60 to 64-year-old men compared with 36 per cent of 55 to 59-year-old women). A contributory factor to this may be that working-age men are more likely than working-age women to have an occupational or personal pension and can therefore afford to retire earlier having accumulated higher pension funds (see Chapter 8: Social protection).

Figure 4.1 showed the increase in the number of people in employment in the UK. One of the outcomes of the increasing levels of employment is a rise in the number of working-age households that are working (that is, households including at least one person of working age where all persons of working age are in employment). There were 10.7 million working households in spring 2006, an increase of 1.9 million since spring 1992. Working households as a proportion of all working-age households rose from 50 per cent in spring 1992 to 57 per cent in 2000 – and remained at this level to spring 2006.

Labour Force Survey (LFS)

The LFS is the largest regular household survey in the UK and much of the labour market data published in this chapter are measured by the LFS. Calendar quarter 2 (Q2) data from the LFS refers to the months April to June in a given year, whereas seasonal spring data refers to the months March to May. For more information on the survey, including differences between calendar and seasonal quarters, see Appendix, Part 4: Labour Force Survey.

Glossary

Economically active (or the labour force) – those aged 16 and over who are **in employment** or are **unemployed**.

Economic activity rate – the percentage of the population, for example in a given age group, which is **economically active**.

In employment – a measure, obtained from household surveys and censuses, of those aged 16 and over who are **employees, self-employed**, people doing unpaid work for a family-run business, and participants in government employment and training programmes. The number of participants in government employment and training programmes includes those who said they were participants on Youth Training, Training for Work, Employment Action or Community Industry, or a programme organised by the Learning and Skills Council in England, the National Council for Education and Training for Wales, or Local Enterprise Companies in Scotland.

Employment rate – the proportion of any given population group who are **in employment**. The main presentation of employment rates is the proportion of the population of working age (16 to 64 for men and 16 to 59 for women) who are in employment.

Employees (Labour Force Survey measure) – a measure, obtained from household surveys, of people aged 16 and over who regard themselves as paid employees. People with two or more jobs are counted only once.

Self-employed – a measure, obtained from household surveys, of people aged 16 and over who regard themselves as self-employed, that is, who in their main employment work on their own account, whether or not they have employees.

Unemployment – a measure, based on International Labour Organisation guidelines and used in the Labour Force Survey, which counts as unemployed those aged 16 and over who are without a job, are available to start work in the next two weeks, who have been seeking a job in the last four weeks or are out of work and waiting to start a job already obtained in the next two weeks.

Unemployment rate – the percentage of the **economically active** who are **unemployed**.

Economically inactive – those aged 16 and over who are neither **in employment** nor **unemployment**. For example, those looking after a home; retirees, or those unable to work because of long term sickness or disability.

Economic inactivity rate – the proportion of a given population group who are **economically inactive**. The main presentation of economic inactivity rates is the proportion of the population of working age (16 to 64 for men and 16 to 59 for women) who are economically inactive.

Working-age household – a household that includes at least one person of working age (16 to 64 for men and 16 to 59 for women).

Working household – a household that includes at least one person of working age and where all the people of working age are **in employment**.

Workless household – a household that includes at least one person of working age where no one aged 16 and over is **in employment**.

Figure **4.2**

Economic activity and inactivity status: by sex and age, 2006[1]

United Kingdom

Thousands

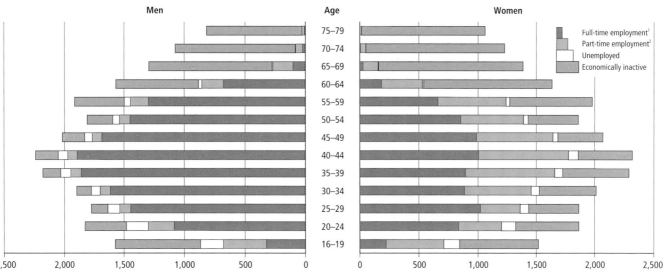

1 Data are at Q2 and are not seasonally adjusted. See Appendix, Part 4: Labour Force Survey.
2 The Labour Force Survey asks people to classify themselves as either full time or part time, based on their own perceptions.

Source: Labour Force Survey, Office for National Statistics

Figure **4.3**

Children living in workless working-age households[1,2]

United Kingdom
Percentages

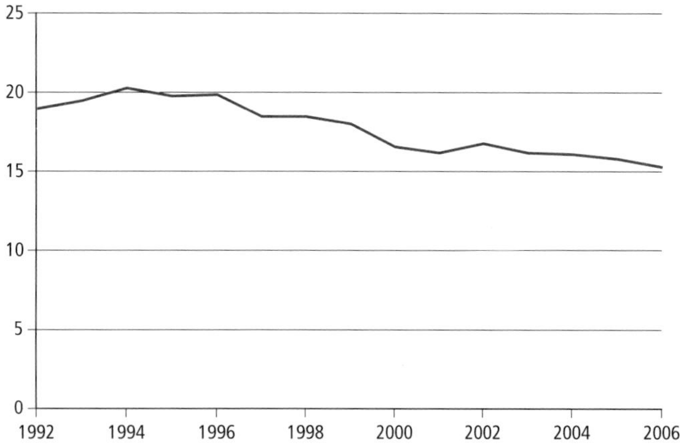

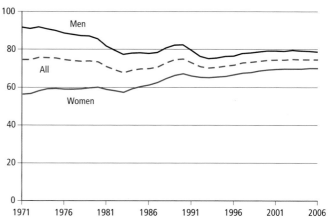

1 Children aged under 16 in workless working-age households as a
   proportion of all children aged under 16 in working-age households.
2 Data are at spring each year and are not seasonally adjusted. See
   Appendix, Part 4: Labour Force Survey.

Source: Labour Force Survey, Office for National Statistics

In spring 2006 there were 3.0 million workless households,
(that is, households where at least one person is of working age
but no one is in employment). The proportion of households
that are workless has remained stable at around 16 per cent
since 2003 having fallen from 19 per cent in spring 1996.

The fall in the proportion of workless households is also
reflected in the fall in the number and proportion of children
living in workless households. There were 2.2 million children
living in workless households in the UK in spring 1992
compared with 1.7 million in spring 2006. This represented
a decrease of 4 percentage points from 19 per cent of all
children in working-age households in spring 1992, to 15 per
cent in spring 2006 (Figure 4.3). Children living in working-
age households in inner London were more likely to be living
in workless households (36 per cent) than children living in
equivalent households in any region of the UK.

Employment

Although Figure 4.1 showed an increase in the levels of
employment in the UK, this should be considered in relation to
the steady growth of the population since 1971 (see Chapter 1:
Population). The proportion of the working-age population in
the UK who were in employment (the employment rate)
decreased from 76 per cent in the mid-1970s to a low of 68 per
cent in Q2 1983 (Figure 4.4). Since then employment rates have
generally risen, although there was a slight fall following the

recession of 1990 and 1991. The employment rate in Q2 2006
was 75 per cent, the same as in Q2 1971.

Before 1993 there were different trends in the employment
rate between the sexes. The male employment rate fell from
92 per cent in Q2 1971 to 86 per cent in Q2 1980. Over the
same period the female employment rate generally rose from
56 per cent to 60 per cent. During the early 1980s the
employment rates for both sexes fell although the fall was
more pronounced among men than women. The employment
rate then recovered and increased for both sexes until the
beginning of the 1990s, with the increase being more evident
for women. Following the recession in the early 1990s
employment rates for men fell to a low of 75 per cent in 1993
– the lowest male rate since LFS records began in 1971. The
employment rates for working-age men and women since
1993 have shown a similar pattern.

Between 1971 and 2006 the UK employment rate of working-
age men fell from 92 per cent in Q2 1971, to 79 per cent in
Q2 2006, while the rate for working-age women rose from
56 per cent to 70 per cent.

Employment rates differ throughout the UK. Table 4.5 shows
working-age employment rates by region and country, and the
highest and lowest local or unitary authority employment rates
within these regions and countries. In 2005, the highest regional
working-age employment rate in England was in the South East
(79 per cent) and the lowest was in London (69 per cent). Rates
in England and Scotland were both 75 per cent with Wales and
Northern Ireland at 71 per cent and 69 per cent respectively.

Figure **4.4**

Employment rates:[1] by sex

United Kingdom
Percentages

1 Data are at Q2 each year and are seasonally adjusted. Men aged 16 to
   64, women aged 16 to 59. See Appendix, Part 4: Labour Force Survey.

Source: Labour Force Survey, Office for National Statistics

Table 4.5

Employment rates:[1] by region and local area,[2] 2005[3]

United Kingdom   Percentages

	Regional rate	Unitary authority/local authority district			
		Lowest rate		Highest rate	
England	74.6	Hackney	53.2	South Northamptonshire	87.3
North East	70.9	Middlesbrough	66.4	Tynedale	77.5
North West	72.6	Manchester	59.6	Eden	84.7
Yorkshire and the Humber	74.1	Kingston upon Hull	66.8	Craven	84.9
East Midlands	75.8	Nottingham	64.1	South Northamptonshire	87.3
West Midlands	73.4	Birmingham	64.1	Shrewsbury & Atcham; Wychavon	81.7
East	78.0	Luton	67.5	St. Edmundsbury	85.1
London	69.1	Hackney	53.2	City of London	84.0
South East	79.0	Southampton	71.0	West Oxfordshire	86.4
South West	77.8	Penwith	68.1	South Gloucestershire	84.4
Wales	71.2	Merthyr Tydfil	62.5	Monmouthshire	78.8
Scotland	74.9	Glasgow City	65.9	Shetland Islands	85.3
Northern Ireland	68.7	..	..	..	..

1 Men aged 16 to 64, women aged 16 to 59.
2 Excludes the Isles of Scilly as the sample size is too small to provide an estimate.
3 January to December. See Appendix, Part 4: Annual Population Survey.

Source: Annual Population Survey, Office for National Statistics

Differences in employment rates between local or unitary authorities within Great Britain are often greater than differences between the English regions and between England, Wales and Scotland. In 2005, the greatest contrast between local authorities was in London, with a difference of 31 percentage points between the highest and lowest working-age employment rates. The London region contains areas with the lowest working-age employment rates in Great Britain; Hackney (53 per cent), Tower Hamlets (56 per cent) and Newham (57 per cent). The local authority with the highest employment rate in Great Britain was South Northamptonshire with a rate of 87 per cent. One hundred local and unitary authorities (25 per cent) had an employment rate of 80 per cent or higher.

One of the factors that can affect employment rates is educational attainment. In Q2 2006, 88 per cent of working-age people in the UK with a degree or equivalent were in employment compared with 47 per cent of those with no qualifications. This relationship was more marked for women than for men – 87 per cent of women who had a degree were in employment compared with 40 per cent of women who did not have any qualifications, whereas 90 per cent of men who had a degree were in employment compared with 54 per cent of men who did not have any qualifications.

Another factor that underlies the different employment rates of men and women (see Figure 4.4) is whether they have dependent children. In Q2 2006, there were clear differences in employment rates between parents and non-parents, between mothers and fathers, and between couple parents and lone parents (Table 4.6 overleaf). Working-age mothers in the UK with dependent children were less likely to be in employment than working-age women without dependent children (67 per cent compared with 73 per cent). For men the opposite was true. Working-age fathers with dependent children were more likely to be in employment than working-age men without dependent children (90 per cent compared with 73 per cent). This pattern was true of all age groups and was prevalent in the 16 to 24 and 50 to 64 age groups.

Variations in employment rates are also present between parents and non-parents, and between different types of parent, and are observed across all age groups. Overall, fathers had higher employment rates than mothers (90 per cent compared with 67 per cent); couple parents had higher employment rates than lone parents (81 per cent and 56 per cent); and lone fathers had higher employment rates than lone mothers (69 per cent and 55 per cent).

Table 4.6

Employment rates of people[1] with and without dependent children:[2] by age and sex, 2006[3]

United Kingdom
Percentages

	16–24	25–34	35–49	50–59/64	All
Mothers with dependent children	32	61	74	69	67
Married/cohabiting mothers	40	65	76	73	71
Lone mothers	23	49	66	56	55
Women without dependent children	60	88	82	69	73
Fathers with dependent children	71	90	92	85	90
Married/cohabiting fathers	72	91	93	86	91
Lone fathers	*	64	73	61	69
Men without dependent children	57	87	84	70	73
All parents with dependent children	39	71	82	79	77
Married/cohabiting parents	50	76	84	82	81
Lone parents	23	50	66	57	56
All people without dependent children	58	88	83	70	73

Note: Shaded cells indicate the estimates are unreliable due to small sample size and any analysis using these figures may be invalid. Any use of these shaded figures must be accompanied by this disclaimer.
1 Men aged 16 to 64 and women aged 16 to 59. Excludes people with unknown employment status.
2 Children aged under 16 and those aged 16 to 18 who have never been married and are in full-time education.
3 Data are at Q2 and are not seasonally adjusted. See Appendix, Part 4: Labour Force Survey.

Source: Labour Force Survey, Office for National Statistics

Patterns of employment

In Q2 2006, 15 per cent of employees in the UK were employed as managers or senior officials – the largest occupational group (see Appendix, Part 4: Standard Occupational Classification 2000 (SOC2000)). This compared with 7 per cent who were employed in process, plant and machine occupations, which was the smallest group (Table 4.7).

The pattern of occupations followed by men and women is quite different; male employees were most likely to be employed as managers or senior officials while female employees were most likely to be employed in administrative and secretarial work. Around one in seven (14 per cent) of female employees worked in personal service (for example hairdressers and child care assistants) and one in eight (12 per cent) worked in sales and customer service – occupations which were far more uncommon among male employees. Only the professional occupations, associate professional and technical occupations (such as nurses, financial advisers and IT technicians), and the elementary occupations (such as catering assistants, bar staff and shelf fillers) were almost equally likely to be followed by both male and female employees: between around one in seven and one in nine were employed in each of these occupations.

Employees most likely to have a degree or equivalent were in the professional occupation group with over two-thirds (69 per

Table 4.7

Employees: by sex and occupation, 2006[1]

United Kingdom
Percentages

	Men	Women	All
Managers and senior officials	19	11	15
Professional	14	12	13
Associate professional and technical	13	15	14
Administrative and secretarial	6	21	13
Skilled trades	15	1	8
Personal service	3	14	8
Sales and customer service	5	12	9
Process, plant and machine operatives	13	2	7
Elementary	13	12	12
All occupations	100	100	100

1 Data are at Q2 and are not seasonally adjusted. People aged 16 and over. See Appendix, Part 4: Labour Force Survey.

Source: Labour Force Survey, Office for National Statistics

cent) qualified to at least degree level in Q2 2006. Around one-third (34 per cent) of employees who worked as managers or senior officials were qualified to at least this level, as were around one-third (32 per cent) who worked in the associate professional and technical occupations. Process, plant and machine operatives, and those in elementary occupations were least likely to have a degree or the equivalent (2 per cent and 3 per cent respectively) and most likely to have no qualifications (17 per cent and 25 per cent respectively) (see also Chapter 3: Education and training).

In 2005, according to data from the Annual Population Survey, 28 per cent of those in employment in Great Britain were in managerial or professional occupations. White British people had a lower proportion of people working in managerial or professional occupations (27 per cent) than those from the Chinese (38 per cent), Indian (36 per cent) and White Irish (34 per cent) groups – the ethnic groups with the highest proportions. The groups with the lowest proportions employed in these occupations were the Black Caribbeans, Black Africans and Bangladeshis (between 19 per cent and 22 per cent).

These overall proportions mask the differences between the sexes in the proportions in employment who were managers

Figure **4.8**

Managers, senior officials and professionals:[1] by ethnic group[2] and sex, 2005[3]

Great Britain
Percentages

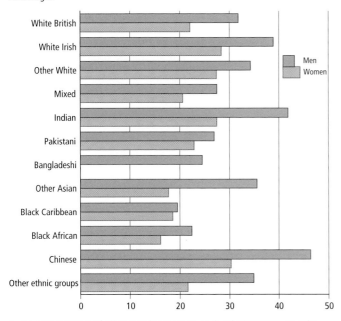

1 As a proportion of all in employment in each ethnic group. People aged 16 and over.
2 The estimates for the Other Black group and Bangladeshi women have been excluded due to a small number of respondents.
3 January to December. See Appendix, Part 4: Annual Population Survey.
Source: Annual Population Survey, Office for National Statistics

or professionals. The largest gap between the sexes was in the Other Asian ethnic group. Of all those in employment from this group, around one-third of men were managers or professionals compared with nearly one-fifth of women (Figure 4.8).

Over the last 25 years the UK economy has experienced structural change. The largest increase in employee jobs has been in the banking, finance and insurance industry, where the number of employee jobs doubled between June 1981 and June 2006 from 2.7 million to 5.4 million. There were also large increases in employee jobs in public administration, education and health (up by 40 per cent) and in the distribution, hotels and restaurants industry (up by 34 per cent). In contrast, the extraction and production industries, made up of agriculture and fishing, energy and water, manufacturing, and construction showed a combined fall of 43 per cent from 8.2 million jobs in 1981 to 4.7 million jobs in 2006. Manufacturing alone accounted for 81 per cent of this decline, with the number of employee jobs in this sector nearly halving from 5.9 million in 1981 to 3.0 million in 2006.

These overall changes are reflected in the industry breakdown of employee jobs by sex. In June 1981, 31 per cent of male employee jobs were in manufacturing but by 2006 this had fallen to 17 per cent (Table 4.9 overleaf). The proportion of female employee jobs in the manufacturing sector also fell over the period, from 18 per cent to 6 per cent. The largest increase in both male and female employee jobs over the period has been in the banking, finance and insurance industry, which accounted for around one in five of both male and female employee jobs in June 2006, compared with around one in ten in June 1981.

In 1981, a higher number of employee jobs were performed by men (13.1 million) compared with women (10.2 million). However, by 2006 the gap between the sexes had narrowed with 13.5 million employee jobs being performed by men compared with 13.3 million being performed by women. Note that Table 4.9 is based on jobs rather than people – one person may have more than one job, and jobs may vary in the number of hours' work they involve.

Not all people in employment work as employees. Since 1992 (the earliest year for which Q2 calendar year data are available), between one in seven and one in eight people in employment have been self-employed. In Q2 2006, there were 3.7 million self-employed people in the UK, accounting for 13 per cent of all those in employment. Men are more likely than women to be self-employed. In Q2 2006, 73 per cent of self-employed people were men. The self-employed are also more likely than employees to work longer hours on a usual basis. In Q2 2006, 34 per cent of self-employed people worked over 45 hours a week compared with 19 per cent of employees.

Table **4.9**

Employee jobs:[1] by sex and industry

United Kingdom   Percentages

	Men				Women			
	1981	1991	2001	2006	1981	1991	2001	2006
Distribution, hotels and restaurants	16	19	22	22	26	26	26	26
Banking, finance and insurance	11	16	20	21	12	16	19	19
Manufacturing	31	25	21	17	18	12	8	6
Public administration, education and health	13	14	14	15	34	36	36	39
Transport and communication	10	10	9	9	2	2	3	3
Construction	9	8	8	8	2	2	1	2
Agriculture and fishing	2	2	1	1	1	1	1	1
Energy and water	4	3	1	1	1	1	-	-
Other services[2]	3	4	5	5	5	5	5	5
All employee jobs (=100%) (millions)	13.1	12.0	13.1	13.5	10.2	11.8	12.9	13.3

1 Data are at June each year and are not seasonally adjusted.
2 Community, social and personal services including sanitation, dry cleaning, personal care, and recreational, cultural and sporting activities.

Source: Short-term Turnover and Employment Survey, Office for National Statistics

There are considerable differences in the type of self-employed work done by men compared with that done by women. Almost one-third of self-employed men worked in the construction industry in Q2 2006, compared with very few

Figure **4.10**

Self-employment: by industry and sex, 2006[1]

United Kingdom
Percentages

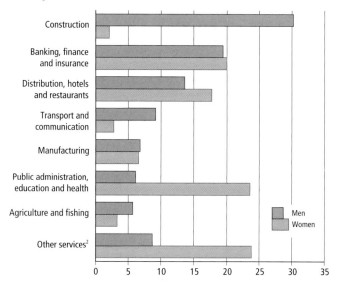

1 Data are at Q2 and are not seasonally adjusted. People aged 16 and over. See Appendix, Part 4: Labour Force Survey.
2 Community, social and personal services including sanitation, dry cleaning, personal care, and recreational, cultural and sporting activities.

Source: Labour Force Survey, Office for National Statistics

women (Figure 4.10). In contrast, nearly one-quarter of self-employed women worked in 'other services' – for example community, social and personal services (such as textile washing and dry cleaning, hairdressing and other beauty treatments) – and another quarter worked in public administration, education and health. This compares with 9 per cent of self-employed men who worked in other services and 6 per cent who worked in public administration, education and health industries.

Although the majority of people in employment work in the private sector, around one in five people in employment work in the public sector (for example central government, local government and public corporations). Public sector employment has grown in recent years following a period of decline in the early to mid-1990s (Figure 4.11). Employment within the public sector fell every year between 1992 and 1998 reducing by 742,000 in total. Between 1998 and 2005 public sector employment increased year on year by a total of 686,000 but in the 12 months to June 2006, it fell by 9,000. There were 5.8 million public sector workers in June 2006, 13 per cent higher than in 1998, but still below the level in 1992 (5.9 million).

Although the level of public sector employment remains far lower than employment in the private sector, the annual percentage growth in public sector employment has been stronger than in the private sector since 2000. In the 5 years to June 2005 the annual percentage growth in the public sector was between 1.6 per cent and 2.8 per cent each year compared with increases of between 0.3 per cent and 1.5 per cent in the private sector. However in the 12 months to June 2006 the number of public sector workers fell by 0.2 percentage points.

Data from the Labour Force Survey show that public sector workers are more likely to be women and to work part time. In 2004, 65 per cent of public sector workers were women, compared with 41 per cent of private sector workers. Around 30 per cent of public sector workers worked part time compared with 24 per cent of the private sector workforce.

Table 4.6 showed the different employment rates of men and women relative to whether they had dependent children. As well as influencing people's participation in employment, having dependent children is also a factor that affects whether someone in employment works full time or part time. In Q2 2006, 30 per cent of married or cohabiting mothers with dependent children worked full time while 41 per cent worked part time (Table 4.12). Among women without dependent children a higher proportion (51 per cent) worked full time and a smaller proportion (22 per cent) worked part time. For men, a higher proportion of married or cohabiting fathers with dependent children worked full time (87 per cent) than men without dependent children (64 per cent).

The Labour Force Survey asks people to classify themselves as either full time or part time, based on their own perceptions, but distinguishing only between full time and part time masks differences in usual working hours which are also asked for in the survey. The 1998 Working Time Regulations are used to implement an EC Directive on working time in the UK. The regulations apply to full-time, part-time and temporary workers and provide for a maximum working week of 48 hours (on average), although individual workers can choose to work longer hours. In Q2 2006, 18 per cent of full-time employees in the UK usually worked over 48 hours a week. However, a higher proportion of male employees (22 per cent) than female (11 per cent) usually worked these longer hours.

The opportunity to work flexibly can improve people's ability to balance home and work responsibilities. Regulations introduced across the UK in April 2003 give parents of children under 6, or parents of disabled children under 18, the right to request a flexible work pattern. This could be either a change to the hours they work; a change to the times when they are required to work; or the opportunity to work from home. Employers have a statutory duty to consider such requests seriously and may only refuse on business grounds. According to the Second Flexible Working Employee Survey in 2005, an employee with dependent children in Great Britain was more likely than an employee who was not a parent of dependent children to be aware of these regulations (67 per cent and 63 per cent respectively).

Figure **4.11**

Public and private[1] sector employment[2]

United Kingdom

Millions

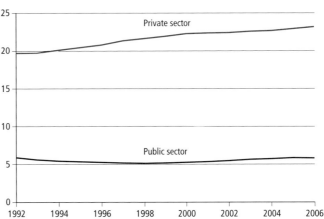

1 Public sector totals are provided by central and local government, and public sector organisations. Private sector totals are estimated as the difference between Labour Force Survey total employment and the data from public sector organisations. See Appendix, Part 4: Public sector employment.
2 Data are at June each year and are not seasonally adjusted. Headcount of people aged 16 and over.

Source: Labour Force Survey, Office for National Statistics; Public sector organisations

Table **4.12**

Employment rates of people[1] with and without dependent children:[2] by work pattern and sex, 2006[3]

United Kingdom   Percentages

	Full time	Part time	All
With dependent children			
Married/cohabiting mothers[4]	30	41	71
Married/cohabiting fathers[4]	87	4	91
Lone parents	30	27	56
All parents[4]	54	23	77
Without dependent children			
Women	51	22	73
Men	64	9	73
All people	58	15	73

1 Men aged 16 to 64 and women aged 16 to 59. Excludes people with unknown employment status.
2 Children aged under 16 and those aged 16 to 18 who have never been married and are in full-time education.
3 Data are at Q2 and are not seasonally adjusted. See Appendix, Part 4: Labour Force Survey.
4 Includes same sex cohabiting couples and civil partners with dependent children.

Source: Labour Force Survey, Office for National Statistics

In spring 2005, over one-fifth of full-time employees and around one-quarter of part-time employees had some form of flexible working arrangement. The most common form of flexible working for full-time employees of both sexes was flexible working hours. It was the most common arrangement among men who worked part time and second most common for women – exceeded only by term-time working (this may because of the higher proportion of female to male teachers in public sector mainstream schools – see Chapter 3: Education and training).

Flexible working arrangements among employee mothers and fathers with dependent children in spring 2005 show a similar story. One-third of full-time working mothers used some form of flexible working pattern compared with around one-fifth of full-time working fathers (Table 4.13). Of all employees, mothers were slightly more likely to use flexible working hours than fathers; one in seven mothers worked flexible working hours compared with one in ten fathers.

Table **4.13**

Employees with dependent children[1] and flexible working patterns:[2] by sex and type of employment,[3] 2005[4]

United Kingdom   Percentages

	Fathers	Mothers	All parents
Full-time employees			
Flexible working hours	10.1	17.4	12.5
Annualised working hours[5]	4.6	5.2	4.8
Four and a half day week	1.2	0.8	1.1
Term-time working	1.4	9.2	3.9
Nine day fortnight	0.2	0.3	0.3
Any flexible working pattern[6]	17.7	33.1	22.7
Part-time employees			
Flexible working hours	9.3	11.9	11.8
Annualised working hours[5]	4.9	4.6	4.7
Term-time working	6.4	14.2	13.8
Job sharing	1.0	2.6	2.5
Any flexible working pattern[6]	21.7	33.9	33.2

1 Children aged under 16 and those aged 16 to 18 who have never been married and are in full-time education.
2 Percentages are based on totals that exclude people who did not state whether or not they had a flexible working arrangement. Respondents could give more than one answer. Men aged 16 to 64 and women aged 16 to 59.
3 The Labour Force Survey asks people to classify themselves as either full-time or part-time, based on their own perceptions.
4 Data are at spring and are not seasonally adjusted. See Appendix, Part 4: Labour Force Survey.
5 The number of hours an employee has to work are calculated over a full year allowing for longer hours to be worked over certain periods of the year and shorter hours at others.
6 Includes other categories of flexible working not separately identified.

Source: Labour Force Survey, Office for National Statistics

Table **4.14**

Sickness absence:[1] by sex of employee and age of youngest dependent child,[2] 2005[3]

United Kingdom   Percentages

	Men	Women	All
Age of youngest dependent child			
Under 5	2.6	2.9	2.7
5–10	2.2	3.6	2.9
11–18	1.7	2.6	2.2
All dependent children	2.2	3.0	2.6
No dependent children	2.1	3.0	2.5

1 Proportions of employees aged 16 and over who were absent from work for at least one day in the Labour Force Survey interview week.
2 Children aged under 16 and those aged 16 to 18 who have never been married and are in full-time education.
3 Data are at autumn and are not seasonally adjusted. See Appendix, Part 4: Labour Force Survey.

Source: Labour Force Survey, Office for National Statistics

Employers are becoming increasingly aware of the costs of sickness absence to their organisations. These include direct costs (such as statutory sick pay, cost of replacement staff, and loss of output) as well as indirect costs (such as low morale among staff who have to carry out additional work to cover a colleague's absence, and the cost of managing absence) which are harder to quantify. Data from the Labour Force Survey show that during winter 2005, 2.4 per cent of male and 3.1 per cent of female employees interviewed had been away from work sick for at least one day in the previous week. Younger employees were more likely to take sickness absence than older employees. Among men, those aged between 16 and 24 were most likely to be off sick, with 2.6 per cent of employees taking at least one day off work in the reference week because of sickness. Among women, those aged between 25 and 34 had the highest rate, at 3.5 per cent.

Overall, female employees with no dependent children had the same sickness absence rate as mothers with dependent children in autumn 2005 (3.0 per cent) (Table 4.14). Mothers whose youngest dependent child was aged between 5 and 10 were most likely of all women to take sickness absence (3.6 per cent). Fathers with dependent children were most likely of all men to take sickness absence where their youngest dependent child was aged under 5 (2.6 per cent).

Unemployment

During periods of economic growth the number of jobs generally grows and unemployment falls, though any mismatches between the skill needs of the new jobs and the skills of those available for work may slow this process.

Conversely, as the economy slows and goes into recession so unemployment tends to rise. During the early 1970s, unemployment was relatively low, at around 1 million people aged 16 and over (equivalent to an unemployment rate of around 4 per cent) (Figure 4.15). Unemployment increased from 1974 before levelling off at around 1.4 million in the late 1970s. In 1980, unemployment began to rise and peaked at 3.3 million in 1984 (equivalent to an unemployment rate of 11.9 per cent). The late 1980s saw an economic recovery and unemployment fell back to around 2 million before a recession in 1990/91 drove it up to nearly 3 million in 1993. Since then unemployment has decreased gradually to reach similar levels to the late 1970s, although in the 12 months to Q2 2006 the number of unemployed people in the UK increased by over 240,000, the first increase in four years.

The first peak in male unemployment since LFS records began in 1971, was in Q2 1983 when 1.9 million men were unemployed. The peak for female unemployment was in Q2 1984 when 1.3 million women were unemployed. The recession in the early 1990s had a much greater effect on unemployment among men than among women, and male unemployment peaked for a second time in 1993 when 1.9 million men were unemployed.

In 2005, the lowest regional unemployment rate in the UK was in the South West of England (3.4 per cent) and the highest was in London (7.1 per cent). The unemployment rates for Wales, Scotland and Northern Ireland were 5.1 per cent, 5.3 per cent and 4.5 per cent respectively.

As with employment rates, differences in unemployment rates within the English regions and countries of the UK are greater than differences between them (Figure 4.16). The local authority areas with the lowest unemployment rates in Great Britain were Eden in the North West (2.0 per cent) and Craven in Yorkshire and the Humber, Purbeck in the South West, and West Oxfordshire in the South East (all at 2.1 per cent). The areas with the highest unemployment rates were Tower Hamlets (11.3 per cent), Hackney (10.5 per cent), Barking and Dagenham (9.2 per cent), all of which are in London, and Liverpool (9.2 per cent) in the North West.

Economic inactivity

People aged 16 and over who are neither in employment nor unemployed are classified as economically inactive. There were 7.0 million people of working age in the UK who were economically inactive in Q2 1971. By Q2 2006 this had risen to 7.8 million people of working age, of whom 60 per cent were women. If those over state pension age (65 for men and 60 for women) are included, the number of economically inactive people in the UK rises to 17.5 million.

Figure 4.15

Unemployment:[1] by sex

United Kingdom
Millions

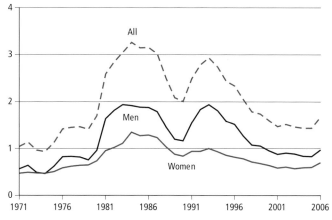

1 Data are at Q2 each year and are seasonally adjusted. People aged 16 and over. See Appendix, Part 4: Labour Force Survey.

Source: Labour Force Survey, Office for National Statistics

Figure 4.16

Unemployment rates:[1] by region,[2] 2005[3]

Great Britain
Percentages

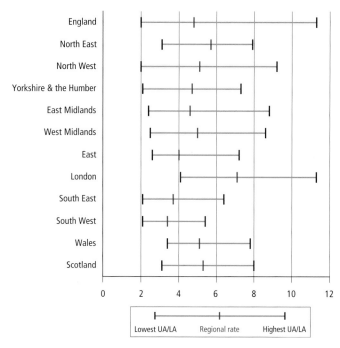

1 People aged 16 and over. See Appendix, Part 4: Model-based estimates of unemployment.
2 By region and lowest and highest unitary authorities or local authority districts. Excludes City of London and the Isles of Scilly.
3 January to December. See Appendix, Part 4: Annual Population Survey.

Source: Office for National Statistics

Figure **4.17**

Economic inactivity rates:[1] by sex

United Kingdom
Percentages

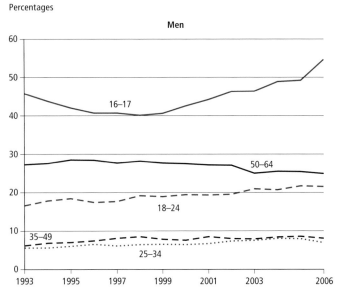

1 Data are at Q2 each year and are seasonally adjusted. Men aged 16 to 64, women aged 16 to 59. See Appendix, Part 4: Labour Force Survey.

Source: Labour Force Survey, Office for National Statistics

The proportion of the working-age population who were economically inactive fluctuated around 21 and 22 per cent throughout the 1970s (Figure 4.17). Economic inactivity increased during the early 1980s and peaked at 23 per cent in Q2 1983. As the economy improved in the late 1980s the inactivity rate began a downward trend, dropping to 19 per cent in 1990 before rising again following the recession in the early

1990s. Since 1992, the rate has returned to similar levels to the 1970s with the inactivity rate at 21 per cent in Q2 2006 among working-age people in the UK. However, this masks differences in the trends for men and women. The inactivity rate among men rose from 5 per cent in Q2 1971 to 16 per cent in Q2 2006. Over the same period, the rate for women was higher than that for men; however it fell from 41 per cent to 26 per cent.

Although Figure 4.17 showed a general rise in economic inactivity rates for working-age men, these rates vary by age (Figure 4.18). From 1993 onwards (the earliest year for which economic inactivity rates by age are available), there was a slight increase in rates for men aged 35 to 49 while for men aged 50 to 64 there was a slight decrease. The biggest change during this period was for 16 to 17-year-old men, where the economic inactivity rate decreased in the mid-1990s and then rose from 1998 to reach 55 per cent in Q2 2006. Although a smaller proportion of 18 to 24-year-old men than 16 to 17-year-olds, were economically inactive between Q2 1993 and Q2 2006, the rate for this group also increased – by 5 percentage points to 21 per cent.

The inactivity rates for working-age women over the period showed a different pattern. Between Q2 1993 and Q2 2006, inactivity rates among women aged 25 and over fell, particularly for those aged between 50 and 59, where there was a fall of 8 percentage points. Inactivity rates for women aged 18 to 24 were relatively stable over the period although

Figure **4.18**

Economic inactivity rates: by sex and age[1]

United Kingdom
Percentages

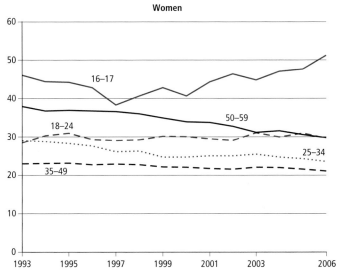

1 Data are at Q2 each year and are seasonally adjusted. Men aged 16 to 64, women aged 16 to 59. See Appendix, Part 4: Labour Force Survey.

Source: Labour Force Survey, Office for National Statistics

Table **4.19**

Reasons for economic inactivity: by sex and age, 2006[1]

United Kingdom

Percentages

	16–24	25–34	35–49	50–59/64	All aged 16–59/64
Men					
Long-term sick or disabled	5	39	62	49	36
Looking after family or home	1	11	16	5	6
Student	81	25	5	-	30
Retired	0	*	*	33	14
Other	13	25	18	12	14
All men	100	100	100	100	100
Women					
Long-term sick or disabled	4	10	23	41	20
Looking after family or home	22	71	61	27	45
Student	66	11	4	1	21
Retired	0	0	-	13	3
Other	9	8	11	18	11
All women	100	100	100	100	100

1 Data are at Q2 and are not seasonally adjusted. See Appendix, Part 4: Labour Force Survey.

Source: Labour Force Survey, Office for National Statistics

they had increased to 30 per cent in Q2 2006 from 28 per cent in 1993. The rate for young women aged 16 to 17 has shown a trend similar to young men in this age group – from Q2 1993 the rate fell, but since 1997 there has been a gradual rise. By Q2 2006 over one-half (51 per cent) of these young women were economically inactive.

Data from the LFS has shown that the economically inactive student group has grown in recent years. The number of inactive students as a proportion of the working-age inactive population, increased from 18 per cent in summer 1998, the lowest figure since 1993 when this information was first collected, to 23 per cent in autumn 2005. This equates to a growth in the number of economically inactive students of approximately 493,000.

There are of course, reasons for economic inactivity other than being a student and these vary by age (when considering all people of working age). In Q2 2006, long-term sickness or disability was the main reason for economic inactivity among working-age men in the UK, particularly for 35 to 49-year-olds (62 per cent) (Table 4.19). Looking after the family or home was the most common reason for inactivity among working-age women: 45 per cent said this was their main reason for not seeking work. Women aged 25 to 34 were most likely (71 per cent) to cite this as the main reason for their economic inactivity.

Industrial relations at work

In autumn 2005, an estimated 6.4 million employees in the UK were members of a trade union. This represents a fall of approximately 119,000 employees (or 1.9 per cent) compared with autumn 2004. Nevertheless union density among employees (membership as a proportion of all employees) increased slightly over the same period from 28.8 per cent to 29.0 per cent. Among female employees, union density rose between autumn 2004 and autumn 2005 by 0.8 percentage points to 29.9 per cent. For male employees, union density over the same period fell by 0.3 percentage points to 28.2 per cent.

The take up of trade union membership among employees varies by both sex and occupation. In 2005, men and women working within professional occupations (which include lawyers, accountants and teachers) were more likely to be trade union members than those in all other occupations, with nearly one-half of all employees in this group being union members (Table 4.20 overleaf). The proportion of female union members within professional occupations was around one and a half times greater than their male counterparts, 62 per cent compared with 39 per cent (see also Table 4.7). The associate professional and technical occupations (which include nurses, financial advisers and IT technicians) had the second highest proportion of female union members, at 47 per cent, while men working in personal service had the second highest proportion of male

Table **4.20**

Trade union membership[1] of employees: by occupation and sex, 2005[2]

United Kingdom
Percentages

	Men	Women	All
Managers and senior officials	17	22	19
Professional	39	62	49
Associate professional and technical	37	47	42
Administrative and secretarial	32	23	25
Skilled trades	25	24	25
Personal service	38	28	30
Sales and customer service	9	13	12
Process, plant and machine operatives	36	25	34
Elementary	25	16	21
All occupations	28	30	29

1 Union membership (including staff associations) as a proportion of all employees.
2 Data are at autumn and are not seasonally adjusted. See Appendix, Part 4: Labour Force Survey.

Source: Labour Force Survey, Office for National Statistics

Figure **4.21**

Labour disputes:[1] working days lost

United Kingdom
Millions

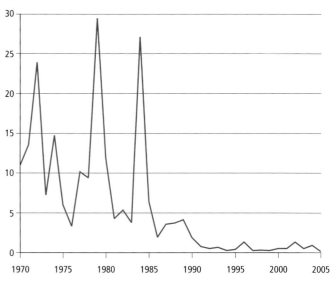

1 See Appendix, Part 4: Labour disputes.

Source: Office for National Statistics

union members, at 38 per cent. The lowest proportions of union members among both men and women were in sales and customer service (9 per cent and 13 per cent respectively).

In 2005, 157,400 working days in the UK were lost from 116 recorded stoppages associated with labour disputes (see Appendix, Part 4: Labour disputes). This was almost six times less than the number of working days lost in 2004 and was the lowest annual total on record (Figure 4.21). The average number of working days lost per year in the 1990s was 660,000. In the 1980s it was 7.2 million working days and in the 1970s, 12.9 million working days were lost. Single disputes during the 1970s and 1980s accounted for large proportions of the total working days lost; a miners' strike

in 1972 accounted for 45 per cent of the 24 million days lost during that year and a strike by engineering workers resulted in just over one-half of the 29 million days lost in 1979. Another miners' strike in 1984 was responsible for over 80 per cent of the 27 million days lost that year.

In 2005, the number of working days lost in the private sector fell from 163,100 to 58,900 and the number of working days lost in the public sector fell from 741,800 to 98,600. However, the proportion of working days lost by the private sector has increased from 18 per cent in 2004 to 37 per cent in 2005. This is still considerably lower than in 1999 when 71 per cent of days lost were in the private sector.

Income and wealth

- Between 2004 and 2005, UK household disposable income grew by 1.4 per cent in real terms, while GDP per head grew by 1.2 per cent. (Figure 5.1)

- In 2004/05 benefits, including the state retirement pension, accounted for just over one-half the gross income of pensioner families in the UK, but personal pensions were the fastest growing source of pensioner income between 1994/95 and 2004/05. (Figure 5.4)

- In 2004/05, people in single and couple households in the UK where all members were in full-time work were nearly twice as likely as the population as a whole to be in the top fifth of the disposable income distribution. (Table 5.12)

- In 2004/05, 86 per cent of children in Pakistani/ Bangladeshi households in the UK were in the bottom 40 per cent of households ranked by disposable income compared with 49 per cent of all children. (Table 5.13)

- The proportion of single people with children experiencing persistent low income in Great Britain has fallen from 40 per cent in 1991–1994 to 21 per cent for the period 2001–2004. (Table 5.18)

- In 2003, one-quarter of the adult UK population owned nearly three-quarters of the total wealth. (Table 5.21)

Chapter 5

People's income plays an important role in their social well-being, because it determines how much they have to spend on the goods and services that together make up their material standard of living. Household income depends on the level of activity within the economy as a whole each year – the national income – and on the way in which national income is distributed. Income represents a flow of money over a period of time, whereas wealth describes the ownership of assets, such as housing or pension rights, valued at a point in time.

Household income

The level of economic activity in a country is usually measured by its gross domestic product (GDP). The total income generated is shared between individuals (in the form of wages and salaries), companies and other organisations (for example in the form of profits retained for investment), and government (in the form of taxes on production). If GDP is growing in real terms (after adjustment to remove inflation), this means that the economy is expanding. GDP per head in the UK more than doubled in real terms between 1971 and 2005 (Figure 5.1). Over this period there were times when the economy contracted, for example in the mid-1970s at the time of international oil crisis, and again during periods of world recession in the early 1980s and early 1990s. However, the UK economy has grown each year since 1992, at an annual average of 2.5 per cent.

Figure **5.1**

Real household disposable income per head[1] and gross domestic product per head[2]

United Kingdom

Index numbers (1971=100)

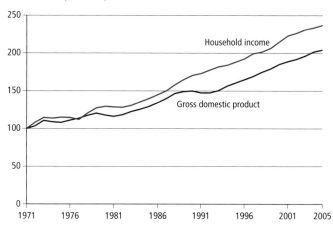

1 Adjusted to real terms using the expenditure deflator for the household sector. See Appendix, Part 5: Household income data sources.
2 Adjusted to real terms using the GDP deflator.

Source: Office for National Statistics

If the country's economy is growing, then there is more 'cake' available for distribution. Household disposable income per head represents the amount of this cake that ends up in

Table **5.2**

Composition of household income

United Kingdom

Percentages

	1987	1991	1996	2001	2004	2005
Source of income						
Wages and salaries[1]	52	50	48	51	51	50
Operating income[2]	11	11	12	13	13	14
Property income	15	16	15	14	12	13
Social benefits[3]	19	19	20	18	19	19
Other current transfers[4]	3	4	5	5	5	5
Total household income (=100%)(£ billion at 2005 prices[5])	704	827	876	1,038	1,103	1,145
As a percentage of total household income						
Taxes on income	11	11	10	12	11	11
Social contributions[1]	9	8	7	7	7	7
Other current taxes	3	2	2	2	3	2
Other current transfers	2	3	4	3	3	3

1 Excludes employers' social contributions.
2 Includes self-employment income for sole-traders and rental income.
3 Comprises pensions and benefits.
4 Mostly other government grants, but including transfers from abroad and non-profit making bodies.
5 Adjusted to 2005 prices using the expenditure deflator for the household sector. See Appendix, Part 5: Household income data sources.

Source: Office for National Statistics

people's pockets – in other words the amount they have available to spend or save – and this measure is commonly used to describe people's 'economic well-being'. It is derived directly from economic activity in the form of wages and salaries and self-employment income, and through transfers such as social security benefits. It is then subject to a number of deductions such as income tax, council tax (domestic rates in Northern Ireland), and contributions towards pensions and national insurance.

Household disposable income per head, adjusted for inflation, increased more than one and a third times between 1971 and 2005 (Figure 5.1). During the 1970s and early 1980s growth fluctuated, and in five of these years there were small year on year falls. Since 1982 there has been growth each year. Although between 1971 and 2005, growth in household disposable income per head was greater than that in GDP per head, there were years when this pattern was reversed, most recently in 2002, 2003 and 2004. However, between 2004 and 2005 the growth in real household disposable income per head was again greater than that in GDP per head (1.4 per cent compared with 1.2 per cent).

Alongside strong growth in household disposable income, since 1987 (the earliest year for which comparable data on the composition of household income are available) there has been considerable stability in its composition (Table 5.2). Although the proportion derived from wages and salaries fell from 52 per cent in 1987 to 48 per cent in 1996, this has since risen to around 51 per cent between 2001 and 2005.

Figure **5.3**

Median individual total income:[1] by sex and age, 2004/05

United Kingdom

£ per week

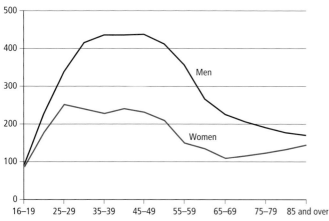

1 See Appendix, Part 5: Individual income.

Source: Family Resources Survey, Department for Work and Pensions

In addition, the proportion of income derived from social benefits has remained at around 19 per cent over the last decade. Taxes on income as a proportion of household income have also remained stable since 1987, at around 11 per cent. Social contributions (that is, employees' national insurance and pension contributions) fell between 1987 and 1996, but have since been stable at around 7 per cent of household income.

The data in Figure 5.1 and Table 5.2 are derived from the UK National Accounts. There are a number of definitional differences between these statistics and statistics derived directly from surveys of households or surveys of businesses, which are used for the tables and charts in most of the remainder of this chapter. Appendix, Part 5: Household income data sources, describes the main differences between household income as defined in the National Accounts and as defined in most survey sources.

The level of an individual's income varies according to a range of factors such as their age, sex and employment status. In the UK in 2004/05, people's incomes tended to be lowest in the youngest age groups, to peak in early middle age, and then to decline in the older age groups (Figure 5.3). Men's incomes outstripped those of women in all age groups, though for those aged 16 to 19 the gap was very small. Although these data represent a snapshot of the various age groups in 2004/05 rather than a longitudinal perspective, they do indicate that income rises with age, particularly for the younger age groups. The median total income of both men and women aged 20 to 24 was more than twice that of those aged 16 to 19 (see Appendix, Part 5: Individual income, for details of how these estimates were derived and their limitations, and the analysing income distribution box on page 63 for an explanation of median). For men, income continued to rise until they reached their mid-30s when it stabilised, and then declined through their 50s and 60s. In contrast, women's incomes were highest for those in their mid- to late-20s, and then showed little variation until their late-40s. Median income was higher for women aged 80 and over than for those in their late-60s and in their 70s, mainly because the older age band includes a higher proportion of widows who have higher individual incomes than women in pensioner couples.

As well as the level of income, the composition of income varies according to age. Pensioners in particular tend to have different sources of income from the working-age population. Benefits, including the state retirement pension and pensioner credit, were the most important component in their gross (pre-tax) income in 2004/05, accounting for just over one-half of the average gross income of pensioner families in the UK (pensioner couples where the man is aged 65 or over, or single pensioners over state pension age – see Appendix, Part 5: Pensioners' income) (Figure 5.4). However, the vast majority of pensioner families had some private income as well (94 per cent of pensioner couples and 82 per cent of single pensioners). A further one-quarter of their gross income was derived from occupational pensions (pensions paid from group schemes organised by their former employer(s)), while investment income and earnings each accounted for just under one-tenth. Personal pensions (pensions provided through a contract between the individual and a pension provider) play a relatively minor role overall in pensioners' incomes – only 11 per cent of pensioner families received them in 2004/05. However, they have been the fastest growing source of pensioner income. Between 1994/95 and 2004/05 average receipts increased over three and a half times. Average receipts of investment income fell in real terms between 2000/01 and 2002/03, reflecting the fall in stock market values over this period. Although they have since recovered, they have not yet regained their 2000/01 level. More information on investments and private pension entitlement may be found in the Wealth section at the end of this chapter. Information on pensions and benefit receipts of older people may be found in Chapter 8: Social protection.

Pensioner incomes have grown faster than average earnings across the economy as a whole over the last ten years. Overall, the gross income of pensioner families rose by 33 per cent in real terms between 1994/95 and 2004/05, compared with an increase of about 16 per cent in real average earnings. It should be noted that changes in average income do not simply reflect changes experienced by individual pensioners; they also reflect changes in the composition of the group, for example as new retirees with greater entitlement to occupational and personal pensions join the group.

At the other end of the adult life cycle, students have experienced changes in the structure of their income caused mainly by changes in the way they are financed through public funds. Student loans were introduced in 1990 to replace the student maintenance grant, and further changes were introduced by the *Teacher and Higher Education Act 1998*. The Act introduced means-tested grants towards tuition fees and provided support for living costs through loans that are in part income-assessed.

Overall, the average income of full-time students studying at higher and further education institutions in England rose from £5,702 (at 2004/05 prices) in 1998/99 to £8,333 in 2004/05, an increase of 46 per cent in real terms. Income from paid work more than doubled, from £822 to £1,821. However, the main source of income in both years was student support: in 1998/99 this was mainly student loans and maintenance grants

Figure **5.4**

Pensioners'[1] gross income: by source

Great Britain/United Kingdom[2]

£ per week at 2004/05 prices[3]

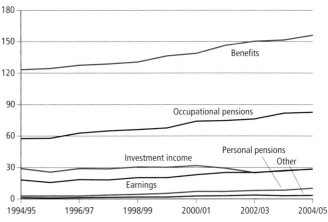

1 Pensioner couples where the man is aged 65 or over, or single pensioners over state pension age (65 for men, 60 for women).
2 Geographic coverage changed from Great Britain to United Kingdom in 2002/03.
3 Adjusted to 2004/05 prices using the retail prices index less local taxes.

Source: Pensioners' Income Series, Department for Work and Pensions

(£1,576 and £1,062 at 2004/05 prices respectively). In 2004/05 average income from student loans had increased to £2,713. Maintenance grants were no longer available but tuition fee support averaged £489, and other sources of student income such as employer support and bursaries had risen sixfold to average £629.

Earnings

Income from employment is the most important component of household income (see Table 5.2). If earnings across the economy as a whole rise rapidly, this may indicate that the labour market does not have enough employees with the right skills to meet the level of demand within the economy. In addition, a rapid rise may indicate that wage settlements are higher than the rate of economic growth can sustain and thus create inflationary pressures. Slower earnings growth may be a reflection of reduced demand within the economy and may be a warning that GDP is about to fall and unemployment is about to increase. The relationship between earnings and prices is also important. If earnings rise faster than prices, this means that employees' pay is increasing faster than the prices they have to pay for goods and services and that all things being equal, their purchasing power will rise and they will be 'better off'.

Between April 2005 and April 2006, median gross weekly earnings of full-time employees in the UK increased by 3.7 per cent to £447, compared with an increase of 2.6 per cent in prices as measured by the retail prices index (RPI) and indicating an increase in purchasing power in real terms. Between 2005 and 2006, the bottom decile point of the earnings distribution increased by 3.7 per cent and the top decile point grew by 4.2 per cent, both outpacing inflation as measured by the RPI (Figure 5.5). Median gross weekly earnings of full-time employees at both the top and bottom decile points (see the analysing income distribution box on page 63) of the earnings distribution increased above the RPI throughout the period shown on the chart, with the sole exception of 2005, and the patterns of growth at the top and bottom were generally similar. The particularly high growth in earnings at the top decile point in 2001 is largely attributed to exceptional bonuses among senior managers and professionals, notably in the financial sector.

A variety of factors influence the level of earnings that an employee receives, such as their skills and experience, their occupation, the economic sector in which they work and the hours they work. The area of the UK in which they work and their sex may also have an impact. The remainder of this section explores some of these factors. However, it should be noted that all factors are interlinked, and no attempt is made here to disentangle the effect that any single factor may have.

Legislation in the 1970s established the principle of equal pay for work that can be established to be of equal value to that done by a member of the opposite sex, employed by the same employer, under common terms and conditions of employment. The impact of this legislation, together with other factors such as the opening up of higher paid work to women, has been to narrow the differential between the hourly earnings of men and women (Figure 5.6). The pay gap between men and women, defined as the difference between the two as a percentage of men's earnings, fell from 17.4 per cent in 1997 to 14.5 per cent

Annual Survey of Hours and Earnings

The source of data in this section is the Annual Survey of Hours and Earnings (ASHE), which replaced the New Earnings Survey (NES) in 2004 – see Appendix Part 5: Earnings surveys, for a summary of the differences between the two. In Figures 5.5 and 5.6, a series has been used that applies ASHE methodology to NES data for 1997 to 2003. ASHE includes supplementary information that was not available in the NES (for example on employees who changed jobs between the time the survey sample was identified and the survey reference date), and data for 2004 are presented both with and without this supplementary information. Results for 2005 onwards are only available including the supplementary information and so care should be taken in comparing these estimates with those for 2003 and earlier.

Figure **5.5**

Growth in weekly earnings[1] at the top and bottom decile points

United Kingdom

Percentages

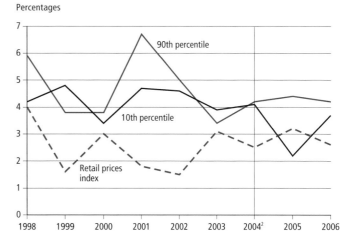

1 Weekly earnings of full-time employees on adult rates at April each year, whose pay for the survey period was unaffected by absence.
2 Vertical line represents discontinuity in 2004 ASHE data. See Appendix, Part 5: Earnings Surveys.

Source: Annual Survey of Hours and Earnings, Office for National Statistics; Retail prices index, Office for National Statistics

in 2004, and then fell a further 1.9 percentage points between 2004 and 2006. In April 2006, the median hourly earnings of women working full time in the UK were £10.24 compared with £11.71 for men.

Figure **5.6**

Pay gap between men's and women's median hourly earnings[1]

United Kingdom

Percentages

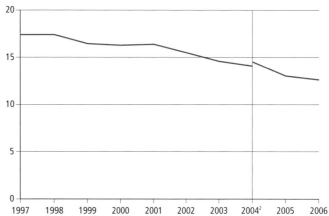

1 Full-time employees on adult rates at April each year, whose pay for the survey period was unaffected by absence. Excludes overtime.
2 Higher percentage includes supplementary information. See Appendix, Part 5: Earnings Surveys.

Source: Annual Survey of Hours and Earnings, Office for National Statistics

On average, part-time employees receive lower hourly earnings than full-time employees, and the hourly earnings differential between men and women working part time is smaller than that for full-time workers. For example, in April 2006 part-time women's median hourly earnings excluding overtime at £7.00 were slightly higher than those of men (£6.85). This is partly because a higher proportion of women than men work part time throughout their careers.

Factors such as occupation and age also affect the level of earnings that employees can command. In April 2006, median weekly earnings for full-time employees rose steadily with age for the younger age groups of both men and women, irrespective of their occupation (Table 5.7). However, men's earnings peaked during their 40s in all occupations except sales and customer services, where they peaked in their 30s. Generally, women's earnings peaked in their 30s, though for women in the associate professional and technical occupations, earnings peaked in their 40s and for those in professional occupations earnings peaked in their 50s.

Young people aged 18 to 21 were the least well paid, with weekly earnings considerably below the median for all of working age in each occupational group. However, even within this age group, earnings varied considerably by occupation and also between men and women. For example, male managers and senior officials aged 18 to 21 earned 36 per cent more than men of that age in sales and customer service occupations. Similarly, women aged 18 to 21 working in professional occupations earned 68 per cent more than women of that age in elementary occupations such as bar staff, and their earnings exceeded those of women in any of the age groups shown working in the skilled trades, personal service, sales and customer service, elementary occupations, and process, plant and machine operatives. For further details of the occupational classification used in Table 5.7, see Appendix, Part 4: Standard Occupational Classification 2000 (SOC2000).

Table **5.7**

Median weekly earnings:[1] by sex, occupation[2] and age, April 2006

United Kingdom

Median gross weekly earnings excluding overtime (£)

	18–21	22–29	30–39	40–49	50–59	60 and over	All employees
Men							
Managers and senior officials	305	485	698	786	754	620	709
Professional	274	537	676	722	721	677	677
Associate professional and technical	307	437	535	578	550	460	521
Administrative and secretarial	251	317	381	397	385	345	354
Skilled trades	258	351	404	422	404	376	390
Personal service	254	289	322	324	300	289	303
Sales and customer service	225	273	316	314	300	262	277
Process, plant and machine operatives	263	320	360	375	355	330	352
Elementary	230	272	318	327	319	302	296
Women							
Managers and senior officials	292	460	586	580	521	434	546
Professional	355	492	613	637	664	650	608
Associate professional and technical	278	420	486	499	496	464	467
Administrative and secretarial	249	310	349	342	331	327	325
Skilled trades	231	290	326	277	255	255	273
Personal service	225	271	289	289	287	286	276
Sales and customer service	231	267	281	249	236	232	251
Process, plant and machine operatives	236	263	274	268	253	247	261
Elementary	211	237	252	247	238	243	236

1 Full-time employees on adult rates, whose pay for the survey period was unaffected by absence.
2 Classified according to the Standard Occupational Classification 2000. See Appendix, Part 4: Standard Occupational Classification 2000 (SOC2000).

Source: Annual Survey of Hours and Earnings, Office for National Statistics

Young people are more likely to be in jobs paid below the national minimum wage, partly because they are more likely to be in a job that is exempt from it. From October 2005, there were three rates for the national minimum wage: one for those aged between 16 and 17 (£3.00 an hour, increased to £3.30 an hour from 1 October 2006), one for those aged between 18 and 21 (£4.25 per hour, increased to £4.45 from October 2006) and one for those aged 22 and over (£5.05 per hour, increased to £5.35 from October 2006). In April 2006, 4.3 per cent of jobs held by those aged 16 to 17 were paid below the relevant minimum wage rate. For those aged 18 to 21 and 22 and over, the figures were 2.5 per cent and 1.2 per cent respectively. Part-time jobs were more likely to pay less than the minimum wage. However, it is important to note that these estimates do not measure non-compliance with the national minimum wage legislation as the ASHE does not indicate whether jobs such as apprentices or new trainees are exempt from the legislation.

Taxes

Taxation is the main means by which governments raise revenue and a wide variety of taxes are levied on both individuals and institutions. The major taxes paid by individuals are income tax and taxes on expenditure. Every individual is entitled to a personal allowance and those with an annual income below this do not pay any income tax. For 2006/07, the personal allowance was set at £5,035 for those aged under 65, with further allowances for people aged 65 and over. The income tax regime on earnings for 2006/07 includes three different rates of tax. Taxable income of up to £2,150 (that is, after the deduction of allowances and any other tax relief to which the individual may be entitled) is charged at 10 per cent. Taxable income above £2,150 but less than £33,300 is charged at 22 per cent, while income above this level is charged at 40 per cent. Special rates apply to income from savings and dividends.

HM Revenue and Customs estimates that in 2006/07 there were around 29.7 million taxpayers in the UK (Table 5.8), 0.5 million more than in 2005/06. Given the progressive nature of the income tax system, the amount of tax payable increases as income increases – both as a proportion of income and in cash terms. The average rate of income tax for taxpayers with taxable incomes between the personal annual allowance of £5,035 and £7,499 was 1.8 per cent compared with average rates in excess of 30 per cent for taxpayers with incomes of £100,000 and over.

National insurance (NI) contributions are paid according to an individual's earnings rather than their total income, and for employees, payments are made both by the individual and

Table **5.8**

Income tax payable: by annual income,[1] 2006/07[2]

United Kingdom

	Number of taxpayers (thousands)	Total tax liability after tax reductions[3] (£ million)	Average rate of tax (percentages)	Average amount of tax (£)
£5,035–£7,499	2,700	306	1.8	114
£7,500–£9,999	3,370	1,390	4.7	411
£10,000–£14,999	5,970	6,990	9.4	1,170
£15,000–£19,999	4,890	10,800	12.7	2,200
£20,000–£29,999	6,440	24,000	15.2	3,720
£30,000–£49,999	4,450	29,000	17.5	6,540
£50,000–£99,999	1,460	24,500	25.3	16,800
£100,000–£199,999	350	14,500	31.3	41,500
£200,000–£499,999	100	9,930	34.2	99,500
£500,000–£999,999	18	4,350	35.4	239,000
£1,000,000 and over	6	4,750	34.2	734,000
All incomes	29,700	131,000	17.9	4,390

1 Total income of the individual for income tax purposes including earned and investment income. Figures relate to taxpayers only.
2 Based on projections in line with the December 2006 Pre-budget Report.
3 In this context tax reductions refer to allowances given at a fixed rate, for example the Married Couple's Allowance.

Source: HM Revenue and Customs

by their employer. In 2006/07, employees with earnings less than £97 per week paid no contributions, and neither did their employers. Employees paid Class 1 contributions equal to 11.0 per cent of their earnings between £97 and £645 per week, and an additional 1.0 per cent on earnings above £645 per week. Employers paid contributions equal to 12.8 per cent of earnings above £97 per week.

Table 5.9 overleaf indicates the impact of income tax and NI contributions on people at different points in the earnings distribution. In this table, income tax payments have been calculated assuming that an individual is entitled to a personal allowance only and that they have no income other than their earnings. It illustrates how income tax liabilities increase as a proportion of earnings as earnings increase, whereas NI contributions decrease in percentage terms once an employee crosses the level of earnings at which the ceiling on contributions applies.

Between 1997/98 and 2001/02, employees at each of the points of the income distribution shown in Table 5.9 experienced a fall in NI contributions as a percentage of their earnings, with the largest fall being for those at the lowest decile point. Employees at the lowest decile point and at

Table **5.9**

Earnings paid in income tax and national insurance contributions:[1] by level of earnings[2]

United Kingdom
Percentages

	1997/98	2001/02	2002/03	2003/04	2004/05	2005/06
Lowest decile point of annual earnings						
Tax	11.3	10.5	10.8	11.2	11.3	11.1
National insurance contributions	7.1	5.8	5.8	6.6	6.7	6.6
Median annual earnings						
Tax	16.6	15.7	15.9	16.0	16.1	16.1
National insurance contributions	8.5	7.7	7.7	8.6	8.6	8.6
Highest decile point of annual earnings						
Tax	20.2	20.7	21.3	21.7	21.6	21.8
National insurance contributions	6.9	6.7	6.5	7.3	7.2	7.2

1 Employee's contributions. Assumes contributions at Class 1, contracted in, standard rate.
2 Average earnings for full-time employees at the start of each financial year in all occupations working a full week on adult rates.

Source: HM Revenue and Customs

median earnings also experienced a fall in income tax as a proportion of their earnings over this period, but since 2001/02 the proportion has risen again, to reach a level in 2005/06 only slightly below that of 1997/98. Those at the top decile point experienced a small rise between 1997/98 and 2001/02 in income tax as a proportion of their earnings, from 20.2 per cent to 20.7 per cent and this rising trend continued up to 2003/04, since which the percentage has remained fairly stable.

In addition to direct taxes such as income tax, households pay indirect taxes through their expenditure. Indirect taxes include value added tax (VAT), customs duties and excise duties, and are included in the prices of consumer goods and services. These taxes are specific to particular commodities. For example, in 2004/05, VAT was payable on most consumer goods at 17.5 per cent of their value, though not on most foods, books and newspapers, and children's clothing; and was payable at a reduced rate on heating and lighting. Customs and excise duties paid on goods such as alcohol and tobacco products tend to vary by the volume rather than value of goods purchased.

On average, households paid 19 per cent of their income in indirect taxes in 2004/05 (Figure 5.10). High income households are more likely to devote a larger proportion of their income to investments or repaying loans, and low income households may be funding their expenditure through taking out loans or drawing down savings. As a result, the proportion of income paid in indirect taxes tends to be higher for those on low incomes than for those on high incomes. In 2004/05 households in the top quintile or top 'fifth' of the income distribution were paying 14 per cent of their disposable income

in indirect taxes, compared with 30 per cent for those in the bottom fifth of the distribution.

A further means of raising revenue from households is through council tax (domestic rates in Northern Ireland). These taxes are raised by local authorities to part-fund the services they provide. For both council tax and domestic rates, the amount payable by a household depends on the value of the property

Figure **5.10**

Indirect taxes as a percentage of disposable income: by income grouping[1] of household, 2004/05

United Kingdom
Percentages

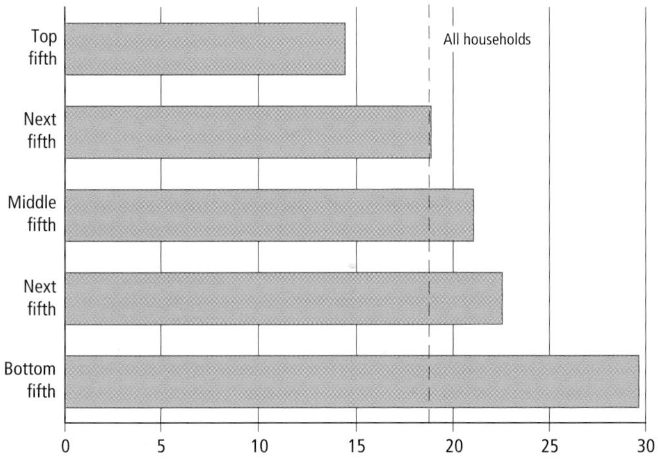

1 Equivalised disposable income has been used to rank the households into quintile groups. See Appendix, Part 5: Equivalisation scales.

Source: Office for National Statistics

they occupy. For those on low incomes, assistance is available in the form of council tax benefits (rates rebates in Northern Ireland). In 2004/05, the average council tax/domestic rate payable (excluding payments for water and sewerage) in the UK was £830 per household, after taking into account the relevant benefit payments. Net council tax varied from £960 per year in the South East of England to £620 in Wales. Net domestic rates in Northern Ireland, which are based on a quite different valuation system, averaged £490, representing 1.9 per cent of gross income. Within Great Britain, council tax as a percentage of gross household income varied from 2.3 per cent in London and in Wales to 3.2 per cent in Scotland.

Income distribution

The first two sections of this chapter demonstrated how the various components of income differ in importance for different household types and how the levels of earnings vary between individuals. The result is an uneven distribution of total income between households, although the inequality is reduced to some extent by the deduction of taxes and social contributions and their redistribution to households in the form of social security benefits. The analysis of income distribution is therefore usually based on household disposable income. In the analysis of Households Below Average Income (HBAI) carried out by the Department for Work and Pensions (DWP), on which most of the tables and figures in this and the next

section are based, payments of income tax, council tax (domestic rates in Northern Ireland) and employee national insurance contributions are deducted to obtain disposable income. For more details see Appendix, Part 5: Households Below Average Income.

In the HBAI analysis, disposable income is also presented both before and after the deduction of housing costs. It can be argued that the costs of housing at a given time may or may not reflect the true value of the housing that different households actually enjoy. For example, the housing costs of someone renting a property from a private landlord may be much higher than those for a local authority property of similar quality for which the rent may be set without reference to a market rent. Equally, a retired person living in a property that they own outright may enjoy the same level of housing as their younger neighbour in an identical property owned with a mortgage, though their housing costs will be very different. Estimates are presented on both bases to take into account variations in housing costs that do not correspond to comparable variations in the quality of housing. Neither is given pre-eminence over the other.

The income distribution and the extent of inequality have changed considerably over the last three decades. In Figure 5.11, the closer the percentiles are to the median line, the greater the

Analysing income distribution

Equivalisation – in analysing the distribution of income, household disposable income is usually adjusted to take account of the size and composition of the household. This recognises that, for example, to achieve the same standard of living a household of five requires a higher income than a single person. This process is known as equivalisation (see Appendix, Part 5: Equivalisation scales).

Quintile and decile groups – the main method of analysing income distribution used in this chapter is to rank units (households, individuals or adults) by a given income measure, and then to divide the ranked units into groups of equal size. Groups containing 20 per cent of units are referred to as 'quintile groups' or 'fifths'. Thus the 'bottom quintile group' is the 20 per cent of units with the lowest incomes. Similarly, groups containing 10 per cent of units are referred to as 'decile groups' or tenths.

Percentiles – an alternative method also used in the chapter is to present the income level above or below which a certain proportion of units fall. Thus the 90th percentile is the income level above which only 10 per cent of units fall when ranked by a given income measure – this is also known as the top decile point. The median is then the midpoint of the distribution above and below which 50 per cent of units fall.

Figure **5.11**

Distribution of real[1] disposable household income[2]

United Kingdom/Great Britain[3]

£ per week at 2004/05 prices

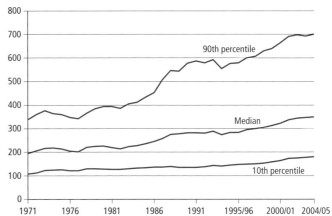

1 Adjusted to 2004/05 prices using the retail prices index less local taxes.
2 Equivalised household disposable income before deduction of housing costs. See Appendix, Part 5: Households Below Average Income, and Equivalisation scales.
3 Data from 1993/94 onwards are for financial years. Source of data changed in 1994/95, definition of income changed slightly and geographic coverage changed from United Kingdom to Great Britain. Geographic coverage changed from Great Britain to United Kingdom in 2002/03.

Source: Institute for Fiscal Studies from Family Expenditure Survey, Office for National Statistics (1971 to 1993/94); Households Below Average Income, Department for Work and Pensions (1994/95 onwards)

equality within the distribution. During the early 1970s the distribution of disposable income among households was broadly stable. Around the mid-1970s there was a gradual move towards equality, but this was reversed during the late 1970s and inequality in the distribution continued to grow throughout the 1980s. During the first half of the 1990s the income distribution appeared to be stable again, although at a much higher level of income dispersion than in the 1970s. The early 1990s were a period of economic downturn when there was little real growth in incomes anywhere in the distribution. Between 1995/96 and 2004/05, income at the 90th and 10th percentiles and at the median all grew in real terms. The Gini coefficient – a widely used measure of inequality (see Appendix, Part 5: Gini coefficient) – increased between 1994/95 and 2000/01 (implying an increase in inequality) with indications of a fall (implying an increase in equality) between 2000/01 and 2004/05.

Researchers at the Institute for Fiscal Studies (IFS) have investigated some of the possible explanations for the changes in inequality. They found that changes to the labour market played an important role. In particular, inequality rose during the 1980s when the incomes of the higher paid grew much more rapidly than those of the lower paid or of households where no one was working. Growth in self-employment income and in unemployment were also found to be associated with periods of increased inequality. It appears that demographic factors such as the growth in one-person households made a relatively unimportant contribution compared with labour

market changes. However, the IFS found that changes in the tax and benefit system had made an impact. The income tax cuts of the 1970s and late 1980s worked to increase income inequality while direct tax rises in the early 1980s and 1990s – together with the increases in means-tested benefits in the late 1990s – produced the opposite effect.

Between 1996/97 and 2003/04, income growth was much more evenly spread across the whole of the income distribution, with exceptions at the very top and bottom of the distribution. Changes at the bottom of the distribution are difficult to disentangle from measurement error. However, there is evidence from these data, based on the Family Resources Survey (FRS), and also from data from tax returns, that there was much more rapid growth in the top 1 per cent of incomes than for the rest of the distribution. The reasons for this growth are not yet well understood, but possible explanations include changes in the nature of executive remuneration.

People in single and couple households where all members were in full-time work were nearly twice as likely as the population as a whole to be in the top quintile group of disposable income in the UK in 2004/05 (Table 5.12). Only 3 per cent of people in full-time work were in the lowest quintile group. The self-employed were also more likely than the population as a whole to be in the highest income group. At the other end of the distribution, people in households where the head or spouse was unemployed were more than three times as likely as all individuals to be in the bottom

Table **5.12**

Distribution of household disposable income:[1] by economic status of family, 2004/05

United Kingdom

Percentages

	Bottom fifth	Next fifth	Middle fifth	Next fifth	Top fifth	All (=100%) (millions)
Self-employed[2]	21	15	17	19	28	5.6
Single/couple, all in full-time work	3	9	19	31	38	14.5
Couple, one in full-time work, one in part-time work	5	18	30	26	22	8.5
Couple, one in full-time work, one not working	17	25	22	19	17	6.9
Single/couple, one or more in part-time work	26	26	21	15	12	5.5
Workless, head or spouse aged 60 or over	28	31	20	13	8	10.1
Workless, head or spouse unemployed	69	18	7	4	2	1.4
Workless, other inactive[3]	52	27	12	6	3	6.3
All individuals	20	20	20	20	20	58.8

1 Equivalised household disposable income before deduction of housing costs has been used to rank the individuals into quintile groups. See Appendix, Part 5: Households Below Average Income, and Equivalisation scales.
2 Those in benefit units which contain one or more adults who are normally self-employed for 31 or more hours a week.
3 Includes long-term sick and disabled people and non-working single-parents.

Source: Households Below Average Income, Department for Work and Pensions

quintile group. The section below on low incomes examines the characteristics of those at the lower end of the income distribution in more depth.

Economic status is one of a variety of factors that influence an individual's position in the income distribution. For example, in 2004/05 in Great Britain, all ethnic minority groups had greater than average likelihood of being in the bottom quintile group, with the Pakistani/Bangladeshi group being particularly at risk. In addition, groups with greater than average risks of being in the bottom quintile group in the UK were single parent families and families where one or more adults and one or more of the children were disabled. Couples without children had a greater than average likelihood of being in the top quintile group.

In the UK in 2004/05, children were more likely to be in the bottom two quintile groups and less likely to be in the top two quintile groups of the income distribution among all individuals (Table 5.13). This was true whatever the ethnic group of the head of the household in which they were living. However, children living in households headed by someone from an ethnic minority group had a greater risk of being in the lowest two quintile groups. Those in the Pakistani/Bangladeshi group were most at risk, with 86 per cent of children in this group being in the lowest 40 per cent of the income distribution.

Material deprivation is generally defined as wanting particular types of goods and services but being unable to afford to buy them. The DWP's Families and Children Study analyses the affordability of 34 'deprivation items', covering four dimensions of material deprivation: food and meals; clothing and shoes; consumer durables; and leisure activities. From these data, a relative material deprivation score can be derived that calculates the number of items a family would like but cannot afford, weighted according to the proportion of families that own these items. The higher the score, the higher the deprivation (for more details see Appendix, Part 5: Material hardship). The study also provides data on income that allow the same definition of household disposable income to be applied as for the Households Below Average Income series used above. It is therefore possible to use this data source to explore the relationship between income and material hardship.

Table 5.14 shows that being in material hardship is related to income, though the relationship is not altogether straightforward. Relative deprivation scores fall as income increases, with families in the lowest two quintile groups being, on average, much more likely to be deprived. However, some families in the top quintile group had non-zero scores, particularly in relation to leisure activities. Throughout the income distribution there appears to be prioritisation in the purchase of items and activities. Families were more likely to go without leisure activities such as a one-week holiday or money for trips or outings and less likely to go without food and meal items, such as a main meal every day; and consumer durables such as a telephone and a washing machine.

Table **5.13**

Position of children within the distribution of household disposable income:[1] by ethnic group,[2] 2004/05

United Kingdom					Percentages
	Bottom fifth	Next fifth	Middle fifth	Next fifth	Top fifth
White	23	24	22	18	14
Mixed	31	33	20	9	7
Asian or Asian British	45	27	11	7	9
Indian	34	22	15	11	18
Pakistani/Bangladeshi	55	31	8	4	2
Black or Black British	32	22	19	15	12
Black Caribbean	23	25	21	18	13
Black African/Other Black	41	20	16	11	11
Chinese or Other ethnic group	37	21	21	11	10
All children	25	24	21	17	13

1 Equivalised household disposable income before deduction of housing costs has been used to rank the individuals into quintile groups. See Appendix, Part 5: Households Below Average Income, and Equivalisation scales.
2 Of household reference person.

Source: Households Below Average Income, Department for Work and Pensions

Table **5.14**

Relative material deprivation score[1] among families with children, 2004

Great Britain					Percentages
	Quintile group of disposable income				
	Bottom fifth	Next fifth	Middle fifth	Next fifth	Top fifth
Food and meals	11.2	6.8	2.8	1.3	0.4
Clothes and shoes	15.0	10.9	4.8	2.3	0.6
Consumer durables	10.1	6.8	3.0	1.5	0.7
Leisure activities	29.0	20.7	10.0	5.3	2.0
All items	14.5	10.0	4.5	2.3	0.8

1 Material deprivation is defined as wanting an item or activity but being unable to afford it. Relative material deprivation weights each item according to how widely it is owned. The higher the score the greater the deprivation. See Appendix, Part 5: Material hardship.

Source: Families and Children Study, Department for Work and Pensions

Low incomes

Low income could be defined as being in the bottom quintile or decile group, but these definitions are not generally used because of their relative nature. It would mean that 20 or 10 per cent of the population would always be defined as poor, even if everyone's income increased. Other approaches generally involve fixing a threshold in monetary terms, below which a household is considered to be 'poor'. This threshold may be calculated in a variety of ways. In countries at a very low level of development it may be useful to cost the bare essentials to maintain human life and use this as the yardstick against which to measure low income. This 'basic needs' measure is of limited usefulness for a developed country such as the UK.

The approach generally used in more developed countries is to fix a low income threshold in terms of a fraction of the median income of the population. This threshold may then be fixed in real terms for a number of years, or it may be calculated in respect of the income distribution for each successive year. The Government's Opportunity for All (OfA) indicators use both approaches. The proportions of people living in households with incomes below various fractions of contemporary median income are monitored, and are referred to as those with relative low income. The proportions with incomes below various fractions of median income in 1996/97 (the reference year for which the threshold was set), known as those with absolute low income, are also monitored. A third OfA indicator measures the number of people with persistent low income, defined as being in a low income household in three out of the last four years. In addition, the Government has announced that to monitor progress against its target of halving the number of children in low income households by 2010 compared with 1998/99 and eradicating child poverty by 2020, there will be another measure that combines material deprivation and relative low income for families with children.

The low income threshold generally adopted and used in the remainder of this section is 60 per cent of contemporary equivalised median household disposable income before the deduction of housing costs, see Appendix, Part 5: Equivalisation scales. In 2004/05, this represented an income of £210 per week. Using this threshold, the Institute for Fiscal Studies calculates that the proportion of the population living in low income households rose from 11 per cent in 1982 and 1983 to reach a peak of 21 per cent in 1992 (Figure 5.15). Official estimates made by DWP indicate that it fell back to 17 per cent in each of the four years 2000/01 to 2003/04 and to 16 per cent in 2004/05. This pattern is also reflected in the proportion of people with incomes less than 50 per cent of the

Figure **5.15**

Proportion of people whose income is below various percentages of median household disposable income[1]

United Kingdom/Great Britain[2]
Percentages

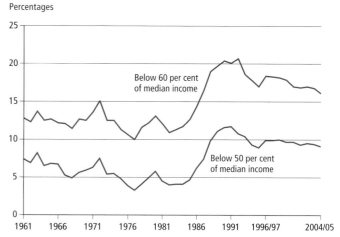

1 Equivalised contemporary household disposable income before deduction of housing costs. See Appendix, Part 5: Households Below Average Income, and Equivalisation scales.
2 Data from 1993/94 onwards are for financial years. Source of data changed in 1994/95, definition of income changed slightly and geographic coverage changed from United Kingdom to Great Britain. Geographic coverage changed from Great Britain to United Kingdom in 2002/03.

Source: Institute for Fiscal Studies from Family Expenditure Survey, Office for National Statistics (1961 to 1993/94); Households Below Average Income, Department for Work and Pensions (1994/95 onwards)

median. Note that between 1994/95 and 2001/02 these figures exclude Northern Ireland, but this is estimated to have only minimal impact on the trends.

The threshold of 60 per cent of median equivalised disposable income was adopted by the Laeken European Council in December 2001 as one of a set of 18 statistical indicators of social exclusion and poverty. Using data from the EU Survey of Income and Living Conditions or comparable national sources analysed as far as possible to a common set of concepts and definitions, Eurostat have calculated the proportion of the population in each EU member state in 2003 that is at risk of poverty, measured against 60 per cent of median equivalised disposable income in the country in which they live. On average, 16 per cent of the EU population were at risk of poverty (Figure 5.16), representing 72 million people. Countries with the highest rates of low income included Ireland, Portugal, and Slovakia each at 21 per cent, followed by Greece and Spain at 20 per cent. At the other end of the scale, the proportion of the population at risk of poverty was 8 per cent in the Czech Republic (though data are for 2002 rather than 2003) and 10 per cent in Slovenia.

Figure **5.16**

Individuals with incomes[1] below 60 per cent of median disposable income:[2] EU comparison, 2003

Percentages

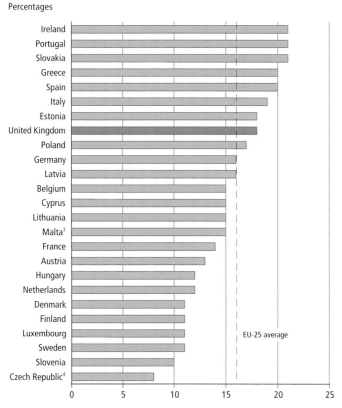

1 Equivalised disposable income in each country.
2 National median used in each country.
3 Data are for 2000.
4 Data are for 2002.

Source: Eurostat

Since these rates are calculated in relation to national median income, they may represent very different standards of living across the EU below which an individual is considered to be on a low income. The threshold of 60 per cent of median equivalised disposable income in the ten countries that joined the EU in 2004 is generally much lower than in the pre-2004 EU-15 member states. This reflects the poorer living conditions that prevail in the newer member states. It is also true that the income distribution is relatively narrow in most of these ten newer member states. This means that the difference in living standards between someone on an income below the low income threshold and someone above the threshold may be much smaller than in some EU-15 member states. Note that slightly different definitions of income have been used for the UK in this figure compared with Figure 5.15, for example Eurostat use different equivalisation scales from those used by DWP in calculating the Households Below Average Income series.

Table **5.17**

Individuals in households with incomes below 60 per cent of median disposable income:[1] by selected risk factors[2]

Great Britain		Percentages
	1994/95	2004/05
Economic status of adults in the family		
Workless, head or spouse unemployed	*58*	*62*
Workless, other inactive	*38*	*43*
Family type		
Single with children	*30*	*29*
Ethnic group of head of household		
Asian or Asian British	*41*	*33*
Black African/Other Black	*37*	*27*
Disability		
One or more disabled children and one or more disabled adults in family	*28*	*28*
All individuals	*18*	*16*

1 Equivalised contemporary household disposable income before deduction of housing costs has been used to rank individuals. See Appendix, Part 5: Households Below Average Income, and Equivalisation scales.
2 Factors have been included in this table if they give rise to proportions of individuals 10 percentage points or more greater than the 'all individuals' proportion of 16 per cent in 2004/05.

Source: Households Below Average Income, Department for Work and Pensions

In Great Britain, being workless and unemployed increased the risk of being in a low income household nearly fourfold in 2004/05, while being economically inactive (see Glossary in Chapter 4: Labour market) and under pension age nearly trebled the risk (Table 5.17). All ethnic minority groups had greater than average likelihood of being in a low income household, with the Asian or Asian British and Black non-Caribbean groups particularly at risk. Other groups with greater than average risks of being in a low income household were single-parent families and families with one or more disabled children and one or more disabled adults.

Over the ten years since 1994/95, the overall risk of living in a low income household fell 2 percentage points, from 18 to 16 per cent. However, for workless households the likelihood of living in a low income household increased by 4 percentage points for those where the head or spouse was unemployed and by 5 percentage points for families where the adult(s) were economically inactive. On the other hand, the risk for those in households where the head was Asian or Asian British fell over the decade by 8 percentage points.

Table **5.18**

Persistent low income: by family type,[1] 1991–2004

Great Britain

Percentages

	3 out of 4 years below 60 per cent of median income[2]			Entry rate into persistent low income[3] 1991–2004	Exit rate from persistent low income[3] 1991–2004
	1991–94	1996–99	2001–04		
Pensioner couple	13	17	15	2	9
Single pensioner	21	23	18	3	10
Couple with children	13	11	9	1	18
Couple without children	3	3	4	1	20
Single with children	40	27	21	4	15
Single without children	6	7	7	1	34
All individuals	12	11	10	1	17

1 Families are classified according to their type in the first year of the relevant period.
2 Equivalised contemporary household disposable income before housing costs. See Appendix, Part 5: Households Below Average Income, and Equivalisation scales.
3 Persistent low income is defined as experiencing low income for at least three consecutive years. An entry occurs during the first year of a persistent low income period, following a period of two years not in low income. An exit occurs as the first year of two not in low income, following a persistent low income period.

Source: Department for Work and Pensions from British Household Panel Survey, Institute for Economic and Social Research

When income is measured after the deduction of housing costs, the proportions of individuals with low incomes are generally higher than before the deduction of housing costs, whatever their economic status. This is principally because housing costs for low income households are large in relation to their income as a whole.

For some people, such as students and those unemployed for a brief period, the experience of low income may be a relatively transient one, but for others it may be more permanent. The British Household Panel Survey (BHPS) provides longitudinal data that allow income mobility and the persistence of low income to be analysed. The definition of the Government's Opportunity for All indicator for persistent low income is 'at least three years out of four below thresholds of 60 or 70 per cent of median income'. Between 1991–1994 and 2001–2004, the proportion of individuals experiencing persistent low income has fallen slightly from 12 per cent to 10 per cent (Table 5.18). However, over the last decade the risk of different family types experiencing persistent low income has changed. In particular the proportion of single people with children experiencing persistent low income has fallen substantially, from 40 per cent during 1991–1994 to 21 per cent during 2001–2004. Those living in couple households without children were at least risk of persistent low income.

The prevalence of low income differs considerably across the country. For example, the risk of being in a low income household, averaged over the period 2002/03 to 2004/05, varied within Great Britain from 12 per cent in the South East to 22 per cent in Inner London. However, there are often greater income differences between local areas within regions than between regions. In the absence of a question on household income in the 2001 Population Census, the Office for National Statistics has produced a set of model-based estimates for average household income in England and Wales based on the 2003 Census Area Statistics ward boundaries. The methodology allows survey data to be combined with census and administrative data, to enable estimation at lower geographical levels such as wards. Estimates for four different income definitions were produced to meet user requirements; for more details see Appendix, Part 5: Model-based estimates of income. Wards where equivalised household disposable income (before deduction of housing costs) was less than £250 per week in 2001/02 were concentrated in the North East and North West, with smaller pockets in south Wales, the Island of Anglesey, and the Midlands.

Wealth

Although the terms 'wealthy' and 'high income' are often used interchangeably, they relate to quite distinct concepts. Income represents a flow of resources over a period received either in cash or in kind, for example earnings or the use of a company car, while wealth describes the ownership of assets valued at a particular point in time. Wealth can be held in the form of financial assets, such as savings accounts or shares, which provide a flow of current income, or pension rights that provide entitlement to a future income flow. These types of asset form financial wealth. Ownership of non-financial wealth may provide financial security even if it does not provide a current income flow; a house or a work of art, for example, could be sold to provide income if necessary. In this section the term 'wealth' includes both financial and non-financial assets. There is a further distinction sometimes made between marketable and non-marketable wealth. Marketable wealth comprises assets that can be sold and their value realised, whereas non-marketable wealth comprises mainly pension rights that often cannot be cashed in. Wealth may be accumulated either by the acquisition of new assets, through saving, by inheritance, or by the increase in value of existing assets.

There are a variety of ways in which individuals can hold financial assets, ranging from a current account to individual savings accounts (ISAs) and stocks and shares. In 2004/05, nine out of ten adults aged 16 and over in the UK had a current account, with young people aged 16 to 24 and those over state pension age only marginally less likely to have one than those aged 25 to 64 (Table 5.19). Around one-quarter of adults aged 16 and over had an ISA, and one-sixth held stocks and shares.

Ownership of savings instruments such as these tended to increase with age. For example, only 10 per cent of males aged 16 to 24 had an ISA compared with 27 per cent of those aged 25 to 64 and 35 per cent of those aged 65 and over. Premium Bonds were more popular among those aged 65 and over compared with the younger age groups.

Aggregate data on the wealth of the household sector compiled in the UK National Accounts indicate that of total assets of over £7,600 billion in 2005, 44 per cent were held in the form of residential buildings (Table 5.20 overleaf). Even when account is taken of the loans outstanding on the purchase of housing, this form of wealth grew strongly between 1991 and 2004. This reflects the buoyant state of the housing market, as well as the continued growth in the number of owner-occupied dwellings. However, between 2004 and 2005 there was a small fall in the real value of residential buildings less loans outstanding on their purchase.

Table **5.19**

Adults holding selected forms of wealth: by sex and age, 2004/05

United Kingdom   Percentages

	Men				Women				All individuals aged 16 and over
	16–24	25–64	65 and over	All aged 16 and over	16–24	25–64	65 and over	All aged 16 and over	
Current account	81.0	89.9	86.1	88.2	84.1	89.3	80.8	86.9	87.5
ISAs	10.2	26.8	35.1	26.3	13.5	29.0	30.5	27.6	26.9
Basic bank account	2.9	3.8	5.2	3.9	4.2	4.9	6.1	5.1	4.5
TESSA	0.1	4.1	9.2	4.5	-	4.2	7.7	4.5	4.5
Post Office account	2.3	2.5	3.3	2.6	2.8	3.3	4.6	3.5	3.1
Other Bank/Building society account	23.4	44.9	49.4	43.0	27.2	47.3	48.8	45.4	44.2
Stocks and shares	3.2	18.7	23.0	17.5	2.2	14.7	17.2	13.9	15.6
PEPs	0.3	5.4	10.0	5.6	0.1	4.7	7.0	4.7	5.2
Unit trusts	0.4	3.8	6.5	3.9	0.5	2.9	4.5	3.0	3.4
Endowment policy not linked	0.1	3.1	0.3	2.2	-	2.4	0.2	1.7	1.9
Gilts	-	0.3	1.3	0.4	-	0.3	1.4	0.5	0.5
Premium Bonds	4.7	16.1	24.4	16.2	4.5	15.6	22.1	15.8	16.0
National Savings Bonds	0.8	1.3	6.5	2.2	0.5	1.6	7.5	2.7	2.5
Guaranteed Equity Bonds	-	0.2	0.6	0.2	-	0.3	0.6	0.3	0.3
Company Share Scheme	0.6	4.7	0.4	3.4	0.6	2.7	0.1	1.9	2.6
Credit Unions	0.3	0.7	0.1	0.5	0.4	0.8	0.1	0.6	0.5
Save as you earn	0.2	0.6	-	0.4	0.2	0.6	0.1	0.4	0.4
Any form of wealth	86.5	94.2	93.7	93.1	90.1	94.6	92.4	93.6	93.4
No form of wealth	13.5	5.9	6.3	6.9	9.9	5.4	7.7	6.4	6.6

Source: Family Resources Survey, Department for Work and Pensions

Table **5.20**

Composition of the net wealth[1] of the household sector

United Kingdom

£ billion at 2005 prices[2]

	1991	2001	2002	2003	2004	2005
Non-financial assets						
Residential buildings	1,605	2,272	2,716	2,985	3,297	3,356
Other	472	527	600	648	695	688
Financial assets						
Life assurance and pension funds	844	1,644	1,464	1,570	1,641	1,842
Securities and shares	360	634	484	527	564	659
Currency and deposits	541	731	773	825	875	920
Other assets	113	136	134	137	146	152
Total assets	3,935	5,943	6,171	6,692	7,218	7,617
Financial liabilities						
Loans secured on dwellings	449	634	708	804	896	966
Other loans	120	171	189	193	212	219
Other liabilities	63	66	79	92	91	92
Total liabilities	633	870	976	1,089	1,200	1,276
Total net wealth	**3,302**	**5,073**	**5,194**	**5,603**	**6,019**	**6,341**

1 At end of each year. See Appendix, Part 5: Net wealth of the household sector.
2 Adjusted to 2005 prices using the expenditure deflator for the household sector. See Appendix, Part 5: Household income data sources.

Source: Office for National Statistics

The second most important element of household wealth is financial assets held in life assurance and pension funds, amounting to £1,842 billion in 2005. This element of household wealth grew strongly in real terms during the 1990s, as a result of increases in the contributions paid into occupational pension schemes as well as increased take-up of personal pensions. It fell by 11 per cent in real terms between 2001 and 2002, reflecting the fall in stock market values over this period, but had recovered to exceed its 2001 level in 2005.

Occupational and private pensions are important determinants of where older people appear in the income distribution, and so the extent to which people of working age are making provision for their retirement is of considerable policy interest – one of the Government's Opportunity for All indicators is the proportion of working-age people contributing to a non-state pension. In 2004/05, the Family Resources Survey found that 43 per cent were doing so in Great Britain, with more men (46 per cent) than women (39 per cent) making contributions. Men and women in their 40s were most likely to be making contributions. In the 45 to 49 age band, 59 per cent of men

and 47 per cent of women were doing so, as were 60 per cent of men and 45 per cent of women aged 40 to 44. Young people aged 20 to 24 were least likely to be contributing (15 per cent of men and 17 per cent of women) but this was the only age band where the proportion of women contributing was greater than that of men.

Over the 20th century as a whole, the distribution of wealth became more equal. It is estimated that in 1911 the wealthiest 1 per cent of the population held around 70 per cent of UK wealth. By 1936–38, this proportion had fallen to 56 per cent, and it fell again after the Second World War to reach 42 per cent in 1960. Using different methodology from the historic data, the share of the wealthiest 1 per cent of the population fell from around 22 per cent in the late 1970s to reach 17 to 18 per cent during the second half of the 1980s, then appears to have grown again, with proportions of 20 to 24 per cent recorded during the period 1996 to 2003 (Table 5.21).

Even during the 1970s and 1980s when the distribution was at its most equal, these estimates indicate that wealth is very much

Table **5.21**

Distribution of marketable wealth[1]

United Kingdom   Percentages

	1991	1996	2001	2002	2003
Percentage of wealth owned by:[2]					
Most wealthy 1%	17	20	22	24	21
Most wealthy 25%	71	74	72	75	72
Most wealthy 50%	92	93	94	94	93
Total marketable wealth (£ billion)	1,711	2,092	3,477	3,588	3,783

1 See Appendix, Part 5: Distribution of personal wealth. Estimates for individual years should be treated with caution as they are affected by sampling error and the particular pattern of deaths in that year.
2 Adults aged 18 and over.

Source: HM Revenue and Customs

Figure **5.22**

Median net financial wealth: by age and highest qualification, 2002

Great Britain

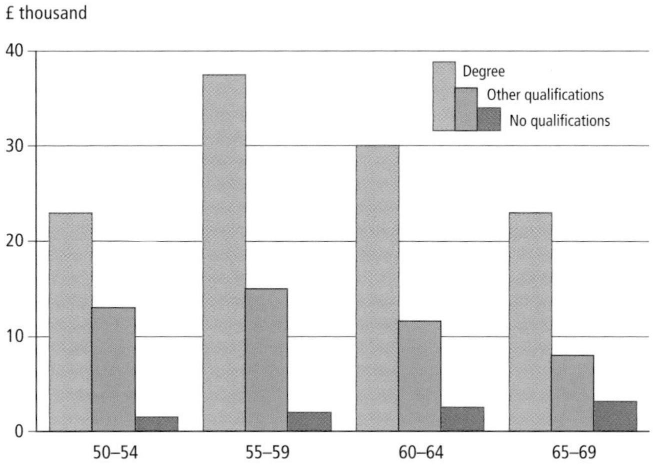

£ thousand

Source: Factors affecting the labour market participation of older workers, Department for Work and Pensions

less evenly distributed than income. One-half the population owned only 7 per cent of total wealth in 2003. To some extent this is because of life cycle effects. It usually takes time for people to build up assets during their working lives through savings and then draw them down during the years of retirement, with the residue passing to others after their death. If the value of housing is omitted from the wealth estimates, then wealth is even more concentrated among a small proportion of the population indicating that housing wealth is rather more evenly distributed than the remainder. These wealth distribution estimates are based on inheritance and capital transfer taxes rather than direct measurement through sample surveys. As such they cover only marketable wealth and so some important elements such as pension rights are excluded.

Although age is an important factor in determining the amount of wealth an individual has been able to build up, particularly pension wealth, there are other factors too. For example, it appears that there is a positive relationship between the level of educational attainment and financial wealth net of debt (other than mortgage debt) (Figure 5.22). For individuals in Great Britain aged 50 to 54, median net financial wealth in 2002 was £23,000 for those with a degree, compared with £13,000 for those with qualifications at a lower level and £1,500 for those with none. The gap between those with a degree and those with other or no qualifications was wider still for the older age groups, with the largest gap for the 55 to 59 age group.

Expendirure

- The volume of goods consumed by UK households increased by 73 per cent between 1991 and 2005, compared with a rise of 28 per cent for services, although services accounted for a greater proportion of their expenditure in 2005. (Table 6.3)

- UK household spending in 2005/06 was 16 per cent higher among couple households with children than in couple households without. (Table 6.4)

- In 2005/06, housing, fuel and power accounted for 19 per cent of spending by UK households in the bottom fifth of the income distribution, compared with 7 per cent for those in the top fifth. (Table 6.6)

- The value of Internet sales to UK households rose fourfold to £21.4 billion between 2002 and 2005. (Table 6.9)

- The proportion of debit card spending in the UK at food and drink outlets nearly halved between 1996 and 2005, although it was still the largest category at 23 per cent of spending. (Table 6.12)

- The number of individual insolvencies in England and Wales rose to 67,600 in 2005, an increase of 45 per cent from 2004. (Figure 6.14)

Chapter 6

There have been substantial changes over the last 30 years in the types of goods and services on which households have chosen to spend their income. Spending patterns provide an insight into society and give an indication of a household's standard of living and material well-being. They also reflect changes in society, consumer preference, and the growth in choices available to consumers not only in what they buy but also how they make their purchases, for example as a result of technological developments, such as internet shopping.

Household expenditure

In 2005, the consumption of goods and services by UK households was two and a half times the consumption in 1974 (Figure 6.1). The volume of spending increased every year over the period, except 1974, 1980, 1981 and more notably in 1991. These years correspond to periods of contraction in the UK economy. The increasing demand for goods and services is a reflection of the rise in real household incomes. The increase in household disposable income per head over the same period was very similar (see also Figure 5.1).

Figure **6.1**

Volume of domestic household expenditure[1] on goods and services

United Kingdom
Index numbers (1971=100)

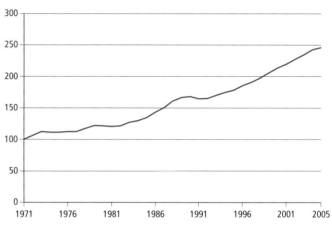

1 Chained volume measure. See Appendix, Part 6: Household expenditure.

Source: Office for National Statistics

Table **6.2**

Household expenditure: by purpose[1]

United Kingdom   Percentages

	1971	1981	1991	2001	2005
Food and non-alcoholic drink	21	17	12	9	9
Alcohol and tobacco	7	6	5	4	4
Clothing and footwear	9	7	6	6	6
Housing, water and fuel	15	17	18	18	19
Household goods and services	7	7	6	6	6
Health	1	1	1	2	2
Transport	12	15	15	15	15
Communication	1	2	2	2	2
Recreation and culture	9	10	11	12	12
Education	1	1	1	1	1
Restaurants and hotels[2]	10	11	12	11	12
Miscellaneous goods and services	7	7	11	11	11
Total domestic household expenditure	100	100	100	99	98
of which goods	65	61	53	49	48
of which services	35	40	47	50	51
Less foreign tourist expenditure	2	2	2	2	2
UK tourist expenditure abroad	1	2	3	4	4
All household expenditure[3] (=100%) (£ billion, current prices)	34	147	360	636	761

1 Classified to COICOP ESA95. See Appendix, Part 6: Classification Of Individual Consumption by Purpose.
2 Includes purchases of alcoholic drink in restaurants and hotels.
3 Includes expenditure by UK households in the UK and abroad.

Source: Office for National Statistics

Table **6.3**

Volume of household expenditure[1]

United Kingdom

Index numbers (1971=100)

	1971	1981	1991	2001	2005	£ billion (current prices) 2005
Food and non-alcoholic drink	100	105	117	137	147	67
Alcohol and tobacco	100	99	92	88	91	28
Clothing and footwear	100	120	187	344	460	44
Housing, water and fuel	100	117	139	152	158	148
Household goods and services	100	117	160	262	293	44
Health	100	125	182	188	203	12
Transport	100	128	181	246	269	113
Communication	100	190	307	790	927	17
Recreation and culture	100	158	279	545	742	94
Education	100	160	199	255	226	10
Restaurants and hotels[2]	100	126	167	193	212	89
Miscellaneous goods and services	100	121	231	282	299	83
Total domestic household expenditure	100	121	165	220	246	749
of which goods	100	117	156	227	270	363
of which services	100	128	180	218	230	386
Less foreign tourist expenditure	100	152	187	210	240	-17
UK tourist expenditure abroad	100	193	298	668	746	29
All household expenditure[3]	100	121	167	227	254	761

1 Chained volume measure. See Appendix, Part 6: Household expenditure. Classified to COICOP ESA95. See Appendix, Part 6: Classification Of Individual Consumption by Purpose.
2 Includes purchases of alcoholic drink in restaurants and hotels.
3 Includes expenditure by UK households in the United Kingdom and abroad.

Source: Office for National Statistics

This rise in the volume of expenditure has been accompanied by substantial changes in the way households allocate expenditure to different goods and services. Between 1971 and 2005, the proportion of total household expenditure on services in the UK increased from around one-third to just over half, while expenditure on goods made up a falling proportion of total expenditure (Table 6.2). In 2000, the proportion of total household expenditure spent on services had exceeded that for goods and this trend continued to 2005. There have been substantial shifts in the pattern of expenditure between 1971 and 2005. In 1971, food and non-alcoholic drink was the largest category, accounting for 21 per cent of expenditure, but by 2005 this had fallen to 9 per cent. This is not to say that real expenditure on food and non-alcoholic drink is falling, merely that expenditure on goods and services is rising much more rapidly, so that the proportion of expenditure on food is falling. The proportion of expenditure on housing, water and fuel increased from 15 per cent to 19 per cent over the same period to become the biggest category in 2005. Other categories

showing a marked increase were transport, and recreation and culture, rising from 12 per cent to 15 per cent, and 9 per cent to 12 per cent, respectively.

Among the categories for which the proportion of total spending fell between 1971 and 2005 were clothing and footwear, from 9 per cent to 6 per cent, and alcohol and tobacco, from 7 per cent to 4 per cent. The declining trend in adult cigarette smoking is described in Figure 7.11.

Changes in the level of consumption of goods and services are measured using volume indices. Volume indices are calculated by adjusting the total value of expenditure within each category, to account for the corresponding price changes. Between 1971 and 1991 the consumption of services increased more quickly than the consumption of goods (by 80 per cent compared to 56 per cent) (Table 6.3), which would be expected given the increased proportion of expenditure allocated to services as discussed above. However, after 1991 and particularly after 2001, the consumption of goods increased much more quickly than the consumption of services. Between 1991 and 2005 consumption of goods increased by 73 per cent, compared with an increase of just 28 per cent in the consumption of services. This is despite the proportion of expenditure allocated to goods falling slightly during this period. These seemingly conflicting patterns can be explained by the fact that since the mid-1990s the prices of goods have generally increased much more slowly (or in some cases fallen), whereas the prices of services have generally increased more quickly (see Figure 6.16). So while the balance of spending has continued to move from goods towards services, the reduced price of goods has enabled an increasing volume of goods to be purchased for a smaller proportion of total expenditure. Conversely, although an increasing proportion of expenditure has been on services, the overall increase in prices of those services has led to a relatively smaller volume being purchased.

Although the proportion of total spending on food and non-alcoholic drink decreased, the volume of household expenditure on these items still increased by 47 per cent between 1971 and 2005 in the UK. Other categories showed much larger increases, for example communication (which includes mobile phone equipment and services, and internet subscription charges) with a ninefold increase, and recreation and culture with a sevenfold increase. Within the recreation and culture category, goods that had the greatest increase in growth in spending between 1975 and 2005 were information processing equipment (which includes personal computers), photographic equipment, audio-visual and recording equipment, and games, toys and hobbies that include electronic and video games. The volume of spending by UK tourists abroad in 2005 was more than seven times that in 1971. The only category showing a decline in the volume of spending over the period was alcohol and tobacco. However, analysis of the breakdown for this category showed that only the tobacco component had decreased by 55 per cent between 1975 and 2005. During this period there were increases in the volume of spending on wine (174 per cent), spirits (129 per cent) and beer (30 per cent).

There are substantial variations in the levels of expenditure for different household types in the UK (Table 6.4). Retired households generally spend less than non-retired households.

Table 6.4

Household expenditure:[1] by selected household types, 2005/06

United Kingdom							£ per week
	Couple		Single				
	With children	No children	With children	No children	Retired couple[2]	Retired single[2]	All households
Food and non-alcoholic drink	62.80	46.70	38.60	22.50	46.00	23.70	45.30
Alcohol and tobacco	13.00	13.90	8.70	7.60	9.00	3.90	10.80
Clothing and footwear	33.60	24.50	23.30	11.50	14.00	6.10	22.70
Housing, fuel and power[3]	48.50	46.90	44.70	41.30	31.80	28.80	44.20
Household goods and services	39.00	38.80	25.50	15.00	31.40	14.50	30.00
Health	5.60	7.00	2.10	5.30	5.90	2.80	5.50
Transport	85.60	77.80	30.80	38.70	45.20	12.40	61.70
Communication	15.10	12.70	11.50	8.90	7.00	5.10	11.90
Recreation and culture	79.00	68.10	39.60	34.90	52.90	21.10	57.50
Education	14.30	3.90	6.10	2.40	1.30	-	6.60
Restaurants and hotels[4]	47.20	45.50	22.80	23.20	24.40	9.50	36.70
Miscellaneous goods and services	50.40	38.70	24.10	18.50	26.90	17.50	34.60
Other expenditure items	120.40	102.80	42.60	58.30	37.70	21.20	75.80
All household expenditure (=100%) (£ per week)	614.20	527.30	320.40	288.20	333.50	166.60	443.40

Note: Shaded cells indicate the estimates are unreliable due to small sample size and any analysis using these figures may be invalid. Any use of these shaded figures must be accompanied by this disclaimer.
1 See Appendix, Part 6: Household expenditure. Expenditure rounded to the nearest 10 pence.
2 Mainly receiving state pension and not economically active.
3 Excludes mortgage interest payments, water charges, council tax and domestic rates in Northern Ireland. These are included in 'Other expenditure items'.
4 Includes purchases of alcoholic drink in restaurants and hotels.
Source: Expenditure and Food Survey, Office for National Statistics

In 2005/06, retired couple households spent 37 per cent less than non-retired couples without children, while single retired households spent 42 per cent less than single non-retired households without children. Expenditure levels were 16 per cent higher among non-retired couples with children, compared with those without. Single non-retired households with children had expenditure levels that were 11 per cent higher compared with those without children.

The proportions of expenditure for different purposes also vary by household type. Households with children spend a higher proportion on food and non-alcoholic drink, clothing and footwear, and education than households without children. There are some distinct differences between retired couple and retired single households. In 2005/06, retired couple households spent a higher proportion of their total expenditure on recreation and culture (16 per cent) than retired single households (13 per cent). Retired couple households also spent a higher proportion on transport (14 per cent) than retired single households (7 per cent). However, retired single households spent a higher proportion (17 per cent) on housing, fuel and power (excluding mortgage interest payments, water charges, council tax and Northern Ireland domestic rates), than retired couple households (10 per cent).

The expenditure of students is measured in the 2004/05 Student Income and Expenditure Survey (SIES), commissioned by the Department for Education and Skills and the Welsh Assembly Government. It covers home students, both full-time and part-time.

There are important differences between the characteristics of full-time and part-time students, which go some way to explaining why their expenditure patterns tend to be quite different. For example, 84 per cent of full-time students in England were under 25 years of age compared with 23 per cent of part-time students. Part-time students were on average much older, with 31 per cent aged 40 years and above. In terms of their family type, 87 per cent of full-time students were single, 6 per cent were living as a couple without children, 5 per cent were in a two-adult family and 3 per cent were lone parents. By comparison, 38 per cent of part-time students were single, 22 per cent were in a couple relationship without children, 31 per cent were in a two-adult family and 8 per cent were lone parents.

Since 1998, means-tested tuition fees have been an integral part of higher education in England. In 2004/05 when the survey was carried out, annual tuition fees were £1,150 for full-time students (although from September 2006, institutions were able to charge annual tuition fees up to £3,000). In 2004/05, tuition fees constituted an average of 11 per cent of

expenditure for full-time students, and this is likely to increase. The SIES showed that the average total expenditure of full-time students in England in 2004/05 was £10,273 (Table 6.5) while expenditure for part-time students was 40 per cent higher at £14,413. Most of the difference in total expenditure can be explained by the higher living costs among part-time students, in particular for non-course related travel and food. Around 19 per cent of the total expenditure of full-time students was accounted for by participation costs (which include tuition fees, books, equipment, travel to the place of study and childcare costs); for part-time students it was 11 per cent. A similar survey in 1998/99, which covered the whole of the UK, found that for both full-time and part-time students, only 13 per cent of expenditure was on participation costs. In 2004/05, the majority of total expenditure was on living costs (57 per cent for full-time students and 63 per cent for part-time students). Personal items, food, entertainment and non-course related travel made up the bulk of living costs for both full- and part-time students.

Table 6.5

Student[1] expenditure: by type of expenditure, 2004/05

England		£ per year per student
	Full time	Part time
Living	**5,870**	**9,056**
Food	1,491	2,313
Household goods	239	735
Personal[2]	1,710	2,224
Travel[3]	1,092	2,193
Other	139	292
Entertainment	1,199	1,298
Housing	**2,276**	**3,042**
Participation	**1,980**	**1,614**
Tuition fee	1,150	725
Direct[4]	426	367
Facilitation[5]	403	522
Children[6]	**147**	**701**
Total expenditure	**10,273**	**14,413**

1 Students attending or registered in higher education.
2 Includes clothes, toiletries, mobile phones, CDs, magazines and cigarettes.
3 Non-course-related.
4 Includes course-related books, computers, equipment, printing, photocopying and stationery.
5 Includes travelling costs to and from place of study, and childcare costs.
6 Expenditure by students on their children and non-course-related childcare.

Source: Student Income and Expenditure Survey, National Centre for Social Research and Institute for Employment Studies

Variations in levels of expenditure exist between full-time students according to their housing arrangements. Students living independently incurred substantially higher housing costs than those living with parents or relatives (£2,742 and £321 respectively). Facilitation costs, which included course related travel costs and childcare costs, were more than double for students living with parents or relatives (including a partner) compared to students living independently (£762 and £318 respectively).

For all households, income is likely to be the factor with the biggest influence on the level of expenditure. In the UK, in 2005/06, households in the top quintile or top 'fifth' of the income distribution spent five times more than households in the bottom 'fifth' (Table 6.6) (see the analysing income distribution box on page 63). Households in the bottom 'fifth' of the income distribution spent a higher proportion of their total expenditure on essential items such as housing (which includes rent but not mortgage interest payments), fuel and power (19 per cent) and food and non-alcoholic drink (16 per cent), than higher income households. Households with lower incomes also spent a higher proportion of their total income on alcohol and tobacco (4 per cent for the bottom fifth

compared with 2 per cent for the top fifth). The proportion of total expenditure spent on transport by households in the top fifth was double that for those in the bottom fifth. Other expenditure items, which include additional housing costs (specifically mortgage interest payments and council tax) and holiday spending, also form a much higher proportion of expenditure by high income households.

Household expenditure varies across the regions of England and the four countries of the UK. For the period 2003/04 to 2005/06, households in England spent more than the other UK countries, per person (Figure 6.7). There were four regions within England, where the households spent considerably more than the other English regions: the South East, London, the East and the South West.

In 2005/06, for some items, household expenditure at large supermarket chains was more than double that at other outlets (Table 6.8). In contrast, more was spent at other outlets on cigarettes (three times the amount spent at supermarkets) and petrol (one and three-quarter times the amount spent at supermarkets). The amounts spent on newspapers at other outlets far exceeded the amounts spent at large supermarket chains (ninefold difference).

Table 6.6

Household expenditure:[1] by gross income quintile group,[2] 2005/06

United Kingdom   Percentages

	Bottom fifth	Next fifth	Middle fifth	Next fifth	Top fifth	All households
Food and non-alcoholic drink	16	13	11	10	8	10
Alcohol and tobacco	4	3	3	3	2	2
Clothing and footwear	5	5	5	5	5	5
Housing, fuel and power[3]	19	14	11	9	7	10
Household goods and services	7	8	7	6	7	7
Health	1	1	1	1	1	1
Transport	8	11	13	14	16	14
Communication	4	3	3	3	2	3
Recreation and culture	11	13	13	14	13	13
Education	1	1	1	1	2	1
Restaurants and hotels[4]	7	7	8	9	9	8
Miscellaneous goods and services	8	7	8	8	8	8
Other expenditure items	9	14	16	17	20	17
All household expenditure (=100%) (£ per week)	166.30	287.30	395.60	531.60	836.10	443.40

1 See Appendix, Part 6: Household expenditure. Expenditure rounded to the nearest 10 pence.
2 See Chapter 5: Analysing income distribution box for an explanation of quintile groups.
3 Excludes mortgage interest payments, water charges, council tax and domestic rates in Northern Ireland. These are included in 'Other expenditure items'.
4 Includes purchases of alcoholic drink in restaurants and hotels.

Source: Expenditure and Food Survey, Office for National Statistics

Figure **6.7**

Household expenditure[1] per head: by region, 2003–06[2]

Index numbers (UK=100)

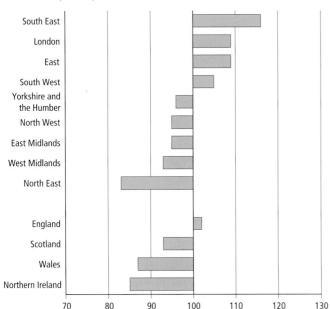

1 See Appendix, Part 6: Household expenditure.
2 Combined data from 2003/04, 2004/05 and 2005/06.

Source: Expenditure and Food Survey, Office for National Statistics

The number of purchases carried out through the internet is increasing rapidly, although in 2005 they still only represented around 3 per cent of total household expenditure. The value of internet sales by UK businesses to households in the UK

Table **6.8**

Household expenditure[1] on selected items: by place of purchase, 2005/06

United Kingdom £ per week

	Large supermarket chains	Other outlets
Alcoholic drinks	4.00	2.20
Non-alcoholic drinks	2.70	1.10
Bread, rice and cereals	2.90	1.20
Fresh fruit	2.20	0.70
Fresh vegetables	2.60	0.80
Chocolate and confectionery products	1.10	0.80
Petrol	5.20	9.10
Cigarettes	1.00	3.10
Newspapers	0.20	1.80

1 See Appendix, Part 6: Household expenditure. Expenditure rounded to the nearest 10 pence.

Source: Expenditure and Food Survey, Office for National Statistics

increased more than fourfold between 2002 and 2005 (Table 6.9). All industrial sectors have substantially increased their internet sales to households over this period from total sales of 5 billion to 21 billion. Transport, travel and tourist assistance activities, and retail trade were the sectors with the highest on-line sales to households in 2005, accounting for 22 per cent and 20 per cent of all internet sales, respectively.

Table **6.9**

Internet sales to households: by industrial sector[1]

United Kingdom £ billion

	2002	2003	2004	2005
Transport, travel and tourist assistance activities	1.3	2.8	3.3	4.7
Retail trade[2]	1.5	1.9	3.4	4.3
Other services	0.5	1.0	2.0	3.8
Construction/manufacturing/ electricity, gas, and water supply	0.4	1.3	2.1	2.8
Wholesale and commission trades[3]	0.3	0.5	0.9	2.0
Post and telecommunications	0.5	0.7	3.6	1.9
Motoring[4]	0.1	0.2	0.5	0.8
Hotels and restaurants	0.2	0.4	0.5	0.7
Computing/other business services	0.1	0.4	0.2	0.6
All internet sales	5.0	9.2	16.5	21.4

1 Excludes businesses with less than 10 in employment.
2 Includes repair of personal and household goods but excludes retail trade of motor vehicles and motorcycles.
3 Excludes trade of motor vehicles and motorcycles.
4 Includes sale, maintenance and repair of motor vehicles and motorcycles and retail sale of automotive fuel.

Source: e-Commerce Survey, Office for National Statistics

Internet sales from the manufacturing, electricity, gas, water supply and construction sectors, accounted for 13 per cent of all internet sales in 2005. For further information on goods and services purchased over the internet, see Chapter 13: Lifestyles and social participation.

Transactions and credit

Purchases from businesses classified as retailers form a considerable part of household expenditure. The retail sales index is a measure of growth in retail sales measured through a monthly survey of retailers. There has been growth in the volume of retail sales in Great Britain every year since 1992 (Figure 6.10). However, in some periods growth has been faster than in others. Growth was particularly low in 1995, late 1998 and early 1999, and again from December 2004 through to November 2005.

The most recent period of low growth from December 2004 to November 2005 can be explained in part by reduced activity in the housing market. This was reflected in a falling volume of sales in household goods stores (including furniture, electrical, and DIY stores) during this period. Also, sales volumes in non-specialised stores (including department stores) were flat over the period after several years of steady growth. However, in the spring of 2006, the volume of sales in these stores, as well as sales more generally, started to grow more strongly again.

While the annual growth rates show how sales increase from year to year, seasonal patterns also exist in retail sales. Sales increase sharply in the build up to Christmas. Between 1991 and 2005, the value of sales in November was about 10 per cent

above average, while in December it was about 30 per cent above average.

The use of debit cards now dominates non-cash transactions within the UK. Between 1991 and 2005 there was an elevenfold increase in the number of payments by debit card (Figure 6.11). The number of automated payments increased threefold during this same period. The volume of transactions using credit and charge cards has also risen steadily, but in 2005 there was a 2 per cent decrease in usage compared with the previous year. This was the first fall since 1991 and may be a reflection of the greater awareness of costs by consumers as other forms of borrowing become more competitive. Only the use of cheques, which includes personal, business and those used for cash acquisition, have shown a steady decline since 1991.

There has been a general increase in the extent of ownership of plastic cards (credit/charge cards, debit cards and ATM cards) in Great Britain, although the pattern differs by age. The sharpest increase in the proportion holding any plastic card was among the 65 and over age group. When looking at specific types of plastic cards, within the population aged 65 and over, 27 per cent held any credit/charge card in 1993, and this increased to 71 per cent in 2005. Among the population aged 25 to 34 years, 41 per cent held any credit/charge card in 1993, increasing to 73 per cent in 2005. Those aged 16 to 24 years were the least likely to hold any credit/charge card with 13 per cent holding

Figure **6.10**

Annual growth in the volume of retail sales[1]

Great Britain

Percentage change over 12 months[2]

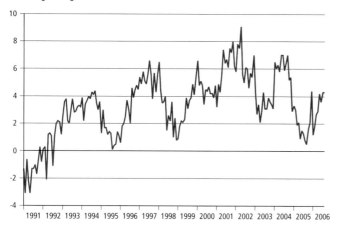

1 See Appendix, Part 6: Retail sales index.
2 In the seasonally adjusted index.

Source: Office for National Statistics

Figure **6.11**

Non-cash transactions:[1] by method of payment

United Kingdom

Billions

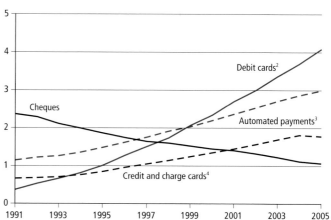

1 Figures are for payments only made by households or businesses. Cheque encashments and cash withdrawals from ATMs and branch counters using credit/charge and debit cards are not included. Based on data supplied by UK card issuers.
2 Visa Debit and Maestro cards in all years; includes Electron cards from 1996 and Solo cards from 1997.
3 Includes direct debits, standing orders, direct credits, inter-branch automated items.
4 Visa, MasterCard and travel/entertainment cards.

Source: APACS – Association for Payment Clearing Services

Table **6.12**

Debit and credit card spending[1, 2]

United Kingdom

Percentages

	Debit cards			Credit cards		
	1996	2001	2005	1996	2001	2005
Food and drink	43	29	23	13	11	11
Motoring	12	13	14	13	13	12
Household	6	9	7	10	12	11
Mixed business	10	7	7	7	6	7
Clothing	6	6	5	6	5	5
Travel	5	7	6	14	12	11
Entertainment	3	5	5	7	7	7
Hotels	1	1	1	6	5	4
Other retail	9	10	10	14	16	16
Other services	4	12	21	10	14	16
of which financial	..	..	10	..	..	7
Total (=100%) (£ billion)	37.0	93.3	169.9	47.7	91.5	122.2

1 By principal business activity of where the purchase was made. Excludes spending outside the United Kingdom by UK cardholders.
2 Based on data reported by the largest UK merchant acquirers, who process plastic card transactions for retailers and other service providers.

Source: APACS – Association for Payment Clearing Services

such a card in 1993, rising to 24 per cent in 2005. Between 1993 and 2005, the largest increases in ATM card holders were among the 65 and over (from 37 per cent to 90 per cent respectively) and 55 to 64 age groups (from 54 per cent to 92 per cent respectively). Among other age groups, ATM cards were already quite widely held in 1993, and so for these age groups the rises have been more modest since then. The slowest rise in ATM card holders during this period was among the population aged 16 to 24, increasing from 71 per cent in 1993 to 86 per cent in 2005.

Differences exist in the ways in which debit and credit cards are used in the UK. In 2005, the largest proportions of spending on debit cards were at outlets whose main business activities were food and drink, 'other services' and motoring (Table 6.12). The largest proportion of total debit card spending is still at food and drink outlets, even though the increasing use of debit cards for a wider range of purchases has seen the proportion spent at food and drink outlets fall from 43 per cent in 1996 to 23 per cent in 2005. By comparison, the proportion of credit card spending was substantially higher than debit card spending for 'other retailers', travel, household retailers and hotels. The 'other retailers' category includes book shops, record stores, pharmacies, jewellers and computer shops. This pattern suggests that credit card usage is more popular for more expensive items. Indeed, the average value of a debit

card purchase in 2005 was £41.40. In comparison, the average value of a credit card purchase was £60.65.

Total net lending to individuals by banks, building societies and other lenders is a measure of the value of new loans less repayments over a given period. The increase in total net lending to individuals between 1993 and 2006, adjusted for inflation, has been driven primarily by loans for house purchases, which are secured against those dwellings. Lending secured against dwellings fell in the recession of the early 1990s and reached its lowest level in the fourth quarter of 1992 (£4.5 billion for that quarter at 2006 prices) (Figure 6.13 overleaf). This type of lending started to increase gradually after 1996, then more rapidly from 2000 onwards with the acceleration in house prices (see Chapter 10: Housing). In the fourth quarter of 2003 net lending secured on dwellings peaked at almost £31 billion per quarter. The fall in late 2004 to mid-2005 reflects the lower number of property transactions in 2005 compared to 2004 (see also Figure 10.17). Mortgage lending started to grow again after mid-2005.

The bulk of total net lending to individuals is secured on dwellings and the remainder consists of consumer credit. Consumer credit covers credit card lending, overdrafts and non-secured loans and advances to individuals. This type of lending fell during the recession of the early 1990s from £2.2 billion in the first

Figure **6.13**

Net lending to individuals[1]

United Kingdom
£ billion at 2006 prices[2]

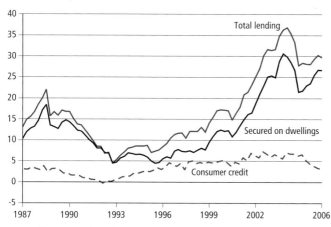

1 Lending secured on dwellings and consumer credit, both to individuals and to housing associations. Seasonally adjusted.
2 Adjusted to 2006 prices using the retail prices index.

Source: Bank of England

Figure **6.14**

Individual insolvencies

England & Wales
Thousands

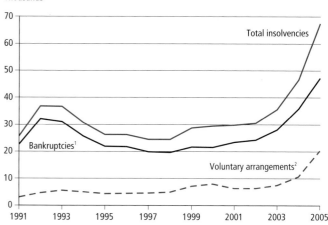

1 Individuals declared bankrupt by a court.
2 Individuals who make a voluntary agreement with their creditors. Includes Deeds of Arrangement, which enable debtors to come to an agreement with their creditors.

Source: Insolvency Service

quarter of 1990 (at 2006 prices) to £0.2 billion in the last quarter of 1992. It then increased gradually from 1993 and remained particularly high from the last quarter of 2001 (£7 billion at 2006 prices) until the first quarter of 2005. During 2005, new consumer credit fell rapidly and by the second quarter of 2006 it had fallen to £3.1 billion, around half its previous level. Through this recent period of high consumer borrowing, there have been regular media reports about the possible risks this level of borrowing could have for consumers and for the economy as a whole.

The high level of net borrowing has meant that the total outstanding amount owed by individuals has risen considerably. In the second quarter of 1993 the total amount owed by individuals was £562 billion at 2006 prices and by the second quarter of 2006 it had reached a record level of £1,228 billion. Over this period, the amount outstanding on loans secured on dwellings had doubled, whereas the amount of outstanding consumer credit had increased nearly threefold.

This increased level of borrowing has been accompanied by an increase in the number of individual insolvencies, which may occur when individuals are unable to meet their debt repayments. Some of the statutory insolvency instruments available to individuals experiencing financial difficulties include bankruptcy and individual voluntary arrangements (IVAs). An individual may be declared bankrupt where the court concludes that there is no likelihood of the debt being repaid. However, in some circumstances the court will encourage the setting up of a voluntary arrangement, to be agreed between the debtor

and the creditors. The total number of individual insolvencies shown in Figure 6.14 covers bankruptcies and IVAs. In England and Wales, there were 67,580 individual insolvencies in 2005. This was an increase of 45 per cent over 2004, and was nearly twice the number in 1992 during the last recession. Figures from the Insolvency Service showed that in England and Wales, in the late 1990s, the number of bankruptcies according to employment status was highest among the self-employed, with 13,300 made bankrupt in 1995, decreasing to 10,800 in 2005. While the number of bankruptcies among the self-employed has decreased, there have been large increases in the number of bankruptcies among employees (from 1,981 in 1995 to 13,600 in 2005) and individuals who were unemployed or had no occupation (from 2,900 in 1995 to 17,100 in 2005). Bank of England figures show that the total number of bad debts written-off by banks for individuals in the UK increased from 1,500 in 1993 to 5,800 in 2005.

Prices

The way in which individuals and households choose to spend their money is affected by the price of goods and services. The retail prices index (RPI) measures the average monthly change in the prices of a variety of goods and services purchased by households, and is the most familiar measure of inflation in the UK. The selection of goods and services represents a 'shopping basket' of items purchased by a typical household. Items are added or removed from the basket each year to ensure that the RPI continues to reflect consumer spending patterns. In 2006, three high technology goods were introduced to the basket of goods and services; personal MP3 players, flat panel televisions and digital camcorders. Music downloads were also introduced in 2006 (see also Chapter 13: Lifestyles and social participation). Meanwhile, personal CD players were removed from the basket of goods and services.

The UK consumer prices index (CPI) is the main domestic measure of inflation used within the government's monetary policy framework. From 10 December 2003, the CPI replaced the all items RPI as the target measure of inflation. Prior to the 10 December 2003, the CPI was published in the UK as the Harmonised Index of Consumer Prices (HICP). Although, the RPI and CPI are broadly similar, there are some differences, for example, council tax and owner occupiers' housing costs (includes mortgage interest payments, house depreciation and buildings insurance) are excluded from the CPI. Since 1989, the CPI inflation rate has usually been lower than the RPI rate.

During the 1970s, inflation was much higher than in more recent years. Inflation as measured by RPI exceeded 20 per cent in 1975, 1976 and 1980 (Figure 6.15). However, the annual change in the RPI remained below 5 per cent from the early 1990s to 2006. From February 1997 to mid-2005, inflation as measured by the CPI was at or below the Government's current 2 per cent target for this measure. By historical standards the level of inflation during this period was very low. From July to November 2005 and during May to December 2006, the CPI was above the target level.

Although the last 14 years has been a period of low overall inflation in the UK, there have been changes in the prices of different categories of goods and services. Figure 6.16 shows the percentage change between 1995 and 2005 in the consumer prices index for each of the major categories of consumption. The greatest increases were for education costs, which include university tuition fees and private school fees, with a 71 per cent increase, and alcohol and tobacco which increased by 43 per cent. Prices for restaurants and hotels also rose by more than twice as much as the all items index. There were two categories that decreased substantially in price, with the largest reduction being for clothing and footwear at 41 per cent followed by communication (which includes postal and telephone services) at 20 per cent. In general, the prices of services have tended to rise faster than the average across all CPI items, while the prices of goods have tended to increase more slowly or have fallen in price. Between 2004 and 2005, there was a rapid increase in price for housing, water and fuels, up 6 per cent over the year compared with the average increase across all items of 2 per cent.

The items within the basket of goods and services are subject to variation over time, but there are certain items, such as cigarettes, sliced white bread and granulated sugar that have continued to

Figure **6.16**

Percentage change in consumer prices index,[1] 1995–2005

United Kingdom

Percentage change over 10 years

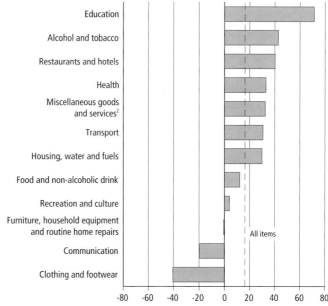

1 Data prior to 1996 are estimates. See Appendix, Part 6: Harmonised index of consumer prices, and Consumer prices index.
2 Includes personal care, personal effects, social protection, insurance and financial services.

Source: Office for National Statistics

Figure **6.15**

Consumer prices index[1,2] and retail prices index[3]

United Kingdom

Percentage change over 12 months

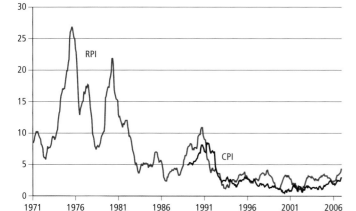

1 Data prior to 1996 are estimates. See Appendix, Part 6: Harmonised index of consumer prices.
2 The percentage change over 12 months in the consumer prices index (CPI) is calculated from unrounded data. The CPI was rebased in January 2006.
3 See Appendix, Part 6: Retail prices index, and Consumer prices index.

Source: Office for National Statistics

Table **6.17**

Cost of selected items

United Kingdom

Pence

	1971	1981	1991	1996	2001	2006
500g back bacon[1]	37	142	235	293	343	377
250g cheddar cheese	13	58	86	115	128	142
Eggs (size 2), per dozen	26	78	118	158	172	181
800g white sliced bread	10	37	53	55	51	81
White fish fillets, per kg	58	245	629	455	866	944
1 pint pasteurised milk[2]	5	19	32	36	36	35
1 kg granulated sugar	9	39	66	76	57	74
100g instant coffee	25	95	130	189	181	189
250g tea bags	..	..	150	134	146	149
Packet of 20 cigarettes (filter tip)[3]	27	97	186	273	412	476
Pint of beer[4]	15	65	137	173	203	251
Whiskey (per nip)	..	..	95	123	148	180
Litre of unleaded petrol	..	..	45	57	76	91

1 In 1971 and 1981 the price is for unsmoked. In 1991 the price is an average of vacuum and not vacuum-packed.
2 Delivered milk included from 1996.
3 Change from standard to king size in 1991.
4 Bottled until 1981 and draught lager after.

Source: Office for National Statistics

be included year on year. Between 1971 and 2006, the price of white fish fillets increased sixteenfold and the price of 250 grams of cheddar cheese increased nearly elevenfold (Table 6.17). The price of a packet of 20 filter tip cigarettes in 2006 was two and a half times the price in 1991 and the price of a pint of beer or a measure of whisky has nearly doubled since 1991. The higher increases in the price of cigarettes than alcohol are a reflection of the heavier increases in duty on cigarettes. The price of unleaded petrol has doubled since 1991. This is largely attributable to a combination of world market price and indirect tax, which includes fuel duty and value added tax (VAT) (see also Figure 12.9).

Rates of inflation in the EU-25, measured by the annual percentage change in the Harmonised Index of Consumer Prices (HICP) from 2004 to 2005 are shown in Table 6.18. The UK had an inflation rate that was similar to the EU-25 average of 2.2 per cent. Latvia and Estonia had the highest inflation rates, at 6.9 per cent and 4.1 per cent respectively, while Finland and Sweden had the lowest rates, both at 0.8 per cent.

The international spending power of sterling depends both on exchange rates, and on the ratios of prices between the UK and other countries, which are measured by purchasing

Table **6.18**

Percentage change in harmonised index of consumer prices:[1] EU comparison, 2005

Percentage change over 12 months[2]

Latvia	6.9	Austria	2.1
Estonia	4.1	Portugal	2.1
Luxembourg	3.8	Cyprus	2.0
Greece	3.5	France	1.9
Hungary	3.5	Germany	1.9
Spain	3.4	Denmark	1.7
Slovakia	2.8	Czech Republic	1.6
Lithuania	2.7	Netherlands	1.5
Malta	2.5	Finland	0.8
Slovenia	2.5	Sweden	0.8
Belgium	2.5	EU-25 average	2.2
Ireland	2.2		
Italy	2.2		
Poland	2.2		
United Kingdom	2.1		

1 See Appendix, Part 6: Harmonised index of consumer prices.
2 Percentage change between the 2004 and 2005 annual averages.

Source: Office for National Statistics

Figure **6.19**

Comparative price levels[1] for household expenditure: EU comparison, 2005

Index numbers (UK=100)

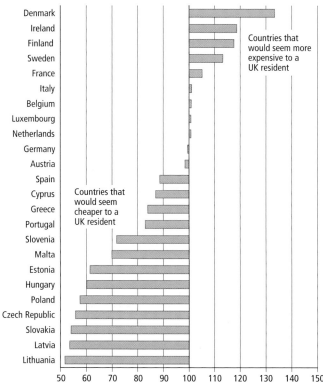

1 Price level indices for private consumption, defined as the ratio of purchasing power parities to exchange rates, provides a measure of the difference in price levels between countries. See Appendix, Part 6: Purchasing power parities.

Source: Office for National Statistics

power parities. These can be used to calculate comparative price levels, which provide a measure of the differences in price levels between countries, and show which countries in the EU-25 would be cheaper or more expensive to UK residents. In December 2006, Denmark, Ireland, Finland, Sweden and France would appear more expensive to a UK visitor (Figure 6.19). Many Eastern European countries would have seemed the least expensive to a UK visitor, with prices just over half those in the UK.

Health

- The expected number of years spent in poor health in Great Britain rose from 6.4 to 8.8 for men between 1981 and 2002, and from 10.1 to 10.6 for women. (Table 7.2)

- The incidence of breastfeeding babies aged six to ten weeks in the UK increased from 62 per cent in 1990 to 76 per cent in 2005. (Page 91)

- Levels of obesity in England increased from 11 per cent to 18 per cent among boys aged 2 to 15 and from 12 per cent to 18 per cent among girls between 1995 and 2005. (Page 93)

- In 2005, 65 per cent of adults supported smoking restrictions in pubs in Great Britain, having increased from 48 per cent in 1996. (Table 7.12)

- In 2004, 18 per cent of boys and 13 per cent of girls aged 5 to 16 in Great Britain, living in households with a gross weekly income of under £100 had a mental disorder. (Figure 7.16)

- There was a threefold increase in the incidence of genital chlamydia between 1996 and 2005 in the UK, with almost 110,000 cases diagnosed in 2005. (Page 99)

Chapter 7

The health of a nation provides some of the most revealing indications of its social and economic characteristics. Today, many of the most common causes of morbidity and premature mortality in the UK are linked to a range of behaviours relating to diet, levels of physical activity, smoking and drinking.

Key health indicators

Life expectancy is a widely used indicator of the state of the nation's health. Large improvements in expectancy of life at birth have been seen over the past century for both males and females. In 1901 males born in the UK could expect to live to around 45 years and females to around 49 years (Figure 7.1). By 2005 life expectancy at birth had risen to 77 years for males and to just over 81 years for females. Since the beginning of the 20th century, female life expectancy at birth has been consistently higher than that of males. The disparity was at its greatest in 1969, when females could expect to live on average 6.3 years longer than males born in the same year. Since then the gap has been steadily narrowing, with this trend projected to continue until around 2014, when the difference is expected to level off at around 3.7 years. Life expectancy at birth is projected to continue rising for both sexes, to reach over 80 years for males and almost 84 years for females by 2021.

In contrast to the long-term improvements seen in life expectancy at birth, it was not until the latter part of the 20th century that life expectancy for adults in the UK showed a continuous improvement. Since the early 1970s, the increase in life expectancy among older adults has been particularly

notable. Between 1971 and 2005 life expectancy for men aged 65 increased by 4.6 years, compared with an increase of only 1.7 years between 1901 and 1971. This improvement can be linked to a rapid decline in death rates among men at these older ages (see Chapter 1: Population).

Despite its use as a general indicator of the population's health, life expectancy takes no account of the quality of life and whether it is lived in good health, with disability or dependency. Summary health measures such as healthy life expectancy and disability-free life expectancy place a greater focus on the population's health-related quality of life. With ever more people living to older ages, when ill-health and disabilities are more common, these indicators are becoming increasingly important to assess the impact that the ageing population may have on future demand for health and social care services. Healthy life expectancy, defined as the expected number of years lived in 'good' or 'fairly good' health, is calculated using life expectancy and self-assessed general health data. For Great Britain, healthy life expectancy data have been published since 1981, with the most recent estimates available for 2002.

Between 1981 and 2002, healthy life expectancy at birth rose for both males and females in Great Britain, but the increases were not as great as those in overall life expectancy. In 2002 healthy life expectancy at birth was 67.2 years for males and 69.9 years for females, increases of 2.8 and 3.2 years respectively since 1981 (Table 7.2). This compares with increases of 5.1 years and 3.7 years in overall life expectancy over the same period. The result is that although people have been living longer, the number of years spent in poor health has been increasing. This was particularly apparent among males. Between 1981 and 2002 the expected number of years in poor

Figure **7.1**

Expectation of life[1] at birth: by sex

United Kingdom

Years

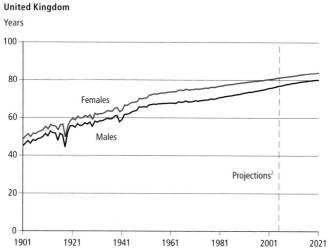

1 See Appendix, Part 7: Expectation of life. The average number of years a new-born baby would survive if he or she experienced age-specific mortality rates for that time period throughout his or her life.
2 2004-based projections for 2006 to 2021.

Source: Government Actuary's Department

Table **7.2**

Life expectancy, healthy life expectancy and disability-free life expectancy[1] at birth: by sex

Great Britain   Years

	Males		Females	
	1981	2002	1981	2002
Life expectancy	70.9	76.0	76.8	80.5
Healthy life expectancy	64.4	67.2	66.7	69.9
Years spent in poor health	6.4	8.8	10.1	10.6
Disability-free life expectancy	58.1	60.9	60.8	63.0
Years spent with disability	12.8	15.0	16.0	17.5

1 See Appendix, Part 7: Expectation of life, Healthy life expectancy and disability-free life expectancy.

Source: Government Actuary's Department; Office for National Statistics

Table **7.3**

Self-reported illness:[1] by sex and age, 2005[2]

Great Britain		Rates per 1,000 population[3]
	Long-standing illness	Limiting long-standing illness
Males		
0–4	140	46
5–14	181	72
15–44	175	90
45–64	401	233
65–74	554	342
75 and over	583	402
All ages	273	150
Females		
0–4	93	28
5–14	160	67
15–44	209	114
45–64	407	245
65–74	589	370
75 and over	545	401
All ages	282	163

1 See Appendix, Part 7: Self-reported illness.
2 Data for 2005 includes last quarter of 2004/05 due to survey change from financial year to calendar year. See Appendix, Part 2: General Household Survey.
3 Data have been age-standardised using the European standard population. See Appendix, Part 7: Standardised rates, and European standard population.

Source: General Household Survey (Longitudinal), Office for National Statistics

health increased from 6.4 to 8.8 years for males, and from 10.1 to 10.6 years for females. By 2002 although females could still expect to spend more years in poor health than males, the gap between the sexes had narrowed.

Disability-free life expectancy, defined as the expected number of years lived free from a limiting long-standing illness, is calculated using life expectancy and self-reported limiting long-standing illness data. Limiting long-standing illness includes such conditions as arthritis, back pain, heart disease and mental disorders. Generally, people can expect to experience more years living with a disability than they can in poor health but the patterns for the two are very similar. In 2002, females could expect to spend 17.5 years of their lives with a disability and males 15.0 years. Between 1981 and 2002 the number of years lived with a disability increased more for males (2.2 years) than it did for females (1.5 years).

As people get older they are more likely to experience a long-standing illness or disability and such conditions may limit their

daily activities in some way. After standardising data to adjust for the age structure of the population in Great Britain in 2005 (see Appendix, Part 7: Standardised rates), 175 per 1,000 males aged 15 to 44 reported having a long-standing illness or disability, rising to 583 per 1,000 aged 75 and over (Table 7.3). There was a similar pattern among females across all age groups, although the highest rate for those reporting a long-standing illness was among those aged 65 to 74, at 589 per 1,000.

The proportion of people reporting a limiting long-standing illness in Great Britain also increased with age. Among those aged 15 to 44, 90 per 1,000 males and 114 per 1,000 females reported such an illness, rising to 233 per 1,000 males and 245 per 1,000 females aged 45 to 64. Among both sexes, rates for limiting long-standing illness peaked among those aged 75 and over at just over 400 per 1,000.

Since the early 1970s, circulatory diseases (which include heart disease and stroke) have remained the most common cause of death among males and females in the UK, however they have also shown by far the greatest decline, particularly among males (Figure 7.4 overleaf). In 1971, age-standardised death rates for circulatory diseases were 6,900 per million males and 4,300 per million females. By 2005 these rates had fallen to 2,600 per million males and 1,700 per million females.

Cancers are the second most common cause of death among both sexes in the UK, but over the past 30 years, different trends have emerged for males and females. Death rates from cancer peaked in the mid-1980s for males at 2,900 per million, and by 2005 had fallen to 2,200 per million. Death rates from cancer for females are typically lower than those for males and did not peak until the late 1980s, since when they have fallen gradually from 1,900 per million in 1989 to 1,600 per million in 2005. These variations in mortality trends partly reflect differences in the types of cancer that men and women are likely to experience, the risk factors associated with developing them and the relative survival rates of different cancers. The incidence of the most common forms of cancer and survival rates from them are examined later on in this chapter.

One of the major factors contributing to an overall increase in life expectancy, particularly in the first half of the 20th century is the reduction in infant mortality. In 1921, 84.0 children per 1,000 live births in the UK died before the age of one. In the years up until the end of the Second World War there was a gradual fall in the infant mortality rate, although the rate fluctuated during the 1920s and again in the early 1940s. There was then a steady fall in the infant mortality rate following the Second World War, from 48.8 per 1,000 in 1945 to half that at 24.4 per 1,000 only 11 years later in 1956. This decline has continued, albeit more

Figure **7.4**

Mortality:[1] by sex and leading cause groups

United Kingdom[2]

Rates per million population

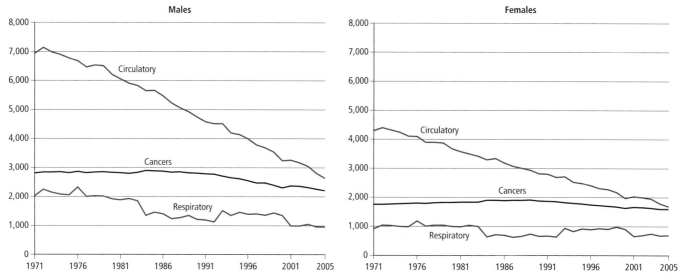

1 Data are for all ages and have been age-standardised using the European standard population. See Appendix, Part 7: Standardised rates, and
  International Classification of Diseases.
2 Data for 2000 are for England and Wales only.

Source: Office for National Statistics

slowly, so that in 2005 there were 5.1 deaths per 1,000 live
births. It is expected that the infant mortality rate will continue
to fall gradually with projections indicating that in 2021, the rate
will be 4.5 per 1,000 live births. The fall in infant mortality rates
can be linked to improvements in diet and sanitation, better
antenatal, postnatal and medical care, and the development of
vaccines and immunisation programmes.

Despite the decline in infant mortality rates, notable socio-
economic inequalities still exist. In England and Wales in 2005,
the infant mortality rate among babies born inside marriage
whose fathers were in semi-routine occupations was 6.1 per
1,000 live births. This was more than twice the infant mortality
rate of 2.7 per 1,000 for those who were born inside marriage
but whose fathers were in large employers and higher
managerial occupations (Table 7.5).

For babies born outside marriage, where the birth was jointly
registered by both parents, there was a similar pattern. The
infant mortality rate for babies whose fathers were in semi-
routine occupations was 6.8 per 1,000 live births, compared
with a rate of 3.1 per 1,000 for those whose fathers were in
large employers and higher managerial occupations.

Over the past 15 years there have been contrasting trends in
the most common childhood infections diagnosed in the UK.
There were epidemics of measles in 1994, when 23,500 cases
were notified, and of rubella (German measles) in 1993 and

Table **7.5**

Infant mortality:[1] by socio-economic classification,[2] 2005

England & Wales		Rates per 1,000 live births[3]
	Inside marriage	Outside marriage[4]
Large employers and higher managerial occupations	2.7	3.1
Higher professional occupations	3.8	3.6
Lower managerial and professional occupations	3.4	3.9
Intermediate occupations	5.0	5.4
Small employers and own account workers	3.9	4.3
Lower supervisory and technical occupations	3.4	4.3
Semi-routine occupations	6.1	6.8
Routine occupations	5.8	6.2
All occupations	4.3	5.5

1 Deaths within one year of birth.
2 Based on father's occupation at death registration of the child. See
  Appendix, Part 7: National Statistics Socio-economic Classification
  (NS-SEC).
3 Figures for live births are a 10 per cent sample coded for father's
  occupation.
4 Jointly registered by both parents.

Source: Office for National Statistics

1996, with around 12,000 notifications in each of these years. Regular mumps epidemics occurred until 1989, when there were 23,500 notifications in Great Britain. After this, the number of notified cases remained low throughout the 1990s at between 2,000 and 5,100 per year. At the beginning of the 21st century there was a rapid increase in the number of notified cases of mumps. Although mumps has historically been a childhood infection, the number of recorded cases among those aged 15 and over showed the most dramatic increase (Figure 7.6). The number of mumps notifications increased sixfold between 2003 and 2004 and more than threefold between 2004 and 2005, reaching almost 52,000 in 2005. This latter increase largely reflects lower immunity rates among older teenagers and young adults, particularly those born between 1983 and 1986 immediately before the introduction of the MMR vaccine in the UK in 1988. In 2004 the number of cases of mumps notified in those under the age of 15, had also risen, to over 3,200, and in 2005 it was almost three times this number. The children affected were mainly at the older end of the age range and only received a single dose of the MMR vaccine, as opposed to the two phase dose introduced in 1996. Among all those under the age of 15 in 2005, exposure to mumps would have been rare in early childhood because of the rapid success of the MMR vaccine in controlling the disease.

Nearly all children in the UK are now immunised against tetanus, diphtheria, poliomyelitis, whooping cough, haemophilus influenzae b, meningitis C and measles, mumps and rubella. From September 2006, a vaccine was also introduced across Great Britain to provide protection against pneumococcal disease. Current government immunisation targets state that 95 per cent of children should be immunised against all of these

diseases before their second birthday. For the MMR vaccine, coverage levels of 90 per cent and over were achieved in the early 1990s. However, in recent years, concerns over the safety of the MMR vaccine have led to a fall in the proportion of children in the UK immunised against measles, mumps and rubella. MMR vaccination coverage levels fell to their lowest level in 2003/04 at 81 per cent. The level then rose to 82 per cent in 2004/05 and to 85 per cent in 2005/06. In 2005/06 uptake in London was the lowest of any region at 74 per cent. In other regions of the UK, variations in uptake were generally small, ranging from 83 to 91 per cent.

Diet and obesity

Good nutrition is important from birth, and studies have shown that breastfeeding gives health benefits to both mother and child. Among babies aged six to ten weeks old, the incidence of breastfeeding in the UK increased from 62 per cent in 1990 to 76 per cent in 2005.

A mother's social class, age and educational level are all strongly associated with the incidence of breastfeeding. When analysed by socio-economic classification, in 2005 the highest incidence of breastfeeding babies aged six to ten weeks in the UK was found among mothers from managerial and professional occupations, at 88 per cent (Figure 7.7). The lowest incidence of breastfeeding was found among mothers in routine and

Figure **7.6**

Mumps notifications: by age

Great Britain

Thousands

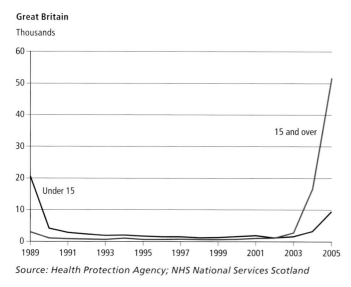

Source: Health Protection Agency; NHS National Services Scotland

Figure **7.7**

Incidence of breastfeeding:[1] by mother's socio-economic classification,[2] 2000 and 2005

United Kingdom

Percentages

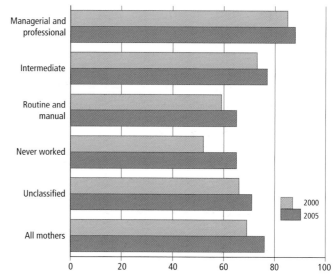

1 Babies breastfed at least once at around six to ten weeks of age.
2 See Appendix, Part 7: National Statistics Socio-economic Classification (NS-SEC).

Source: Infant Feeding Survey 2005: Early Results, The Information Centre for health and social care

manual occupations and mothers who had never worked, both at 65 per cent. Between 2000 and 2005 the incidence of breastfeeding increased among mothers in all socio-economic groups, with the largest increase being seen among those who had never worked, with breastfeeding incidences rising from 52 per cent to 65 per cent. Within the UK, the incidence of breastfeeding varies by country. In 2005 breastfeeding rates were highest in England at 78 per cent and lowest in Northern Ireland at 63 per cent. Since 1990 breastfeeding rates in Northern Ireland have remained lower than in any other country of the UK, however, the rate there rose by 9 percentage points between 2000 and 2005, a greater increase than elsewhere in the UK.

Diet has an important influence on weight and general health. The Department of Health recommends that a healthy diet should include at least five portions a day of a variety of fruit and vegetables (excluding potatoes). In 2005, 26 per cent of men and 30 per cent of women aged 16 and over in England met this target on a daily basis.

Over the past 30 years in the UK there have been notable changes in the amounts of fruit and vegetables consumed, as well as the varieties of each which are eaten. Between 1974 and 2004/05 overall consumption of fresh and processed vegetables (excluding potatoes) fell by 4 per cent to 1,105 grams per person per week (Figure 7.8). Over the same period the amount of fresh potatoes and potato products eaten each week fell by 43 per cent, from 1,430 grams to 822 grams per person. The fall in potato consumption over this period can in part be linked to an increase in consumption of pasta and rice. In contrast to the trends for vegetable consumption, the amount of fresh and processed fruit eaten each week has been rising. Between 1974 and 2004/05 the amount increased by 60 per cent to reach 1,168 grams per person per week.

The increase in fruit consumption between 1974 and 2004/05 reflects an increased public awareness of the health benefits associated with eating more fruit, as well as the availability of a far wider range of fresh fruits throughout the year. Between 1974 and 2004/05 consumption of fresh fruit rose by 56 per cent to reach 805 grams per person per week. In contrast, the amount of fresh vegetables (excluding potatoes) consumed remained steady at around 800 grams per person per week throughout this period. The largest increases in consumption of specific fruits were seen in fresh bananas, grapes, stone fruits and pure fruit juices. There were falls in the quantities of fresh oranges, apples and tinned fruits consumed.

Diets which are high in fat and low in fresh fruit and vegetables can contribute to a person being overweight or obese. Obesity is linked to heart disease, diabetes and premature death. The body mass index (BMI) (see Appendix, Part 7: Body mass index) is a common measure for assessing an individual's weight

Figure **7.8**

Consumption of fruit and vegetables[1] in the home[2]

United Kingdom

Grams per person per week

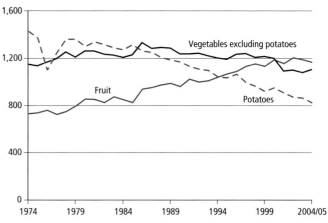

1 Includes fresh and processed fruit and vegetables.
2 Data for 1974 to 2000 are based on adjusted National Food Survey (NFS) results. The NFS ended in March 2001 and was replaced by the Expenditure and Food Survey, which merged together the NFS and Family Expenditure Survey. Data are for financial years from 2001/02.

Source: National Food Survey, Department for Environment, Food and Rural Affairs; Expenditure and Food Survey, Office for National Statistics

relative to their height, and a BMI score of over 30 is taken as the definition of obesity. In recent years the proportion of the adult population in England who are obese has been rising. Between 1993 and 2005 the proportion of men aged 16 and over who were classified as obese increased from 13 per cent to 22 per cent, while among women the proportion rose from 16 per cent to 24 per cent.

The prevalence of obesity tends to rise with age in both sexes, until age 75 and over when there is a noticeable drop. In 2005, 8 per cent of men aged 16 to 24 were obese compared to 29 per cent of men aged 55 to 64 (Table 7.9). The prevalence of obesity in men dropped to 17 per cent for those aged 75 and over. In 2005, 12 per cent of women aged 16 to 24 were obese compared to 34 per cent of women aged 65 to 74. The prevalence of obesity in women dropped to 26 per cent for those aged 75 and over.

A small proportion of the population are classed as underweight by their BMI score with 1 per cent of men and 2 per cent of women in England being so in 2005. Those aged 16 to 24 are more likely than any other age group to be classed as underweight with 7 per cent of men and 5 per cent of women defined as such in 2005. Just over three-fifths of this age group are of 'desirable' weight within the BMI range, the highest proportion among all age groups.

In recent years there has been concern over the proportion of children who are obese or overweight. Between 1995 and 2005

Table **7.9**

Body mass index:[1] by sex and age, 2005

England

Percentages

	Underweight (18.5 or under)	Desirable (over 18.5 to 25)	Overweight (over 25 to 30)	Obese (over 30)	All persons
Men					
16–24	7	61	24	8	100
25–34	-	39	44	17	100
35–44	-	27	46	27	100
45–54	1	25	47	28	100
55–64	0	24	47	29	100
65–74	1	25	47	28	100
75 and over	1	33	49	17	100
All aged 16 and over	1	34	43	22	100
Women					
16–24	5	63	19	12	100
25–34	2	52	27	19	100
35–44	1	44	30	25	100
45–54	1	36	35	28	100
55–64	1	34	37	28	100
65–74	1	23	42	34	100
75 and over	3	32	40	26	100
All aged 16 and over	2	42	32	24	100

1 Using the body mass index (BMI) for people aged 16 and over. See Appendix, Part 7: Body mass index.

Source: Health Survey for England, The Information Centre for health and social care

levels of obesity among boys aged 2 to 15 in England increased from 11 per cent to 18 per cent, and among girls in this age group from 12 per cent to 18 per cent.

Alcohol and smoking

Excessive alcohol consumption can lead to an increased likelihood of developing health problems such as high blood pressure, cancer and cirrhosis of the liver. The Department of Health advises that consumption of three to four units of alcohol a day for men and two to three units a day for women should not lead to significant health risks. Consistently drinking more than these levels is not advised because of the associated health risks.

In 2005, just over one-third of men and one-fifth of women in Great Britain reported exceeding the recommended amount of alcohol on at least one day during the week before interview. Young people were more likely than older people to have exceeded the recommended daily amount (Table 7.10). In 2005, 43 per cent of young men aged 16 to 24 had exceeded four units on at least one day during the previous week, compared with 16 per cent of men aged 65 and over. Among women, 36 per cent of those in the youngest age group had

Table **7.10**

Adults exceeding specified levels of alcohol:[1] by sex and age, 2005[2]

Great Britain

Percentages

	16–24	25–44	45–64	65 and over	All aged 16 and over
Men					
More than 4 units and up to 8 units	13	17	19	12	16
More than 8 units	30	25	16	4	19
More than 4 units	43	42	35	16	35
Women					
More than 3 units and up to 6 units	14	15	14	3	12
More than 6 units	22	11	4	1	8
More than 3 units	36	26	18	4	20

1 On at least one day in the previous week. See Appendix, Part 7: Alcohol consumption.
2 Data for 2005 includes last quarter of 2004/05 due to survey change from financial year to calendar year. See Appendix, Part 2: General Household Survey.

Source: General Household Survey (Longitudinal), Office for National Statistics

exceeded three units on at least one day compared with only 4 per cent of those aged 65 and over.

Men aged 16 to 24 are the most likely to binge drink (defined as the consumption of twice the recommended daily amount). In 2005, 30 per cent had done so on at least one day in the previous week, a slightly higher proportion than among the 25 to 44 age group. Among women aged 16 to 24, 22 per cent had consumed twice the recommended daily amount on at least one day during the preceding week, twice the proportion of those in the 25 to 44 age group, who were the next most likely age group to have consumed at least twice the recommended daily level.

In 2005 there was little variation by socio-economic group of household reference person in the proportion of men who consumed more than the recommended levels of alcohol on at least one day in the week before interview. In contrast among women, those who headed large employer and higher managerial households were the most likely to have exceeded the recommended limits, with 26 per cent having done so in the previous week. This compares with only 16 per cent of women in the semi-routine and routine groups.

There now appears to be a pattern of drinking alcohol among children. In 2005, 22 per cent of children aged 11 to 15 in England reported drinking alcohol at least once in the week before interview. The prevalence of drinking increased with age: 4 per cent of boys and 2 per cent of girls aged 11 had consumed an alcoholic drink in the last week, while 46 per cent of boys and 45 per cent of girls aged 15 had done so. The average weekly consumption among 11 to 15 year olds who reported drinking alcohol in the previous week increased from 5.3 units of alcohol in 1990 to 10.4 units in 2000, and has fluctuated around this level since then.

Smoking is related to a range of health problems, including lung cancer, heart disease, stroke, chronic bronchitis and emphysema. Over the past 35 years there has been a substantial decline in the proportion of adults aged 16 and over in Great Britain who smoke cigarettes. In 1974, 51 per cent of men aged 16 and over smoked compared with 41 per cent of women. By 2005, 25 per cent of men and 23 per cent of women were smokers (Figure 7.11). Among both men and women much of the decline occurred in the 1970s and early 1980s, after which the rate of decline slowed. The reduction in the difference between the proportion of men and women who smoke, partly reflects different cohort patterns for smoking, as smoking became common among men several decades before it did among women.

Since the early 1990s, the prevalence of cigarette smoking has been higher among those aged 20 to 24 than among those in

Figure **7.11**

Prevalence of adult[1] cigarette smoking:[2] by sex

Great Britain

Percentages

1 People aged 16 and over.
2 From 1988 data are for financial years. Between 1974 and 2000/01 the surveys were run every two years. Data for 2005 includes last quarter of 2004/05 due to survey change from financial year to calendar year. See Appendix, Part 2: General Household Survey.
3 From 1998/99 data are weighted to compensate for nonresponse and to match known population distributions. Weighted and unweighted data for 1998/99 are shown for comparison.

Source: General Household Survey (Longitudinal), Office for National Statistics

other age groups. In 2005, 34 per cent of men and 30 per cent of women in this age group were smokers.

Smoking prevalence varies markedly by socio-economic group. In 2005, around one-third of men and women in routine and manual occupation households in Great Britain were smokers, compared with just under one-fifth of men and women in managerial and professional households. The Government target set out in the NHS *Cancer Plan* of 2000, is to reduce the proportion of smokers in manual occupation groups in England to 26 per cent by 2010.

Under legislation in the *Health Act 2006* all public places and workplaces in England will become smoke-free from the summer of 2007. In Scotland, all enclosed public places have been smoke-free since March 2006. In recent years public support for smoking restrictions in public places has been growing. Between 1996 and 2004 the proportion of adults in Great Britain supporting restrictions in the workplace increased from 81 per cent to 88 per cent, and were similarly high at 86 per cent in 2005. The proportion supporting restrictions in restaurants rose from 85 per cent to 91 per cent between 1996 and 2005 (Table 7.12). The largest increase was in support of restrictions in pubs, which rose from 48 per cent in 1996 to 65 per cent in 2005.

Views on restricting smoking in certain places varied by socio-economic group. Those in managerial and professional

Table **7.12**

Adults agreeing with smoking restrictions in certain places

Great Britain   Percentages

	1996	2001	2002	2003	2004	2005
At work	81	86	86	86	88	86
In restaurants	85	87	88	87	91	91
In pubs	48	50	54	56	65	65
In other public places[1]	82	85	87	90	93	92

1 Includes places such as banks and post offices.

Source: Omnibus Survey, Office for National Statistics

occupations were far more likely to be in favour of restrictions than those in routine and manual occupations, perhaps reflecting the likelihood of them being non-smokers themselves (see page 94). In 2005, 92 per cent of those in managerial and professional occupations agreed with restrictions on smoking in the workplace compared with 80 per cent of those in routine and manual occupations. Lower proportions in each group felt that there should be smoking restrictions in pubs, but there was still a higher proportion in support of the restrictions among the managerial and professional group (72 per cent) than among those in the routine and manual group (59 per cent).

Cancer

About one-third of the population develop cancer at some time in their lives, and in its various forms it was responsible for around one-quarter of all deaths in the UK in 2003 (See Figure 7.4). In both sexes the overall incidence rates of cancer increase continuously from around the age of 30 (Figure 7.13). Among those below the age of 45 the increase is far more rapid among females. For instance, in 2003 the overall incidence rate of cancer among females aged 30 to 34 in the UK was 88 per 100,000, almost 70 per cent higher than the rate for males in this age group (52 per 100,000). This difference can largely be attributed to the incidence of cancers of the breast and cervix among females, which are more likely to be developed at an earlier age than the most common cancers diagnosed among males. In contrast, among those aged 65 and over there is a far steeper rise in the incidence of cancer among males. In 2003, incidence rates were over 40 per cent higher in males than females aged 65 to 69 (1,575 per 100,000 compared with 1,100 per 100,000), and almost 70 per cent higher in those aged 80 to 84 (3,091 per 100,000 for males compared with 1,839 per 100,000 for females). This is mainly because the cancers with the highest incidence rates among males (lung and prostate) are more likely to develop and be diagnosed at a later age.

Figure **7.13**

Age-specific incidence of all cancers:[1] by sex, 2003

United Kingdom

Rates per 100,000 population

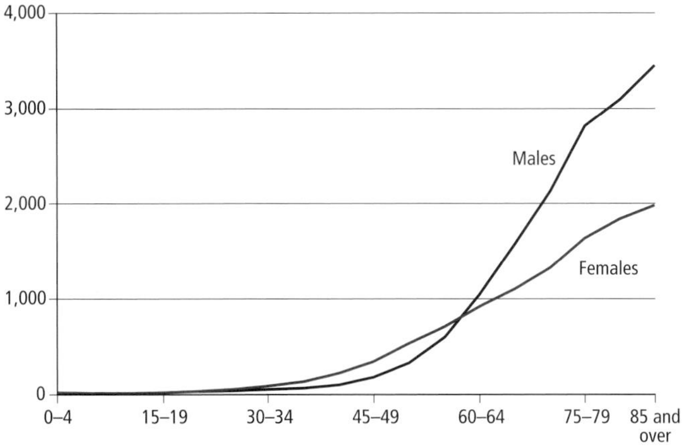

1 All malignant neoplasms excluding non-melanoma skin cancer.

Source: Office for National Statistics

The incidence of some of the most common types of cancer in Great Britain has changed since the early 1980s (Figure 7.14 overleaf). Trends in lung cancer incidence are strongly linked to those for cigarette smoking, which is by far the greatest single risk factor for the disease. The incidence of lung cancer has fallen sharply in males since the early 1980s, mainly as a result of the decline in cigarette smoking (see Figure 7.11). In 1981 the age-standardised lung cancer incidence rate in Great Britain was 112 per 100,000 males. By 2003 the rate had fallen by 45 per cent to 61 per 100,000. Lung cancer incidence rates among females are far lower, largely as a consequence of historically lower incidences of smoking. The age-standardised incidence rate for lung cancer reached its peak of 36 per 100,000 females in the early 1990s. Since then it has remained at a similar level.

The incidence of both prostate cancer among males and breast cancer among females has risen considerably over the past 20 years and they are the most commonly diagnosed cancers for males and females respectively. The incidence rate for prostate cancer rose from 38 per 100,000 males in 1981 to 90 per 100,000 in 2003. In 1999 prostate cancer overtook lung cancer as the most commonly diagnosed cancer among males. Although there is no NHS screening programme currently available for prostate cancer, the increase in incidence rates is mainly due to the large increase in the number of men presenting for unorganised screening using the PSA (prostate-specific antigen) test. This has increased the likelihood of earlier diagnosis. Throughout the past 20 years breast cancer has been the most commonly diagnosed form of cancer among females. In 1981 the incidence rate was 78 per 100,000 females.

Figure **7.14**

Standardised incidence rates[1] of major cancers: by sex

Great Britain
Rates per 100,000 population

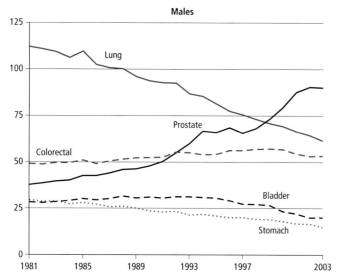

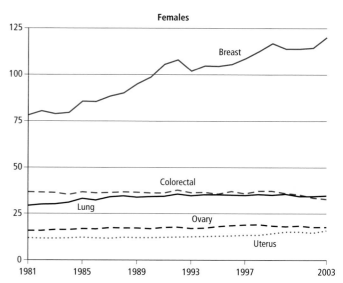

1 Age-standardised to the European standard population. See Appendix, Part 7: European standard population, Standardised rates, and International Classification of Diseases.

Source: Office for National Statistics

By 2003 this had risen to 120 per 100,000. The increase in the incidence of breast cancer is in part due to the introduction of the NHS breast cancer screening programme between 1989 and 1993. This resulted in a large number of cases being diagnosed earlier than they would otherwise have been.

In recent years, survival rates from the time of diagnosis in England and Wales have been improving in both sexes for most of the major cancers. For the majority of cancers common to both sexes, a slightly higher proportion of females than males aged 15 to 99 diagnosed during 1996 to 1999 survived for at least five years (Table 7.15). Age at diagnosis is an important factor as well as advances in treatment and care. Among adults, the younger the age at diagnosis, the higher the survival rate for most cancers.

Survival rates from lung cancer are very low compared with the other most common cancers. For those diagnosed with lung cancer in England and Wales during 1996–1999, the five-year survival rate for both males and females was around 6 per cent. The five-year survival rates for patients diagnosed in England during 1998–2001 remained at a similar level to this for males and showed a slight improvement for females, rising to 7.5 per cent.

Survival rates for prostate cancer in men and breast cancer in women have shown a greater improvement. The five-year survival rate for men diagnosed with prostate cancer in England during 1998–2001 was 71 per cent, compared with a rate of

Table **7.15**

Five year relative survival rates[1] for major cancers: by sex

	England & Wales 1996–1999		England 1998–2001[2]	
	Survival rate (percentages)	Number of cases	Survival rate (percentages)	Number of cases
Males[3]				
Prostate	64.8	73,921	70.8	88,802
Lung	5.8	67,862	6.3	67,502
Colon	46.9	31,977	49.4	33,368
Bladder	64.4	29,252	60.3	27,395
Rectum	46.8	24,702	50.0	25,613
Stomach	12.6	19,555	12.6	19,162
Females[3]				
Breast	77.5	125,093	79.9	132,292
Lung	6.4	39,455	7.5	41,774
Colon	47.9	32,243	50.2	32,687
Ovary	36.4	20,177	38.3	20,945
Uterus	73.3	16,549	76.2	18,114
Rectum	51.1	17,264	53.6	17,556

1 See Appendix, Part 7: Relative survival rates.
2 Latest survival rates only available for England. Comparison with earlier period will be reasonably reliable as England accounts for almost 95 per cent of the England and Wales population.
3 Aged 15 to 99 years. Data have been age-standardised using the European standard population. See Appendix, Part 7: Standardised rates, and European standard population.

Source: Office for National Statistics

65 per cent for England and Wales for the period 1996–1999. The breast cancer survival rate at five years among women diagnosed in England during 1998–2001 was 80 per cent, around 2 percentage points higher than for women diagnosed in England and Wales during 1996–1999.

Mental health

In recent years there has been an increasing awareness of the mental health problems experienced by children and young people. In 2004, 10 per cent of 5 to 16 year olds living in private households in Great Britain had a clinically diagnosed mental disorder. These included: 4 per cent with an emotional disorder, 6 per cent with a conduct disorder, 2 per cent with a hyperkinetic disorder (characterised by hyperactive, impulsive or inattentive behaviour) and 1 per cent with a less common disorder (including autism, tics and eating disorders). Boys in this age group were more likely to have some form of mental disorder (11 per cent) than girls (8 per cent).

There appears to be a close association between mental disorder in children and economic disadvantage in their household. Among both boys and girls the prevalence of mental disorder tends to rise as household income falls. In 2004 in Great Britain the highest prevalence of mental disorder was found among children who lived in a household with a gross weekly income of under £100,

Figure **7.16**

Prevalence of mental disorders[1] among children:[2] by sex and gross weekly household income, 2004

Great Britain

Percentages

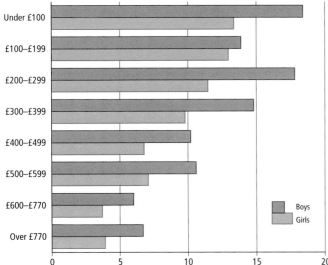

1 See Appendix, Part 7: Mental disorders.
2 Aged 5 to 16 years and living in private households.

Source: Mental Health of Children and Young People Survey, Office for National Statistics

among whom 18 per cent of boys and 13 per cent of girls had some type of mental disorder (Figure 7.16). In contrast, children living in households with a gross weekly income of £600 or more were the least likely to experience any type of mental disorder, at between 6 and 7 per cent of boys and 4 per cent of girls.

In 2000 (the latest year for which data are available), about one in six people aged 16 to 74 living in private households in Great Britain reported experiencing a neurotic disorder (self-diagnosed), such as depression, anxiety or a phobia, in the seven days before interview for the Psychiatric Morbidity Survey. A higher proportion of women (19 per cent) than men (14 per cent) experienced such a disorder.

Mental illness is the major risk factor for suicide. Trends in suicide rates have varied by age group and sex in the UK over the last 30 years. Until the end of the 1980s older men aged 65 and over had the highest suicide rates (Figure 7.17 overleaf). In 1986 the suicide rate among men aged 65 and over peaked at 26 per 100,000 population and then fell to 14 per 100,000 in 2005. In contrast, suicide rates for younger men rose, in particular for those aged 25 to 44, for whom the suicide rate almost doubled from 14 per 100,000 in 1971 to a peak of 27 per 100,000 in 1998. The suicide rate among men in this age group has since declined, but in 2005 remained the highest, at 22 per 100,000.

There is a clear difference in suicide rates between men and women. In 2005 the age-standardised rate for all men aged 15 and over was 18 per 100,000, three times that of women at 6 per 100,000. This gap has widened considerably since 1973, when the suicide rate among all men aged 15 and over was around one and a half times that of all women. Among women aged 45 and over, suicide rates have more than halved since the early 1980s. However for younger women the rates have remained fairly stable since the mid-1980s.

Between 1991 and 2004, there were large variations in regional suicide rates within the UK. During this period, suicide rates in Scotland were consistently higher than the rates for the other constituent countries of the UK for both men and women. For most of this period, suicide rates for men in Scotland were over 50 per cent higher than the overall UK rate and in the period 2000–2002 were 67 per cent higher at 32 per 100,000 population. The suicide rate for women in Scotland remained relatively stable between 1991–1993 and 2002–2004 at around 10 deaths per 100,000 population, but this was consistently higher than the rates for the other countries. The difference was greatest in 2001–2003 when the suicide rate for women in Scotland was around double the rates for both England and Wales (10 per 100,000 compared to 5 and 6 per 100,000 in England and Wales respectively). Within England, the highest

Figure **7.17**

Suicide rates:[1] by sex and age

United Kingdom
Rates per 100,000 population

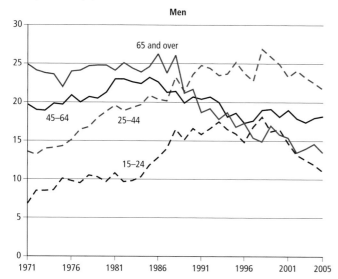

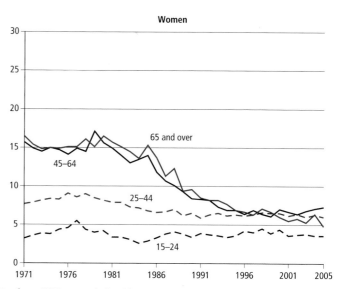

1 Includes deaths with a verdict of undetermined intent (open verdicts). Rates from 2002 are coded to ICD-10. See Appendix, Part 7: International Classification of Diseases. Rates are age-standardised to the European standard population. See Appendix, Part 7: Standardised rates.

Source: Office for National Statistics; General Register Office for Scotland; Northern Ireland Statistics and Research Agency

suicide rates were generally seen in the North West and North East for men, and the North West and London for women.

Sexual health

Since the late 1990s the increase in notifications of sexually transmitted diseases, especially among young people, has become a major public health concern across the UK. Those who have unprotected sex and multiple sexual partners are at the greatest risk of contracting a sexually transmitted infection. During 2005/06 men were more likely than women in Great Britain to have had more than one sexual partner in the previous year for all age groups aged under 50 (Table 7.18). Among both sexes, multiple sexual partnerships were most common among those below the age of 25. Among men, those aged 16 to 19 were the most likely to report having had more than one sexual partner in the previous year and also the most likely to have had none. Among women, those aged 20 to 24 were the most likely to report having more than one sexual partner in the previous year.

Among men and women, those aged 25 and over were the most likely to have had one sexual partner and the least likely to have had none. This in part reflects marital status among the

Table **7.18**

Number of sexual partners[1] in the previous year: by sex and age, 2005/06

Great Britain

Percentages

	16–19	20–24	25–34	35–44	45–49
Men					
No partners	38	21	10	10	11
1 partner	26	54	72	82	82
2 or 3 partners	26	17	11	5	5
4 or more partners	10	9	7	3	2
All aged 16–49	100	100	100	100	100
Women					
No partners	36	14	7	11	14
1 partner	48	67	84	85	84
2 or 3 partners	12	16	7	3	2
4 or more partners	4	3	2	-	-
All aged 16–49	100	100	100	100	100

1 Self-reported in the 12 months prior to interview.

Source: Omnibus Survey, Office for National Statistics

Figure **7.19**

Diagnoses of genital chlamydia infection: by sex and age

United Kingdom

Rates per 100,000 population

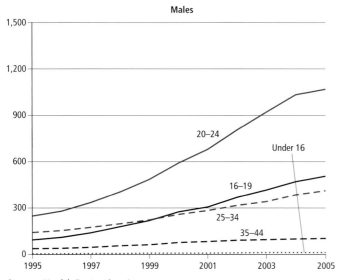

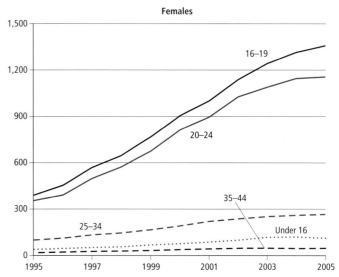

Source: Health Protection Agency

older age groups, as 93 per cent of married or cohabiting men and 97 per cent of married or cohabiting women reported having only one sexual partner in the previous year.

Sexually transmitted infections (STIs), including HIV infection, are the most prevalent infectious disease problem in the UK today. In 2005 almost 800,000 diagnoses were made in genito-urinary medicine (GUM) clinics in the UK. Genital chlamydia was the most common STI diagnosed in GUM clinics in the UK in 2005: almost 110,000 cases were diagnosed, 5 per cent more than in 2004 and three times the number in 1996. As in previous years the highest rates of diagnoses in 2005 were among women aged 16 to 19, at 1,359 per 100,000, and those aged 20 to 24 at 1,156 per 100,000 (Figure 7.19). Among men, the highest rates of diagnoses were in those aged 20 to 24 at 1,070 per 100,000.

The continued increase in diagnoses of genital chlamydia infection in the UK since the mid-1990s is probably due to several factors including increases in unprotected sexual intercourse, increased awareness of the infection through health awareness campaigns, and the increased availability of testing services. The National Chlamydia Screening Programme was introduced in England in April 2003. During the third year there were over 100,000 screenings between April 2005 and March 2006, compared with 63,000 in the second year and 18,000 in the first.

In 2005 uncomplicated gonorrhoea was the second most common bacterial STI diagnosed in GUM clinics in the UK. In contrast to genital chlamydia there has been a gradual decline in the number of diagnoses since 2002, and between 2004 and 2005, there was a 13 per cent decrease from just over 22,000 cases to just over 19,000 in 2005. In 2005 the rate of diagnoses in men (47 per 100,000) was more than twice that seen in women (18 per 100,000). The highest rates of diagnoses in 2005 were among men aged 20 to 24, at 196 per 100,000, and women aged 16 to 19 at 133 per 100,000. The recent decline in the number of diagnoses of uncomplicated gonorrhoea may have resulted from several factors such as awareness campaigns and NHS initiatives in areas of concern.

For those who have multiple sexual partnerships, condom use can help reduce the risk of contracting sexually transmitted infections. In 2005/06 in Great Britain, both men and women who had had more than one sexual partner in the previous 12 months, were more than twice as likely to have used condoms to prevent infection (75 per cent of men and 85 per cent of women respectively) than those who had just one sexual partner (36 per cent of men and 34 per cent of women respectively).

Although the use of condoms is important in preventing sexually transmitted infections among people who have multiple sexual partners, the most common reason cited by

Table **7.20**

Regularity of condom use: by age, 2005/06[1]

Great Britain

Percentages

	16–19	20–24	25–29	30–34	35–39	40–44	45–49
Always	59	40	30	34	27	16	22
Usually	17	9	11	7	7	6	3
Sometimes	11	22	16	13	9	9	6
Never	13	29	44	47	57	69	69
All adults	100	100	100	100	100	100	100

Note: Shaded cell indicates the estimate is unreliable due to small sample size and any analysis using this figure may be invalid. Any use of this shaded figure must be accompanied by this disclaimer.
1 Men and women currently in a sexual relationship or had one in the last 12 months.

Source: Omnibus Survey, Office for National Statistics

all those who had used them in the previous 12 months was to prevent pregnancy. In 2005/06, 88 per cent of men aged 16 to 69 and 90 per cent of women aged 16 to 49 who had used a condom in the previous 12 months gave this as a reason.

In 2005/06 the regularity of condom use in Great Britain varied considerably by age. Younger adults aged 16 to 19 were more likely than those in older age groups to say they always used condoms (59 per cent) and less likely to say they never used them (13 per cent) (Table 7.20). The proportion of men and women who reported always using a condom during intercourse generally declined with age. This in part reflects marital status and the number of sexual partners people may have had during the past 12 months (see Table 7.18).

Social protection

- Spending on social protection in the UK was £4,710 per person in 2003, higher than the EU-25 average of £4,160 per person. (Figure 8.2)

- In 2005, local authorities provided 3.6 million hours of home care (in a survey week) in Great Britain; nearly three-quarters of which were purchased from the independent sector. (Figure 8.7)

- In 2004/05, 53 per cent of single female pensioners in the UK had an occupational or personal pension in addition to the state pension, compared with 66 per cent of single male pensioners and 83 per cent of pensioner couples. (Table 8.14)

- In 2004/05, 89 per cent of lone parents with dependent children and 62 per cent of couples with children in the UK were receiving income-related benefits. (Table 8.16)

- In 2004 in Great Britain, childcare arrangements included formal childcare for less than one-third of children aged under five where the mother was working. (Table 8.17)

- In 2005, over 77,000 children were being looked after by local authorities in the UK, with over 60 per cent cared for in foster homes. (Table 8.18)

Chapter 8

Social protection is the term used to describe the help available to people who are in need or are at risk of hardship for reasons such as illness, low income, family circumstances or age. Central government, local authorities and private bodies (such as voluntary organisations) can provide help and support. Help may be provided through direct cash payments such as social security benefits or pensions; payments in kind such as free prescriptions or bus passes; or the provision of services, for example through the National Health Service (NHS). Unpaid care, such as that provided by family members, also plays a part.

Expenditure

Information about expenditure on social protection within the EU is collated by Eurostat as part of the European System of integrated Social Protection Statistics (ESSPROS). The main components of expenditure on social protection benefits which protect people against common sources of hardship include: government expenditure on social series, health services and personal social services; sick pay paid by employers; and payments made from occupational and personal pension schemes.

Total UK expenditure on social protection in 2004/05 was £294 billion. This is equivalent to 25 per cent of gross domestic product (GDP) at market prices. Expenditure on benefits for old age and 'survivors' (defined as those whose entitlement derives from their relationship to a deceased person, for example

widows, widowers and orphans) accounted for 46 per cent of the UK total. Spending on sickness, healthcare and disability accounted for 38 per cent, and that on families and children accounted for 7 per cent. In real terms, after allowing for inflation, there was a 22 per cent rise in total social protection expenditure between 1994/95 and 2004/05. Over this period, expenditure on sickness, healthcare and disability increased by 33 per cent and spending on benefits for old age and survivors increased by 31 per cent (Figure 8.1). Expenditure on families and children showed a 3 per cent decrease although it remained above that of housing, unemployment and other expenditure, at £20 billion. Spending on unemployment showed a steady decline over the period with the exception of 2001/02 when it rose before falling again the following year.

In 2003, UK spending on social protection was equivalent to £4,710 per person which was higher than the EU-25 average of £4,160 per person (Figure 8.2). Among the EU-25 member

Figure **8.2**

Expenditure[1] on social protection per head: EU-25 comparison, 2003[2]

£ thousand per head

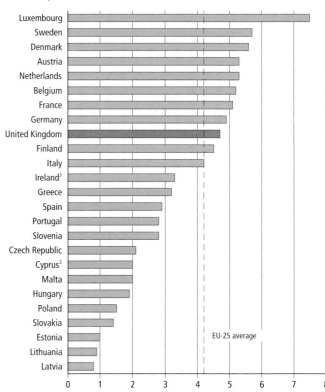

1 Before deduction of tax, where applicable. Tax credits are generally excluded. Figures are purchasing power parities per inhabitant. Includes administrative and other expenditure incurred by social protection schemes.
2 Only partial data are available for the 10 countries which joined the EU in 2004 but are still considered reliable for comparison.
3 Data for Ireland excludes funded occupational pension schemes for private sector employees. Data for Cyprus are for 2002.

Source: Eurostat

Figure **8.1**

Expenditure on social protection benefits in real terms:[1] by function

United Kingdom
£ billion at 2004/05 prices[1]

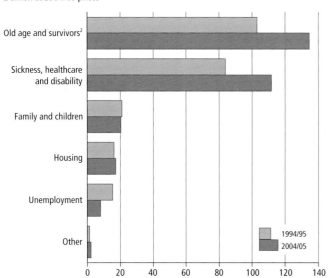

1 Adjusted to 2004/05 prices using the GDP market prices deflator.
2 Survivors are those whose entitlement derives from their relationship to a deceased person (for example, widows, widowers and orphans).

Source: Office for National Statistics

Figure **8.3**

Social security benefit expenditure in real terms[1]

United Kingdom
£ billion at 2005/06 prices[1]

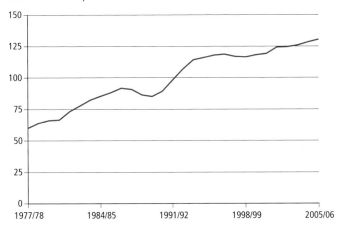

1 Adjusted to 2005/06 prices using the GDP market prices deflator (second quarter 2006).

Source: Department for Work and Pensions; HM Revenue and Customs; Veterans Agency; Department for Social Development, Northern Ireland

Figure **8.4**

Local authority personal social services expenditure:[1] by recipient group, 2004/05

England
Percentages

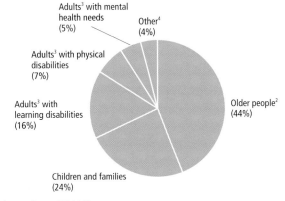

Total expenditure: £18.2 billion

1 All figures include overhead costs.
2 Aged 65 and over.
3 Adults aged under 65.
4 Includes expenditure on asylum seekers and overall service strategy.

Source: The Information Centre for health and social care

states, Luxembourg spent the most when expressed as per head of the resident population, at £7,540. However, a large proportion of benefits in Luxembourg are paid to people living outside the country (primarily on healthcare, pensions and family allowances) which inflates the per head figure. Sweden and Denmark spend the next highest on social protection at £5,710 and £5,610 per head respectively. Only partial data are available for the ten countries which joined the EU in May 2004. In 2003 Slovenia spent the most on social protection per head, at £2,820, while Latvia spent the least, at £810. Of the pre-2004 EU-15 countries, Spain and Portugal spent the least at around £2,800 to £2,900 per head.

In order for meaningful comparisons to be made across the countries, levels of expenditure shown in Figure 8.2 have been adjusted to take account of differences in the general level of prices for goods and services within each country. These differences reflect variations in social protection systems, demographic structures, unemployment rates and other social, institutional and economic factors.

The Department for Work and Pensions (DWP) in Great Britain and the Department for Social Development in Northern Ireland are responsible for managing social security benefits, for example the state retirement pension, disability allowance, income support and pension credit. After allowing for inflation, social security benefit expenditure in the UK more than doubled from £60 billion in 1977/78 to £130 billion in 2005/06 (Figure 8.3). In addition to social security benefits, since 1999/2000 financial assistance has also been provided in the form of tax credits which are administered by HM Revenue and Customs (HMRC)

and which reached £17 billion in 2005/06. Spending on social security benefits can be influenced by the economic cycle, demographic changes and government policies. After falling between 1986/87 and 1989/90, spending on social security benefits rose to £114 billion in 1993/94, reflecting increases in the number of people who were unemployed or economically inactive (see Glossary on page 43). Since 1994/95, there has been a more gradual increases in expenditure, this may be a result of increases in expenditure on benefits aimed specifically at pensioners and children.

Of the £130 billion UK benefit expenditure in 2005/06, nearly £116 billion was managed by the DWP in Great Britain, 65 per cent of which was directed at people of state pension age and over (age 60 for women and 65 for men), 31 per cent was directed at people of working age and 4 per cent at children. Of the benefit expenditure provided to adults with responsibility for children, 2 per cent was paid in income support, 1 per cent was paid in disability living allowance and the largest part of the remainder was paid in housing and council tax benefits. In Northern Ireland, nearly £4 billion was spent by the Department for Social Development on pensions and income related pension credit; contributory and disability benefits; job seekers allowance and income support and social fund payments such as winter fuel payments. The remaining £11 billion of UK benefit expenditure comprised nearly £10 billion on child benefit, paid by HMRC and £1 billion on War Pensions paid by the Veterans Agency.

In 2004/05, local authorities in England spent £18.2 billion on personal social services (Figure 8.4). This includes expenditure on

Figure **8.5**

Expenditure on social protection by the top 500 charities:[1] by category,[2] 2004/05

United Kingdom
£ million

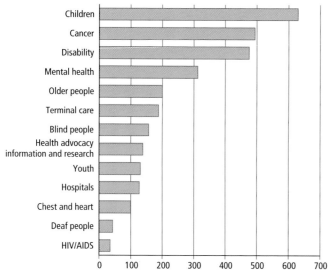

1 Charities Aid Foundation top 500 fundraising charities. Direct charitable expenditure.
2. Category is self-classified by charity.

Source: Charities Aid Foundation

home help and home care, looked after children, children on child protection registers and foster care. A total of nearly £8 billion was spent on older people (those aged 65 and over), the largest single portion at 44 per cent. Spending on children and families accounted for around one-quarter of total personal social services expenditure at £4.4 billion. The combined spending on adults with learning difficulties, adults with physical disabilities, and those with mental health needs accounted for 28 per cent (£5 billion) of local authority spending. Total expenditure on personal social services increased by 8 per cent in cash terms compared with 2003/04, with expenditure on children and families showing the largest increase (11 per cent) over the period.

Charities are another source of social protection assistance in the UK, although this is not counted in ESSPROS and is small in comparison to total social protection expenditure. The top 500 fundraising charities, based on income generated during the year, spent over £3 billion on social protection in 2004/05, an increase of 7 per cent (£190 million) from 2003/04. Of the charities in the top 500, children's charities spent the most on social protection (£630 million, or 21 per cent of the total), followed by cancer related charities (£494 million) and those for people with disabilities (£475 million) (Figure 8.5).

Carers and caring

The *Community Care Reforms Act* was introduced in 1993 to enable more people to continue to live in their own homes as independently as possible. Services are offered by the local authority and may involve routine household tasks within or outside the home, personal care of the client or respite care in support of the client's regular carers.

Councils and Local Authorities provide a range of services from in-home care to equipment, depending on the circumstances and requirements of those being assessed. In 2004/05 it was estimated that nearly 2 million adults in England were referred to councils with social services responsibilities (Table 8.6) for the first time, a 2 per cent fall on the year before. Around 1 million of these contacts resulted in further assessment or the commissioning of ongoing services which include home care, day care, meals, equipment and direct payments. Twenty seven per cent of all contacts were self-referrals. Referrals to councils with social services responsibilities from secondary health sources such as hospitals, accounted for 25 per cent of contacts and referrals from families, friends and neighbours accounted for 14 per cent. Referrals from primary health providers such as GPs or community health centres accounted for 13 per cent of contacts. Referrals from local authorities rose by 14 per cent between 2003/04 and 2004/05 although they still accounted for only 2 per cent of all referrals in 2004/05.

Table **8.6**

New contacts with councils:[1] by source of referral, 2004/05

England   Thousands

Self referral	536
Secondary health	492
Family/friend/neighbour	265
Primary health/Community health	260
Internal[2]	133
Other departments of own local authority or other local authority	45
Local authority housing department or Housing association	32
Legal agency	30
Not known	49
Other	116
All contacts	1,960

1 Councils with social services responsibilities.
2 Council's own social services department.

Source: The Information Centre for health and social care

Local authority home care services assist people – principally those with physical disabilities (including frailty associated with ageing), dementia, mental health problems and learning difficulties – to continue living in their own home and to function as independently as possible. The number of home help hours purchased or provided by local authorities in England increased between 1993 and 2005 (Figure 8.7). In September 2005, local authorities provided or purchased 3.6 million hours of home care services during the survey week, compared with 3.4 million hours in September 2004 and 2.4 million hours in September 1995, an increase of almost 50 per cent over the decade to 2005. There has also been a change in the way in which these services are sourced. In 1995, the majority of home help contact hours were directly provided by local authorities in England (70 per cent); this had more than halved to 27 per cent in 2005. Instead, the number of hours of care that have been purchased by local authorities from the independent sector (both private and voluntary) has increased more than threefold over the decade from 0.71 million in 1995 to 2.62 million in 2005 and has become the main source of provision.

Of households where some form of home help or home care contact is provided, the proportion receiving more than five hours of home help or home care contact and six or more visits per week, has increased steadily from 21 per cent in 1995 to 48 per cent in 2005. This reflects an increased focus by councils with social services responsibilities on increasing the number

Figure **8.7**

Number of contact hours of home help and home care:[1] by provider

England

Millions

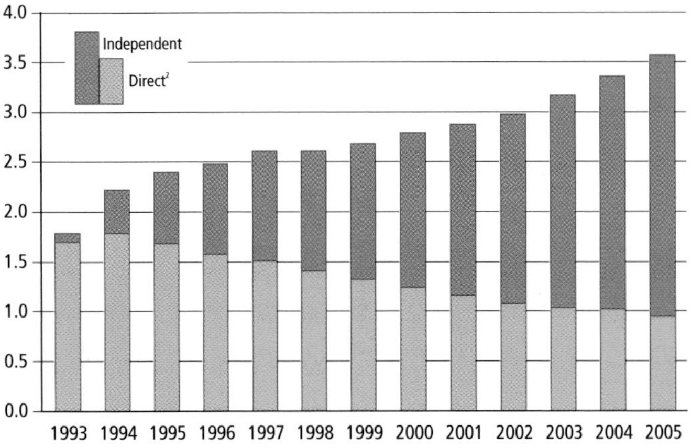

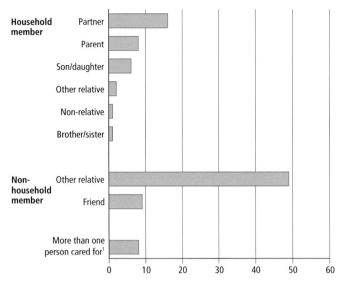

1 During a survey week in September. Contact hours provided or purchased by local authorities. Households receiving home care purchased with a direct payment are excluded.
2 Directly provided by local authorities.

Source: The Information Centre for health and social care

Figure **8.8**

Informal care received: by relationship to care provider, 2004/05

Great Britain

Percentages

1 For example, those who care for both a partner and parent. Includes both household and non-household members.

Source: Family Resources Survey, Department for Work and Pensions

and intensity of home care visits. The number of households receiving low intensity care (two hours or less of home help or home care and one visit per week) as a proportion of all households receiving care has fallen from 32 per cent in 1995 to 12 per cent in 2005.

Informal carers are adults or children who provide any regular service or help to someone who is sick, disabled or elderly and excludes those who give this help as part of a formal job. In 2004/05, the Family Resources Survey found that in Great Britain, more than half of informal carers were providing care to someone living outside of their own household (58 per cent) (Figure 8.8). The majority (49 per cent) of care given outside the household was provided by relatives. Care provided to partners within the household accounted for 16 per cent of all help provided. Those in full-time employment (31 per cent) made up the largest group of carers, regardless of whether care was provided inside or outside the household, followed by those in retirement (22 per cent) and those who were otherwise inactive or in part-time employment (both 15 per cent).

Sick and disabled people

There are a number of financial benefits available to sick and disabled people. Disability living allowance (DLA) is a benefit for people who are disabled, have personal care needs, mobility needs, or both and who are aged under 65. Attendance allowance (AA) is paid to people who become ill or disabled on or after their 65th birthday and due to the extent or severity of their physical or mental condition, need someone to help with their personal care. In 2002/03 in Great Britain shows that there were 4.4 million people in 2005/06 in receipt of DLA and/or AA compared with 4 million in 2002/03. This increase reflects changes in entitlement conditions for benefits, demographic changes and increased take-up.

In February 2006, 2.8 million people in Great Britain were in receipt of DLA and 1.6 million were receiving AA (Table 8.9). The most common condition for which each type of allowance was received was arthritis (489,000 and 495,000 people for DLA and AA respectively). For recipients of DLA, other common conditions included 'other mental health causes' such as psychosis and dementia, learning difficulties and back ailments. Other common conditions for people receiving AA included frailty, mental health causes and heart disease. Incapacity benefit (IB) and severe disablement allowance (SDA) are claimed by those of working age who are unable to work because of illness and/or disability. The number of people receiving IB or SDA or those benefits they replaced was lower in 2005/06 than in 2002/03.

In addition to financial assistance, people who are sick and disabled are provided with health services through the National Health Service. The NHS offers a range of health and care services to sick and disabled people. Primary care services include those provided by GPs, dentists, opticians and the England and Wales NHS Direct telephone, website and digital TV service and NHS 24 in Scotland. Secondary care services such as NHS hospitals provide acute and specialist services, and treat conditions that normally cannot be dealt with by primary care specialists.

The NHS is increasingly using technology in patient care. NHS Direct, the telephone helpline launched in England and Wales in 1998, provides access to health advice and information. In 2005/06 the service handled over 6.8 million calls. In addition, the NHS Direct Online website provides evidence based health information. Since its launch in December 1999, usage has increased steadily year on year. In 2001/02 the average number of visits per month to the website was 169,000. By 2005/06 this had risen to just over 1.1 million visits.

In 2005, there were just over 1.2 million full-time equivalent direct care staff employed in NHS hospital and community health services in the UK, offering secondary care. Of these 510,000 were nursing, midwifery and health visiting staff; 100,000 were medical and dental staff; and 624,000 were other non-medical staff such as therapists, admin support, management and infrastructure support. A further 283,000 people were employed in personal social services, and there were around 39,000 general medical practitioners and 25,000 general dental practitioners, offering primary care. The number of full-time equivalent staff throughout health and personal social services showed a 2.9 per cent increase between 2004 and 2005 in the UK. Scotland recorded a 3.1 per cent increase, Northern Ireland and England both showed increases of 2.9 per cent and Wales recorded a 1.8 per cent increase.

Table **8.9**

Recipients of selected benefits for sick and disabled people[1]

Great Britain				Thousands
	2002/03	2003/04	2004/05	2005/06
Incapacity benefit only	852	829	818	777
Severe disability allowance	325	309	296	283
Incapacity benefit and disability living allowance	502	518	526	532
Incapacity benefit and income support	681	673	645	625
Incapacity benefit, income support and disability living allowance	423	448	467	480
Disability living allowance[2]	2,516	2,625	2,713	2,786
Attendance allowance[3]	1,515	1,556	1,595	1,642

1 See Appendix, Part 8: Expenditure on social protection benefits. At February each year.
2 Includes those in receipt of an allowance, but excludes people with entitlement where the payment has been suspended (for example if they are in hospital).
3 Includes those cases with entitlement but where payment is currently suspended (for example, because of an extended stay in hospital or an overlapping benefit).

Source: Work and Pensions Longitudinal Study, Department for Work and Pensions

Table **8.10**

NHS GP consultations:[1] by site of consultation

Great Britain					Percentages
	1975	1985	2003/04	2004/05	2005[2]
Surgery[3]	78	79	86	87	87
Telephone	3	7	10	9	10
Home	19	14	4	4	3

1 NHS GP consultations in the 14 days prior to interview. Data for 1975 and 1985 are unweighted.
2 Data for 2005 includes last quarter of 2004/05 due to survey change from financial year to calendar year. See Appendix, Part 2: General Household Survey.
3 Includes consultations with a GP at a health centre and those who had answered 'elsewhere'.

Source: General Household Survey (Longitudinal), Office for National Statistics

People consult their GP for a number of services including vaccinations, general health advice and secondary care services. The majority of consultations take place in GPs' surgeries, with smaller numbers taking place over the telephone or in the home (Table 8.10). Since 1975 home visits have declined, from 19 per cent to 3 per cent of all consultations, while consultations over the telephone and at the surgery have both increased, from 3 per cent to 10 per cent and 78 per cent to 87 per cent respectively.

An out-patient is a person who is seen by a hospital consultant for treatment or advice but who is non-resident at the hospital. In 2005/06 in Great Britain, 14 per cent of people reported visiting an out-patient or casualty department at least once in the preceding three months, when questioned as part of the General Household Survey. With the exception of children aged under five, the likelihood of having been an out-patient generally increased with age (Figure 8.11). Women aged between 16 and 44 were more likely than men in the same age group to have been out-patients although the reverse was true for those aged 65 and over. Among those under 16, boys are more likely than girls to have been an out-patient.

An in-patient is a person who is admitted to hospital and spends at least one night there. In the UK between 1991/92 and 2004/05, the number of finished consultant episodes classified as 'acute' (those where the patient has completed a period of

Figure **8.11**

Out-patient or casualty department attendance:[1] by sex and age, 2005[2]

Great Britain

Percentages

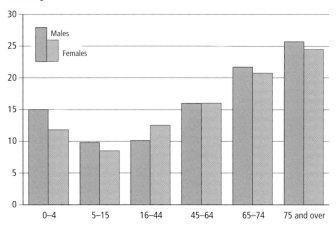

1 In the three months before interview.
2 Data for 2005 includes last quarter of 2004/05 due to survey change from financial year to calendar year. See Appendix, Part2: General Household Survey.

Source: General Household Survey (Longitudinal), Office for National Statistics

care under one consultant with one hospital provider) rose by 78 per cent in the UK to reach 12.4 million (Table 8.12). The number of finished consultant episodes for the mentally ill has

Table **8.12**

NHS in-patient activity for sick and disabled people[1]

United Kingdom

	1981	1991/92	2001/02	2002/03	2003/04	2004/05
Acute[2]						
Finished consultant episodes[3] (thousands)	5,693	6,974	11,184	11,488	11,958	12,434
In-patient episodes per available bed (numbers)	31.1	51.4	87.0	89.2	91.9	95.9
Mean duration of stay (days)	8.4	6.0	3.7	3.7	3.7	3.6
Mentally ill						
Finished consultant episodes[3] (thousands)	244	281	259	255	238	232
In-patient episodes per available bed (numbers)	2.2	4.5	6.6	6.5	6.1	6.2
Mean duration of stay[4] (days)	..	114.8	34.2	34.2	40.7	42.5
People with learning disabilities						
Finished consultant episodes[3] (thousands)	34	62	41	42	34	31
In-patient episodes per available bed (numbers)	0.6	2.4	5.7	6.8	5.4	5.7
Mean duration of stay[4] (days)	..	544.0	105.8	94.6	53.0	71.7

1 See Appendix, Part 8: In-patient activity.
2 General patients on wards, excluding elderly, maternity and neonatal cots in maternity units.
3 All data for Wales and Scotland except acute after 1986 are for deaths, discharges and transfers between specialities and for Northern Ireland are for deaths, discharges and transfers between hospitals.
4 Scotland data unavailable from 2001/02 onwards.

Source: The Information Centre for health and social care; Welsh Assembly Government; National Health Service in Scotland; Department of Health, Social Services and Public Safety, Northern Ireland

Table **8.13**

Satisfaction with NHS GPs and hospitals in their area, 2005[1]

Great Britain
Percentages

	In need of a lot of improvement	In need of some improvement	Satisfactory	Very good
GP services				
Being able to choose which GP to see	14	29	45	12
Quality of medical treatment by GPs	6	22	49	22
Hospital services				
Staffing level of nurses in hospitals	22	45	28	5
Staffing level of doctors in hospitals	21	45	29	5
Quality of nursing care in hospitals	15	34	37	13
Quality of medical treatment in hospitals	14	34	41	11

1 Respondents aged 18 and over were asked 'From what you know or have heard, please tick a box for each of the items below to show whether you think the National Health Service in your area is, on the whole, satisfactory or in need of improvement.' Excludes those who responded 'Don't know' or did not answer.

Source: British Social Attitudes Survey, National Centre for Social Research

fallen in recent years and in 2004/05 was 17 per cent lower than in 1991/92.

Between 1991/92 and 2004/05 the average length of stay in hospital for the mentally ill more than halved from 115 days to around 43 days. Over the same period the average duration of stay for people with learning disabilities fell by 87 per cent from 544 days to around 72 days. This reflects in part the change in legislation to help people with such difficulties to live with independence in the community, rather than in NHS hospitals.

The British Social Attitudes survey includes questions on attitudes towards various aspects of NHS care. In 2005, over half (57 per cent) of adults in Great Britain aged 18 and over thought that their degree of choice in which GP to see was either satisfactory or very good (Table 8.13). Furthermore, nearly three-quarters (71 per cent) thought that the quality of medical treatment delivered by GPs was either satisfactory or very good. In comparison, around two-thirds believed that staffing levels of nurses and doctors in hospitals were in need of some or a lot of improvement. When asked about the quality of medical treatment in hospital, 52 per cent of people thought that it was either satisfactory or very good and 50 per cent thought that the quality of nursing care in hospital was either satisfactory or very good.

Older people

In the UK, much of central government expenditure on social protection for older people is through payment of the state retirement pension. Nearly everyone over state pension age

(age 60 for women and 65 for men) receives this pension. Some also receive income related state benefits, such as council tax or housing benefit. However, there is an increasing emphasis on people making their own provision for retirement, and this can be through an occupational, personal or stakeholder pension (See also Figure 5.4).

In 2004/05, 49 per cent of single female pensioners in the UK had an occupational pension in addition to the state pension, compared with 55 per cent of single male pensioners and 64 per cent of pensioner couples (Table 8.14). Much smaller proportions had a personal pension as well as the state pension, 8 per cent of single male pensioners and 3 per cent of single female pensioners. The lower percentages for women may be due in part to women traditionally having lower employment rates than men (see also Figure 4.4) and also having been less likely to have been in pensionable jobs. Women were also less likely to have been self-employed and therefore to have had a personal pension.

There is a range of state benefits available for older people in the UK including pension credit, which replaced the minimum income guarantee in 2003. Pension credit provided a minimum income of £114.05 a week for single pensioners and £174.05 for pensioner couples in 2006/07. In addition it provided a means tested income top up for those saving towards retirement where either a single person, or where either partner in a couple was aged over 65. Single pensioners entitled to the top up can receive an additional £17.88 a week, and pensioner couples could be entitled to an additional £23.58.

Table **8.14**

Pension receipt: by type of pensioner unit,[1] 2004/05

United Kingdom

Percentages

	Pensioner couples	Single male pensioners	Single female pensioners	All pensioners
Includes retirement pension[2]/minimum income guarantee/pension credit only	17	32	44	31
Plus				
Occupational, but not personal pension[3]	64	55	49	56
Personal, but not occupational pension[3]	10	8	3	7
Both occupational and personal pension[3]	9	3	1	5
Other combinations, no retirement pension /minimum income guarantee/pension credit	0	0	1	1
None	1	1	2	1
All people	100	100	100	100

1 A pensioner unit is defined as either a single person over state pension age (65 for men, 60 for women), or a couple where the man is over state pension age.
2 Includes receipt of other contributory benefits. See Appendix, Part 8: Pension schemes.
3 Occupational and personal pensions include survivors benefits.

Source: Pensioners' Income Series, Department for Work and Pensions

Table **8.15**

Receipt of selected social security benefits among pensioners: by type of benefit unit,[1] 2004/05

United Kingdom

Percentages

	Single		Couple
	Men	Women	
Income-related			
Council tax benefit	31	39	17
Income support/minimum income guarantee/pension credit	22	30	12
Housing benefit	21	24	8
Any income-related benefit[2]	36	46	19
Non-income-related[3]			
Incapacity or disablement benefits[4]	21	24	25
Any non-income-related benefit[2]	100	100	100
Any benefit[2]	100	100	100

1 Pensioner benefit units. See Appendix, Part 8: Benefit units.
2 Includes benefits not listed here. Components do not sum to totals as each benefit unit may receive more than one benefit.
3 Includes state pension.
4 Includes incapacity benefit, disability living allowance (care and mobility components), severe disablement allowance, industrial injuries disability benefit, war disablement pension and attendance allowance.

Source: Family Resources Survey, Department for Work and Pensions

Single pensioners are more likely than pensioner couples to receive any type of income-related benefit. In 2004/05, 36 per cent of single male pensioners and 46 per cent of single female pensioners in the UK received income-related benefits, compared with 19 per cent of pensioner couples (Table 8.15). Among single pensioners, more women than men were in receipt of income support or pension credit (30 per cent compared with 22 per cent). For pensioner couples the figure was 12 per cent. Compared with 2003/04, the proportions of pensioner families receiving income support and/or pension credit had increased across all pensioner groups. Similar proportions (between one-fifth and one-quarter) of pensioners received disability-related benefits, whether single or in a couple and these proportions were unchanged between 2003/04 and 2004/05.

Families and children

There are a number of benefits available to families with children in the UK. They include income related benefits paid to low income families such as housing and council tax benefit and income support; and non income-related benefits such as child benefit and incapacity or disablement benefits. In 2004/05, in the UK 89 per cent of lone parents with dependent children and 62 per cent of couples with children were receiving income-related benefits. Among lone parents with children, 71 per cent received working tax credit or income support compared with 15 per cent of couples with dependent children (Table 8.16). This may reflect the employment status of lone mothers, who head the majority of lone-parent families, and are less likely to be employed than mothers with a partner. According to the 2004 Families and Children Study (FACS 2004) 48 per cent of lone mothers do not work compared with 28 per cent of mothers with a partner (see also Table 4.6).

Childcare is essential in supporting parents to take up or return to employment. There is a Government target to increase the take-up of formal childcare places by lower-income families in England, to 738,000 by 2008, from 615,000 in 2005. Childcare can be provided by formal paid sources such as nurseries and crèches; nursery schools and playgroups; registered childminders; after school and breakfast clubs or holiday play schemes. Across the UK parents can receive financial support from the Government if they use these services as long as the service providers are registered and approved. In March 2006, there were around 13,000 providers offering 566,000 registered full day-care places and 11,000 providers offering nearly 367,000 out of school day-care places in England (see also Chapter 3: Education and training). Childcare can also be

Table **8.16**

Receipt of selected social security benefits among families below pension age: by type of benefit unit,[1] 2004/05

United Kingdom Percentages

	Lone parent with dependent children	Couple with dependent children
Income-related		
Council tax benefit	46	8
Housing benefit	44	7
Working tax credit, income support or pension credit	71	15
Jobseeker's allowance	-	2
Any income-related benefit	89	62
Non-income-related		
Child benefit	97	97
Incapacity or disablement benefits[2]	8	8
Any non-income-related benefit	97	97
Any benefit or tax credit[3]	98	98

1 Families below pension age. See Appendix, Part 8: Benefit units.
2 Includes incapacity benefit, disability living allowance (care and mobility components), severe disablement allowance, industrial injuries disability benefit, war disablement pension, attendance allowance and disabled persons tax credit.
3 Includes all benefits not listed here. Components do not sum to totals as each benefit unit may receive more than one benefit.

Source: Family Resources Survey, Department for Work and Pensions

provided informally by grandparents, older children, partners, ex-partners and other relatives and friends. In 2004, 28 per cent of all dependent children in Great Britain received childcare from their grandparents, 24 per cent received care from their parent's partner, 12 per cent of care came from other relatives and friends and 4 per cent from older siblings.

Use of formal childcare in Great Britain reduces as children get older (Table 8.17); around 30 per cent of children under five whose mothers were working used formal childcare. This fell to 16 per cent for children aged five to ten, when children are of primary school age, and decreased further when they started secondary education. Around nine in ten children aged under five with working mothers in Great Britain received some form of childcare in 2004. Use of informal childcare decreases more slowly with age, with around half of children between the ages of five and 10 and around one-third of children between 11 and 15 receiving this form of childcare.

The hours per week that parents work may determine or be determined by the type of childcare used. The childcare patterns of working lone mothers are similar to those of couples where both parents work for 16 or more hours a week. In 2004 in Great Britain, around one-fifth of working lone mothers used formal childcare and around half used informal childcare. For couples where only one parent worked 16 or more hours a week, around one-tenth used formal childcare. This may be because the other parent was at home looking after the child. Formal types of childcare were less likely to be used when parents (lone or couples) worked less than 16 hours per week.

Parental perceptions of the affordability of local childcare provision vary between lone parents and couples. In the 2004 Families and Children Study (FACS), almost one-third (32 per cent) of lone parents in Great Britain described their local childcare provisions as 'not at all affordable' compared with one-quarter (25 per cent) of couples. A further 33 per cent of lone parents found the provisions 'fairly affordable' compared with 42 per cent of couples. Couples where both worked 16 hours or more per week were more likely than those where either partner worked between 1 and 15 hours to consider local childcare to be 'fairly affordable' – 45 per cent compared with 29 per cent.

The 2004 FACS showed that where families receive financial help from relatives, it was most common when children were at young ages. Such help may include being given or loaned money or receiving financial help towards bills, clothing, holidays or other items. The most financial help from relatives was received by lone parents working up to 15 hours per week (63 per cent). Lone parent families were more likely to receive financial help from their family (54 per cent) than couples

Table **8.17**

Childcare arrangements for children with working mothers:[1] by family characteristics, 2004

Great Britain   Percentages[2]

	Formal childcare[3]	Informal childcare[4]	Childcare not required
Family type			
Lone parent	22	48	36
Couple	19	54	35
Family type working status			
Lone parent: 1 to 15 hours	17	36	55
Lone parent: 16 hours and above	23	50	34
Couple - both: 16 hours and above	21	54	33
Couple - one only: 16 hours and above	12	51	41
Age of child			
0–4 years	30	68	15
5–10 years	16	54	35
11–15 years	8	31	64

1 All children where the mother is in work.
2 Percentages do not add up to 100 per cent as respondents could give more than one answer.
3 Includes nurseries/creches, nursery schools, playgroups, registered childminders, after school clubs/breakfast clubs, and holiday play schemes.
4 Provided by the main respondent's partners/ex-partners, parents/parents-in-law, other relatives and friends, and older children.

Source: Families and Children Study, Department for Work and Pensions

(29 per cent). The largest source of help for both groups was that family bought clothes for the parent/children – 16 per cent of couples and 35 per cent of lone parents received such help.

In cases where parents have difficulty in looking after their children, local authorities can take them into care. These children are usually described as being 'looked after'. In 2005, over 77,000 children were being looked after by local authorities in the UK (Table 8.18), an increase of 6 per cent since 2000. Over 60 per cent of children were cared for in foster homes and this category recorded the largest increase (10 per cent) since 2000. The next largest increase was in children cared for in children's homes (6 per cent). In Scotland, children who have committed offences or are in need of care and protection may be brought before a Children's Hearing, which can impose a supervision requirement if it thinks that compulsory measures are appropriate. Under these requirements, most children are allowed to remain at home under the supervision of a social worker. In Scotland, in 2005, around 12,000 children were being looked after either in a children's home or with parents and 3,500 were cared for in foster homes in the same year.

Children may be placed on a local authority child protection register when a social services department considers they are at continuing risk of significant harm. As at March 2005 there

were 27,900 children on child protection registers in England and Wales, with around 600 more boys than girls. Neglect was the most common reason to be placed on the register, for 45 per cent of boys and 42 per cent of girls. Emotional abuse was the second most common reason, with around one-fifth of both boys and girls on the register because of this.

Table **8.18**

Children looked after by local authorities:[1] by type of accommodation

United Kingdom   Thousands

	2000	2005
Foster placements	45.2	50.0
Children's homes[2]	7.9	8.4
With parents[2]	12.6	12.0
Placed for adoption[3]	3.4	3.5
Other accommodation	3.9	3.6
All looked after children	73.0	77.5

1 At 31 March.
2 See Appendix, Part 8: Children looked after by local authorities.
3 'Placed with prospective adopters' in Scotland. Not collected for Northern Ireland.

Source: Department for Education and Skills; Welsh Assembly Government; Scottish Executive; Department of Health, Social Services and Public Safety, Northern Ireland

Table **8.19**

Calls and letters to Childline: by type of problem/concern and sex, 2005

United Kingdom   Numbers

	Boys	Girls
Bullying	9,329	23,359
Family tensions, including divorce and separation	3,881	13,653
Physical abuse	3,722	8,791
Facts of life, including other issues around growing up	2,771	6,557
Sexual abuse	2,099	6,538
Sexuality	2,079	1,720
Health (physical and emotional)	1,732	5,332
Concern for others	1,527	8,448
Partner relationship	1,177	3,674
Run away or homeless	1,099	2,507
Problem with friends	772	4,671
Alcohol, drugs, solvent abuse and smoking	760	1,311
School problem	705	1,556
Other abuse (risk, neglect and emotional)	693	2,481
Pregnancy	384	5,459
In care	215	714
Suicide	182	857
Self-harm	115	1,907
Other[1]	1,958	4,389
Total	35,200	103,924

1 Includes a range of problems, for example; bereavement, domestic violence, offending, legal, adoption, racism, financial, cultural and religious.

Source: Childline

Voluntary organisations and charities play a role in providing help to children with problems. Childline was launched in 1986 and between 1986 and 2005 nearly 1.8 million children and young

Table **8.20**

Use of health services[1] by children: by age, 2005[2]

Great Britain   Percentages[3]

	0–4	5–15
Health visitor at the GP surgery	6	1
Practice nurse at the GP surgery	5	2
Child health or welfare clinic	5	1
None of the above	86	97

1 Services used in the 14 days prior to interview.
2 Data for 2005 includes last quarter of 2004/05 due to survey change from financial year to calendar year. See Appendix, Part 2: General Household Survey.
3 Percentages do not add up to 100 per cent as respondents could give more than one answer.

Source: General Household Survey (Longitudinal), Office for National Statistics

people were counselled and provided with confidential advice and protection. In 2005, Childline provided counselling to almost 140,000 children and young people (Table 8.19), around three-quarters of whom were girls. The most common reported problem for both girls and boys was bullying, accounting for 23 per cent of all calls. The next most common problems were family tensions, including divorce and separation, and physical abuse, at 13 per cent and 9 per cent respectively. Childline called ambulances for 28 children who telephoned while making suicide attempts, more than 1000 children were referred to social services and more than 200 children were referred to the police.

Children also make use of services available to the whole population. In 2005, 15 per cent of all children aged under 5 years in Great Britain were seen by an NHS GP in the 14 days before interview. Six per cent of all children under five saw a health visitor at the GP surgery (Table 8.20) and a further 5 per cent visited a child health or welfare clinic. Older children are less likely to make use of these services with only 1 per cent of 5 to 15-year-olds seeing a health visitor at the GP surgery or attending a child health or welfare clinic in the 14 days before interview.

Crime and justice

- The British Crime Survey (BCS) showed that there were 10.9 million crimes committed against adults living in private households in England and Wales, 8.4 million fewer crimes than in 1995. (Figure 9.1)

- Property crime accounted for the majority (73 per cent) of all offences recorded by the police in 2005/06 in England and Wales. (Table 9.2)

- The total value of all card fraud in the UK in 2005 was £439 million, a decrease of 13 per cent compared with 2004. (Page 117)

- The risk of becoming a victim of crime fell from 40 per cent of the population in 1995 to 23 per cent in 2005/06 in England and Wales, the lowest recorded level since the BCS began. (Page 119)

- In 2004, over four in ten juveniles in England and Wales re-offended within one year of their original conviction. (Page 123)

- Full-time equivalent police officer numbers in England and Wales reached record levels in 2006, with 167,170 officers on 31 March. (Table 9.21)

Chapter 9

Crime affects many people during the course of their lives. It can affect people directly through loss and suffering or it can have indirect effects such as raising fear of crime, or needing increased security measures around the home or in everyday life. Dealing with crime and its associated problems is an ever-present concern for society and the Government. There are two main sources of statistics on levels of crime: household population surveys of crime, and police recorded crime (see Measures of crime box below).

Crime levels

After a long period of annual reductions in crime, the British Crime Survey (BCS) in 2005/06 showed that the level of crime in England and Wales was stable compared with 2004/05. The 2005/06 BCS estimated that 10.9 million crimes were committed against adults living in private households, a similar number to the previous year. The number of crimes reported to the BCS rose steadily through the 1980s and into the 1990s before falling progressively back again to levels similar to the early 1980s. In 2005/06 there were 8.4 million fewer crimes than the peak of 19.4 million in 1995, representing a fall in BCS crime of 44 per cent (Figure 9.1). In 2005/06 police recorded crime showed a 1 per cent reduction from 2004/05 in the number of crimes recorded.

The Scottish Crime Survey estimated that just under 1 million crimes were committed against individuals and households in Scotland in 2003/04, a similar amount to that from the previous survey which covered 2002. The 2005 Northern Ireland Crime Survey estimated that 200,000 offences were committed against adults living in private households in Northern Ireland. This is a decrease from the 300,000 offences committed in both 2003/04 and 2001.

In 2005/06, 53 per cent of offences reported to the BCS in England and Wales involved some type of theft or attempted theft. Vehicle-related theft was the most prevalent with 1.7 million thefts in 2005/06. This represented a fall of 60 per cent in all vehicle related theft since 1995 and accounted for 16 per cent of all thefts. The second most common BCS offence group was vandalism, which accounted for one-quarter (25 per cent) of all crime in the 2005/06 survey. Vandalism offences have fallen by 19 per cent from 3.4 million to 2.7 million between the 1995 and 2005/06 BCS respectively. Violent incidents were the third most common type of BCS crime, accounting for 22 per cent of all crime in the 2005/06 survey. Between 1995 and 2005/06 the number of violent offences reported to the BCS fell by 43 per cent, from 4.3 million to 2.4 million.

The Northern Ireland Crime Survey (NICS) showed that in 2005, 36 per cent of offences in Northern Ireland involved

Figure **9.1**

British Crime Survey offences[1]

England & Wales
Millions

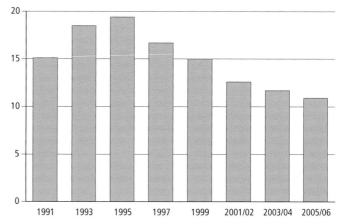

1 Until 2000, respondents were asked to recall their experience of crime in the previous calendar year. From 2001/02 the British Crime Survey (BCS) became a continuous survey and the recall period was changed to the 12 months before interview.

Source: British Crime Survey, Home Office

Measures of crime

There are two main measures of the extent of crime in the UK: surveys of the public, and the recording of crimes by the police. The British Crime Survey (BCS) interviews adults aged 16 and over who are living in households in England and Wales. The BCS, the Scottish Crime Survey (SCS) and the Northern Ireland Crime Survey (NICS), are thought to give a better measure of many types of crime than police recorded crime statistics. These surveys are able to find out about the large number of offences that are not reported to the police. They also give a more reliable picture of trends, as they are not affected by changes in levels of reporting to the police or by variations in police recording practice (see Appendix, Part 9: Types of offences in England and Wales and in Northern Ireland).

Recorded crime data collected by the police are a by-product of the administrative procedure of completing a record for crimes investigated. The National Crime Recording Standard (NCRS) was introduced in England and Wales in 2002 with the aim of taking a more victim-centred approach and providing consistency between police forces (see Appendix, Part 9: National Crime Recording Standard).

Police recorded crime and survey measured crime have different coverage. Unlike crime data recorded by the police, the surveys are restricted to crimes against adults living in private households and their property, and do not include some types of crime (for example, fraud, murder and victimless crimes such as drug use where there is not a direct victim).

See also Appendix, Part 9: Availability and comparability of data from constituent countries.

some type of theft or attempted theft. Of the theft related offences, other household theft was the most common with 33,000 thefts in 2005. As in England and Wales, the second most common NICS offence group in Northern Ireland was vandalism, which accounted for 30 per cent of all crime in the 2005 survey.

Over half of crimes reported to the BCS (58 per cent) are not reported to the police. This lack of reporting is the main reason why BCS estimates of crime are higher than the actual recorded crime figures. Victims may not report a crime for a number of reasons. These include thinking the crime was too trivial or that there was no loss. In 72 per cent of incidents reported to the BCS but not to the police, the victims believed the police would not or could not do much about them. In almost one in five cases (19 per cent) the victim felt the incident was a private matter. The proportion of crimes reported to the police varied considerably according to the type of offence. Of the comparable crimes (see Appendix, Part 9: Comparable crimes) thefts of vehicles were the most likely crimes captured in the BCS to be reported to the police in 2005/06 (94 per cent). Burglaries in which something was stolen had the second highest reporting rate (81 per cent). This is unsurprising as both these crimes need to be reported to the police if the victim is to make an insurance claim.

In 2005/06, police recorded 5.6 million crimes in England and Wales (Table 9.2). Almost three-quarters (73 per cent) of these offences were property crimes. The offence category of theft and handling stolen goods comprised 36 per cent of all recorded crime. This includes thefts of, or from, vehicles, which comprised 13 per cent of all recorded crime. Criminal damage, burglary and fraud and forgery are the other property offences. Following the introduction of the National Crime Recording Standard (NCRS) in 2002 (see Measures of crime box opposite) there was an increase in the number of minor crimes recorded (including vandalism, minor theft, petty assault, breach of the peace) which contributed to an overall increase in the number of crimes recorded that year. The introduction of the Scottish Crime Recording Standard (SCRS) in April 2004 resulted in similar increases in the number of minor crimes recorded in Scotland, but had no impact on the figures for the more serious crimes such as serious assault, sexual assault, robbery or housebreaking.

In Scotland the term 'crime' is reserved for the more serious offences (broadly equivalent to 'indictable' and 'triable-either-way' offences in England and Wales), while less serious crimes are called 'offences' (see Appendix. Part 9: Types of offences in England and Wales and Northern Ireland, and Offences and crimes). Recorded crime in Scotland decreased by 5 per cent between 2004/05 and 2005/06, when a total of 418,000 crimes

Table 9.2

Crimes recorded by the police: by type of offence,[1] 2005/06

Percentages

	England & Wales	Scotland	Northern Ireland
Theft and handling stolen goods	36	34	24
Theft of vehicles	4	3	3
Theft from vehicles	9	6	4
Criminal damage	21	31	28
Violence against the person	19	2	25
Burglary	12	7	10
Fraud and forgery	4	3	4
Drugs offences	3	11	2
Robbery	2	1	1
Sexual offences	1	1	1
Other offences[2]	1	10	3
All notifiable offences (=100%) (thousands)	5,557	418	123

1 See Appendix, Part 9: Types of offences in England and Wales, and in Northern Ireland; and Offences and crimes.
2 Northern Ireland includes 'offences against the state'. Scotland excludes 'offending while on bail'.

Source: Home Office; Scottish Executive; Police Service of Northern Ireland

were recorded by the police. Theft and handling stolen goods comprised 34 per cent of recorded crime in Scotland, criminal damage 31 per cent, and drugs offences 11 per cent (Table 9.2).

The definition of crimes in Northern Ireland are broadly comparable with those used in England and Wales. Crime recorded by the police in Northern Ireland increased by 4 per cent from 2004/05 to 2005/06, to 123,000 incidents. Criminal damage comprised over one-third (35 per cent) of recorded crime in Northern Ireland, and violence against the person accounted for 31 per cent, increasing from 27 per cent and 25 per cent respectively from 2004/05. These crimes made up a greater proportion of all recorded crime in Northern Ireland than for similar crime types in England and Wales. Theft and handling stolen goods comprised 21 per cent of recorded crime in Northern Ireland, a smaller proportion than in England and Wales (Table 9.2).

Recorded crime data for England and Wales and for Northern Ireland indicate that crime is not evenly distributed across the country. In England and Wales in 2005/06 the number of crimes recorded ranged from 60 offences per 1,000 population in Dyfed Powys, to between 130 and 134 offences per 1,000 in Nottinghamshire; Humberside, Cleveland and the Metropolitan Police area in London. It should be noted that crime rates

Map **9.3**

Recorded crime: by police force area,[1,2] 2005/06

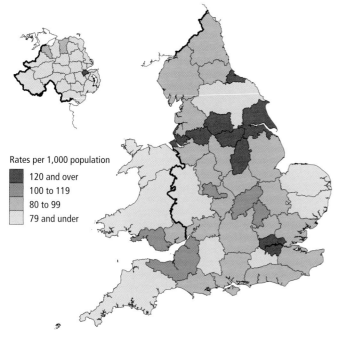

Rates per 1,000 population

- 120 and over
- 100 to 119
- 80 to 99
- 79 and under

1 In Northern Ireland, data are shown for Police District Command Units (PDCUs). For Belfast, the combined total for the four PDCUs is shown, as separate population figures are not available.
2 Figures for London do not include City of London as the crime rate for this area is misleading due to the high day time population but very low resident population.

Source: Home Office; Police Service of Northern Ireland

recorded in London and larger cities will be effected by the influx of commuters and tourism. In Northern Ireland in 2005/06 the number of crimes recorded ranged from 38 offences per 1,000 population in Ballymoney (rural area), to 125 per 1,000 in Belfast (Map 9.3).

Both the BCS and police statistics suggest that crime is lower in rural areas than in urban areas (see Appendix: Part 9, Urban and Rural). The 2005/06 BCS found that households in rural areas were at a lower risk of vehicle theft than those in urban areas (4 per cent of rural households were victims of vehicle theft compared with 8 per cent of urban households). People living in households in urban areas in England and Wales were also more likely than those in rural areas to have been a victim of violent crime in the previous year, at 4 per cent and 2 per cent respectively. A similar pattern was seen for burglary, with 3 per cent of households in urban areas compared with 2 per cent of households in rural areas, having been victims in the previous year.

The likelihood of being a victim of crime also varies by the level of deprivation in the area. Generally people living in deprived areas are more likely to be a victim of crime than those in other areas (see Appendix, Part 9: Indices of Deprivation). The 2005/06 BCS found that households in employment-deprived areas in England were at a higher risk of vehicle crime than those

households in areas with higher levels of employment. In the area with the lowest level of employment in England and Wales, 12 per cent of households had been a victim of at least one vehicle theft in 2005/06 compared with 7 per cent of households in the area with the highest level of employment. Rates of burglary and violent crime were also higher in employment-deprived areas.

Offences

According to the BCS, offences relating to household and personal crime in England and Wales remain at statistically significantly lower levels compared with their highpoint in 1995 (Table 9.4). Since 1995 the number of vehicle thefts has fallen by 60 per cent and instances of domestic burglary have fallen by 59 per cent. Other household theft, which includes thefts and attempted thefts from domestic garages, outhouses and sheds, has fallen by 49 per cent since 1995. The BCS shows that common assault has decreased by almost half (49 per cent) and that violent crime has fallen by 43 per cent over the same period.

The BCS and police recorded crime have both shown overall falls in the number of burglary offences in England and Wales since the peaks in the early to mid-1990s. Between 2003/04 and 2004/05 the number of domestic burglaries as measured by the BCS remained stable and showed further signs of decline between 2004/05 and 2005/06. Since 1995 the number of domestic burglaries reported to the BCS has decreased by 59 per cent from 1.8 million to 733,000, in 2005/06. In 2005/06, 60 per cent (440,000) of domestic burglaries involved entry into the house (burglary includes entry and attempted entry, with or without loss) (Table 9.5). Burglaries were more likely to result in no loss than in anything being taken and this finding has been broadly consistent over time in the BCS. According to the 2005/06 BCS, 57 per cent of burglaries resulted in nothing being taken.

The risk of becoming a victim of burglary, measured as the percentage of households who were victims of burglary at least once in the 12 months before interview, varied by the characteristics of the household. Households with no home security measures in place were much more likely to be victims of burglary; 19 per cent of these households interviewed during 2005/06 had been victims of one or more burglaries in the past year compared with 2 per cent of households with security measures such as burglar alarms, security lights or window bars. Households where the reference person (see Reference person box on page 16) was aged 16 to 24 were more likely to have been burgled (6 per cent) than those where the reference person was older. For households where the reference person was aged between 45 and 64, the proportion of those burgled was 2 per cent. Single-parent households

Table **9.4**

Incidents of crime: by type of offence[1]

England & Wales

Millions

	1981	1991	1995	2001/02	2003/04	2005/06
Vandalism	2.7	2.8	3.4	2.6	2.5	2.7
All vehicle thefts	1.8	3.8	4.4	2.5	2.1	1.7
Minor injuries	1.4	1.8	2.9	1.7	1.7	1.5
Other household theft[2]	1.5	1.9	2.3	1.4	1.3	1.2
Other thefts of personal property	1.6	1.7	2.1	1.4	1.3	1.2
Burglary	0.7	1.4	1.8	1.0	0.9	0.7
Theft from the person	0.4	0.4	0.7	0.6	0.6	0.6
Wounding	0.5	0.6	0.9	0.6	0.7	0.5
Bicycle theft	0.2	0.6	0.7	0.4	0.4	0.4
Robbery	0.2	0.2	0.3	0.4	0.3	0.3
All violence reported to BCS	2.2	2.6	4.3	2.8	2.7	2.4
All household crime	6.9	10.4	12.4	7.9	7.2	6.8
All personal crime	4.1	4.7	6.9	4.7	4.5	4.1
All crimes reported to BCS	11.0	15.1	19.4	12.6	11.7	10.9

1 Until 2000, respondents were asked to recall their experience of crime in the previous calendar year. From 2001/02 the British Crime Survey (BCS) became a continuous survey and the recall period was changed to the 12 months before interview.
2 Includes thefts and attempted thefts from domestic garages, outhouses and sheds, not directly linked to the dwelling, as well as thefts from both inside and outside a dwelling.

Source: British Crime Survey, Home Office

were at a high risk of burglary, compared with other family types, as were households with a low income compared with households with a higher income. This is consistent with crime levels being higher in the most deprived areas of the country. The risk of burglary was also higher for those who had moved recently (within the 12 months before the survey) than for those who had lived at the address for a longer period of time.

In 2005/06, 233,000 fraud and forgery offences were recorded by the police, a decrease of 17 per cent compared with 2004/05. Of these, 87,900 were cheque and credit card frauds, a 28 per cent decrease compared with 2004/05. However, cheque and credit card frauds are often not reported to the police, either as the victims are unaware they are being deceived, or because the card holders are more likely to inform their bank or card company than the police. The banking and credit card industry records a considerable amount of information on fraudulent misuse of its services, which may provide a better indication of the extent and trends in fraud. The data collected by the Association for Payment and Clearing Services (APACS), the UK payments association, put the total value of all card fraud at £439 million in 2005, a decrease of 13 per cent compared with 2004.

The number of defendants found guilty of fraud-related offences has fallen between 1999 and 2005. Around 14,600

Table **9.5**

Domestic burglary:[1,2] by type

England & Wales

Thousands

	Burglary		Burglary		All burglary
	With entry	No entry	With loss	No loss	
1981	474	276	373	376	749
1991	869	511	712	668	1,380
1995	998	772	791	979	1,770
1997	852	768	651	970	1,621
1999	767	523	551	739	1,290
2001/02	552	416	396	573	969
2002/03	561	412	407	566	973
2003/04	533	410	417	526	943
2004/05	469	287	327	429	756
2005/06	440	293	315	418	733

1 Burglary with no entry and with entry add up to all burglary. Burglary with no loss and with loss also add up to all burglary.
2 Until 2000, respondents were asked to recall their experience of crime in the previous calendar year. From 2001/02 the British Crime Survey (BCS) became a continuous survey and the recall period was changed to the 12 months before interview.

Source: British Crime Survey, Home Office

Table **9.6**

Defendants found guilty of indictable fraud offences

England & Wales

Numbers

	1998	1999	2000	2001	2002	2003	2004	2005
Obtaining property by deception	11,440	11,480	10,540	9,440	9,350	8,460	7,520	6,470
Dishonest representation for obtaining benefit	240	710	1,350	1,950	1,990	1,840	2,460	3,450
Making off without payment	1,250	1,440	1,410	1,320	1,300	1,810	1,690	1,790
Obtaining services by deception	980	1,030	880	880	830	800	750	650
False accounting	1,690	1,620	1,160	870	750	650	730	630
Conspiracy to defraud	470	420	430	450	410	450	520	500
Other offences	1,130	1,100	1,100	1,000	940	1,030	1,130	1,110
All offences	17,200	17,800	16,870	15,910	15,570	15,040	14,800	14,600

Source: Office for Criminal Justice Reform

defendants were found guilty of indictable fraud offences in England and Wales in 2005, a fall of 18 per cent compared with the peak of around 17,800 defendants in 1999 (Table 9.6). Obtaining property by deception was the most common type of fraud offence in 2005, committed by 44 per cent of offenders found guilty of indictable fraud. The number of people found guilty of this offence has fallen by 44 per cent since 1999. The number of offences for dishonest representation for obtaining benefit is nearly five times higher than it was in 1999 and fourteen times higher than it was in 1998, and was the second most commonly prosecuted fraud offence in 2005. Almost one-quarter (24 per cent) of all defendants found guilty of an indictable fraud offence in 2005 were guilty of dishonest representation for obtaining benefit, increasing from 4 per cent of all defendants in 1999 and 8 per cent in 2000. This was the largest increase over a single year over the whole time period for any category of indictable fraud offence.

Violent crime as measured by the BCS has fallen by 43 per cent since a peak in 1995. The BCS estimated that there were 2.4 million violent incidents against adults in England and Wales in 2005/06. The number of violent crimes experienced by adults remained stable between 2004/05 and 2005/06 BCS interviews. Violent crime recorded by the police increased by 2 per cent over the same period. Almost half (49 per cent) of all violent incidents reported to the BCS did not result in injury to the victim. There were 765 homicides in 2005/06, 12 per cent less than in 2004/05. This figure includes 52 homicide victims of the 7 July 2005 suicide bombings in London.

In England and Wales, between 2004/05 and 2005/06 the number of offences involving firearms other than air weapons such as air guns, air rifles and air pistols recorded by the police remained stable. Firearms are taken to be involved in an incident if they are fired, used as a blunt instrument against a person, or

used in a threat. Most offences involving firearms other than air weapons are violent crimes. Over half of all crimes involving firearms other than air weapons (55 per cent) occurred in the areas covered by the Greater Manchester, West Midland and Metropolitan police forces. Between 1998/99 and 2001/02 there was a substantial increase in the number of crimes reported to the police where a firearm had been used (Figure 9.7). Between 2003/04 and 2004/05 the number of firearm offences involving air weapons decreased from 13,800 to 11,800. Nevertheless the number of offences where an air weapon had been used, continued to account for the highest proportion of all firearm offences.

Figure **9.7**

Crimes[1] reported to the police in which a firearm had been used

England & Wales

Thousands

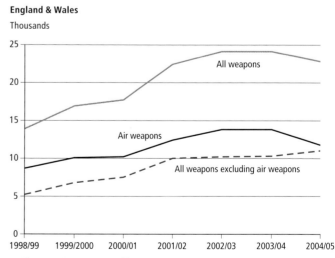

1 Changes in counting offences were made in April 1998 and the National Crime Recording Standard was implemented in April 2002. See Appendix, Part 9: National Crime Recording Standard.

Source: Home Office

In 2005/06 there were 46 homicides involving firearms in England and Wales, 40 per cent less than in 2004/05. Although a provisional figure, this is the lowest recorded number of homicides involving firearms since the late 1980s. In 2005/06, 3 per cent of more serious incidents of violence against the person (other than homicide) involved firearms. In 2005/06, 474 firearm offences resulted in serious injury, a 16 per cent increase from 2004/05. Over the same period, the number of firearm robberies increased by 10 per cent and the number of offences involving handguns and shotguns both increased by 7 per cent but the number of imitation weapon offences fell by 4 per cent. In England and Wales in March 2005 there were 126,400 firearm certificates and 572,400 shotgun certificates on issue. A total of 358,400 firearms and 1,384,000 shotguns were covered by the certificates issued.

It is not possible to identify offences involving the use of weapons other than firearms, using crime statistics recorded by the police (apart from homicide statistics). The 2005/06 BCS estimated that the most common type of weapons used in England and Wales were knives and hitting implements such as sticks and clubs, both used in 7 per cent of all incidents of violence reported to the BCS.

Glass bottles were used in 4 per cent of all incidents of violence reported to the BCS. A National Knife Amnesty, which ran from 24 May to 30 June 2006, encouraged people to dispose of knives and other weapons in secure bins at police stations across the UK. The public were advised that nobody who voluntarily handed over a weapon would be prosecuted. Nearly 90,000 knives were handed over in England and Wales during the programme, according to figures compiled by police forces.

Victims

Following a sharp rise between 1981 and the mid-1990s, the risk of being a victim of crime fell from 40 per cent of the population in 1995 to 23 per cent in 2005/06. This represents just over 6 million fewer victims in 2005/06 than in 1995 and is the lowest recorded level since the BCS began in 1981.

The 2005/06 BCS showed that women were almost three times as likely as men to be very worried about being a victim of violence (24 per cent compared with 9 per cent), however, there was no real difference in the proportions of men and women who were victims of violent crime (4 per cent compared with 3 per cent) (Table 9.8). Young men aged 16 to 24 were most at risk; 13 per cent had experienced a violent crime in the

Table **9.8**

Victims of violent crime:[1] by sex and age, 2005/06

England & Wales
Percentages

	Domestic	Mugging	Stranger	Acquaintance[2]	All violence
Males					
16–24	0.3	3.0	6.5	4.2	12.6
25–34	0.2	1.1	2.9	1.5	5.5
35–44	0.3	0.7	1.8	1.3	3.9
45–54	0.3	0.4	1.3	1.2	3.1
55–64	-	0.2	0.6	0.3	1.1
65–74	-	0.2	0.2	0.2	0.5
75 and over	-	0.2	0.1	-	0.3
All aged 16 and over	0.2	0.9	2.1	1.4	4.3
Females					
16–24	1.4	2.1	2.0	2.3	7.0
25–34	0.6	0.4	1.3	0.5	2.8
35–44	1.1	0.4	0.6	1.2	3.0
45–54	0.6	0.2	0.5	0.9	2.2
55–64	0.2	0.3	0.2	0.3	1.0
65–74	-	0.2	0.2	0.1	0.5
75 and over	-	0.3	-	-	0.4
All aged 16 and over	0.6	0.5	0.7	0.8	2.5

1 Victimised once or more in the previous 12 months.
2 Assaults in which the victim knew one or more of the offenders at least by sight.

Source: British Crime Survey, Home Office

previous 12 months according to the 2005/06 BCS, compared with 7 per cent of young women in the same age group. The proportions of victims also varied by type of crime. Young men aged 16 to 24 were most likely to be a victim of violence committed by strangers (6.5 per cent), whereas young women in the same age group were more likely to be a victim of violence committed by an acquaintance (2.3 per cent). Older people were less likely than younger people to be a victim of a violent crime; less than 1 per cent of those aged 65 and over reported that they had been victims of violent crime in the previous 12 months.

The nature of violence can vary considerably. Violent crime as measured by the BCS can be divided into a typology based on the relationship between the victim and the offender, and includes domestic violence, mugging, acquaintance violence and stranger violence. Domestic violence includes all violent incidents (except mugging), which involves partners, ex-partners or other relatives. Mugging includes robbery, attempted robbery, and snatch theft. Stranger violence includes common assaults and woundings in which the victim did not know any of the offenders in any way. Acquaintance violence includes common assaults and woundings in which the victim knew one or more of the offenders, at least by sight. Using this typology, over one-third (36 per cent) of all incidents of violent crime in the 2005/06 BCS were categorised as stranger violence. A further one-third (34 per cent) were accounted for by acquaintance violence, around one-sixth of incidents were muggings (16 per cent) and the remainder were incidences of domestic violence (15 per cent). Men were more likely than women to experience violence committed by strangers (45 per cent compared with 21 per cent) and young men aged 16 to 24 were more likely to be victims of violence committed by strangers, than men aged over 24 (7 per cent compared to 3 per cent or less for all other age groups). In contrast, according to the BCS there are six times as many incidents of domestic violence among women than men. Of women who were victims of violent crime, 31 per cent were victims of domestic violence (285,000) in 2005/06, compared with 5 per cent of men (72,000).

Almost half of all violent incidents reported to the BCS in 2005/06 involved no injury (49 per cent). Of those victims of violent incidents who were injured, the most common injury type was minor bruising or a black eye (34 per cent of women and 28 per cent of men). These were the most common injuries across the different categories of violent crime. For example, victims of violence by strangers were around twice as likely to suffer from minor bruising or a black eye (27 per cent of male victims and 29 per cent of female victims) as they were to suffer from severe bruising (16 per cent of male victims and 12 per cent of female victims). Broken bones, or concussion/loss of consciousness were the least common injuries following a violent crime, both with less than 4 per cent of male victims and 3 per cent of female victims suffering these injuries. Incidents of wounding during violent incidents have been generally decreasing over the last decade, with a statistically significant fall of 40 per cent since 1995. There were 547,000 incidents of wounding in this circumstance based on the 2005/06 BCS, compared with 914,000 in 1995.

Table 9.9

Anti-social behaviour indicators[1]

England & Wales   Percentages

	1992	1996	2000	2001/02	2002/03	2003/04	2004/05	2005/06
High level of perceived anti-social behaviour[2,3]	-	-	-	19	21	16	17	17
Abandoned or burnt-out cars[3]	-	-	14	20	25	15	12	10
Noisy neighbours or loud parties	8	8	9	10	10	9	9	10
People being drunk or rowdy in public places	-	-	-	2	23	19	22	24
People using or dealing drugs	14	21	33	31	32	25	26	27
Teenagers hanging around on the streets	20	24	32	32	33	27	31	32
Rubbish or litter lying around	30	26	30	32	33	29	30	30
Vandalism, graffiti and other deliberate damage to property	26	24	32	34	35	28	28	29
Total(=100%)[4] (thousands)	10.1	8.0	9.7	32.8	36.5	37.9	45.1	47.7

1 People saying anti-social behaviour is a 'very/fairly big problem' in their area. See Appendix, Part 9: Anti-social behaviour indicators.
2 This measure is derived from responses to the seven individual anti-social behaviour strands reported in the table.
3 Question only asked of one-quarter of the sample in 2001/02 and 2002/03.
4 Percentages do not add up to 100 per cent as respondents could give more than one answer.

Source: British Crime Survey, Home Office

The *Crime and Disorder Act (1998)* defined anti-social behaviour as 'acting in a manner that caused or was likely to cause harassment, alarm or distress to one or more persons not of the same household (as the defendant)'. Overall perceptions of anti-social behaviour remained unchanged between the 2004/05 and 2005/06 BCS, with one in six people (17 per cent) perceiving a high level of disorder in their local area.

Almost one-third of people believed that teenagers and young people hanging around on the streets (32 per cent), and rubbish or litter (30 per cent) were anti-social behaviour problems in their area, according to the 2005/06 BCS. A further three in ten perceived vandalism and graffiti (29 per cent) to be a problem and one-quarter (27 per cent) perceived illicit drug use or dealing to be a problem in their area (Table 9.9). The 2005 Northern Ireland Crime Survey found a similar pattern, with 29 per cent of people believing teenagers hanging around on the streets were an anti-social behavioural problem in their area and 28 per cent of people believing rubbish or litter were problems. Just over one-quarter (26 per cent) perceived vandalism and graffiti to be a problem and 28 per cent thought illicit drug use or dealing were problems in their area.

The proportion of people saying each of these behaviours were a very or fairly big problem in their area generally increased across all the behaviour indicators between 1992 and 2002/03 in England and Wales. The proportions fell for most indicators in 2003/04. Between 2003/04 and 2005/06 the percentage of people who perceived teenagers hanging around to be a problem, increased from 27 to 32 per cent, while those who perceived people behaving in an anti-social way by being drunk or rowdy, increased from 19 per cent to 24 per cent. Some 27 per cent of people believed illicit drug use or dealing was a problem in 2005/06, almost double the proportion in 1992 (14 per cent). In the same time period, there was an increase in the proportion of people who believed teenagers hanging around was a problem, from 20 per cent in 1992 to 32 per cent in 2005/06.

People's perceptions of anti-social behaviour vary by socio-demographic and socio-economic characteristics. The proportion who perceived high levels of anti-social behaviour in their area in 2005/06, decreased with age for both men and women, from 21 per cent of young men aged 16 to 24, to 6 per cent of men aged 75 and over; and from 28 per cent of young women aged 16 to 24, to 4 per cent of women aged 75 and over. People from a non-White background were more likely than those from a White background to perceive high levels of anti-social behaviour in their area (26 per cent and 16 per cent respectively). Unemployed or economically inactive people of working age (see Glossary on page 43) were more likely than those in employment to perceive high levels of anti-social behaviour in their area (24 per cent and 18 per cent respectively).

Offenders

In 2005, 1.8 million offenders were found guilty of, or cautioned for, indictable and summary offences in England and Wales, (see Appendix, Part 9: Types of offences in England and Wales) 1 per cent less than in 2004. Most of the offenders were male (79 per cent), of whom around 12 per cent were aged 17 and under.

Of nearly half a million people found guilty of, or cautioned for, an indictable offence in England and Wales in 2005, four-fifths were males. According to the cautions and court proceedings data compiled by the Office for Criminal Justice Reform, the number of young offenders as a proportion of the population, is highest for males between the ages of 10 and 17. In 2005 in England and Wales, 6 per cent of all 17-year-old males were found guilty of, or cautioned for, indictable offences, the highest rate for any age group and four times the corresponding rate for females (Figure 9.10). As young men and women entered their 20s, the proportion of offenders started to decline. Less than 1 per cent of men in each age group over the age of 43, and of women over the age of 19 were found guilty of, or cautioned for, an indictable offence.

Theft and handling stolen goods was the most common offence category committed by both male and female offenders in

Figure **9.10**

Offenders[1] as a percentage of the population: by sex and age,[2] 2005

England & Wales
Percentages

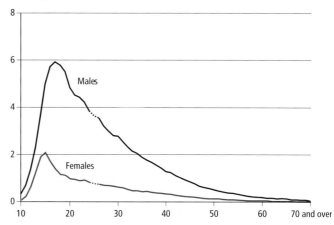

1 People found guilty of, or cautioned for, indictable offences.
2 Age 25 is plotted as the mid-point between ages 24 and 26, as it is used for offenders who did not give an age.

Source: Office for Criminal Justice Reform

121

Figure **9.11**

Offenders found guilty of, or cautioned for, indictable offences:[1] by sex and type of offence, 2005

England & Wales
Thousands

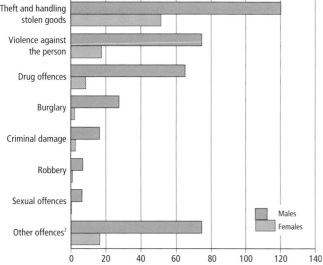

1 See Appendix, Part 9: Types of offences in England and Wales, and Offenders cautioned for burglary.
2 Includes fraud and forgery and indictable motoring offences.

Source: Office for Criminal Justice Reform

England and Wales in 2005. Although 70 per cent of these offences were committed by males, just over half (52 per cent) of female offenders were found guilty of, or cautioned for, theft-related offences, compared with almost one-third (31 per cent) of male offenders (Figure 9.11). Between 10 and 20 per cent of offenders found guilty of, or cautioned for, all other indictable offences were female, apart from burglary and sexual offences, with 7 per cent and 2 per cent of females respectively.

The 2005/06 BCS found that victims of violent offences believed the offender or offenders to be under the influence of alcohol in 44 per cent of incidents (Table 9.12). The estimated number of alcohol-related violent incidents in 2005/06 was just over 1 million. The offender was judged by the victim to be under the influence of alcohol in 57 per cent of all violent incidents causing wounding, and in 54 per cent of all violence committed by strangers. Almost half of the offenders involved in incidents of domestic violence were thought to be under the influence of alcohol, compared with 21 per cent of offenders involved in muggings.

In 23 per cent of violent incidents in 2005/06, the victim believed the offender to be under the influence of drugs. This was up from 18 per cent from the previous year's survey. The offender was believed to be under the influence of drugs in the majority of incidents of violence committed by an acquaintance (30 per cent), robbery (28 per cent) and in almost one-quarter of muggings (24 per cent). The offender was judged to be under the influence of drugs in one in five incidents of violence committed by strangers and in one in eight incidents of domestic violence. One-quarter of victims of violence stated that they did not know whether the offender was under the influence of drugs.

A relatively small number of offenders are responsible for a large number of offences. Two-thirds (66 per cent) of adults released from prison in England and Wales in the first quarter of 2003 reoffended within two years (by the first quarter of 2005) and were subsequently reconvicted in court. Almost nine in ten men and over eight in ten women previously convicted of theft, re-offended (in any offence) within two years of discharge from prison in the first quarter of 2003, and almost eight in ten men

Table **9.12**

Offenders[1] perceived to be under the influence of drink or drugs in violent incidents, 2005/06

England & Wales
Percentages

	Under the influence of drink				Under the influence of drugs		
	Yes	No	Don't know		Yes	No	Don't know
Domestic	46	53	1		12	83	6
Mugging	21	59	20		24	44	32
Stranger	54	34	12		20	44	37
Acquaintance	44	53	3		30	51	19
Wounding	57	36	8		24	47	29
Robbery	24	57	19		28	39	33
Common Assault	45	49	6		22	57	22
All violence	44	47	8		23	53	25

1 Not asked if offender identified was of school age.

Source: British Crime Survey, Home Office

convicted for domestic burglary re-offended within two years. Around half of men convicted were re-offenders for violence, and nearly one in three men convicted were reconvicted for sexual offences within two years of release.

In 2004 the proportion of those re-offending within one year of their original offence was 41 per cent for juveniles (those aged 10 to 17) in England and Wales, a fall of 2 percentage points compared with 2000. However, unlike adult reoffending data, just over half of juveniles receive pre-court disposals such as cautions, reprimands and final warnings, so convictions alone would undercount their offending and reoffending. Therefore, juvenile re-offending information includes those given pre-court disposals. Almost six in ten juveniles involved in a theft from vehicle offence re-offended by the first quarter of 2005, within one year of their original pre-court disposal or conviction for the same offence. This compares with just over five in ten who re-offended within one year of their original pre-court disposal or conviction in the first quarter of 2000 (Table 9.13).

Table **9.13**

Juvenile reconviction[1] within one year: by original offence

England & Wales		Percentages
	2000	2004
Violence	37	38
Robbery	52	49
Public order or riot	47	44
Sexual	38	29
Domestic burglary	58	54
Other burglary	47	46
Theft	40	34
Handling stolen goods	47	47
Fraud and forgery	43	37
Absconding or bail offences	66	70
Taking and driving away a vehicle and related offences	54	52
Theft from vehicles	52	57
Other motoring offences	64	62
Drink driving offences	40	44
Criminal or malicious damage	41	42
Drug possession/small-scale supply	40	37

Note: Shaded cells indicate the figures are unreliable due to small number of offenders and any analysis using these figures may be invalid. Any use of these shaded figures must be accompanied by this disclaimer.
1 Juvenile offenders aged 10 to 17 who received pre-court disposals, non-custodial court disposals or were released from custody in the first quarter of 2000 or 2004, and who reoffended during a one year follow-up period and subsequently received a pre-court disposal or were convicted in court.

Source: Home Office

Around half of juveniles involved in domestic burglary, robbery or handling stolen goods re-offended within one year after their original conviction in 2004. Almost two in five juveniles who received pre-court disposals, non-custodial court disposals (such as probation orders, community service and fines), or were released from custody in 2004 for drugs possession or small-scale supply, re-offended within the following year.

The Offending, Crime and Justice Survey 2005 showed that one-quarter (25 per cent) of children and young people aged between 10 and 25 in England and Wales said they had committed at least one core offence in the 12 months before interview (see Appendix, Part 9: Crime and Justice Survey core offences). The most common offence categories were assault (committed by 16 per cent of young people aged between 10 and 25) and other thefts (committed by 11 per cent). Criminal damage, drug selling offences and vehicle related thefts were less commonly committed (4 per cent, 4 per cent and 2 per cent respectively).

Police and courts action

Under the National Crime Recording Standard counting rules (see Appendix, Part 9: National Crime Recording Standard), a crime is defined as 'detected' if a suspect has been identified and interviewed and there is sufficient evidence to bring a charge. There does not have to be a prosecution; for example, the offender may accept a caution or ask for the crime to be taken into consideration by a court, or the victim may not wish to give evidence.

Of the 1.5 million total crimes detected in England and Wales in 2005/06, there were just over 1.3 million crimes subject to sanction detections. Sanction detections include charges, summonses, cautions, offences taken into consideration, penalty notices for disorder (PNDs) or formal warnings (FWs) for cannabis possession. A little under 200,000 crimes were detected through other methods (non-sanction detections where the offence is counted as detected but no further action is taken). Detections are counted on the basis of crimes rather than offenders. A robbery, for example, is one detection even if it involved ten offenders. Care must therefore be taken when comparing detection rates with conviction data. Cautions accounted for just over one-fifth (21 per cent) of all detections, and 7 per cent of detected offences resulted from the issuing of a penalty notice for disorder. Formal warnings for cannabis possession accounted for 4 per cent of all detections. Offences detected through a charge or summons accounted for almost half (48 per cent) of all detections.

In England and Wales the overall crime detection rate was 27 per cent in 2005/06. Detection rates vary according to the type of offence group. Drug offences were the most likely

Table **9.14**

Recorded crimes detected by the police: by type of offence,[1] 2005/06[2]

Percentages

	England & Wales	Scotland	Northern Ireland
Drug offences	95	98	75
Violence against the person	54	67	57
Sexual offences	35	74	43
Rape (including attempted)	28	72	46
Fraud and forgery	29	76	34
Robbery	18	37	16
Theft and handling stolen goods	18	35	20
Theft of vehicles	15	37	20
Theft from vehicles	9	15	6
Criminal damage	15	23	15
Burglary	14	26	13
Other crimes[3]	71	95	66
All recorded crime detected	27	46	31

1 See Appendix, Part 9: Types of offences in England and Wales, and in Northern Ireland, and Offences and crimes.
2 Some offences cleared up/detected may have been initially recorded in an earlier year.
3 The Northern Ireland figure includes 'offences against the state'.

Source: Home Office; Scottish Executive; Police Service of Northern Ireland

offence group to be detected in 2005/06 in England and Wales (95 per cent) and burglary was the least likely (14 per cent) (Table 9.14). The overall detection rate in Northern Ireland in 2005/06 was 31 per cent.

In Scotland detection rates are known as clear-up rates. The clear-up rates have been increasing steadily since the early 1980s, from 30 per cent in 1982 to 46 per cent in 2005/06, with drug offences the most likely to be detected. Fraud and forgery also had a high clear-up rate, with three-quarters of offences being detected. Even with the introduction of the new crime recording standards in Scotland, and England and Wales care should be taken when making comparisons of detection rates in Great Britain because of the different legal systems and crime recording practices which exist across the constituent countries.

The *Police and Criminal Evidence Act (PACE)*, which was implemented in January 1986, gave the police certain powers covering stop and searches of people or vehicles, road checks, detention of people, and intimate searches of people. Stop and searches in England and Wales under Section 1 of PACE rose quickly from 118,000 in 1987 to a peak of nearly 1.1 million in 1998/99. In 2004/05 there were 852,000 stop and searches of people and vehicles; this was 102,000 more stop and searches than in the previous year. Looking for stolen property was the most common reason for a stop and search throughout the 1990s. From 2002/03 looking for illicit drugs became the most common reason, with 363,000 stopped for this reason, falling to 346,000 in 2004/05.

Three-quarters of people who were stopped and searched in 2004/05 in England and Wales were White (Table 9.15). In 2004/05 the main reason for stopping and searching across all ethnic groups was illicit drugs, followed by stolen property. Until 2003/04, White people were more likely to have been searched for stolen property than for illicit drugs. In 2004/05, over one-fifth of people searched for firearms and just under

Table **9.15**

Ethnic[1] composition of stop and searches, 2004/05

England & Wales

Percentages

	Drugs	Stolen property	Going equipped[2]	Offensive weapons	Firearms	Criminal damage	Other reasons	Total
White	69	79	83	67	67	93	83	75
Black	18	12	9	19	22	2	6	14
Asian	10	5	4	10	8	2	4	7
Other	1	2	1	2	1	1	1	2
Not recorded	2	3	2	2	3	2	6	3
Total (=100%) (thousands)	342.0	234.6	106.9	74.8	12.2	11.7	57.8	840.0

1 Ethnicity of the person stopped and searched as perceived by the police officer concerned.
2 Persons found in possession of an article capable of being used in connection with a crime.

Source: Home Office

one-fifth of people searched for offensive weapons were Black. Overall, Black people accounted for 14 per cent of those stopped and searched in 2004/05.

Anti-social Behaviour Orders (ASBOs) were introduced in England and Wales under the *Crime and Disorder Act 1998* and have been available since April 1999. ASBOs are civil orders that impose restrictions on the behaviour of individuals who have behaved in an anti-social way, to protect communities from often longstanding and intimidating activity. They can be made against anyone aged ten and over.

The number of ASBOs issued in England and Wales has increased from 135 in the period June to December 2000 to 7,360 in September 2005, most notably from 2002 onwards. This increase was in line with the introduction of the *Anti-social Behaviour Act* that came into effect in 2003. As well as strengthening the ASBO by expanding the number of categories for which ASBOs can be awarded, enhancing their legal status, and banning spray paint sales to people under the age of 16, the Act gave local councils the power to order the removal of graffiti from private property. It also covers truancy, people making false reports of emergency, misuse of fireworks, public drunkenness and gang activity.

The Crown Prosecution Service (CPS) is the government agency that handles the bulk of prosecutions (charging individuals with committing a crime) in England and Wales. The CPS prosecutes most of its cases in the Crown Court although it can also

prosecute in magistrates' courts. Magistrates' courts deal with criminal and some civil cases and usually only deal with cases that arise in their own area. The Crown Court deals with serious criminal offences that are tried by judge and jury, appeals from the magistrates' courts, and convictions in the magistrates' courts that are referred to the Crown Court for sentencing. The Crown Court has the power to impose more severe sentences than the magistrates' courts.

Almost 1.9 million defendant cases were seen in magistrates' courts by the CPS in 2005. The majority of all cases at the magistrates' courts resulted in a conviction (75 per cent), while 18 per cent of cases were terminated early without trial, 4 per cent were committed to the Crown Court for trial and 2 per cent resulted in an acquittal (includes dismissal or discharge). The CPS dealt with 76,000 defendant cases in the Crown Court in 2004, just over three-quarters (76 per cent) of which resulted in a conviction.

When an offender has been found guilty, the court imposes a sentence. Sentences in England, Wales and Northern Ireland can include immediate custody, a community sentence, a fine or, if the court considers that no punishment is necessary, a discharge. In 2005, 306,600 people were sentenced for indictable offences in England and Wales (Table 9.16). The form of sentence varied according to the type of offence committed. In 2005 a community sentence was the most common type of sentence; almost half of those sentenced for burglary, violence

Table **9.16**

Offenders sentenced for indictable offences: by type of offence[1] and type of sentence,[2] 2005

England & Wales

Percentages

	Discharge	Fine	Community sentence	Fully suspended sentence	Immediate custody	Other	All sentenced (=100%) (thousands)
Theft and handling stolen goods	21	16	40	1	20	3	103.3
Drug offences	17	35	25	1	20	2	38.9
Violence against the person	8	7	47	3	32	3	40.8
Burglary	4	2	49	2	42	2	22.7
Fraud and forgery	16	14	40	3	25	2	18.3
Criminal damage	21	12	49	1	11	5	11.5
Motoring	3	30	33	3	30	1	6.7
Robbery	-	-	36	1	62	1	7.1
Sexual offences	4	4	30	3	57	2	4.7
Other offences	8	37	23	1	20	11	52.6
All indictable offences	14	19	36	2	25	4	306.6

1 See Appendix, Part 9: Types of offences in England and Wales.
2 See Appendix, Part 9: Sentences and orders.

Source: Home Office

against the person or criminal damage were given a community sentence. Those sentenced for drug offences were the most likely to be fined, with 36 per cent receiving this form of sentence.

The proportion of people in England and Wales in the BCS who thought that sentencing was too lenient fell from just over one-half in 1996 to just under one-third in 2002/03 (32 per cent) and then increased to 37 per cent in 2005/06. There was relatively little change in the proportion who thought that sentencing by the courts was about right, at around one in five people (19 per cent in 1996 and 21 per cent in 2005/06).

In England and Wales a formal caution may be given by a senior police officer when an offender has admitted his or her guilt, there is sufficient evidence for a conviction, and it is not in the public interest to institute criminal proceedings. Cautions are more severe than a reprimand and details are put on the individual's record. In 2005, 182,900 cautions for indictable offences in England and Wales were given, an increase of 26,600 (17 per cent) on 2004. The number of cautions has been rising since 2001 following a fall in the 1990s. The offence category receiving the highest number of cautions in 2005 was theft and handling stolen goods. In 2004 a higher number of cautions were received for violence against the person than for drug offences for the first time since the 1980s. This pattern continued into 2005, when there were 16,600 more offenders cautioned for violence against the person, than for drug offences.

As well as information on crime, the BCS respondents were asked about their confidence in the criminal justice system (CJS). The 2005/06 BCS reported that compared with 2004/05, public

Figure **9.17**

Confidence in the criminal justice system, 2005/06

England & Wales
Percentages

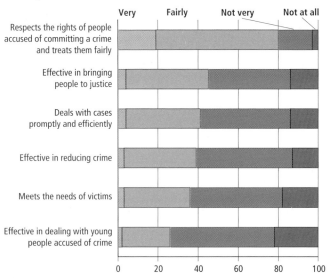

Source: British Crime Survey, Home Office

confidence in the CJS has improved in five of the seven areas covered, continuing a general improvement from 2002/03. In 2005/06, four-fifths of respondents (80 per cent) were very or fairly confident that the CJS respects the rights of people accused of committing a crime and treats them fairly (Figure 9.17). The general public's confidence is lowest for the way in which the CJS is perceived to deal with young people accused of crime, with only 26 per cent of people expressing confidence in the way the CJS deals with this. The Northern Ireland Crime Survey 2005/06 shows similar proportions for all categories.

Confidence in the CJS varied by age. Levels of confidence were higher among younger people than older people and there was no real difference in views expressed by men and women in the younger age group. For example, among young people aged 16 to 24, 54 per cent of men and 55 per cent of women were very or fairly confident that the CJS meets the needs of victims, compared with 21 per cent of men and 27 per cent of women aged 65 to 74.

Prisons and probation

Prison is the usual destination for offenders given custodial sentences and those who break the terms of their non-custodial sentences. Sentenced prisoners are classified into different risk-level groups for security purposes. Women prisoners are held in separate prisons or in separate accommodation in mixed prisons. Young offenders receiving custodial sentences have traditionally been separated from adult offenders, so that they can receive additional educational and rehabilitative treatment.

In September 2006 the prison population in England and Wales was 79,400. A further 270 people were in Secure Training Centres (privately run, education-focused centres for offenders up to the age of 17), and 230 were in Local Authority Secure Children's Homes (run by social services and focused on attending to the physical, emotional and behavioural needs of vulnerable young people). The prison population in Great Britain was relatively stable in the 1980s and early 1990s (averaging between 48,000 and 55,000). In the mid-1990s the prison population began to increase and rose to just over 84,000 by 2005, an increase of 68 per cent since 1993 (Figure 9.18). Over the same period, the average number of sentenced prisoners increased by 80 per cent, while the number of remand prisoners rose by 21 per cent. Remand prisoners comprised almost one-fifth of the total prison population in 2005. Northern Ireland's prison population fell during the 1980s and 1990s to 910 in 2001. Reasons for the decrease in the late 1990s include the implementation of the *Northern Ireland (Sentences) Act 1998*, arising from the Good Friday Agreement. This Act resulted in just over 430 prisoners being released between 1998 and 2000. The number of prisoners in Northern Ireland has since increased by 42 per cent to 1,300 in 2005.

Figure **9.18**

Average prison[1] population

Great Britain

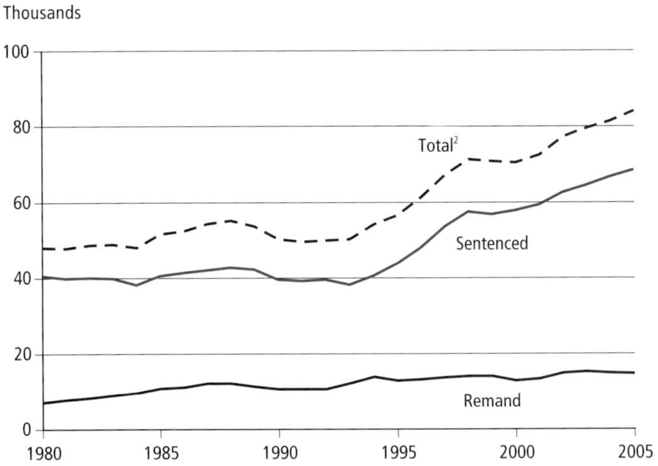

Thousands

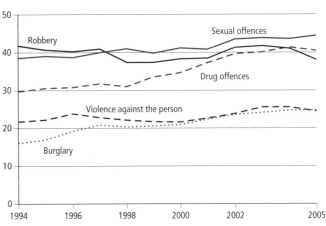

1 Includes prisoners held in police cells.
2 Includes non-criminal prisoners (for example, those held under the 1971 Immigration Act).

Source: Home Office; Scottish Executive

Figure **9.19**

Average length of Crown Court custodial sentence:[1] by offence group

England & Wales

Months

1 Excludes life sentences and indeterminate sentences for public protection.

Source: Court Proceedings Data, Home Office

The young adult population (aged 18 to 20) in prisons in England and Wales was 8,480 at 30 June 2006 (the latest date, at the time of writing, for which data were available), a decrease of 2 per cent from September 2005. The population of 15 to 17 year olds in prison decreased by 6 per cent from 2,500 in September 2005 to 2,350 in June 2006.

The increased prison population in England and Wales may be a result of the rise in the use of longer prison sentences. Between 1997 and 2005 the number of sentences of four years and over (including life) has increased at a faster rate than shorter sentences of under 12 months. The proportional increase has been much greater for women than for men. The number of female adult prisoners serving sentences of at least four years (including life) more than doubled from 680 in 1997 to 1,430 in 2005, while the number of male adult prisoners serving this type of sentence increased by half from 19,270 in 1997 to 28,890 in 2005. The proportion of male adult prisoners serving sentences of less than 12 months increased by 10 per cent, while the proportion of female adult prisoners serving this length of sentence increased by 52 per cent.

The average custodial sentence length (which excludes life and indeterminate sentences) given by the Crown Court in England and Wales has increased from 20.1 months in 1994 to 25.6 months in 2005. This rise is driven by an increase in the duration of sentences for drug offences and burglary (Figure 9.19). Throughout the 1990s the highest average custodial sentence lengths were for sexual offences and robbery. In 2004 and 2005, for the first time the average custodial sentences for drug offences were higher than for

robberies. There was a small decrease in average custodial sentence length between 2004 and 2005 for violence against the person, robbery and drug offences. This decrease was the result of the new sentences introduced by the *Criminal Justice Act 2003* coming into effect in April 2005. One of the new sentences is an indeterminate sentence for public protection (IPP), available for the more serious offences. Offenders receiving an indeterminate sentence for public protection are, like those given life sentences, not included in the quantification of average custodial sentence lengths. The average length of custodial sentences given by magistrates' courts remained stable at around three months.

At the end of December 2005 the National Probation Service in England and Wales was supervising 89,440 people or 'caseloads' either before or after being released from prison, 7 per cent more than a year earlier. It was also supervising 137,380 people under a court order, 7 per cent more than at the end of December 2004. The three probation areas with the largest caseloads were London (17 per cent of total court orders and 21 per cent of pre- and post-release supervision caseloads), the West Midlands (8 and 9 per cent respectively) and Greater Manchester (7 per cent for both).

Civil justice

In England and Wales, individuals or a company can bring a case under civil law. The majority of these cases are handled by the county courts and the High Court in England, Wales and Northern Ireland, and by the sheriff court and the Court of Session in Scotland (see Appendix, Part 9: Civil courts). The High Court and Court of Session deal with the more substantial and complex cases. Civil cases may include breach of contract, claims for debt, negligence and recovery of land. Tribunals deal with cases that involve the rights of private citizens against decisions of the state in areas such as social security benefits, income tax and mental health; and with other disputes involving private citizens, such as employment rights and unfair dismissal. There are some 80 tribunals in England and Wales, which dealt with over 1 million cases in 2005.

Once a writ or summons claim has been issued, many cases are settled without the need for a court hearing. There was an overall fall in the number of claims issued in county courts in England and Wales of 57 per cent, between the 1991 peak of 3.7 million and 1.6 million in 2003. Since 2003 the number of writs and summonses issued has been increasing with 1.6 million issued in 2005 (Figure 9.20). The increase between 1988 and 1991, from 2.3 million to 3.7 million may be explained in part by the increase in lending following financial deregulation. Money claims represented 86 per cent of the total number of writs and summonses issued in 2003.

Police Resources

A large share of expenditure on the criminal justice system has traditionally been spent on the police service. Full-time equivalent police officer numbers reached record levels, with 167,200 officers in the UK on 31 March 2006 (Table 9.21). Almost 16,400 of these police officers were in police forces in Scotland and 7,500 were in police forces in Northern Ireland. The eight metropolitan forces in England (City of London, Greater Manchester, Merseyside, Metropolitan Police, Northumbria, South Yorkshire, West Midlands and West Yorkshire) accounted for almost half of all officers (46 per cent) in England and Wales. The Metropolitan Police Service (London) is the largest force; accounting for 22 per cent of all officers in England and Wales at 31 March 2006.

At the same time there were 36,800 female police officers in the UK, representing 22 per cent of the total police force. One in ten officers at the rank of chief inspector and above were female compared with almost one-quarter at the rank of constable.

The Government sets employment targets for the recruitment, retention and progression of ethnic minority officers in England and Wales. These are intended to ensure that by 2009, forces reflect their ethnic minority populations. At 31 March 2006 there were 5,300 ethnic minority officers, representing 3.7 per cent of the total police service. This compares with 3.5 per cent on 31 March 2005 and 2.9 per cent at 31 March 2003. The number of ethnic minority officers increased by 280 (6 per cent) in the 12 months to 31 March 2006. Ethnic minority recruits to the Metropolitan Police accounted for 42 per cent of this increase.

Figure **9.20**

Writs and summonses issued[1]

England & Wales
Millions

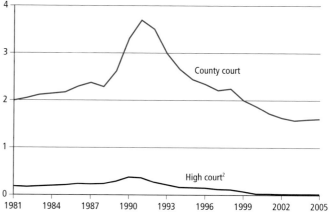

1 See Appendix, Part 9: Civil courts.
2 Queen's Bench Division.

Source: Court Service

Table **9.21**

Police officer strength:[1] by rank and sex, 2005/06

United Kingdom   Numbers

	Males	Females	All
ACPO[2] ranks	230	32	262
Chief superintendent	708	61	769
Superintendent	1,056	101	1,157
Chief inspector	2,081	261	2,341
Inspector	7,534	983	8,517
Sergeant	21,483	3,491	24,974
Constable	97,276	31,879	129,156
All ranks	130,368	36,807	167,174
Police staff	42,003	50,904	92,907
Police community support officers	3,936	2,833	6,769
Traffic wardens[3]	847	567	1,414
Designated officers	778	550	1,328
Total police strength	164,925	88,025	252,949
Special constabulary[4]	10,210	5,104	15,314

1 At 31 March 2006. Full-time equivalents. Includes staff on secondment to NCOS (Non-commissioned officer in the armed forces), NCIS (National Criminal Intelligence Service), central services, and staff on career breaks or maternity/paternity leave. Figures excludes British Transport Police.
2 Police officers who hold the rank of Chief Constable, Deputy Chief Constable or Assistant Chief Constable, or their equivalent.
3 Excludes local authority traffic wardens.
4 Headcounts.

Source: Home Office; Scottish Executive; Police Service of Northern Ireland

Housing

- Between 2001/02 and 2005/06, the proportion of newly built homes with two bedrooms rose from 25 per cent to 42 per cent in England, replacing homes with four or more bedrooms as the most common new build. (Figure 10.4)

- The number of owner-occupied dwellings in the UK increased by 48 per cent to 18.4 million between 1981 and 2005, representing nearly three-quarters of total dwelling stock. (Figure 10.5)

- Half of lone-parent households with dependent children in Great Britain rented social sector housing in 2005, compared with one in seven households containing a couple with dependent children. (Table 10.8)

- In 2005/06, 94,000 households were accepted as homeless by local authorities in England, 22 per cent less than in 2004/05. (Page 135)

- The number of non-decent homes in England fell from 9.1 million to 6.3 million between 1996 and 2004. (Page 136)

- The average price paid by first-time buyers in the UK rose by 204 per cent between 1995 and 2005. Their average incomes increased by 92 per cent. (Figure 10.19)

Chapter 10

A person's home and housing conditions will be strongly influenced by a range of socio-economic factors such as their income, employment status and household type. The type of home a person lives in, its tenure and condition can have a major impact upon their health and well-being.

Housing stock and housebuilding

Since the early 1950s the number of dwellings in Great Britain has almost doubled from 13.8 million in 1951 to 25.5 million in 2005. The rise in housing stock reflects a greater demand for homes caused by the increase in the population (see Chapter 1: Population) and more particularly, a trend towards smaller households which has emerged since the 1970s (see Appendix, Part 2: Households). Between 1971 and 2005 the number of dwellings in Great Britain increased by 34 per cent. During the same period the number of households increased by 30 per cent from 18.6 million to 24.2 million (see also Table 2.1), whereas the population increased by only 8 per cent.

The damage caused to the nation's housing stock during the Second World War led to the provision of new housing being a post-war government priority. In the early post-war years local authorities undertook the majority of housing construction. During the mid-1950s, private enterprise housebuilding increased dramatically and has been the dominant sector for new housebuilding since 1959. Housebuilding completions in the UK peaked in 1968 when 426,000 dwellings were

Figure **10.1**

Housebuilding completions:[1] by sector

United Kingdom
Thousands

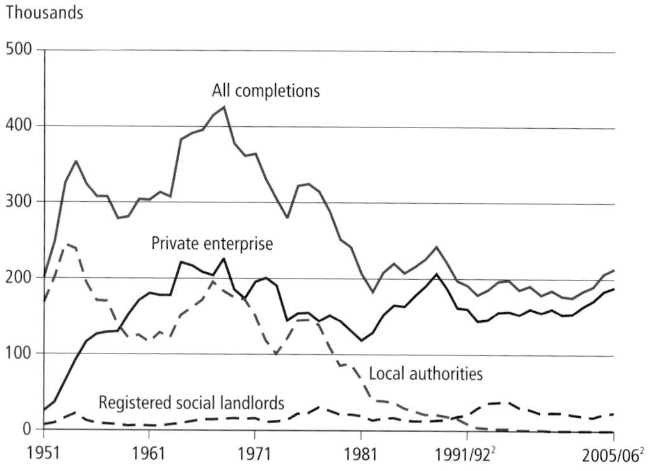

1 See Appendix, Part 10: Dwelling stock, and Dwellings completed.
2 From 1990/91 data are for financial years.

Source: Communities and Local Government; Welsh Assembly Government; Scottish Executive; Department of the Environment, Northern Ireland

completed (Figure 10.1). Fifty three per cent of these were built by private enterprise and 47 per cent were built by the social sector, primarily local authorities. Since the 1990s registered social landlords (RSLs) – predominantly housing associations – have dominated building in the social sector, accounting for 99 per cent of social sector completions in 2005/06. In 2005/06 there were 214,000 completions, of which 88 per cent were by the private enterprise sector.

Much of the existing housing stock in England reflects over 100 years of housebuilding, with 19 per cent having been built before the end of the First World War (Table 10.2). Sixty two per cent of dwellings in England were built after the Second World War, the highest proportion of which were built between 1965 and 1984. There are notable regional variations in the age of dwelling stock. London has the oldest housing stock: in 2005/06, 26 per cent of dwellings were built before 1919 and 30 per cent were built between 1919 and 1944. In contrast, 50 per cent of the dwellings in the East have been built since 1965, as have over 40 per cent in the South East, South West, West Midlands and East Midlands. The patterns in recent years are in part associated with inter-regional population movements within the UK (see also Table 1.11).

There are also wide variations in the age of properties by tenure. Just over one-third of households who rented privately in 2005/06 lived in homes built before 1919. In contrast, only one in five households who were owner-occupiers, one in ten of those renting from housing associations and one in twenty five renting from a council lived in a home built before 1919. One-quarter of households renting from a housing association lived in a home built since 1985. This was a higher proportion than among any other tenure group.

There is an increasing focus on using land for housebuilding more efficiently both to maximise the number of homes available and to make them more affordable, especially in areas of high demand. In recent years an increasing proportion of new homes have been built on previously developed land – usually referred to as 'brown field sites'. The Government target for England is that by 2008, 60 per cent of new dwellings should be built on previously developed land including through conversions of existing buildings. Between 1995 and 2005 the proportion of new dwellings in England built on previously-developed land (including conversions of existing buildings) rose from 57 per cent to 74 per cent (see also Table 11.20). In 2005 London had the highest proportion of new dwellings built on previously developed land, at 98 per cent. The region with the lowest proportion was the East Midlands at 55 per cent.

Table **10.2**

Dwelling stock:[1] by region and year built, 2005/06

England   Percentages

	Before 1919	1919– 1944	1945– 1964	1965– 1984	1985 or later	All
England	19	19	22	25	14	100
North East	15	23	28	23	11	100
North West	21	22	23	20	14	100
Yorkshire and the Humber	20	19	24	25	12	100
East Midlands	19	15	23	27	15	100
West Midlands	12	19	26	28	15	100
East	15	11	23	32	18	100
London	26	30	17	19	8	100
South East	16	16	21	29	17	100
South West	23	15	19	25	18	100

1 See Appendix, Part 10: Dwelling stock.

Source: Survey of English Housing, Communities and Local Government

Since the mid-1990s, another way in which land has been used more efficiently has been to build new homes at a higher density. Between 1995 and 2005 the average density of new dwellings built in England increased from 24 to 40 per hectare. During this period there were increases in the density of newly built homes in each of the English regions, but the increase was particularly large in London where the number of new dwellings per hectare rose from 48 to 110 (Figure 10.3).

Figure **10.3**

Density of new dwellings:[1] by region

England
Dwellings per hectare

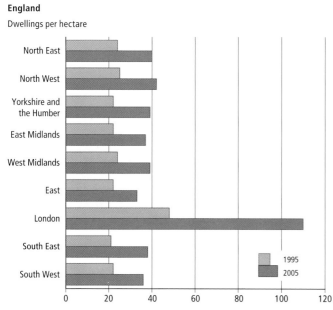

1 See Appendix, Part 10: Dwellings completed.

Source: Communities and Local Government

The increase in the density of new dwellings constructed has been reflected in changes to the type and size of home. During the 1990s and into the early years of the 21st century the proportion of large newly built homes (which includes houses and flats) in England increased steadily. This trend was particularly evident for homes with four or more bedrooms. Between 1991/92 and 2001/02 the proportion of all newly built homes of this size increased from 20 per cent to 37 per cent (Figure 10.4). However the proportion has since risen to 21 per cent in 2005/06. In contrast, the proportion of newly built homes with two bedrooms fell from 32 per cent in 1991/92

Figure **10.4**

Housebuilding completions:[1] by number of bedrooms

England
Percentages

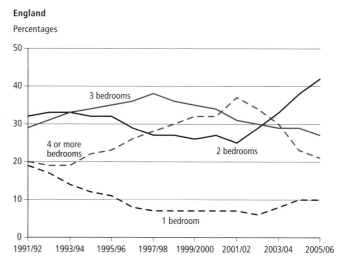

1 All houses and flats. See Appendix, Part 10: Dwellings completed.

Source: Communities and Local Government

to 25 per cent in 2001/02, since when it has risen steadily to reach 42 per cent in 2005/06 and is now the most common type of new build. The proportion of newly built homes with one bedroom (which were mostly flats), also fell between 1991/92 and 2002/03 but has since risen. In recent years there has been a shift away from house building to flat building. In 2005/06, 46 per cent of new dwellings completed in England were flats, compared with 26 per cent in 1991/92 and 15 per cent in 1997/98. The recent trend of building smaller homes can be linked to the increasing numbers of one-person households (see Chapter 2: Households and families) and Government initiatives to increase the supply and affordability of homes in areas of high demand. These include four 'Growth Areas' in London and the South East where population density and demand for housing places an ever increasing pressure on land use (see Appendix, Part 10: Sustainable Communities Plan).

Tenure and accommodation

One of the most notable housing trends in the UK since the early 1980s is the increase in owner occupation. Between 1981 and 2005 the number of owner-occupied dwellings increased by 48 per cent to reach 18.4 million, representing nearly three-quarters of all dwellings in 2005 (Figure 10.5). Over the same period the number of homes rented from local authorities fell by 56 per cent to 2.8 million. The decline in renting from a local authority is partly explained by the increase in owner occupancy, but there has also been a

growing number of homes rented from registered social landlords (RSLs) – predominantly housing associations – and this has been steadily increasing since the early 1990s. By 2005, 2.2 million homes were rented from RSLs compared with 0.5 million in 1981. The number of dwellings rented privately has been growing steadily in recent years, increasing from around 2.5 million in 2001 to 2.8 million in 2005.

A number of schemes that aim to increase low-cost home ownership have accompanied the growth in the number of owner-occupied dwellings in Great Britain. Since the early 1980s, public tenants with secure tenancies of at least two years' standing have been entitled to purchase their home. This scheme, known as 'right to buy' was particularly popular during the 1980s, following a period of stabilisation in the housing market and changes in legislation that enabled more tenants to buy. There were peaks of over 180,000 sales in both 1982 and 1989 (Figure 10.6). In 2005 there were 42,000 sales of right to buy properties, a decrease of 44 per cent on the previous year and the lowest number since the scheme was introduced.

Another type of scheme which aims to increase low-cost home ownership is shared ownership, in which tenants buy a share of a property from an RSL and pay rent for the remainder. Since the late 1990s large scale voluntary transfers have been the main contributors to the transfer of ownership from local authorities to other owners, mainly housing associations (see Appendix, Part 10: Sales and transfers of local authority dwellings).

Figure **10.5**

Stock of dwellings:[1] by tenure

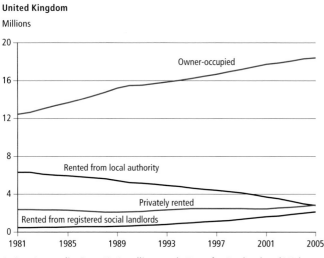

United Kingdom
Millions

1 See Appendix, Part 10: Dwelling stock. Data for England and Wales are at 31 March, and for Scotland and Northern Ireland they are at 31 December the previous year, except for 1991, where Census figures are used.

Source: Communities and Local Government

Figure **10.6**

Sales and transfers of local authority dwellings[1]

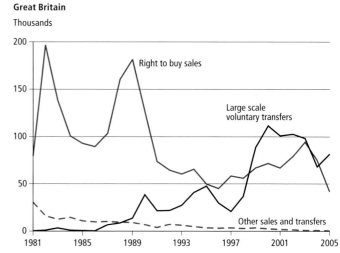

Great Britain
Thousands

1 Excludes new town and Scottish Homes sales and transfers. See Appendix, Part 10: Sales and transfers of local authority dwellings.

Source: Communities and Local Government; Welsh Assembly Government; Scottish Executive

In 2003 in the UK, the proportion of people living in households that owned their accommodation, or lived in it rent-free, was 73 per cent, just below the EU-25 average of 76 per cent (Table 10.7). There were particularly high rates of owner occupiers among the ten countries which became EU members in May 2004. Among these, Hungary, Lithuania, Slovenia and Cyprus all had proportions of owner occupiers in excess of 90 per cent. Accommodation in many of the Central and Eastern European countries which joined the EU in 2004 was traditionally supplied by the state or via cooperatives. On transition to the EU, many governments pursued active privatisation policies, developing laws on property rights and housing finance to underpin an emerging market in residential housing. Precise policies differed from country to country. Among the fifteen countries which were members of the EU before May 2004, Greece and Spain had high rates of owner occupation at 90 per cent and 89 per cent respectively. Germany had the lowest recorded level at 57 per cent.

Tenure varies markedly according to the type of household. In 2005 in Great Britain, lone-parent households with dependent children were more likely than any other type of household to rent their property rather than own it (Table 10.8). Two-thirds of lone-parent households with dependent children were

Table **10.7**

People in owner-occupied or rent-free households:[1] EU-25 comparison, 2003

Percentages

Hungary[2]	94	Austria[3]	71
Lithuania[2]	94	Finland	71
Slovenia[2]	94	Poland[2]	71
Cyprus	91	Denmark[3]	67
Greece[3]	90	Sweden[2]	67
Estonia	89	France[2]	62
Spain	89	Netherlands[2]	58
Ireland[3]	83	Germany[3]	57
Italy[3]	83	Czech Republic	..
Belgium[3]	81	Slovakia	..
Malta[3]	80	EU-25 average[4]	76
Latvia[2]	78		
Portugal[3]	77		
Luxembourg	75		
United Kingdom	73		

1 People living in households that own their accommodation, either outright or with a mortgage, or live in it rent-free.
2 Data are as at 2002.
3 Data are as at 2001.
4 Population weighted average based on the available individual national figures for 2001.

Source: Eurostat

Table **10.8**

Household composition: by tenure, 2005[1]

Great Britain   Percentages

	Owned outright	Owned with mortgage	Privately rented[2]	Rented from social sector	All tenures
One person					
Under pensionable age	18	39	20	22	100
Over pensionable age	58	4	6	33	100
One family households					
Couple[3]					
No children	46	35	9	10	100
Dependent children[4]	8	70	8	14	100
Non-dependent children only	35	52	2	10	100
Lone parent[3]					
Dependent children[4]	6	29	14	52	100
Non-dependent children only	32	29	6	33	100
Other households[5]	20	22	44	14	100
All households[6]	30	38	12	20	100

1 Data for 2005 includes last quarter of 2004/05 due to survey change from financial year to calendar year. See Appendix, Part 2: General Household Survey.
2 Includes tenants in rent-free accommodation and squatters.
3 Other individuals who were not family members may also be included.
4 See Appendix, Part 2: Families. May also include non-dependent children.
5 Comprising two or more unrelated adults or two or more families.
6 Includes a very small number of same sex couples.

Source: General Household Survey (Longitudinal), Office for National Statistics

renting their home, mostly from social sector landlords (RSLs or local authorities), while just over one-third were living in owner-occupied accommodation. In contrast, four-fifths (78 per cent) of couple households with dependent children were owner occupiers and only one in seven (14 per cent) rented from the social sector. Households consisting of one person under state pension age (age 65 for men and age 60 for women) were more likely than any other type of one-person or one-family household to live in privately rented accommodation. Almost three-fifths of one person households over state pension age owned their home outright, compared with just under one-fifth of those under state pension age. This in part reflects the time it can take to pay off a mortgage.

In Northern Ireland in 2005/06, tenure patterns by household type were generally similar to those in Great Britain. However, there was a larger proportion of lone-parent households with dependent children living in privately rented accommodation, at just over one-fifth (22 per cent), compared with one in seven (14 per cent) such households in Great Britain.

Within Great Britain tenure varies by socio-economic status. In 2005, 58 per cent of households where the reference person (see Appendix, Part 10: Household reference person) was economically

active were buying their home with a mortgage and 18 per cent owned their home outright. Households where the reference person was in the large employers and higher managerial occupational group were the most likely to be buying their home with a mortgage (74 per cent). Those who had retired formed the majority (67 per cent) of those owning their home outright.

In 2005 those in routine and semi-routine occupations and those who had never worked or were long-term unemployed were the least likely to be owner occupiers and the most likely to rent from the social sector. This was particularly true for those who had never worked or were long-term unemployed, with 27 per cent owning their home and 50 per cent renting from the social sector. In contrast to other tenures, the proportions of households renting privately were far less variable across the socio-economic groups.

The type of home that people live in often reflects the size and type of their household and what they can afford or are provided with. Overall, 80 per cent of households in Great Britain lived in a house or a bungalow in 2005 (Table 10.9). Among households with dependent children, couples were more likely than lone parents to live in a house or bungalow (92 per cent and 77 per cent respectively). The majority of couples

Table 10.9

Household composition: by type of dwelling, 2005[1]

Great Britain
Percentages

	House or bungalow			Flat or maisonette		
	Detached	Semi-detached	Terraced	Purpose-built	Other[2]	All dwellings[3]
One person						
Under pensionable age	11	20	30	29	10	100
Over pensionable age	17	29	24	27	3	100
One family households						
Couple[4]						
No children	30	33	24	10	3	100
Dependent children[5]	28	37	27	6	1	100
Non-dependent children only	30	39	27	4	1	100
Lone parent[4]						
Dependent children[5]	8	29	40	20	3	100
Non-dependent children only	14	36	34	13	2	100
Other households[6]	12	25	36	19	7	100
All households[7]	22	31	28	16	4	100

1 Data for 2005 includes last quarter of 2004/05 due to survey change from financial year to calendar year. See Appendix, Part 2: General Household Survey.
2 Includes converted flats, part of a house and rooms.
3 Includes other types of accommodation, such as mobile homes.
4 Other individuals who were not family members may also be included.
5 See Appendix, Part 2: Families. May also include non-dependent children.
6 Comprising two or more unrelated adults or two or more families.
7 Includes a very small number of same sex couples.

Source: General Household Survey (Longitudinal), Office for National Statistics

with dependent children lived in detached or semi-detached houses (65 per cent). Over one-quarter (27 per cent) lived in terraced houses compared with 40 per cent of lone parents with dependent children. Lone parents with dependent children were over three times as likely as couples with dependent children to live in a purpose-built flat or maisonette (20 per cent compared with 6 per cent).

Compared with family households, one-person households were more likely to live in a flat. Among those under state pension age, 39 per cent lived in either a purpose-built or converted flat compared with 30 per cent of those over state pension age.

In Northern Ireland in 2005/06, a higher proportion of households lived in a house or bungalow (93 per cent) than did so in Great Britain (80 per cent) in 2005. Households in Northern Ireland were almost twice as likely as those in Great Britain to live in a detached house (40 per cent compared with 22 per cent). The higher proportion of households living in houses in Northern Ireland compared with Great Britain may partly reflect the availability of land for building and lower population density (see also Map 1.10).

Among lone parents with dependent children, those in Great Britain were far more likely to be living in a flat or maisonette (23 per cent) than those in Northern Ireland (3 per cent). In contrast, a higher proportion of such households in Northern Ireland lived in a terraced house (55 per cent) than did so in Great Britain (40 per cent).

Homelessness

Homelessness can result from changes in personal circumstances, such as the reluctance or inability of relatives or friends to continue to provide accommodation, the breakdown of relationships, or financial hardship leading to rental or mortgage arrears. Local housing authorities in England have a statutory obligation known as the 'main homeless duty' to ensure that suitable accommodation is available for applicants who are eligible for assistance, have become homeless through no fault of their own, and who fall within a priority need group. Such groups include families with children, and households that include someone who is vulnerable, for example because of pregnancy, domestic violence, old age, or physical or mental disability.

During 2005/06, 94,000 households were accepted as homeless and in priority need in England under the homelessness provisions of the *Housing Act 1996*. This was 22 per cent less than in 2004/05 and represented 44 per cent of all decisions on applications. The primary reason for households that were accepted as being in priority need was the presence of dependent children (53 per cent). A further 12 per cent of acceptances were households that included a pregnant woman.

Figure **10.10**

Homelessness:[1] by household composition, 2004/05

England
Percentages

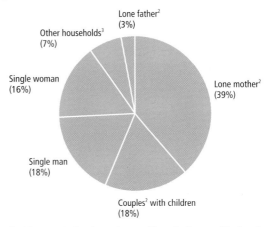

1 Households accepted as homeless and in priority need by local authorities.
2 With dependent children.
3 Includes couples without children, families with dependent children and extended families.
Source: Communities and Local Government

Other acceptances included applicants who were vulnerable young people (9 per cent) or vulnerable because of mental illness (8 per cent), physical disability (5 per cent), domestic violence (4 per cent) or old age (2 per cent).

Among those households that were accepted as homeless in England in 2004/05 (the latest year for which these data are available), there were 13 times as many lone mothers with dependent children accepted as there were lone fathers (39 per cent compared with 3 per cent) (Figure 10.10). This in part reflects the higher number of lone mothers than lone fathers in the population in general; in spring 2006, nine out of ten lone-parent families in Great Britain were headed by a woman (see Table 2.5). The proportions of household types accepted as homeless in Scotland in 2005/06 were different to those in England in 2004/05, although in Scotland the priority need criterion does not apply. In Scotland the largest proportion of households accepted as homeless were those comprising single men (38 per cent). Lone-mother households made up 25 per cent and lone-father households 5 per cent of the acceptances. In Wales in 2005/06, the largest proportion of households accepted as homeless were lone mothers (34 per cent) compared with 3 per cent of lone fathers; similar proportions to those in England in 2004/05. However, compared with England, single person households formed a higher proportion of those accepted as homeless in Wales: 24 per cent compared with 18 per cent for single men, and 21 per cent compared with 16 per cent for single women.

In 2005/06, 21 per cent of those accepted as homeless by local authorities in England were from ethnic minorities, although they represented only 11 per cent of all households in 2001. In every region of England in 2005/06, the proportion of homeless households that were from an ethnic minority was greater than the proportion of all households that were from an ethnic minority. This was most marked in London, where ethnic minority households made up almost one-quarter (23 per cent) of all households in 2001 but accounted for over half (54 per cent) of those accepted as homeless by local authorities in 2005/06.

Around half the households accepted as homeless in England in 2005/06 were provided with temporary accommodation. There had been a steady rise in the number of households in temporary accommodation in England, from 41,000 in 1996/97 to 101,000 in 2004/05, before numbers fell to 97,000 in 2005/06. This recent decrease has mainly resulted from housing authorities providing settled housing for those in temporary accommodation through support from both housing association partners and the private rented sector. In 2005/06, over half (52 per cent) of the households living in temporary accommodation in England were living in self-contained properties leased in the private sector and a further one-quarter (23 per cent) were accommodated in self-contained social housing let on a temporary basis (Figure 10.11). Under the *Homelessness (Suitability of Accommodation) (England) Order 2003*, local authorities can no longer place families with children in bed and breakfast (B&B) accommodation for longer than six weeks. Between March 2003 and March 2006 the total number of homeless households in England living in B&B hotels fell by 59 per cent to 5,200. Over the same period, the use of self-contained property leased from the private sector increased by 75 per cent, and by March 2006, it accounted for over half of all temporary accommodation.

In Scotland and Wales the total number of homeless households provided with temporary accommodation has been rising since the late 1990s. In Scotland the number rose from 3,800 in 1997/98 to 8,100 in 2005/06, while in Wales the number increased from 700 to 2,500 over the same period. In Scotland the number of households accommodated temporarily in B&B hotels levelled off at around 1,500 in 2005/06, but had been rising since the mid-1990s when the number was around 400. In Scotland, local authorities cannot place households with children or pregnant women in temporary accommodation which fails to meet standards relating to physical quality, access to services and safety. While the aim must always be to adhere to the safety standard, accommodation which would usually be deemed unsuitable may be used in exceptional circumstances, including emergency presentations or households wishing to stay

Figure **10.11**

Homeless households in temporary accommodation[1]

England

Thousands

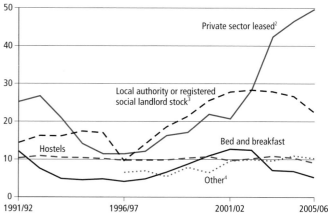

1 Excludes 'homeless at home' cases. See Appendix, Part 10: Homeless at home. Data as at 31 March, and include households awaiting the outcome of homeless enquiries.
2 Prior to March 1996, includes those accommodated directly with a private sector landlord.
3 Prior to March 1996, includes all 'Other' types of accommodation.
4 From March 1996, includes mobile homes (such as caravans and portacabins) or being accommodated directly with a private sector landlord.

Source: Communities and Local Government

in accommodation despite it being unsuitable. Some exceptions, such as the first one, have a time limit of 14 days, while others do not. If more than one exception applies, the time limit is determined by the one with the longest exemption period. In Wales the number of homeless households in temporary B&B accommodation had also been rising since the late 1990s, but fell by 22 per cent between 2004/05 and 2005/06 from 760 to around 600. In Wales, from April 2007 local authorities will only be able to place vulnerable households with children and young people in B&B accommodation for up to two weeks before finding them other accommodation. From April 2008 this limited use of B&B accommodation will apply to all priority need groups.

Housing condition and satisfaction with area

Between 1996 and 2004 the number of 'non-decent' homes in England fell from 9.1 million to 6.3 million (from 45 per cent to 29 per cent of all dwellings). During this period the proportion of non-decent homes in the social sector fell at a faster rate than in the private sector. To be considered 'decent' a dwelling must meet the statutory minimum standard for housing: it must be in a reasonable state of repair; have reasonably modern facilities and services; and provide a reasonable degree of thermal comfort. In 1996, 53 per cent of social sector stock and 43 per cent of private sector stock was considered non-decent.

Table **10.12**

Dwellings that fail the decent home standard:[1] by tenure and reason for failure, 2004

England   Percentages

| | Reason for failure | | | | |
	Thermal comfort	Disrepair	Fitness	Modernisation	All non-decent[2]
Private sector					
Owner-occupied	20	7	4	1	27
Privately rented	30	14	10	4	43
All private sector	21	8	5	2	29
Social sector					
Local authority	24	8	6	5	35
Registered social landlords	21	4	4	2	26
All rented from social sector	23	6	5	4	31
All tenures	21	8	5	2	29

1 See Appendix, Part 10: Decent home standard.
2 Homes may fail standard for more than one category.

Source: English House Condition Survey, Communities and Local Government

By 2004 these proportions had fallen to 31 per cent and 29 per cent respectively. Government targets state that by 2010, all social housing must be in a 'decent' condition and the proportion of vulnerable households in private sector housing living in homes that are in decent condition should be increased.

In 2004 the most common reason dwellings in England failed to meet the decent home standard was that they did not provide a reasonable level of thermal comfort. This affected 4.6 million dwellings in England, representing 21 per cent of the total stock (Table 10.12). Of those dwellings failing the thermal comfort standard, 57 per cent failed through a lack of adequate insulation.

Compared with dwellings in other tenure groups, privately rented homes were the most likely to fail to meet the decent home standard in 2004 either for thermal comfort, disrepair or fitness.

Poor housing is one aspect of disadvantage. A number of factors, such as age, long-term illness or disability, may increase the likelihood of households living in poor housing conditions, and such groups may have limited resources to improve their housing situation.

The likelihood of living in poor housing conditions is strongly related to household income. Households in the lowest fifth of the income distribution are the most likely to live in non-decent homes and experience poor quality environments. In 2004, 37 per cent of households in England in the lowest fifth of the income distribution lived in non-decent homes and 20 per cent

experienced poor quality environments (see Appendix, Part 10: Poor quality environments) (Table 10.13). Households in the highest fifth of the income distribution were the least likely to live in non-decent homes (20 per cent) or experience a poor quality environment (11 per cent).

Table **10.13**

Poor living conditions: by income grouping[1] of household, 2004

England   Percentages

	Bottom fifth	Next fifth	Middle fifth	Next fifth	Top fifth	All house-holds
Non-decent homes[2]	37	32	29	24	20	28
Poor quality environments[2]	20	17	15	14	11	15
Energy inefficient homes[2]	12	9	8	6	7	8
Homes in serious disrepair[3]	13	11	9	8	6	10

1 Net household income has been used to rank the households into quintile groups.
2 See Appendix, Part 10: Decent home standard, Poor quality environments, and (for energy inefficient homes) Standard Assessment Procedure (SAP).
3 Based on the 10 per cent of all households whose dwellings have the highest repair costs per square metre.

Source: English House Condition Survey, Communities and Local Government

Table **10.14**

Aspects of their area that householders would like to see improved[1]

England

Percentages

	1995/96	2000/01	2001/02	2002/03	2003/04	2004/05
Opportunities and facilities for children and young people	39	45	38	39	38	39
Crime and vandalism	39	47	32	32	31	31
Local amenities, parks and leisure facilities	27	38	31	31	31	30
Public transport service	22	30	28	29	28	26
Shopping and commercial facilities	14	26	21	21	21	20
Local health services	11	20	18	18	19	18
Quality of environment	17	25	18	18	18	18
Amount and quality of housing	12	14	12	15	16	16
Availability of jobs	30	23	16	17	16	14
Schools and colleges	8	10	9	9	10	9
None of these[2]	18	8	16	15	15	15

1 Respondents were asked to select only from those aspects listed in the table. Percentages do not add up to 100 per cent as respondents could give more than one answer.
2 Includes respondents who had nothing they wished to see improved and those who would like to see improvements in aspects other than those listed.

Source: Survey of English Housing, Communities and Local Government

Particular types of household are more likely to experience poor living conditions than others. In England in 2004, 29 per cent of lone-parent households with dependent children lived in non-decent homes and 22 per cent lived in a poor quality environment. In contrast, 23 per cent of couple households with dependent children lived in non-decent homes and 14 per cent lived in a poor quality environment. Young adult households are also more likely to live in non-decent homes and experience poor quality environments than the average for all households. In 2004, 39 per cent of households where the oldest person was aged 16 to 24 lived in a non-decent home and 27 per cent lived in a poor quality environment. These proportions compared with averages for all households of 28 per cent and 15 per cent respectively. Higher than average proportions of young adult households also lived in energy inefficient homes (11 per cent) and homes in serious disrepair (17 per cent).

The neighbourhood in which people live can influence how content they are with their homes. In 2004/05, the four aspects of their area that householders in England most commonly wished to see improved were: opportunities and facilities for children and young people; levels of crime and vandalism; local amenities, parks and leisure facilities; and public transport services (Table 10.14). These have been the four aspects of greatest concern each year since 2000/2001, but in the mid-1990s there was also considerable concern about the availability of jobs.

Overall satisfaction with the area in which people live varies by tenure. In England in 2004/05, 51 per cent of homeowners

reported that they were 'very satisfied' with their area compared with 38 per cent of those who were renting in the social sector. However, almost twice as many of those living in social rented accommodation (19 per cent) highlighted crime as a serious problem in their area compared with those who were owner-occupiers (10 per cent). Overall the proportion of households who considered crime to be a serious issue in their area has fallen, from 22 per cent in 1994/95 to 12 per cent in 2005/06. The proportion of households who viewed traffic as a serious problem has been growing in recent years, from 15 per cent in 1999/2000 to 20 per cent in 2005/06 (see also Table 12.12).

Housing mobility

The length of time that people remain living at the same address varies with tenure. Private renters are the most mobile tenure group. In 2005/06, 38 per cent of those living in privately rented accommodation in England had been at their current address for less than a year (Table 10.15). For people such as students and young professionals who may need to move frequently, private renting offers flexibility and is the only option for many people who are saving to buy or do not qualify for social rented accommodation. In contrast, the least mobile group are owner-occupiers. However, there are differences in mobility between those who own their homes outright and those buying with a mortgage. In 2005/06, 57 per cent of those who owned outright had lived in the same home for 20 years or more, compared with 12 per cent of those who were buying with a mortgage.

Table **10.15**

Length of time at current address:[1] by tenure, 2005/06

England   Percentages

	Under 1 year	1 year but less than 5 years	5 years but less than 10 years	10 years but less than 20 years	20 years or more	All
Owner-occupied						
Owned outright	2	11	12	19	57	100
Owned with mortgage	7	32	24	24	12	100
All owner-occupied	5	23	19	22	32	100
Privately rented						
Furnished	49	40	6	3	2	100
Unfurnished	34	41	11	6	8	100
All privately rented	38	41	9	5	6	100
Rented from social sector						
Council	8	27	19	20	25	100
Housing association	11	33	22	19	15	100
All rented from social sector	9	29	21	20	21	100
All tenures	10	26	18	20	27	100

1 Of household reference person. See Appendix, Part 10: Household reference person.

Source: Survey of English Housing, Communities and Local Government

In most of the housing moves that occurred in England during 2005/06, households remained within the same type of tenure. More than three-fifths of the households that owned their home outright had previously done so and a further one-fifth had previously owned with a mortgage. Almost two-fifths of all those moving had previously been in privately-rented accommodation, demonstrating the importance of this sector in facilitating mobility within the housing market.

Differences in the mobility of different tenure groups can be measured by the number of times they have moved home in the past year. In 2005/06, over one-third of households in England living in privately rented furnished accommodation had moved once in the past year. In contrast, less than one in twenty households in owner-occupied homes and one in twelve households renting in the social sector had moved once in the past year.

People have different reasons for moving. In 2005/06 the most common reasons given for moving in the year before interview were personal reasons (22 per cent) (Figure 10.16). Around one-third of such moves were because of divorce or separation and a further third were because of marriage or cohabitation. The desire for different accommodation (20 per cent), job-related reasons (12 per cent), and wishing to move to a better area (10 per cent), were also important factors in decisions to move home.

Figure **10.16**

Main reasons for moving, 2005/06

England

Percentages

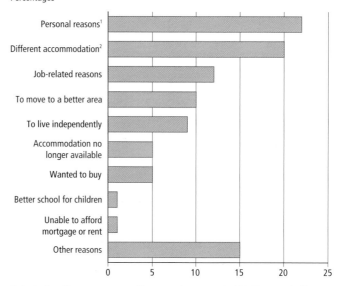

1 Includes divorce or separation, marriage or cohabitation, and other personal reasons.
2 Includes those wanting a larger or better house or flat, and those wanting a smaller or cheaper house or flat.

Source: Survey of English Housing, Communities and Local Government

Reasons for moving also varied by tenure. Among owner occupiers, 25 per cent who owned outright had moved because they wanted a smaller or cheaper house or flat, reflecting the high proportion of this group who had retired. However among those buying with a mortgage, 21 per cent had moved because they wanted a larger or better home. A far higher proportion of private renters than any other tenure group gave job-related reasons for their move (19 per cent).

The mobility of owner occupiers is linked to the state of the housing market. Over the past 40 years trends in the economy and the housing market have followed a similar pattern, with booms and slumps in one tending to contribute to the other. The number of property transactions that took place in England and Wales rose during the 1980s, mainly as a result of existing owner-occupiers moving home (Figure 10.17). Market activity by first-time buyers and public sector tenants (right to buy purchases) (see Figure 10.6) were also factors, but contributed to a lesser extent. Changes to the mortgage lending market in the 1980s may also have been a contributing factor to the 1980s property boom, when new households opted for ownership rather than renting. Following interest rate rises in 1988, the annual number of transactions fell from a peak of 2.2 million to 1.1 million by 1992, after which it fluctuated for several years. In 2005, 1.5 million property transactions took place in England and Wales, 15 per cent fewer than in 2004. Of all the property transactions that took place in England and Wales in 2005, 90 per cent were residential property transactions.

Housing costs and expenditure

In 2005 the average price for a dwelling in the UK was £183,966, an increase of almost 6 per cent compared with 2004 (Table 10.18). This was almost three times the average dwelling price compared with 1995 when it stood at £66,786. Over the same period, UK inflation measured by the all items consumer prices index (see Chapter 6: Expenditure) rose by 16.3 per cent.

Although London, the South East and East of England remained the most expensive regions in which to purchase a property in 2005, they also recorded the lowest year on year price increases. House price inflation was highest in Northern Ireland at 14 per cent, and Scotland and Wales at 12 per cent, although average property prices in Northern Ireland and Scotland were still the lowest of all regions in the UK. House price inflation in 2005 was much lower than in 2004 for all regions and countries except Northern Ireland.

Steep increases in house prices have made affordability a particular concern to first-time buyers. Over the past decade, the rise in average house prices paid by first-time buyers has been far greater than the increase in their average incomes.

Figure **10.17**

Property transactions[1]

England & Wales

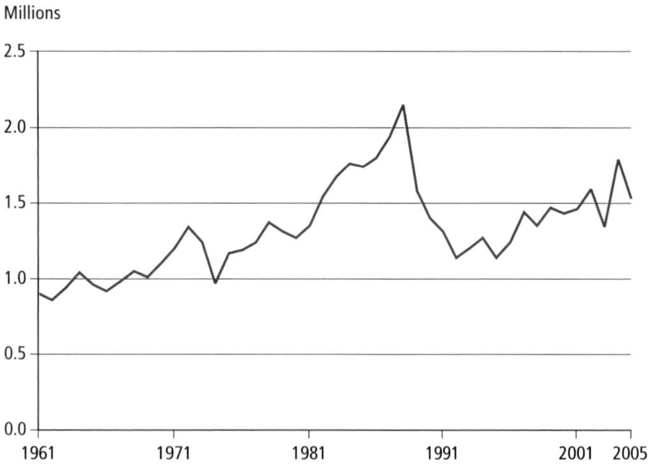

Millions

1 Includes residential and commercial transactions. See Appendix, Part 10: Property transactions.

Source: HM Revenue and Customs

Table **10.18**

Average dwelling prices:[1] by region, 2005

	All dwellings (£)	Percentage change 2004–05
United Kingdom	183,966	5.6
England	193,097	4.8
North East	131,814	10.2
North West	146,111	11.0
Yorkshire and the Humber	143,281	10.2
East Midlands	159,249	6.0
West Midlands	163,945	6.6
East	204,215	3.1
London	266,328	3.0
South East	233,069	2.3
South West	199,230	3.7
Wales	145,825	11.9
Scotland	124,390	12.1
Northern Ireland	129,580	13.6

1 See Appendix, Part 10: Mix adjusted prices.

Source: Survey of Mortgage Lenders; Communities and Local Government; Regulated Mortgage Survey and BankSearch run by Council of Mortgage Lenders

Figure **10.19**

First-time buyers: average dwelling prices,[1] incomes and deposits

United Kingdom

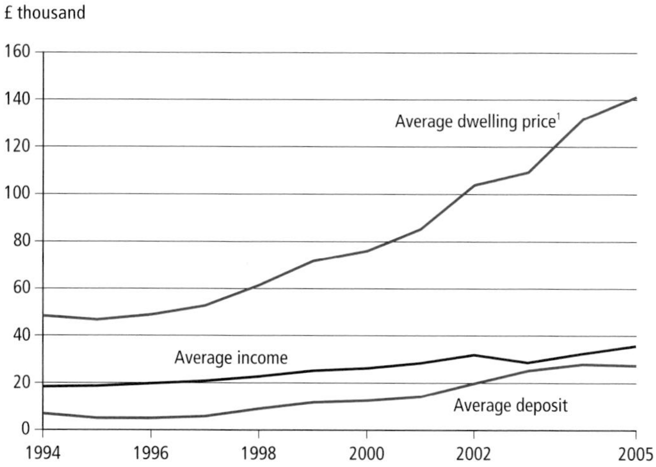

£ thousand

1 Uses simple average prices. See Appendix, Part 10: Mix adjusted prices.

Source: Survey of Mortgage Lenders; Communities and Local Government; Regulated Mortgage Survey, BankSearch run by Council of Mortgage Lenders

Table **10.20**

Expenditure[1] on selected housing costs[2] among households with children, 2005/06

United Kingdom   £ per week

	One adult with children	Two adults with children
Mortgage[3]	32.10	104.50
Household alterations and improvements	21.20	48.40
Charges[4]	14.30	26.50
Net rent	21.30	14.20
Household maintenance and repair	5.90	11.00
Household insurances	2.90	6.10

1 Expenditure rounded to the nearest 10 pence.
2 Includes average expenditure on all items allocated across all households in the sample, with every household being attributed a weekly expenditure on net rent and a mortgage. See Appendix, Part 10: Housing expenditure.
3 Includes interest, protection premiums and capital repayment.
4 Includes council tax or domestic rates, water charges and refuse collection.

Source: Expenditure and Food Survey, Office for National Statistics

Between 1995 and 2005 the average price paid by first-time buyers in the UK rose from £46,489 to £141,229, an increase of 204 per cent (not adjusting for inflation). Over the same period average incomes of first-time buyers increased by 92 per cent to reach £35,900 by 2005 (Figure 10.19).

As the gap between their income and the prices paid by first-time buyers has widened, a higher proportion of the price paid has had to be funded through a deposit. In 1995 the average deposit paid by first-time buyers in the UK was £4,800, equivalent to nearly ten per cent of the average house price in that year. By 2005 the average deposit paid had risen to £27,300, representing 19 per cent of the average price. One consequence of the need to save larger deposits has been that first-time buyers have been entering the housing market at later ages. In 1995, 24 per cent of first-time buyers were under the age of 25. By 2005 this proportion had fallen to 19 per cent and the majority of first-time buyers (53 per cent) were aged 25 to 34.

Regardless of tenure, housing costs constitute a substantial proportion of household budgets. In 2005/06 households in the UK spent an average of £139.60 per week on housing related costs. Among households with children there are notable differences in weekly housing expenditure between those with one and those with two adults. In 2005/06, households containing two adults and children spent £215.40 per week, over twice as much as those containing one adult with children who spent £99.60 (Table 10.20).

Among both types of household, mortgage payments were the largest item of weekly housing expenditure. However, households containing two adults and children spent over three times the amount that those with one adult and children did (£104.50 compared with £32.10). Households containing two adults and children also spent over twice as much per week on household alterations and improvements as those with one adult and children (£48.40 compared with £21.20).

Environment

- The warmest year on record for central England was 2006, with an annual average temperature of 10.8°C. (Page 144)

- Carbon dioxide emissions fell by 18 per cent between 1970 and 2004 in the UK; much of the decline came from industry where emissions fell by 49 per cent. (Figure 11.4)

- The proportion of sensitive habitat areas where critical loads of pollutants delivered as acid rain were exceeded in the UK fell from 73 per cent in 1996 to 56 per cent in 2003. (Page 150)

- Complaints about noise from domestic premises rose almost fivefold between 1984/85 and 2004/05 in England and Wales. (Figure 11.15)

- There was a threefold increase in the volume of household waste collected for recycling or composting in England between 1996/97 and 2004/05. (Page 152)

- In 2005, 62 per cent of new housing in England was built on previously developed land compared with 39 per cent in 1990. (Table 11.20)

Chapter 11

Human activities can affect the physical environment and natural resources at both the local and global level. The move from agricultural communities into industrial towns and conurbations has lead to huge pressures on the land, wildlife, atmosphere and waters. To moderate this often negative influence, many governments have developed environment-related policies and regulations. The UK has a strategy for sustainable development which aims to protect the environment and reduce the negative impact that human activity has upon it.

Global warming and climate change

The temperature of the Earth is determined by a balance between energy from the sun and radiation from the surface of the Earth to space. Some of this outgoing radiation is absorbed by naturally occurring gases such as water vapour and carbon dioxide. This creates a greenhouse effect that keeps the surface of the Earth around 33 degrees Celsius (°C) warmer than it would otherwise be and helps to sustain life.

Both global and local average temperatures have risen over the long term since the late 19th century, though there have been fluctuations around this trend (Figure 11.1). For this purpose, local is defined as the triangular area of the UK enclosed by Bristol, Manchester and London and is otherwise referred to as 'central England'. Average global surface temperatures have increased by around 0.7°C over the last century, beyond the range of estimated average temperatures for the Earth over the last 1000 years. All ten of the hottest years since global records began in 1850 have occurred during the period 1990–2005, with 1998 being the warmest year and 2005 being almost as warm. Current climate

models predict that global temperatures will rise by between 1.4 and 5.8°C by the end of the 21st century, and that this increase in temperature will affect sea levels and weather patterns.

During the 20th century, the annual mean temperature for central England warmed by about 1°C. The 1990s were exceptionally warm in central England by historical standards, and about 0.6°C warmer than the 1961–90 average temperature. The warmest year ever measured in central England was 2006, with an annual average temperature of 10.8°C. Seven of the ten warmest years since records began in the UK in 1772 have occurred since 1990, and 2004 and 2005 were among the top 15 warmest years. The highest single temperature ever recorded in the UK was in August 2003, when temperatures peaked at 38.5°C at the observing station at Brodgate in Kent. Climate change models suggest that the average temperature across the UK could increase by between 2.0 and 3.5°C by the 2080s, with the level of warming dependent on future global greenhouse gas emissions.

The Intergovernmental Panel on Climate Change reported in 2001 that there is new and stronger evidence that most of the warming over the last 50 years is attributable to human activities. The predominant factor among these activities is the emission of 'greenhouse gases', such as carbon dioxide, methane and nitrous oxide.

Under the Kyoto Protocol, the UK has a legally binding target to reduce its emissions of a 'basket' of six greenhouse gases by 12.5 per cent over the period 2008–2012. This reduction is against emission levels in 1990 for carbon dioxide, methane and nitrous oxide, and 1995 for hydrofluorocarbons,

Figure **11.1**

Difference in average surface temperature: deviation from 1961–90 average[1]

Global and central England

Degrees Celsius

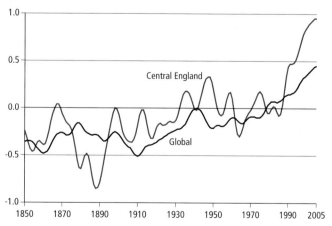

1 Data are smoothed to remove short term variation from a time series to get a clearer view of the underlying changes.

Source: Hadley Centre for Climate Prediction and Research

Figure **11.2**

Emissions of greenhouse gases[1]

United Kingdom

Million tonnes of carbon equivalent

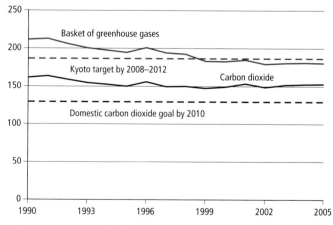

1 See Appendix, Part 11: Global warming and climate change.

Source: Department for Environment, Food and Rural Affairs; AEA Energy & Environment

perfluorocarbons and sulphur hexafluoride. Additionally, the Government intends to move beyond that target towards a goal of reducing carbon dioxide emissions to 20 per cent below 1990 levels by 2010. It is estimated that in 2005, emissions of the 'basket' of six greenhouse gases, weighted by global warming potential (see Appendix, Part 11: Global warming and climate change), were around 15.1 per cent below the base year level (Figure 11.2). However, emissions had not fallen since 2002, mainly a result of increased carbon dioxide emissions from industry and transport.

Similarly, the EU is committed to reducing emissions of these six greenhouse gases to 8 per cent below the 1990 level over the 'commitment period' of 2008–2012. This target only applies to the 15 states (EU-15) that were members of the EU when the Protocol was ratified in May 2002. However, the ten countries that joined the EU in May 2004 have all since ratified the Protocol, and have their own Kyoto targets of between 6 and 8 per cent on the same basis.

Total EU-15 emissions fell from 8.6 tonnes per person in 1990 to 8.3 tonnes per person in 2000, but then rose again so that in 2003, they were the same as in 1990 (Table 11.3). Emissions per head were lower in 2003 than in 1990 in only four countries in the EU-15, namely Luxembourg, Germany, UK and Sweden. However, much of the reduction in Germany and the UK can

The scientific basis for climate change

The case for climate change presented in *Social Trends* is based on the 2001 reports by the Intergovernmental Panel on Climate Change (IPCC). The IPCC was established by the World Meteorological Organization (WMO) and the United Nations Environment Programme (UNEP) in 1988. It is open to all members of the UN and WMO.

The role of the IPCC is to assess the scientific, technical and socio-economic information relevant to understanding the scientific basis of risk of human-induced climate change, its potential impacts and options for adaptation and mitigation. The assessment is based on peer reviewed and published scientific/technical literature.

The IPCC's *Fourth Assessment Report: Climate Change 2007*, providing a comprehensive and up-to-date assessment of the current state of knowledge on climate change, will be completed in 2007, after *Social Trends* has gone to press.

For more details visit *www.ipcc.ch/index.html*

be attributed to one-off factors: economic restructuring following reunification in Germany, and increased use of gas for electricity generation following changes in energy regulation in the UK. The countries that produced the least carbon dioxide per person in 2003 were Portugal (5.5 tonnes), Sweden (5.6 tonnes) and France (6.4 tonnes).

Carbon dioxide (CO_2) accounted for around 84 per cent of greenhouse gas emissions within the UK in 2004. The industry and the transport sectors each accounted for 28 per cent of emissions, and domestic users accounted for a further 27 per cent (Figure 11.4). For these data, emissions from power

Table **11.3**

Carbon dioxide emissions: EU comparison

Tonnes per person

	1990	1995	2000	2003
Luxembourg	27.6	22.1	18.9	22.1
Finland	10.8	10.9	10.6	13.5
Belgium	11.0	11.2	11.1	11.2
Denmark	10.0	11.2	9.5	10.6
Ireland	8.4	9.0	10.9	10.5
Netherlands	9.9	10.4	10.1	10.4
Germany	12.4	10.7	10.2	10.2
Greece	7.6	7.5	8.8	9.2
United Kingdom	9.8	9.0	8.8	9.1
Austria	7.0	7.0	7.2	8.3
Italy	7.0	7.3	7.7	7.9
Spain	5.3	5.9	7.0	7.2
France	6.4	6.3	6.4	6.4
Sweden	5.9	5.9	5.3	5.6
Portugal	3.9	4.7	5.6	5.5
EU-15 average	8.6	8.3	8.3	8.6

Source: European Environment Agency

Figure **11.4**

Carbon dioxide emissions: by end user

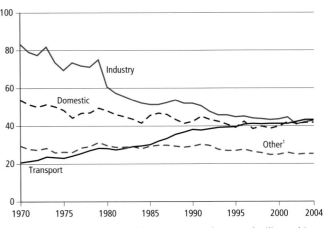

United Kingdom
Million tonnes of carbon equivalent

1 Includes commercial and public sector, agriculture, and military ships and aircraft.

Source: AEA Energy & Environment

stations that generate electricity are allocated to those sectors using that electricity.

Between 1970 and 2004 estimated carbon dioxide emissions fell by 18 per cent. Much of this decline came from a reduction in emissions attributable to industry, which fell steeply in the late 1970s and early 1980s, declined more steadily from that point, and then levelled off from 1997. The overall result has been a 49 per cent reduction in emissions from industry between 1970 and 2004. Emissions by domestic users have declined by 22 per cent over the same period, although they have risen recently, and those attributable to transport have more than doubled. Furthermore, these transport data do not include figures for international aviation and shipping.

Greenhouse gas emissions from aviation and shipping in the UK can be estimated from the refuelling activities at bunkers at UK airports and ports, of both UK and non-UK operators. Emissions attributed to fuel stored in UK shipping bunkers fell slightly, but UK shipping operators purchase most of their bunker fuel outside the UK. Reflecting the growth in air travel (see Chapter 12: Transport), carbon dioxide emissions from aviation fuel use doubled between 1990 and 2004. Additionally, because emissions at high altitude interact directly with the upper atmosphere, the greenhouse effect of aviation is greater than that of emissions at ground level.

The UK was the first country to use nuclear power on an industrial and commercial scale when the Calder Hall power

Table **11.5**

Electricity generation: by fuel used, EU comparison, 2004

Percentages

	Coal and lignite	Petroleum products	Natural and derived gas	Nuclear	Renewable sources	All fuels (=100%) (thousand GWh)
Germany	48	2	12	28	11	606.6
France	5	1	4	78	12	572.2
United Kingdom	33	1	40	20	5	395.3
Italy	15	19	45	-	21	303.3
Spain	28	9	20	23	20	280.0
Poland	92	2	3	0	3	154.2
Sweden	1	1	1	51	46	151.7
Netherlands	23	3	63	4	7	100.7
Finland	27	1	15	26	30	85.8
Belgium	11	2	28	55	4	85.4
Czech Republic	59	-	6	31	4	84.3
Austria	12	3	19	0	66	64.1
Greece	60	14	15	0	11	59.3
Portugal	33	13	26	0	29	45.1
Denmark	46	4	25	0	25	40.5
Hungary	24	2	35	35	3	33.7
Slovakia	19	2	9	56	14	30.6
Ireland	30	13	50	0	7	25.6
Lithuania	-	2	14	78	6	19.3
Slovenia	34	-	2	36	28	15.3
Estonia	93	-	7	0	1	10.3
Latvia	-	1	31	0	68	4.7
Cyprus	-	100	-	0	-	4.2
Luxembourg	-	-	76	0	24	4.1
Malta	-	100	-	0	-	2.2
EU-25 total	29	4	20	31	15	3,178.6

Source: Eurostat

station was commissioned by the United Kingdom Atomic Energy Authority in 1956. The consumption of nuclear energy in the UK has fallen since the late 1990s, and in 2003 the Energy White Paper, 'Our energy future – creating a low carbon economy' made clear the Government priority of developing energy efficiency and renewable energy. While nuclear energy is an important source of carbon-free electricity, the economics of nuclear power have so far limited new generating capacity and there are also important issues regarding how to dispose of nuclear waste that need to be resolved. However, it is possible that new nuclear generation may be developed in the future to meet carbon reduction objectives.

One-fifth (20 per cent) of the electricity produced in the UK in 2004 was generated by nuclear power stations, a similar proportion to that produced by Germany (28 per cent), Finland (26 per cent) and Spain (23 per cent) (Table 11.5). France produces over three-quarters of its electricity from nuclear power. Nearly half of EU-25 member states have no developed nuclear production capacity.

Renewable electricity can be generated from wind (both offshore and onshore), water (hydro, wave and tidal power), sunlight (the direct conversion of solar radiation into electricity, called photovoltaics or PV), biomass (energy from forestry, crops or biodegradable waste) and from the earth's heat (geothermal energy). None of these forms of generation, except biomass, involves the production of carbon dioxide, and biomass generation produces only the carbon that the material has absorbed from the atmosphere while growing.

Around 5 per cent of electricity produced in the UK in 2004 came from renewable sources. This was among the lowest proportions in the EU-25 where the average was 15 per cent. Latvia, Austria and Sweden produced the greatest proportions. The UK figure reflects its historical use of coal and gas, the absence of high mountains, which facilitate large scale hydro generation, and the absence of extensive forests needed for biomass generation. There is, however, scope to develop extensive wind and wave power in the UK. Under its Renewables Obligation, the UK Government is committed to increasing the contribution of electricity from renewable sources. By providing market incentives for renewable energy, it is estimated that by 2010, 10 per cent of licensed electricity sales will be from renewable sources. The EU-wide target is that 22 per cent of electricity should be generated from renewable sources by 2010.

Use of resources

Between 1991 and 2004, the number of households in the UK increased by 10 per cent. Over the same period household waste per person increased by 26 per cent (Figure 11.6).

Household energy consumption in the UK has increased roughly in line with the increase in households, at 9 per cent over the same period, but fell in 2005, representing an overall increase of 5 per cent. Changes such as an increased efficiency of appliances and improved thermal insulation of houses have been counterbalanced by an increased use of appliances and a tendency for people to heat their homes to higher temperatures than previously. Household carbon dioxide emissions fell by 7 per cent between 1991 and 2004, largely due to electricity generators switching away from coal. However because the majority of electricity in the UK is still produced from fossil fuel sources that generate carbon dioxide (see Table 11.5), fluctuations in the overall pattern of household carbon dioxide emissions are similar to those of energy consumption.

Water consumption per person has also grown in line with the growth in households, with particular peaks in 1995 and 2003, when there were droughts (households tend to use more water during droughts, for example to water gardens). In 2005, water consumption was 8 per cent higher than it was in 1991. The increase in water consumption can be linked to greater ownership of appliances such as washing machines, washer-dryers and dishwashers, and the increased use of those appliances within the home, as well as the greater number of smaller households (see Chapter 2: Households and families). In 1991, 87 per cent of households had a washing machine compared with 95 per cent in 2005. The proportion of households with a dishwasher has also risen, from 14 per cent to 29 per cent over the same period.

Figure **11.6**

Environmental impact of households

United Kingdom

Index numbers (1991=100)

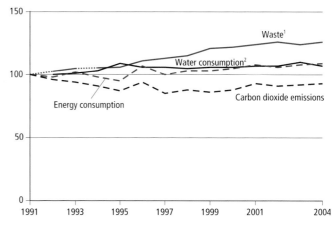

1 Waste data for 1992 and 1994 are not available.
2 Water consumption data are 1992=100.

Source: Department for Environment, Food and Rural Affairs; Department of Trade and Industry; Office for National Statistics; AEA Energy & Environment; The Water Services Regulation Authority (Ofwat)

The UK does not suffer from lack of rain, although levels of precipitation vary both geographically and over time. However, if predicted changes in precipitation patterns occur as a result of climate change – with wetter winters and drier summers – water resources in the UK could become a major concern over the next century.

Over the last 40 years Scotland has been the wettest part of the UK, with a long-term (1961–1990) average of 1,436 mm of precipitation a year. The Anglian region in the east of England has the driest long term average, at 596mm a year. Since 1990, the wettest year was 2001, with a UK average of 1,335 mm, 124 per cent of the long term average. During this year, Wales was actually the wettest area with 1,765 mm of precipitation. The driest year in the UK since 1990 was 2004, with only 901 mm annual rainfall, 83 per cent of the long term average.

The variable rainfall is reflected in overall reservoir stocks. Within-year variations of reservoir capacity in England and Wales can be large, such as in 1995, when water stocks fell to below 50 per cent capacity in October of that year, having been at over 98 per cent of capacity in March (Figure 11.7). There has generally been higher than average rainfall since mid-1997, which increased reservoir stocks, but considerable stress can be placed on water resources in drought years.

There were 315 drought orders issued throughout the UK between 1988 and 2004. Most of these were issued in the drought years of 1989 (93 drought orders), 1990 (61), 1995 (63) and 1996 (44). One way to help conserve water is to encourage greater use of water meters to discourage wastage. Metered water is water measured at the point of delivery to premises (including non-drinkable water). There is considerable variation in the amount of water supplied by the water service companies. In 2005/06, households in the Thames area were supplied with the most metered water per person in England and Wales, receiving 154 litres per person per day, and those in Severn Trent used the least, at 118 litres per person per day (Figure 11.8). In 2005/06, all water service companies supplied more unmetered water per person than metered water.

Most of the energy produced in the UK comes from fossil fuels, such as petroleum, coal and natural gas. In 2005, UK primary fuel production was 9 per cent lower than in the previous year, and 90 per cent of this was accounted for by fossil fuels, petroleum, coal and natural gas (Figure 11.9). The dominant position of coal 30 years ago has been eroded, initially by petroleum and latterly also by natural gas. The sharp drop in production in 1984 was due to the miners' strike of that year. In 2005 coal accounted for 6 per cent of primary fuel production, while natural gas accounted for 41 per cent and

Figure **11.7**

Reservoir stocks[1]

England & Wales
Percentages

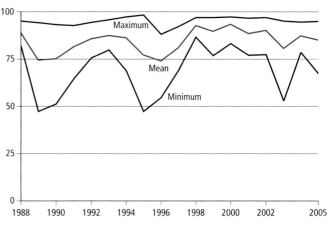

1 The maximum, mean and minimum percentage of overall net capacity based on a network of 27 large reservoir sites.

Source: Centre for Ecology and Hydrology from Environment Agency and water and sewerage companies

Figure **11.8**

Household water consumption:[1] by water and sewerage company,[2] 2005/06

Great Britain
Litres per person per day

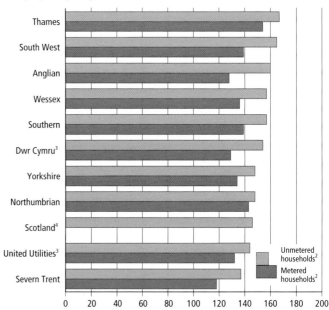

1 Excluding underground supply pipe leakage.
2 See Appendix, Part 11: Water supply.
3 Dwr Cymru formerly Welsh Water, United Utilities formerly North West.
4 Typically households are not metered in Scotland.

Source: The Water Services Regulation Authority (Ofwat); Scottish Executive Water Services Unit

petroleum for 43 per cent. Petroleum production increased sharply between 1976 and 1985 as oilfields were discovered and brought into production, although it fell with the resumption of coal production in 1984. The increase in the production of natural gas from the end of the 1980s resulted in electricity suppliers switching from coal to gas as a cheaper and cleaner source of fuel. The production of both petroleum and natural gas has fallen since the end of the 20th century as North Sea reserves have decreased.

UK oil reserves were estimated at 4,400 million tonnes in 2006, of which 3,100 million tonnes have already been recovered (Table 11.10). This was greater than the estimated reserves of 3,200 million tonnes in 1990, due to both new discoveries and improvements in recovery techniques. Of the remaining oil, only 500 million tonnes were proven. Proven reserves are those estimated to have a 90 per cent chance of being recovered. Probable and possible reserves have a greater than 50 per cent, and less than 50 per cent chance respectively, of being technically and commercially recoverable. Beyond this, there is an estimated 68 to 423 million tonnes of oil reserves that have yet to be discovered but that may exist in areas of the UK continental shelf.

Estimates of how long the remaining UK oil reserves will last are uncertain, but they do show an overall decline between

Table **11.10**

Oil and gas reserves

United Kingdom[1]

	1990		2006	
	Oil (million tonnes)	Gas (billion cubic metres)	Oil (million tonnes)	Gas (billion cubic metres)
Total recoverable reserves	3,189	2,532	4,357	3,013
Already recovered	1,374	752	3,090	2,007
Total remaining reserves in present discoveries	1,815	1,780	1,267	1,006
Proven reserves[2,3]	535	545	516	481
Probable reserves[3]	660	655	300	247
Possible reserves[3]	620	580	451	278
Potential additional reserves	170 to 380	140 to 300	68 to 423	68 to 282

1 Including the UK Continental Shelf, which comprises of those areas of the sea bed and subsoil beyond the territorial sea over which the UK exercises sovereign rights of exploration and exploitation of natural resources.
2 Excludes volumes of oil and gas already recovered.
3 See Appendix, Part 11: Oil and gas reserves.

Source: Department of Trade and Industry

1990 and 2006, as would be expected given the extraction of reserves over the period. Between 2004 and 2005, the life expectancy of oil reserves increased from 13 to 14 years. However, this is a result of lower extraction rates rather than new discoveries. Levels of oil extraction amounted to 85 million tonnes in 2005.

Estimates of gas reserves were 3,000 billion cubic metres for 2006, up from 2,500 billion cubic metres in 1990. Proven reserves amounted to 480 billion cubic metres in 2006. In 2006 gas reserves were expected to last for approximately 11 years, if the rate of extraction remains unchanged. Levels of gas extraction fell after the peak of gas production in 2000. In 2005, 86 billion cubic metres of gas were extracted, 19 per cent lower than the 2000 peak, and the lowest annual amount extracted since 1996.

Pollution

Emissions of the major air pollutants in the UK have generally been falling since the 1970s, and the rate of decline has accelerated since 1989. Carbon monoxide (CO) is harmful because it reduces the capacity of the blood to carry and deliver oxygen around the body. Emissions of carbon monoxide fell by 31 per cent between 1970 and 1990, followed by a 64 per cent

Figure **11.9**

Production of primary fuels[1]

United Kingdom

Million tonnes of oil equivalent

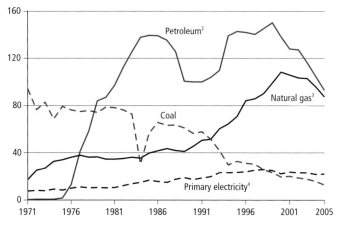

1 See Appendix, Part 11: Production of primary fuels.
2 Includes crude oil, natural gas liquids and feedstocks.
3 Includes colliery methane.
4 Nuclear, natural flow hydro-electricity and, from 1988, generation at wind stations, solar and geothermal heat, solid renewable sources (wood, waste, etc), and gaseous renewable sources (landfill gas, sewage gas).

Source: Department of Trade and Industry

Figure **11.11**

Emissions of selected air pollutants[1]

United Kingdom

Million tonnes

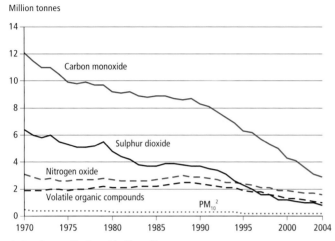

1 See Appendix, Part 11: Air pollutants.
2 Particulate matter that is less than 10 microns in diameter.

Source: Department for Environment, Food and Rural Affairs; AEA Energy & Environment

Table **11.12**

Air pollutants: by source,[1] 2004

United Kingdom   Percentages

	Carbon monoxide	Nitrogen oxides	Volatile organic compounds	Sulphur dioxide	PM$_{10}$[2]
Transport[3]	49	44	15	5	24
Manufacturing industries and construction	22	16	4	19	16
Residential	17	7	5	4	17
Industrial processes	5	-	14	2	12
Energy industries	3	27	1	68	7
Agriculture[3]	1	4	40	-	9
Fugitive emissions[4] from fuels	1	-	20	1	1
Land-use change and forestry	-	-	-	-	9
Commercial and institutional	-	1	-	-	-
Other[3]	1	-	1	-	5
All sources (=100%) (million tonnes)	2.9	1.6	1.0	0.8	0.2

1 See Appendix, Part 11: Air pollutants, and Sources of air pollution.
2 Particulate matter that is less than 10 microns in diameter.
3 Contains a combination of EMEP source categories. See Appendix, Part 11: Sources of air pollution.
4 Emissions resulting from the leakage of gases during various human activities. See Appendix, Part 11: Sources of air pollution.

Source: AEA Energy & Environment

reduction between 1990 and 2004 (Figure 11.11). This was mainly as a result of the introduction of catalytic converters in petrol cars.

Sulphur dioxide (SO_2) is an acid gas that can affect both human and animal health and vegetation. It affects the lining of the nose, throat and lungs, particularly among those with asthma and chronic lung disease, and is one of the pollutants that form 'acid rain'. Sulphur dioxide emissions fell by 77 per cent between 1990 and 2004, largely as a result of a reduction in coal use by power stations and the introduction of the desulphurisation of flue gas at two power stations. Following this change, the rate of decline slowed after 1999. Nitrogen oxides (NOx) are also acid gases that have similar effects to sulphur dioxide. Emissions of nitrogen oxide pollutants fell by 45 per cent between 1990 and 2004.

Particulate matter that is less than 10 microns in diameter, known as PM$_{10}$ is generated primarily by combustion processes, as well as from processes such as stone abrasion during construction, mining and quarrying. Particulate matter can be responsible for causing premature deaths among those with pre-existing heart and lung conditions. Emissions fell by 48 per cent between 1990 and 2004.

Air pollution comes from a variety of different sources. Fossil fuel combustion is the main source of air pollution in the UK, with road transport and power stations the most important contributors. Emissions of other pollutants are more evenly

spread among different sources, although road transport and electricity generation are, again, important contributors.

In 2004 road transport accounted for 49 per cent of carbon monoxide emissions, and 44 per cent of nitrogen oxide emissions (Table 11.12). This compared with 66 per cent of carbon monoxide emissions and 47 per cent of nitrogen oxide emissions in 1990. Although the level of road traffic has continued to grow since 1990 (see Chapter 12: Transport), changes in vehicle technology have reduced the impact of emissions from this sector. Power stations produced 68 per cent of sulphur dioxide and 27 per cent of nitrogen oxide emissions in 2004, compared with 74 per cent and 27 per cent respectively in 1990.

Some pollutants, particularly sulphur dioxide, nitrogen oxides and ammonia (NH_3), can cause harm to the environment through acid deposition. This can occur at the land surface where gases and particles from the atmosphere are absorbed directly or as mentioned previously, through polluted rainfall ('acid rain'). Acid deposition can be found hundreds of kilometres away from the source of emissions. The percentage of areas of sensitive habitats where critical loads (the levels at which significant harm is caused) were exceeded in the UK decreased between 1996 and 2003, from 73 per cent to 56 per cent. The largest reduction, from 68 per cent in 1996 to 44 per cent in 2003, was in Scotland.

The quality and quantity of water supplies are important to the health and well-being of both people and the natural environment. A number of factors can affect the quality of rivers and other areas of water, including fertiliser run-off, industrial and sewage discharge, and climate. Lower than average rainfall can result in low river flows, which can have an adverse effect on river water quality by reducing the dilution of pollutants.

The Environment Agency monitors water pollution in England and Wales. In 2005 it recorded 23,504 incidents, of which 661 were category 1 or category 2 incidents. Category 1 incidents, classified as 'most severe', are defined as those that have a persistent and/or extensive effect on water quality. They may cause major damage to aquatic ecosystems; cause the closure of a drinking water abstraction plant; cause major damage to agriculture and/or commerce; or have a serious impact on the human population. Category 2 incidents, classified as 'severe', have similar but less serious effects. The two most commonly identified sources of the category 1 and 2 incidents in 2005 were agriculture and the sewage and water industry (Figure 11.13).

Rivers and canals in the UK are generally in good or fair condition, and both the chemical and biological quality have improved since 1990. Biological water quality tests

are carried out across the UK by monitoring tiny animals (macro-invertebrates) that live in or on the riverbed. The number and diversity of freshwater species found in samples can be used to make inferences about water quality, since research has shown that there is a relationship between species composition and water quality. In 2005 the proportion of river length in good or fair biological condition as measured by these criterion was 95 per cent in England, 99 per cent in Wales, 97 per cent in Scotland and 98 per cent in Northern Ireland (Table 11.14). Different systems of classification were used in these national surveys so the results are not directly comparable.

The chemical quality of rivers in England has improved since 1990, with 93 per cent of river length classified as being in good or fair condition in 2005. In Wales, Scotland and Northern Ireland, 98 per cent, 97 per cent and 93 per cent of their river lengths were in good or fair chemical condition. Improvements in water quality since 1990 are thought to be largely attributable to the investment programme of the water industry and to pollution control measures.

Table **11.14**

Biological quality[1] of rivers and canals: by country and region[2]

United Kingdom			Percentage of total river length	
	1990[3]		2005	
	Good/ fair	Poor/ bad	Good/ fair	Poor/ bad
England	89	11	95	5
North West	68	32	89	11
North East	85	15	93	7
Midlands	92	8	92	8
Anglian	97	3	99	1
Thames	91	9	96	4
Southern	97	3	99	1
South West	97	3	99	1
Wales	98	2	99	1
Scotland[4]	97	3	97	3
Northern Ireland	100	-	98	2

1 See Appendix, Part 11: Rivers and canals.
2 Environment Agency regions in England and Wales. The boundaries of the Environment Agency regions are based on river catchment areas and not county or country borders.
3 Northern Ireland figures are for 1991.
4 Data for Scotland are collected on a different basis to the rest of the United Kingdom.

Source: Environment Agency; Scottish Environment Protection Agency; Environment and Heritage Service, Northern Ireland

Figure **11.13**

Water pollution incidents:[1] by source, 2005

England & Wales
Numbers

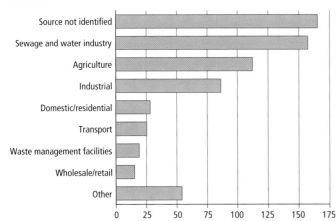

1 Incidents with major or significant impacts (categories 1 and 2). See Appendix, Part 11: Water pollution incidents.

Source: Environment Agency

Noise pollution is an environmental issue that affects people on a personal level. The number of noise complaints to environmental health officers (EHOs) in England and Wales has increased considerably over the last 20 years. However, this may reflect an increased tendency to complain among the public, as well as an increase in the incidence of nuisance. The largest increase in noise complaints over the period was in complaints about neighbours. Between 1984/85 and 2004/05, complaints about noise from domestic premises increased almost fivefold (Figure 11.15). Nearly three-quarters of all noise complaints received by EHOs since the mid-1990s had domestic premises as their source.

The number of complaints about noise from road works, construction and demolition works were three and a half times greater in 2004/05 than in 1984/85, while complaints about noise from industrial and commercial premises nearly doubled over the same period.

The number of complaints about road traffic noise generally rose until 1995/96, but has since fallen. Overall, complaints about traffic noise fell by 22 per cent between 1984/85 and 2003/04, the latest year for which data are available. However, these figures only cover complaints about road traffic noise made to EHOs. They do not include complaints to other government bodies such as the Department for Transport.

Loud music and barking dogs were the most common reasons for complaints to local authorities about noise nuisance from neighbours in England, Wales and Northern Ireland, according

to the National Noise Survey 2005. These sources were given as the cause of most complaints by over two-thirds and over one-quarter of local councils, respectively. Pubs and clubs were the source of most complaints about non-domestic noise, with over half of local councils identifying them as the cause of most complaints.

The local authorities were also asked 'What, in your opinion, is the reason for the continued high level of noise complaints?'. Around 6 in 10 local authorities suggested that 'selfish attitudes' and 'a higher expectation of quiet' were the most common reasons, followed by 'incompatible lifestyles with neighbours', 'inadequate sound insulation' and 'more powerful sound equipment'. There were similar results for the Noise Survey Scotland.

Waste management

The collection and disposal of domestic waste and litter and rubbish from public areas, as well as some commercial waste, is the responsibility of local authorities throughout the UK. Most of this municipal waste has traditionally been disposed to landfill, a method that makes little use of the waste and produces greenhouse gases, mainly carbon dioxide and methane.

The total amount of municipal waste produced in England rose from around 24,600 thousand tonnes in 1996/97 to nearly 29,400 thousand tonnes in 2002/03, before falling slightly in 2003/04. However, in 2004/05 it rose again to a high point of nearly 29,700 thousand tonnes, an increase of 21 per cent since 1996/97 (Table 11.16).

In 2004/05, 67 per cent of this municipal waste was disposed to landfill, down from 84 per cent in 1996/97. Recycling rates increased over the same period, from 7 per cent to 23 per cent. The amount of waste disposed of by incineration (and used to produce energy) doubled, while the amount of waste incinerated without energy production decreased over the period.

Around 86 per cent of municipal waste in England was generated by households in 2004/05. This represented 25.7 million tonnes of waste, equivalent to 513 kilograms per person over the year. The amount of household waste collected for recycling or composting (excluding home-composting) more than trebled between 1996/97 and 2004/05, to 5.8 million tonnes. Recycling or composting includes materials taken to civic amenity sites and other drop-off points such as bottle banks provided by the local authority, as well as material collected directly from households. The government target for Great Britain, set in Waste Strategy 2000, is to recycle or compost 25 per cent of household waste by 2005/06. The recycling rate for household waste rose from 11 per cent in 2000/01 to 22 per cent in 2004/05. Compost,

Figure **11.15**

Noise complaints received by environmental health officers:[1] by source

England & Wales
Index numbers (1984/85=100)

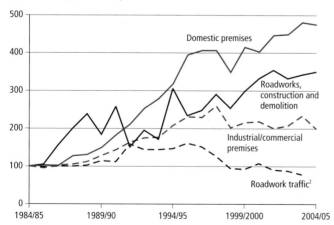

1 See Appendix, Part 11: Noise complaints.
2 Data for 2004/05 not available.

Source: The Chartered Institute of Environmental Health

Table **11.16**

Management of municipal waste: by method

England

Thousand tonnes

	1996/97	1998/99	2000/01	2002/03	2003/04	2004/05
Landfill	20,635	21,517	22,039	22,068	20,936	19,899
Incineration with EfW[1]	1,435	2,139	2,391	2,600	2,596	2,818
Incineration without EfW[1]	619	17	20	7	8	7
RDF[2] manufacture	148	131	67	87	12	19
Recycled/composted[3]	1,751	2,523	3,446	4,572	5,528	6,982
Other[4]	0	10	95	59	26	8
Total	24,588	26,337	28,057	29,394	29,105	29,734

1 Energy from waste.
2 Refuse derived fuel.
3 Includes household and non-household sources collected for recycling or for centralised composting; home composting estimates are not included in this total.
4 Excludes any processing before waste is sent to landfill or materials reclamation.

Source: Department for Environment, Food and Rural Affairs

followed by paper and card, made up the largest proportions of recycled material in 2004/05, accounting for 30 per cent and 28 per cent of recycled materials, respectively.

There was a wide variation in household recycling rates across England and Wales in 2004/05. The rates achieved by local waste disposal authorities varied between 10 per cent in Cardiff, Merthyr Tydfil, Middlesbrough and Sunderland, and 38 per cent in Cambridgeshire, with nearly one-third of authorities achieving a rate between 15 and 20 per cent (Map 11.17).

Most of the authorities with high recycling rates (25 per cent and above) were located in the East, South West, East Midlands and South East regions of England. No waste disposal authority in England and Wales had a household waste recycling rate of less than 10 per cent in 2004/05, compared with 9 per cent of authorities in 2003/04.

A regional comparison of the composition of materials collected for recycling in 2003/04 showed a wide variation, and reflected a combination of differences in local recycling amenities, policy and public attitudes. For example, 17 per cent of materials collected in London and 20 per cent collected in the North East were for composting, compared with 37 per cent in the North West and 35 per cent in the East Midlands.

Countryside, wildlife and farming

Land use is defined as the main activity taking place on an area of land. Over 70 per cent of the total UK land area is under agricultural use, and much of the 'natural' landscape is the result of centuries of agricultural activities. Agricultural land includes grasses and rough grazing, as well as crops, land set

Map **11.17**

Household waste recycling:[1] by waste disposal authority,[2] 2004/05

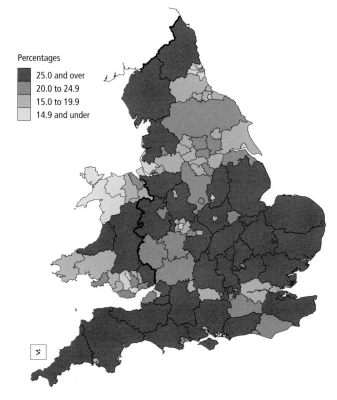

Percentages
- 25.0 and over
- 20.0 to 24.9
- 15.0 to 19.9
- 14.9 and under

1 Includes composting.
2 These boundaries generally match county or unitary authority boundaries, except for metropolitan districts in West Yorkshire, South Yorkshire, Tyne and Wear and West Midlands.

Source: Department for Environment, Food and Rural Affairs; Welsh Assembly Government

Figure **11.18**

Land area: by use,[1] 2005

United Kingdom
Percentages

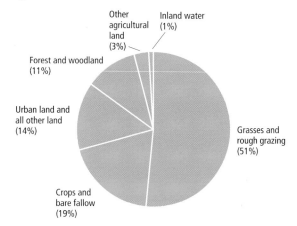

1 See Appendix, Part 11: Land use.

Source: Department for Environment, Food and Rural Affairs

aside under European Commission (EC) agricultural schemes and other agricultural uses. The total area of land under agricultural use decreased by 1 per cent to 51 per cent between 1998 and 2005 (Figure 11.18). The area under crops fell by 12 per cent to 19 per cent during this period, mainly as a result of EC Set-Aside Schemes – the amount of set-aside land rose by nearly 44 per cent between 1998 and 2005. Sole right rough grazing land decreased by 6 per cent and other grassland increased by 4 per cent, while urban and other land use increased by 9 per cent.

Figure **11.19**

Land under organic crop production[1]

United Kingdom
Thousand hectares

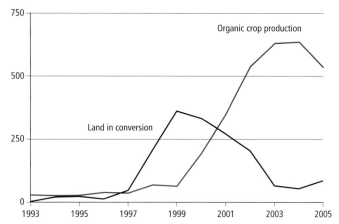

1 Figures for 1993 to 1999 use dates closest to December. From 2000 onwards, data are at December.

Source: Department for Environment, Food and Rural Affairs

The varieties of crops grown in the UK are likely to change if climate change predictions prove correct (see Global warming and climate change section). Between 1998 and 2005 the area covered by most crop types declined, in line with a fall in the overall area under crop production. However the area under oilseed rape increased by 2 per cent over this period.

Over the past ten years, concerns about the possible impacts that the use of pesticides, BSE in cattle, and the development of genetically modified (GM) crops may have on people's health and the environment, have led to an increased interest in organic farming. There has been an overall increase in the area of land under organic production since 1998. By December 2005, 533,900 hectares of land in the UK were under organic production, representing 4 per cent of total area (Figure 11.19). However, this increase had begun to slow by 2002, and the amount of land converting to organic production – a process that takes two to three years – fell after 1999, until 2005 when there was a small rise. Uncertainties about the reform of the Common Agricultural Policy may have been partly responsible for the reduced level of conversion to organic methods.

In 2005, 52 per cent of organically managed land in the UK was in Scotland, covering 360 thousand hectares, 38 per cent was in England, 9.3 per cent was in Wales and 1.0 per cent was in Northern Ireland. Over half of organically managed land in England is situated in the south west and south east of the country. Permanent and temporary pasture accounted for 86 per cent of fully organic or in-conversion land in the UK. The remainder was made up of cereals and other crops; vegetables including potatoes; set-aside; woodland and other uses.

Urban land accounted for 11 per cent of England's land area when last estimated in 1991. In an attempt to minimise the effect of the growth in new house building (see Chapter 10: Housing) on the countryside and other green areas, the Government has a target for 60 per cent of new housing to be built on previously developed land by 2008. In 2005 the proportion of new housing built on previously developed land had increased from 39 per cent in 1990 to 62 per cent in 2005 (Table 11.20). In 2005, 31 per cent of land changing to residential use in England was previously rural, of which 27 per cent was agricultural land. This compared with 52 per cent in 1990, of which 44 per cent was previously agricultural land.

Wild bird populations are good indicators of the condition of wildlife and the countryside, as birds have a wide range of habitats and tend to be at, or near, the top of the food chain. The UK Government's indicator of wild bird populations which looks at 113 different breeds shows that following an increase in the 1990s, the overall population of wild birds in the UK is nearly

Table **11.20**

Land changing to residential use:[1,2,3] by previous use

England   Percentages

	1990	1995	2000	2005
Agriculture	44	35	34	27
Other rural uses	8	4	5	4
All rural uses	52	40	39	31
Residential	21	15	17	20
Previously developed vacant and derelict land	11	23	22	22
Vacant, not previously developed	10	12	9	7
Other urban uses	7	10	13	19
All urban uses	48	60	61	69
All previously developed land	39	48	52	62
All land changing to residential use (=100%) (hectares)	8,755	5,820	5,280	..

1 Information relates to map changes recorded by Ordnance Survey between 1985 and 2005 for which the year of change is judged to have been the year shown. See Appendix, Part 11: Land use change.
2 Excludes conversion of existing buildings.
3 Figures for the most recent years are subject to revision due to the lag between the change occurring and it being recorded.

Source: Communities and Local Government

10 per cent higher than it was in 1970. However, the breeding populations of some common farmland and woodland birds have fallen. Populations of 19 farmland species are at about 60 per cent of their 1970 level but have remained fairly stable since the early 1990s. Between 1994 and 2005, using the most recent consistent measure for individual species, breeding populations of skylark, yellowhammer and starling declined,

Table **11.21**

Breeding populations of selected birds

United Kingdom   Index numbers (1994=100)

	1994	1997	2000	2003	2005
Woodland					
Great tit	100	113	121	128	144
Pheasant	100	100	114	131	132
Blue tit	100	120	104	119	124
Blackbird	100	96	116	120	122
Farmland					
Woodpigeon	100	96	106	120	122
Skylark	100	92	92	87	87
Yellowhammer	100	90	90	84	83
Starling	100	99	97	73	79

Source: British Trust for Ornithology; Joint Nature Conservation Committee, Royal Society for the Protection of Birds

by 13 per cent, 17 per cent and 21 per cent respectively (Table 11.21). However, other species, particularly woodland species such as the great tit, pheasant and blackbird, have increased over the same period.

Changes in farming practices may have contributed to the decline in species, particularly those that mainly breed on farmland. Increased use of chemicals and loss of hedgerows have led to a decline and deterioration in suitable breeding and feeding areas. The Government has set a target to reverse the long term decline in the number of farmland birds by 2020.

Fish are a traditional food resource and are a vital element of the ocean's ecosystem. Trends in spawning stock vary from species to species and stocks can fluctuate substantially over relatively short periods. Biomass estimates are used to evaluate whether the spawning population of each stock is sustainable. In 2005 the percentage of 26 assessed fish stocks around the UK that were categorised as being at full reproductive capacity and harvested sustainably was 35 per cent. This means that for 65 per cent of the assessed stocks, spawning levels were insufficient to guarantee stock replenishment.

Most stocks have been over-exploited over time and some are at near historically low levels. For example, the spawning stock of North Sea cod fell from 157,000 tonnes in 1963 to 38,000 tonnes in 2001, a decrease of 76 per cent, although

Figure **11.22**

North Sea fish stocks

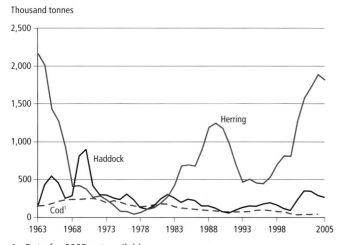

Thousand tonnes

1 Data for 2005 not available.

Source: Centre for Environment, Fisheries and Agriculture Science; International Council for the Exploration of the Sea; Department for Environment, Food and Rural Affairs

it has since increased slightly to 46,000 tonnes in 2004 (Figure 11.22).

The North Sea herring population was seriously affected by over-fishing in the 1970s. The closure of the North Sea fishery between 1978 and 1982 allowed spawning stocks to recover. From the late 1980s there was another decline in stocks of North Sea herring. This recovered again from the mid-1990s and in 2004 the spawning stock was at the highest level recorded for 40 years. In 2005 stocks declined slightly, to an estimated 1,820 thousand tonnes.

Transport

- The total distance travelled by people within Great Britain nearly tripled between 1961 and 2005, from 295 billion to 797 billion passenger kilometres, further than ever before. (Table 12.1)

- In 2005, 43 per cent of trips to school made by 5 to 10-year-olds in Great Britain were made by car, compared with 38 per cent in 1995–97. (Page 160)

- Bus and coach fares rose by 168 per cent between 1987 and 2006 in the UK, compared with a rise in the 'All items' retail price index of 93 per cent. (Figure 12.8)

- The proportion of households with two or more cars increased from 8 per cent to 31 per cent between 1971 and 2004 in Great Britain. (Page 163)

- The number of children killed or seriously injured in road accidents in Great Britain halved between the average for 1994–98 and 2005. (Page 167)

- The UK received 30 million visitors from overseas in 2005, a new high. The last peak was in 1998 with 25.7 million visitors. (Table 12.21)

Chapter 12

Long-term trends have been established in many areas of transport and travel, for example the increase in the average distance each person travels in a year, the rising number of cars on the roads, and an ever increasing reliance on them. Travel overseas, and particularly air travel, has increased substantially in recent years. There are, however, pronounced variations in people's travel patterns depending, for example, on their age, sex, where they live, and their income.

Travel patterns

People in Great Britain are travelling further than ever before. The total distance travelled by people within Great Britain nearly tripled between 1961 and 2005, from 295 billion to 797 billion passenger kilometres per year (Table 12.1). Distance travelled by air in 2005 was 10 times that travelled in 1961, the fastest growth of any means of transport. However, this was from a very low starting point, and the 10 billion passenger kilometres travelled by air in 2005 still only comprised around 1 per cent of the total distance travelled within Great Britain in that year.

The distance travelled by car, van and taxi in Great Britain rose to 678 billion passenger kilometres in 2005, contributing most to the overall increase in distance travelled between 1961 and 2005. Since the early 1960s the car has been the dominant means of transport, accounting for 85 per cent of all passenger kilometres travelled in 2005. However, the rapid rates of increase that occurred particularly in the 1960s and 1980s were replaced by more gradual growth from the late 1980s. The total distance travelled by car rose by an average of nearly

5 per cent a year in the 1980s, compared with an annual average of 1 per cent between 1991 and 2005.

Distances travelled by rail in Great Britain grew from 39 billion to 52 billion passenger kilometres between 1961/62 and 2005/06. However, there was a decline in the number of passenger kilometres travelled for much of the early part of this period, reaching a low point of 31 billion in 1982/83. Passenger kilometres by rail then rose for much of the 1980s to a peak of 41 billion in 1988/89, before declining again in the early 1990s. Between 1994/95 and 2003/04, passenger kilometres travelled, rose by an average of nearly 4 per cent a year.

Travel on buses and coaches fell steadily from 76 billion passenger kilometres in 1961 to a low of around 43 billion in 1992. After remaining broadly steady for much of the 1990s, the distance travelled by bus and coach rose slowly to reach 48 billion passenger kilometres in 2004 and 2005. Travel by bus and coach, and the railway each accounted for just 6 per cent of all passenger kilometres in 2005.

According to the National Travel Survey, British residents travelled an average of 11,600 kilometres per person in Great Britain in 2005, a 3 per cent increase on 1995–97 (the earliest period for which comparable weighted data are available). Most (80 per cent) of this distance was accounted for by car and van journeys, made either as a driver or a passenger, but walking accounted for around 317 kilometres per person, behind surface rail (742 kilometres per person) and local buses (450 kilometres per person). Cycling accounted for 58 kilometres per person in 2005, a decline from 69 kilometres in 1995–97. The average trip length across all modes of transport was 11 kilometres.

Most distances travelled are for leisure or work. In 2005, people travelled an average of 4,657 kilometres per person per year for leisure, and 3,402 kilometres per person commuting to work and on business trips. People travelled a further 1,414 kilometres during the year to shop. The distance people travel in a year varies by their socio-economic group. Professionals, and employers and managers each travelled an average of nearly 22,000 kilometres in 2005, twice as far as semi-skilled and personal service workers, and unskilled manual workers (Figure 12.2).

The increase in distance travelled between 1995–97 and 2005 was mirrored by an increase of 4 per cent in the time spent travelling, which reached 385 hours per person in 2005. However the number of trips has decreased by 4 per cent over the same period to 1,044 trips per person per year.

Females in Great Britain made more trips in 2005 on average (1,056) than males (1,031). There were also differences in the purpose of their trips and the methods of transport used.

Table **12.1**

Passenger transport: by mode

Great Britain					Billion passenger kilometres	
	1961	1971	1981	1991	2001	2005
Road[1]						
Car and van[2]	157	313	394	582	654	678
Bus and coach	76	60	48	44	47	48
Bicycle	11	4	5	5	4	4
Motorcycle	11	4	10	6	5	6
All road	255	381	458	637	710	735
Rail[3]	39	35	34	39	47	52
Air[4]	1	2	3	5	8	10
All modes	295	419	495	681	765	797

1 Road transport data from 1993 onwards are not directly comparable with earlier years. See Appendix, Part 12: Road traffic.
2 Includes taxis.
3 Data relate to financial years.
4 Includes Northern Ireland, Channel Islands and the Isle of Man.

Source: Department for Transport

Figure **12.2**

Average distance travelled per person per year: by socio-economic group,[1] 2005

Great Britain
Kilometres per person

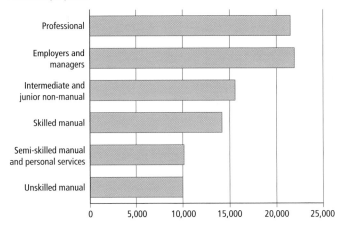

1 See Appendix, Part 12: Socio-economic Group.

Source: National Travel Survey, Department for Transport

While most trips by both males and females were made by car (around two-thirds), females were more likely than males to walk or use buses and coaches (Table 12.3). Similar proportions of trips made by males and females were for entertainment or socialising, but a greater proportion of trips by males were for commuting or business, and a greater proportion of females' trips were for shopping, or for escorting children to school.

Within this overall pattern, there are specific types of trip that show even wider differences. In particular, males were more likely than females to use a car to commute or for business, despite making on average the same number of car trips. Females made more of their car trips for shopping than males. Females were also twice as likely as males to use the train to attend an educational establishment, and over half of rail trips made by men were for commuting to work, compared with under two-fifths of rail trips made by women.

In 2005, residents of Great Britain spent an average of 63 minutes a day travelling (including trips to work), with the average time taken to make one trip being 22 minutes, an increase of 9 per cent since 1995–97. Trips made by car and van drivers took an average of 21 minutes, with surface rail trips averaging 80 minutes and trips made on local buses taking 33 minutes (37 minutes in London). Walking trips were on average 16 minutes long.

Peoples' trips to work took an average of 27 minutes in Great Britain in 2005 compared with an average of 24 minutes in 1995–97. In 2005, it was estimated that just over 1 million people entered Central London daily during the morning peak (7am to 10am), an increase of 6 per cent since 1995. There are variations in travel to work times depending on where people work in Great Britain. Generally, the more built-up the area, the longer the commute to work will take. The area type with the longest commuting times was the London Boroughs, with average commuting times of 33 minutes for men and

Table **12.3**

Trips per person per year: by sex, main mode and trip purpose,[1] 2005

Great Britain   Percentages

	Males						Females					
	Car	Walk	Bus and coach	Rail[2]	Other	All modes	Car	Walk	Bus and coach	Rail[2]	Other	All modes
Social/entertainment	24	21	21	19	26	23	25	17	17	22	28	23
Other escort and personal business	23	14	13	5	9	19	24	15	13	6	12	20
Commuting	20	7	21	52	27	18	13	7	20	38	14	13
Shopping	17	21	21	5	11	18	22	21	31	12	16	22
Education	3	13	19	5	12	7	3	10	12	10	14	6
Business	6	2	1	9	4	5	3	1	1	6	4	2
Holiday/day trip	4	1	3	4	11	4	4	1	3	6	10	4
Escort education	3	4	-	-	-	3	5	11	2	-	-	6
Other, including just walk	-	17	-	-	-	4	-	16	-	-	-	4
All purposes (=100%) (numbers)	671	228	55	27	51	1,031	671	261	72	20	32	1,056

1 See Appendix, Part 12: National Travel Survey.
2 Includes London Underground.

Source: National Travel Survey, Department for Transport

Figure **12.4**

Mean time taken to travel to work: by sex and area type[1] of workplace, 2005

Great Britain

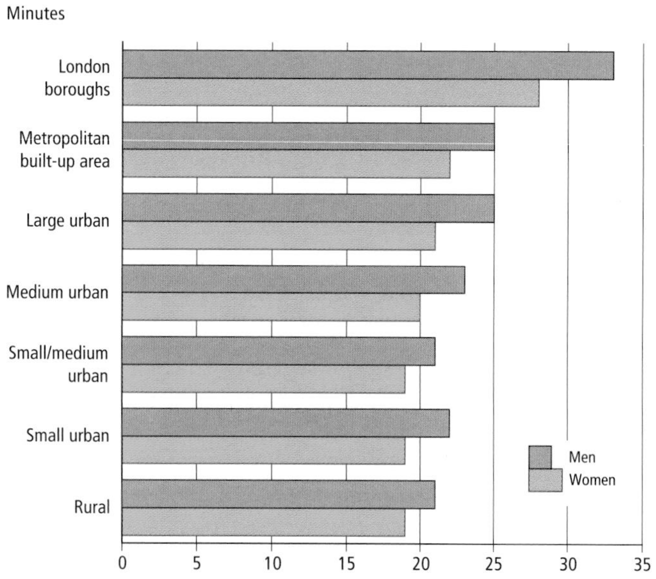

Minutes

1 See Appendix, Part 12: Area type classification.

Source: National Travel Survey, Department for Transport

Table **12.5**

Mean time taken to travel to school: by age of child and area type[1]

Great Britain

Minutes

	Age 5–10		Age 11–16	
	1996–98	2005	1996–98	2005
London boroughs	13	16	26	27
Metropolitan built-up area	12	13	22	23
Large urban	13	12	21	26
Medium urban	11	12	21	20
Small/medium urban	14	10	21	19
Small urban	12	11	20	20
Rural	11	13	20	26

1 See Appendix, Part 12: Area type classification.

Source: National Travel Survey, Department for Transport

28 minutes for women (Figure 12.4). Those working in metropolitan built-up areas faced trips to work of 25 minutes for men and 22 minutes for women. This compares with trips to work of 21 minutes for men and 19 minutes for women for those working in both rural communities of less than 3,000 people and in small/medium towns with populations between 10,000 and 25,000.

Similar travel time patterns exist for children travelling to school. In the period 1996–98, for older children travelling to secondary school, the time taken to travel to school in London took on average 6 minutes longer than those travelling in rural areas (Table 12.5). In 2005, secondary school children in rural areas and large urban areas in Great Britain with populations over 250,000, were taking a similar time to travel to school (26 minutes) as children in London (27 minutes).

The ways in which children travel to school have changed over the last fifteen years or so. In general, fewer are walking and more are travelling in cars. During the period 1995–97, 38 per cent of trips to and from school by 5 to 10-year-olds were in a car; by 2005 this figure had risen to 43 per cent. For 11 to 16-year-olds the proportion travelling by car rose from 20 per cent to 22 per cent over the same period. Private and local bus travel accounted for 6 per cent of journeys to and from school made by 5 to 10-year-olds, and 29 per cent of journeys by 11 to 16-year-olds in 2005. Six per cent of 5 to 10-year-olds and 44 per cent of 11 to 16-year-olds in Great Britain travelled

the main part of their journey unaccompanied. The average length of trips to school also increased over the same period, from 2.0 to 2.5 kilometres for children aged 5 to 10, and from 4.7 to 4.8 kilometres for those aged 11 to 16.

Since trips to and from school usually take place at the same time each morning and evening, those made by car have a major impact on levels of road congestion in residential areas. The peak time for school traffic in Great Britain in 2005 was 8.50am on weekdays during term time, when the school run accounted for one in every five car trips made by residents of urban areas.

Freight transport

The volume of goods transported within Great Britain has grown over the last 30 years, although it has remained broadly stable since 2000. The volume of goods transported by road grew by 86 per cent between 1971 and 1998 and then stabilised to stand at 163 billion tonne kilometres in 2005 (Figure 12.6). This measure combines both the weight of the goods transported and the distance they are carried. The volume of freight carried by water (virtually all of it between sea ports in Great Britain) also rose over the period, although much of this growth occurred between the mid-1970s and early 1980s. In 2005/06, 22 billion tonne kilometres of goods were moved by rail. This was the same as in 1971/72, although it represents an increase of 70 per cent since a low point of 13 billion tonne kilometres in 1994/95.

The increase in the volume of goods moved by road has resulted from increases in both the weight of goods transported and the average distance carried. The weight of freight loaded into vehicles with gross weight over 3.5 tonnes rose by 10 per cent

Figure **12.6**

Goods moved by domestic freight transport: by mode

Great Britain

Billion tonne kilometres

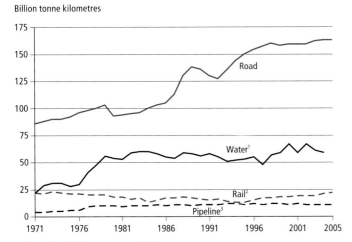

1 Data for 2005 are not available.
2 Data are financial years from 1991.
3 Carrying petroleum products.

Source: Department for Transport

to 1,868 million tonnes between 1995 and 2005. The average distance travelled by vehicles carrying this freight fell by 2 per cent to reach 87 kilometres in 2005 and this was 8 kilometres less on average than the peak in 1999.

Over 156,000 million tonne kilometres of goods were moved by vehicles with gross weight over 3.5 tonnes within the UK in 2005 (Table 12.7). Other foodstuffs (including meat, fish, dairy products, and other processed foods), was the largest single commodity, with over 23,000 million tonne kilometres moved. Additionally, nearly 12,000 million tonne kilometres of agricultural products (including bulk cereals, potatoes, fresh and frozen fruit and vegetables, sugar, and live animals) were moved.

UK registered vehicles exported over 5,000 million tonne kilometres to the EU-25 in 2005. Machinery and transport equipment (935 million tonne kilometres), chemicals (747), other foodstuffs (629) and crude materials (200), accounted for nearly half of the goods moved. More goods were imported to the UK (nearly 6,000 million tonne kilometres) from abroad than were exported in UK registered vehicles. Other foodstuffs was the largest category of goods moved, with 1,024 million tonne kilometres, followed by machinery and transport equipment with 856 million tonne kilometres.

The UK imported more goods by weight by road goods vehicles than it exported to the EU-15 in 2005. The Republic of Ireland and France were the origin of the greatest proportions of freight unloaded in the UK, followed by Belgium and Luxembourg, the Netherlands and Germany. Around half of the goods loaded in the UK and transported to other EU-15 countries were to the Republic of Ireland, and much of this was

Table **12.7**

Domestic and international road haulage by UK registered vehicles:[1] by commodity,[2] 2005

Million tonne kilometres

	Domestic	International Outward journey[3]	International Inward journey[3]
Agricultural products	11,926	124	452
Beverages	6,157	58	298
Other foodstuffs	23,455	629	1,024
Wood, timber and cork	4,706	12	45
Fertiliser	1,157	0	7
Crude minerals (including sand, gravel and clay)	15,272	63	64
Ores	1,735	14	12
Crude materials (including rubber and paper)	2,452	200	59
Coal and coke	1,571	32	34
Petrol and petroleum products	5,813	25	44
Chemicals	7,684	747	343
Building materials (including cement)	11,243	111	355
Iron and steel products, and other metal products	7,378	309	173
Machinery and transport equipment	9,476	935	856
Miscellaneous manufactures (including textiles and clothing)	15,658	572	658
Miscellaneous articles (including packaging and waste)	30,430	1,535	1,560
All freight	156,115	5,366	5,983

1 Over 3.5 tonnes.
2 See Appendix, Part 12: Freight commodity classification.
3 Excludes vehicles travelling between Northern Ireland and the Republic of Ireland only; that is, where the whole journey is confined to the island of Ireland.

Source: Department for Transport

across the border with Northern Ireland. France, which is close in proximity to the UK and has extensive links through port traffic and the Channel Tunnel, was the destination for 17 per cent of freight carried from the UK to the EU-15.

Transport prices

Motoring costs in the UK as measured by the 'All motoring' component of the retail prices index (RPI) rose by 86 per cent between January 1987 and January 2006, compared with a rise in the RPI of 93 per cent. Therefore motoring was relatively less

Figure **12.8**

Passenger transport prices[1]

United Kingdom

Index numbers (1987=100)

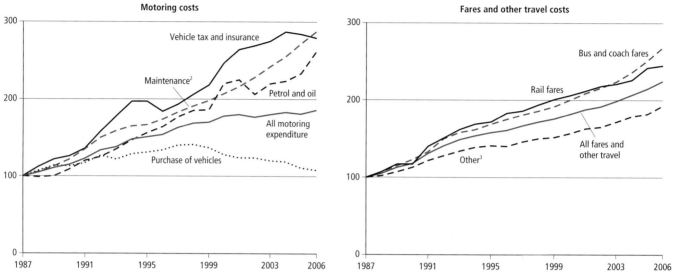

1 At January each year based on the retail prices index (RPI). For comparison, the 'All items' RPI measure of general inflation in January 2006 was 193. See Appendix, Part 6: Retail prices index.
2 Includes spare parts and accessories, roadside recovery services, MOT test fee, car service, labour charges and car wash.
3 Includes taxi and minicab fares, self-drive and van hire charges, ferry and sea fares, air fares, road tolls, purchase of bicycles, boats and car park charges.

Source: Office for National Statistics

expensive in 2006 than it was in 1987 (Figure 12.8). This is mainly because the rise in the price of vehicles (8 per cent) was much less than the rate of inflation. Vehicle tax and insurance rose by 179 per cent after falling in the mid-1990s, and maintenance costs rose by 188 per cent. The cost of petrol and oil rose sharply in 2000 before falling in 2002, and rising again to 2006, resulting in an overall increase of 162 per cent over the period.

Bus and coach fares, and rail fares in the UK rose by considerably more than the rate of general inflation between 1987 and 2006, by 168 and 145 per cent respectively. Overall, the 'All fares and other travel' index rose by 125 per cent, compared with the increase in the 'All items' RPI of 93 per cent.

Reflecting the rise in prices, households spent more on transport and travel in 2005/06 than in 1991, according to the Expenditure and Food Survey. After taking into account the effect of inflation, UK household expenditure on transport and travel increased by 30 per cent between 1991 and 2005/06. This compares with an 18 per cent increase in household spending on all goods and services over the same period (see Chapter 6: Expenditure).

Between 1991 and 2005/06, UK household expenditure on motoring increased by 29 per cent in real terms, although within this total, spending on vehicle insurance and taxation increased by 69 per cent. In 2005/06 household expenditure on motoring was nearly six times greater than expenditure on

fares and other travel costs. Bus and coach fares were the only areas of transport expenditure that decreased, by 17 per cent between 1991 and 2005/06. However, total spending on fares and other non-motoring travel costs increased by 35 per cent during this period. Transport and travel accounted for 17 per cent of all household expenditure in the UK in 2005/06, compared with 15 per cent in 1991.

In January 2006, the average price of premium unleaded petrol in the UK was 88.8 pence per litre, a rise of 132 per cent since January 1990 (Figure 12.9). The average price of diesel rose by 138 per cent to 93.2 pence per litre over the same period. There is considerable volatility in these prices, reflecting the market for crude oil which in turn is influenced by world events. Between January and October 2006, premium unleaded petrol prices fell by 3 per cent, but the period included the highest average price for unleaded petrol at 97.7 pence per litre in August 2006.

The UK has among the cheapest pre-tax petrol prices across the EU-25, due in part to its own reserves (see Chapter 11: Environment) and a competitive domestic fuel market. The price excluding tax in the UK was the third lowest in the EU-25 at 29.1 pence per litre in March 2006, with the Czech Republic having the lowest price at 28.0 pence per litre, and Malta having the highest price at 40.6 pence per litre. However, after adding fuel duty and value added tax, premium unleaded petrol and diesel prices in the UK are among the highest in the EU. In

Figure **12.9**

Premium unleaded petrol[1] and diesel prices

United Kingdom
Pence per litre[2]

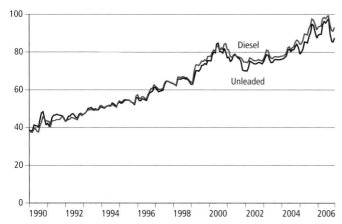

1 Premium unleaded petrol, 95RON.
2 At current prices.

Source: Department of Trade and Industry

March 2006, one litre of unleaded petrol cost 7.0 pence less in the UK than in the Netherlands, the country with the highest price and was 31 pence per litre higher than the price in Latvia, which at 58.4 pence per litre had the lowest price. In March 2006, taxes and duties accounted for 67 per cent of the pump price in the UK, the same as in Germany. The lowest tax component was 44 per cent in Malta. In the second quarter of 2006, 39 per cent of car fuel was sold by supermarkets.

The roads

The number of licensed cars on Britain's roads has continued to increase, reaching over 29.2 million in 2005 (Table 12.10). This was over four and a half times the number in 1961, when there were only 6.2 million licensed cars. The number of licensed motorcycles decreased from 1980 until 1995 when it reached a low of 594,000. There has been a recovery in recent years and in 2003, the total number of currently licensed motorcycles exceeded one million for the first time since 1986, and stood at 1,075,000 in 2005. However, new motorcycle registrations have been declining each year since 2000 and stood at 132,000 in 2005. New registrations of cars increased each year reaching a peak of just over 2.8 million registrations in 2003, but the number has since fallen to 2.6 million in 2005.

The increase in licensed cars is reflected in the growth in the number of households with two or more cars. Since the early 1970s the percentage of households with only one car in Great Britain has been stable at around 45 per cent. However, the percentage with no car fell from 48 per cent in 1971 to 25 per cent in 2004 (Figure 12.11). The percentage of households with two or more cars increased from 8 per cent to 31 per cent

Table **12.10**

Cars[1] and motorcycles[2] currently licensed,[3] and new registrations[4]

Great Britain   Thousands

	Currently licensed		New registrations	
	Cars	Motorcycles	Cars	Motorcycles
1961	6,240	1,577	743	212
1971	11,895	899	1,462	128
1981	16,490	1,371	1,644	272
1991	21,952	750	1,709	77
2001	26,443	882	2,710	177
2005	29,226	1,075	2,604	132

1 Includes light goods vehicles.
2 Includes scooters and mopeds.
3 At 31 December each year.
4 New methods of estimating vehicle stock were introduced in 1992, and changes to the vehicle taxation system were introduced from 1 July 1995.

Source: Department for Transport

over the same period. Most of these households have two cars, but the number of households with 3 or more cars has steadily increased from 1 per cent in 1971 to 5 per cent in 2004. Rural households were more likely than other households to have two or more cars. Over half of all rural households had two or more cars, compared to around one-third of households in most urban areas, and only one-fifth of households in London.

The higher a household's income, the more likely it is to have access to a car. Only 47 per cent of households in the lowest fifth of the income distribution in Great Britain had access to at

Figure **12.11**

Households with regular use of a car[1]

Great Britain
Percentages

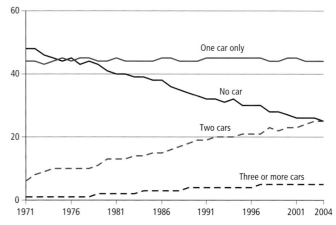

1 See Appendix, Part 12: Car ownership.

Source: Family Expenditure Survey and General Household Survey, Office for National Statistics; National Travel Survey, Department for Transport

least one car in 2005. This proportion compares with 67 per cent for those in the next fifth and 90 per cent for households in the highest fifth of the income distribution (see Chapter 5: Income and wealth).

Historically, men have been much more likely than women to hold full car driving licences. In 1975–76, 69 per cent of men in Great Britain held such a licence compared with only 29 per cent of women. However, the gap is narrowing. In 2005, the proportion of men with a driving licence was 81 per cent (18.1 million), while among women the proportion was 63 per cent (15.2 million). The gap between the sexes is smallest in the youngest age groups and largest in the oldest; 37 per cent of men and 27 per cent of women aged 17 to 20 held licences in 2005, whereas among those aged 70 and over, 73 per cent of men held a licence compared with only 35 per cent of women. The proportion of younger (17 to 20-year-old) men and women holding a licence has decreased from the early 1990s, from nearly one-half to around one-third of young people.

Growth in the number of motor vehicles owned, and the greater distances travelled by individuals and by road haulage vehicles have led to an increase in the average daily flow of vehicles on Great Britain's roads. Between 1993 and 2005 average traffic flows rose by 21 per cent, to 3,500 vehicles per day (Table 12.12). Motorways had the highest flow of vehicles at 75,500 vehicles a day in 2005. This was an increase of 30 per cent since 1993, but nearly two-thirds of this growth occurred between 1993 and 1998. Major roads in rural areas had the second greatest proportional increase in traffic flow between 1993 and 2005 (23 per cent), while urban major roads had an increase of only 5 per cent.

One consequence of increased traffic can be lower average speeds, especially in urban areas. Transport for London found that the average traffic speed for all areas of London during 2003–06 was 14.8 miles per hour in the morning peak period, compared with 18.1 miles per hour in 1968–70.

In 2005, the Department of Transport estimated that between 2000 and 2010 the number of vehicle kilometres travelled by cars in England would increase by between 22 and 29 per cent. The number of vehicle kilometres travelled by goods vehicles over 3.5 tonnes, and light goods vehicles, was forecast to grow by between 10 and 11 per cent and 39 to 40 per cent respectively.

Cars travelled a total of 397 billion passenger kilometres in Great Britain in 2005. This represented an average of 14,452 kilometres per car, 6 per cent less than in 1995–97. Of this, 12 per cent of passenger kilometres were for business, and 32 per cent were for commuting. Company cars however, travelled an average of over 31,000 kilometres, over twice as much as the average for all cars.

Cars belonging to households in rural areas in Great Britain travelled an average of 16,494 kilometres in 2005, compared with 13,597 kilometres in metropolitan areas and 11,612 kilometres in cars belonging to households in London (Figure 12.13). There was a decrease of 7 per cent in the average distances travelled by cars belonging to households in all area types between 1995–97 and 2005.

Table **12.12**

Average daily flow[1] of motor vehicles: by class of road[2]

Great Britain

Thousands

	1993	1998	2001	2005
Motorways[3]	58.2	68.7	71.6	75.5
All major roads	14.4	16.3	16.7	17.5
Urban major roads	19.2	20.2	20.1	20.2
Rural major roads	8.9	10.0	10.3	10.9
All minor roads	1.3	1.3	1.4	1.5
All roads	2.9	3.2	3.3	3.5

1 Flow at an average point on each class of road.
2 See Appendix, Part 12: Road traffic.
3 Includes motorways owned by local authorities.

Source: National Road Traffic Survey, Department for Transport

Figure **12.13**

Average annual distance covered per household car:[1] by area type[2]

Great Britain

Kilometres per car per year

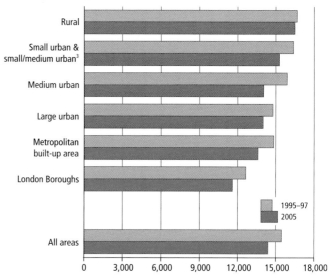

1 Four-wheeled cars only.
2 See Appendix, Part 12: Area type classification.
3 Separate categories were not available in 1995–97.

Source: National Travel Survey, Department for Transport

Public transport

In terms of the number of journeys taken, buses and coaches are the most widely used form of public transport. Over 4.7 billion journeys in Great Britain were made by local bus in 2005/06, more than twice the number of journeys made by rail. Just over one-third of these journeys on local buses took place in London. After a long period of post-war decline which continued into the 1990s, local bus use measured by the number of passenger journeys, stabilised towards the end of the decade and started to increase from 1999/2000 (Figure 12.14). There were substantial increases in the number of passenger journeys on London buses, offsetting further declines in most other areas of Great Britain. The overall distance travelled by buses recovered from a low point of 2.1 billion kilometres in 1985/86 until the mid-1990s when it stabilised at around 2.6 billion kilometres.

The *Transport Act 2000* required all local authorities to provide concessionary fares set at a minimum standard of a half fare for women aged 60 and over, men aged 65 or over (60 since 2003), and disabled people. In 2005, the take-up rate for those aged 60 or more for the scheme was 56 per cent. This compares with a take-up rate of 49 per cent for those of state pension age (age 65 for men and 60 for women) with access to a scheme in 1998–2000.

For households with no, or only limited, access to a car, public transport can be vital. In 2004/05, virtually all households (96 per cent) in Great Britain lived within 13 minutes walk of a

Figure **12.14**

Bus travel[1]

Great Britain

Index numbers (1981/82=100)

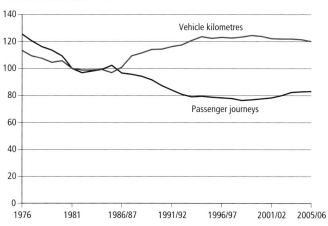

1 Local services only. Includes street-running trams but excludes modern 'supertram' systems. Financial years from 1985/86.

Source: Department for Transport

bus stop, and almost nine in ten lived within 13 minutes walk of a bus stop with a service at least once an hour (Table 12.15). However, there is considerable variation across the regions. In London, 98 per cent of households lived within 13 minutes walk of a bus stop with a service at least once an hour, compared with 81 per cent in the South West. Ninety per cent of households in London lived within a six minute walk of any bus stop, compared with 82 per cent in the neighbouring South East.

Table **12.15**

Time taken to walk to nearest bus stop: by region, 2004–05

Great Britain   Percentages

	6 minutes or less	7 to 13 minutes	4 to 26 minutes	27 minutes or more	Accessibility indicator[1]
Great Britain	86	10	3	1	89
England	86	10	3	1	89
North East	89	7	3	1	94
North West	88	10	2	-	93
Yorkshire and the Humber	88	9	2	1	91
East Midlands	86	10	3	1	88
West Midlands	86	10	3	1	90
East	84	11	4	1	83
London	90	9	1	-	98
South East	82	13	4	1	85
South West	84	11	3	1	81
Wales	84	9	3	3	86
Scotland	86	9	3	2	91

1 Households within 13 minutes walk of a bus stop with a service at least once an hour.

Source: National Travel Survey, Department for Transport

These differences result at least partly from the mix of rural and urban areas within each region. Only 70 per cent of rural households in Great Britain lived within a 6 minute walk of their closest bus stop in 2005, compared with 90 per cent of households in metropolitan built-up areas (see Appendix, Part 12: Area type). Services were also likely to be less frequent, giving rise to an availability indicator of only 54 per cent in rural areas of Great Britain, compared with 98 per cent in metropolitan built-up areas and the London boroughs.

The railways

The number of passenger journeys made on Great Britain's railway network (including underground and metro systems) rose by 138 million between 2001/02 and 2005/06, to 2.2 billion, an increase of 7 per cent (Table 12.16). There were around 1.3 billion passenger journeys per year in the early 1980s and, apart from a period in the early 1990s when journey numbers fell, the number of journeys has generally increased. In 2005/06, more than 1 billion passenger journeys were made on the national rail network for the third year running. This represented 43.2 billion passenger kilometres. Overall, national rail and London Underground accounted for almost all rail journeys in 2005/06 (49 and 44 per cent respectively).

Light railways and trams accounted for 7 per cent of rail journeys in Great Britain in 2005/06, compared with only 1 per cent in 1981. This was a result of the building or extending of several new light railways and tram lines. Over the next decade, further increases in route kilometres for the Docklands Light Railway in London are expected, along with possible new lines and extensions elsewhere in the UK. Passenger journeys by this mode of transport more than doubled between 1996/97 and 2005/06.

The Office of Rail regulation compiles a rail fare price index, which covers all rail services previously operated by franchise holders (Table 12.17). Overall, fares increased by 46 per cent between 1995 and 2006 compared with an increase of 33 per cent in the 'All items' RPI, so the increase in real terms was about 13 per cent. However, prices charged by long distance operators rose by 64 per cent, a 32 per cent increase in real terms.

The National Passenger Survey (NPS) found that in autumn 2006, 34 per cent of passengers were dissatisfied with the value for money of their rail journey, compared with 43 per cent who were satisfied.

The NPS also found that 12 per cent of passengers interviewed in autumn 2006 were dissatisfied with the punctuality of their service. However, 79 per cent were satisfied, up from 59 per cent

Table **12.16**

Rail journeys:[1] by operator

Great Britain

Millions

	1981	1991/92	1996/97	2001/02	2003/04	2005/06
Main line/underground						
National Rail	719	792	801	960	1,012	1,082
London Underground	541	751	772	953	948	970
Glasgow Underground	11	14	14	14	13	13
All national rail and underground	1,271	1,557	1,587	1,927	1,973	2,065
Light railways and trams						
Docklands Light Railway	.	8	17	41	48	52
Tyne and Wear Metro	14	41	35	33	38	36
Croydon Tramlink	.	.	.	18	20	23
Manchester Metrolink	.	.	13	18	19	20
Sheffield Supertram	.	.	8	11	12	13
Nottingham Express Transit	.	.	.	.	.	10
Midland Metro	.	.	.	5	5	5
Blackpool Trams	6	5	5	5	4	4
All light railways and trams	20	54	78	132	147	162
All journeys by rail	1,291	1,611	1,665	2,059	2,119	2,227

1 Excludes railways and tramways operated principally as tourist attractions.

Source: Department for Transport

Table **12.17**

Rail fare prices index[1]

Great Britain						Index numbers (1995=100)
	1995	1999	2001	2003	2005	2006
All operators	100	113	120	126	137	146
London and South East operators	100	112	116	119	130	136
Long distance operators	100	116	127	139	152	164
Regional operators	100	112	117	121	130	137
RPI (all items)	100	112	117	122	129	133

1 As at January each year.

Source: Office of Rail Regulation

Table **12.18**

Passenger death rates:[1] by mode of transport

Great Britain				Rate per billion passenger kilometres	
	1981	1991	1996	2001	2004
Motorcycle	115.8	94.6	108.4	112.1	105.0
Walk	76.9	69.8	55.9	47.5	36.7
Bicycle	56.9	46.5	49.8	32.5	34.7
Car	6.1	3.7	3.0	2.8	2.5
Van	3.7	2.1	1.0	0.9	0.8
Bus or coach	0.3	0.6	0.2	0.2	0.4
Rail[2]	1.0	0.8	0.4	0.3	0.2
Water[3]	0.4	0.0	0.8	0.4	0.0
Air[3]	0.2	0.0	0.0	0.0	0.0

1 See Appendix, Part 12: Passenger death rates.
2 Financial years. Includes train accidents and accidents occurring through movement of railway vehicles.
3 Data are for the UK.

Source: Department for Transport

in spring 2001. In autumn 2006, 81 per cent of passengers were satisfied with their overall journey, the highest level of satisfaction recorded by the NPS since the survey began in 1999. According to the Public Performance Measure, 86.4 per cent of trains arrived on time in the fourth quarter of 2005/06, compared with 85.5 per cent in the previous quarter and 83.6 per cent in the fourth quarter of 2004/05. Operators in London and the South East recorded most services as being on time in the fourth quarter of 2005/06 at 90.8 per cent, while long distance operators recorded the fewest, at 87.0 per cent.

Transport safety

The safety levels of transport in Great Britain have improved since the early 1980s, and improvements in most areas have continued since the early 1990s. Motorcycling, walking and cycling have the highest fatality rates per kilometre travelled of any form of transport (Table 12.18). In 2004, the highest death rate was for motorcycle users, at 105 deaths per billion passenger kilometres travelled, over 40 times greater than the death rate for car users.

Between 1980 and 2004, the total number of road casualties in Great Britain fell by 14 per cent, with a 60 per cent decrease in the number of fatal and serious casualties. In 2005 there were 198,700 road accidents involving personal injury, 4 per cent less than in 2004. Of these, 25,000 road accidents involved serious injury and a further 3,200 caused death. This compares with an annual average of 2,900 deaths caused by road accidents in 1994–98 and 6,000 in 1980.

In 2005, 52 per cent of those killed in road accidents in Great Britain were travelling in cars, 21 per cent were pedestrians, 18 per cent were riders or passengers of two-wheeled motor vehicles and 5 per cent were pedal cyclists. Occupants of

buses, coaches and goods vehicles accounted for the remaining 4 per cent of deaths. Public transport by air, sea, rail and bus or coach continues to be the safest mode of travel. The lowest death rates were for air travel, less than 1 per billion passenger kilometres in each year between 1981 and 1989 and less than 0.1 per billion passenger kilometres since 1990. Death rates for travel by water were similar to air.

The number of pedestrians killed each year has fallen steadily since the mid-1990s. In both 2004 and 2005, 671 pedestrians were killed in road accidents in Great Britain, the lowest totals in over 40 years. The proportion of those killed or seriously injured whilst travelling in cars fell by 56 per cent between 1980 and 2005. They accounted for a little under half of the 32,000 people killed or seriously injured in road accidents in 2005. The number of people killed in drink-drive accidents fell to a low of 460 deaths in 1998, but the number has since risen to an estimated 560 deaths in 2005. The numbers of minor injuries in drink-drive accidents had been increasing since 1993. However an estimated figure for 2005 suggests a fall of 9 per cent from 2004.

There has been a steady fall in the number of children killed or seriously injured in road accidents. In 2005, 3,500 children were killed or seriously injured in road accidents, down 11 per cent from 2004, a 49 per cent reduction compared with the average for 1994–98 and a 68 per cent reduction since 1980. Most children killed or seriously injured in road accidents in 2005 were pedestrians (61 per cent) rather than car passengers (17 per cent). Generally, the risk of children

Figure **12.19**

Casualty rates in children: by age and mode of transport, 2005

Great Britain

Rate per 100,000 population

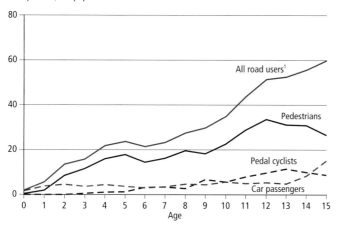

1 Includes casualties from other modes of road transport.

Source: Department for Transport

being killed or seriously injured in a road accident increases with age (Figure 12.19). In 2005, the peak casualty rate for child pedestrians in Great Britain was at age 12, after which the rate fell for 13 to 15-year-olds. However, the casualty rate increased sharply from age 14 for those children travelling as car passengers.

The UK has a good safety record in terms of road accidents involving children. In 2004 the UK road accident death rate for children aged 0 to 14, at 1.3 per 100,000 of population, was one of the lowest in Europe. Luxembourg had the lowest recoreded rate, at less than 0.1 per 100,000 population, while Poland had the highest at 3.6 per 100,000 population.

The member states with the lowest recorded death rates for all persons due to road accidents in 2004 were the Netherlands at 4.9 per 100,000 population, Sweden at 5.3 per 100,000 population and the UK at 5.6 per 100,000 population (Table 12.20). Poland, Greece and the Czech Republic recorded the highest road death rates, with 15.0, 14.6 and 13.5 deaths per 100,000 population, respectively. The UK death rate due to road accidents was also substantially lower than those for other industrialised nations such as Australia which recorded 7.9 deaths per 100,000 population and the US with 14.5 per 100,000 population.

International travel

UK residents are making more trips abroad each year than ever before, over three times as many in 2005 as in 1981 (Table 12.21). In 2005, air travel accounted for 81 per cent of all trips taken abroad, compared with 60 per cent in 1981. Conversely, sea

Table **12.20**

Road deaths: EU comparison, 2004

Rate per 100,000 population

	All persons	Children[1]		All persons	Children[1]
Poland	15.0	3.6	United Kingdom	5.6	1.3
Greece[2]	14.6	..	Sweden	5.3	0.9
Czech Republic	13.5	1.7	Netherlands	4.9	1.2
Hungary	12.8	2.4	Cyprus	..	..
Portugal	12.3	2.9	Estonia	..	..
Belgium	11.2	1.2	Latvia	..	..
Luxembourg	11.1	-	Lithuania	..	..
Spain	11.0	2.0	Malta	..	..
Austria	10.7	1.7	Slovakia	..	..
Italy	9.7	1.4	Slovenia	..	..
France	9.3	1.7	EU-25 average	..	..
Ireland[2]	8.4	1.9			
Finland	7.2	1.4			
Germany	7.1	1.3			
Denmark	6.8	2.0			

1 Children aged under 15.
2 Data are at 2003.

Source: Organisation for Economic Co-operation and Development

travel has declined over the same period, from 41 per cent of all trips in 1981 to just 12 per cent in 2005. The number of trips abroad using the Channel tunnel increased through the 1990s, but has generally declined since 2001.

The number of trips to the UK by overseas residents has also grown, increasing by 125 per cent between 1981 and 1998 when it peaked at 25.7 million. However in the years that followed, numbers fell slightly, and in 2001 visit numbers were severely affected by both the outbreak of foot-and-mouth disease and the terrorist attacks on 11 September that year. Since then numbers have recovered, so that there were 30 million visitors in 2005, a new high.

The Department for Transport has forecasted that demand for air travel will continue rising during the 21st century. Mid-range estimates suggest that between 2005 and 2020, the number of international and domestic terminal passengers at UK airports will grow from 229 million to 401 million. The growth in the number of international passengers at nearly 80 per cent is expected to exceed the growth in domestic passengers of around 70 per cent.

Almost 90 per cent of all air terminal passengers (excluding those in transit) entering or leaving UK airports were travelling

Table **12.21**

International travel: by mode[1]

United Kingdom

Millions

	1981	1991	2001	2005
Visits abroad by UK residents				
Air	11.4	20.4	43.0	53.6
Sea	7.7	10.4	9.7	8.1
Channel Tunnel	.	.	5.6	4.7
All visits abroad	19.0	30.8	58.3	66.4
Visits to the UK by overseas residents				
Air	6.9	11.6	16.1	22.0
Sea	4.6	5.5	4.0	4.7
Channel Tunnel	.	.	2.8	3.3
All visits to the UK	11.5	17.1	22.8	30.0

1 Mode of travel from, and into, the UK.

Source: International Passenger Survey, Office for National Statistics

to or from overseas countries. The increase in the number of people travelling by plane over the last two decades is both a continuation, and an acceleration, of a long-term trend. Between 1980 and 2005, the number of international terminal passengers at UK airports quadrupled from 43 million to 178 million. However, the number of passengers fell in 1991, the year of the first Gulf war, and there was also a marked levelling off of the upward trend in 2001.

Spain, including the Canary Islands, was the most popular destination for travel by plane by UK residents in 2005 (see also Chapter 13: Lifestyles and social participation), as it had been in 1990 (Figure 12.22). However, during this period, the number of passenger movements to and from Spain from UK airports nearly trebled, to 35 million. Trips by air to and from Italy showed the greatest increase, more than trebling to 10.7 million trips between 1990 and 2005. The second and third most popular destinations in 2005 were the US (18.3 million passenger movements) and Ireland (11.8 million passenger movements).

Figure **12.22**

International air passenger movements:[1] by selected country[2]

United Kingdom

Millions

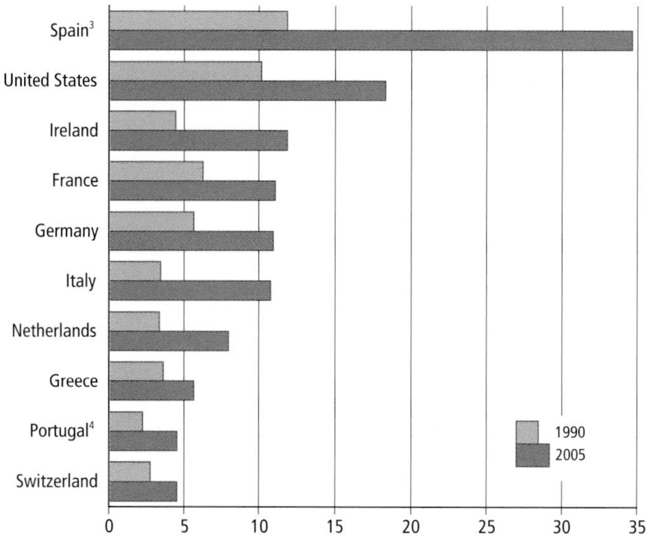

1 Arrivals in and departures from the UK.
2 Country of embarkation or landing.
3 Includes Canary Islands.
4 Includes Madeira, the Azores and Cape Verde Islands.

Source: Civil Aviation Authority

Lifestyles and social participation

- Around half (49 per cent) of children aged 8 to 11 owned a mobile phone in the UK in 2005, compared with four-fifths (82 per cent) of children aged 12 to 15. (Page 172)

- Between January and April 2006, 42 per cent of adults aged 16 and over in Great Britain purchased something online in the 12 months before interview. (Page 174)

- UK residents made a record 44.2 million holiday trips abroad in 2005; 43 per cent were package holidays, down from 53 per cent in 2001. (Page 174)

- Over half of children and young people aged 5 to 17 in England enjoyed reading 'very much' or 'quite a lot' in 2005. (Page 177)

- In 2005/06, 80 per cent of pupils in School Sports Partnership (SSP) schools in England took part in two or more hours of high quality physical education and school sport each week, an increase of 11 percentage points since 2004/05. (Figure 13.14)

- Nearly half of adults aged 16 and over in England participated in some form of volunteering activity in 2005, and over two-thirds participated in an informal voluntary activity. (Page 180)

Chapter 13

People engage in many different activities in their spare time. Some visit places of entertainment and cultural activity, such as the theatre and cinema, or take holidays. Other activities involve interaction with technology, such as the Internet. Although modern technology seems ever more present, traditional forms of leisure, such as reading books remain popular. Many individuals participate in sports or exercise in their leisure time or use their free time for purposes other than entertainment, such as helping other people, participating in politics, or religious worship.

Use of information technology

A period of technological change has brought about the widening application of information and communication technology (ICT). Home ownership of CD players, DVD players, computers and mobile phones has risen substantially between the 1990s and the present day (Figure 13.1). Household ownership of some products has grown more than others. Between 1996/97 and 2005/06, the proportion of households owning a mobile phone increased by over four times from 17 per cent to 79 per cent, although during the last three years the rise has levelled off. The proportion of UK households with a DVD player has risen from 31 per cent in 2002/03 to 79 per cent in 2005/06, a rise of 48 percentage points. Growth in ownership of CD players has occurred more slowly over this period. In 1996/97, 59 per cent of households had a CD player compared with 88 per cent in 2005/06. The annual growth of household Internet connections has slowed since 2000/01 after a sharp rise in the late 1990s. Between 1998/99 and 2002/03 the proportion of households that had an Internet connection grew, with an average annual growth of 9 percentage points. Between 2002/03 and 2005/06, the annual increase in home Internet connection was around 3 percentage points.

Two other media devices have become popular in the last couple of years, namely digital radios and MP3 players. According to the Media Literacy Audit published by Ofcom (see Appendix, Part 13: Media Literacy Audit), 27 per cent of adults in the UK stated that they listen to digital radio services. By far the main reasons for acquiring digital radio, for people that already owned one in 2005 were better sound quality (42 per cent) and receiving more stations (31 per cent). MP3 players are portable personal audio players that support MP3 files. These files that are mainly music tracks can be downloaded via the Internet. According to the Radio Joint Audience Research, over one-quarter (26 per cent) of adults aged 15 and over owned an MP3 player between April and June 2006 in the UK.

In 2005 nearly two-thirds (65 per cent) of children aged 8 to 15 in the UK had their own mobile phone. The older the child, the more likely they were to have a mobile. Nearly half (49 per cent) of children aged 8 to 11 had one compared with just over

Figure **13.1**

Households with selected information and communication technology[1]

United Kingdom
Percentages

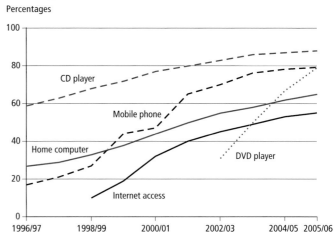

1 Based on weighted data. Data for 1998/99 onwards include children's expenditure.

Source: Family Expenditure Survey and Expenditure and Food Survey, Office for National Statistics

four-fifths (82 per cent) of children aged 12 to 15. The main reasons for having a mobile phone among children aged 12 to 15 were to keep in touch with friends (65 per cent), to keep in touch with family (54 per cent), for emergencies (46 per cent) and peer pressure (30 per cent). The most popular use of a mobile phone for children aged 8 to 15 was sending text messages (89 per cent) and making calls (82 per cent) (Figure 13.2). Girls were

Figure **13.2**

Children's[1] use of mobile phones,[2] 2005

United Kingdom
Percentages

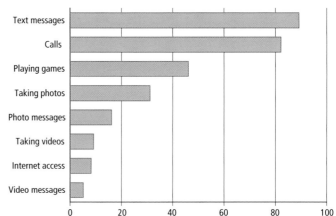

1 Children aged 8 to 15.
2 Percentages do not add up to 100 per cent as respondents could give more than one answer.

Source: Ofcom

more likely to send text messages than boys but there was very little difference between girls and boys in terms of using a mobile phone for making calls.

According to the Office for National Statistics Omnibus Survey, 85 per cent of adults in Great Britain had used a mobile phone between January and April 2006. In May 2006, a record 3.3 billion text messages were sent in the UK according to the Mobile Data Association. This figure equates to 106 million messages sent every day. Despite the large number of texts sent, 64 per cent of adults who had used a mobile phone in Great Britain between January and April 2006 stated that texting had not affected the amount of postal mail they had sent. A further 19 per cent stated that text/picture messaging had substituted a small amount of their postal mail and 11 per cent stated that their postal mail had been mostly replaced by texts.

Between January and April 2006 mobile phones were used by 11 per cent of adults in Great Britain to access the Internet in the three months before interview, although a computer remained the most popular mode of accessing the Internet. At first people were only able to access the Internet at home through a narrowband or 'dial-up' connection. Since broadband has become widely available the proportion of households in Great Britain with a broadband connection has almost quadrupled between 2003/04 and 2006, from 11 per cent to 40 per cent (Figure 13.3). Over the same period, the proportion of households with a narrowband connection fell from 38 per cent to 17 per cent; and the proportion of households with an Internet connection of any type increased from 51 per cent to 57 per cent of all households.

Broadband aims to give faster and more reliable Internet access than narrowband. A greater proportion of people who had broadband access than who had narrowband access used the Internet for tasks that required faster data transferral such as downloading music. Between January and April 2006, 37 per cent of adults that had a broadband connection in their household played or downloaded music compared with 15 per cent who had a narrowband connection. Similarly, 28 per cent of those who had a broadband connection listened to web radios or watched television over the Internet compared with just 9 per cent of those with narrowband.

Two in five (40 per cent) children aged 8 to 11 and just over 7 in ten (71 per cent) of those aged 12 to 15 in the UK with the Internet at home had 'mostly' used the Internet on their own at home. Children aged 8 to 15 who used the Internet at home, at school or elsewhere, used it for an average of 6 hours 12 minutes a week, with those aged 12 to 15 using it for an average of 8 hours and those aged 8 to 11, 4 hours 24 minutes. Both age groups used the Internet mainly for school work and playing games (Figure 13.4). Around 86 per cent of both age groups

Figure **13.3**

Household Internet connection:[1] by type[2]

Great Britain

Percentages

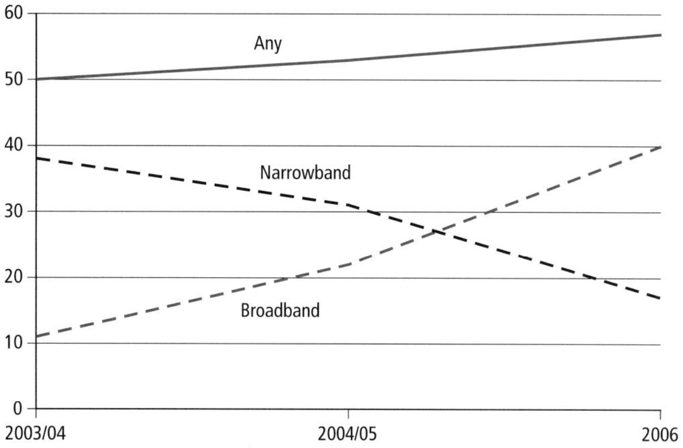

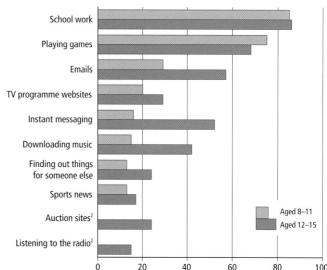

1 See Appendix, Part 13: Internet connection.
2 Data for 2003/04 and 2004/05 were collected in April (May in 2005), July, October and February. Data for 2006 were collected in January, February and April.

Source: Omnibus Survey, Office for National Statistics

used the Internet for school work, and 75 per cent of those aged 8 to 11 and 68 per cent of those aged 12 to 15 used the Internet to play games. Children aged 12 to 15 made broader use of the Internet than those aged 8 to 11, with considerably higher use for each of the other remaining reasons in the top ten, except

Figure **13.4**

Children's top ten Internet uses: by age,[1] 2005

United Kingdom

Percentages

1 Percentages do not add up to 100 per cent as respondents could give more than one answer.
2 The estimates for children aged 8–11 are excluded due to a small number of respondents.

Source: Ofcom

Figure **13.5**

Internet shopping:[1] by items purchased, 2006

Great Britain

Percentages

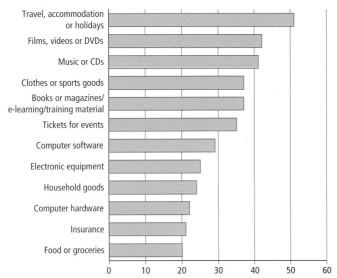

1 Adults aged 16 and over who had bought goods or services in the 12 months prior to interview for private use.

Souce: Omnibus Survey, Office for National Statistics

for 'sports news'. This was particularly evident when using the Internet for instant messaging. Instant messaging is an electronic communication involving immediate correspondence between two or more users who are all online simultaneously. In 2005, instant messaging was used by 52 per cent of children aged 12 to 15 compared with 16 per cent of those aged 8 to 11. Sending emails was also more popular among children aged 12 to 15 (57 per cent) compared with those aged 8 to 11 (29 per cent).

A growing number of people in Great Britain use the Internet to purchase goods and services online. Between January and April 2006, 42 per cent of the adult population aged 16 and over in Great Britain said they purchased something online in the 12 months before interview. The most popular purchase was travel, accommodation or holidays which were bought or ordered online by half (51 per cent) of online shoppers (Figure 13.5). Films, videos or DVDs, and music or CDs were the next most common categories of items purchased online (42 per cent and 41 per cent respectively). Men were more likely than women to buy music or CDs, videos or DVDs, computer software and hardware, and electronic equipment online. Women were more likely to buy clothes or sports goods, and food or groceries.

Some items can be purchased and downloaded directly from the Internet, including films, videos, music, books and computer software. For people who had bought these items from the Internet in the 12 months before interview, 21 per cent

downloaded computer software including games and software upgrades, 18 per cent downloaded films, videos and music, and 5 per cent downloaded books, magazines, e-learning/ training materials and newspaper articles.

The main problems experienced by online shoppers based in Great Britain were that delivery took longer than indicated, reported by 14 per cent, and that damaged goods had been delivered (6 per cent). Among Internet users who did not shop online, 42 per cent said that they preferred to shop in person or liked to see the product, and 37 per cent saw no need to shop online. More than one-third (35 per cent) were worried about security and this stopped them from shopping online.

Social and cultural activities

UK residents made a record 44.2 million holiday trips abroad in 2005. The number of holiday trips taken abroad in 2005 has increased by 65 per cent since 1996 and is a continuation of the rise in overseas holidays over the last three decades from 6.7 million in 1971. Most holiday trips were taken between July and September, when more than twice as many were taken than during January to March. Spain has been UK residents' favourite holiday destination since 1994, accounting for nearly three in ten holidays abroad in 2005 (Figure 13.6). France was the second most popular destination (16.6 per cent). As in previous years, nine of the ten countries most visited by UK residents in 2005 were in Europe. The exception was the US, which accounted for 6 per cent of all holidays (2.6 million visits).

Figure **13.6**

Holidays abroad by UK residents: by selected destination, 2005

United Kingdom

Percentages

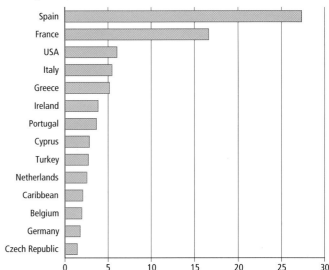

Source: International Passenger Survey, Office for National Statistics

Map **13.7**

Holidays[1] taken within Great Britain by UK residents: by region of destination, 2005

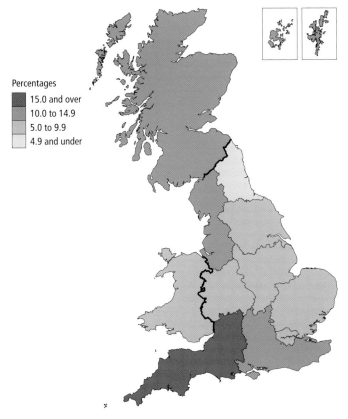

Percentages

- 15.0 and over
- 10.0 to 14.9
- 5.0 to 9.9
- 4.9 and under

1 Lasting one night or more taken by UK residents aged 16 and over.

Source: United Kingdom Tourism Survey, VisitBritain

Package holidays accounted for 43 per cent of holiday trips abroad in 2005, but this proportion has fallen in the last five years from 53 per cent in 2001. Holiday trips to countries other than those in Europe and North America increased from 2.5 million trips in 1996 to 5.0 million trips in 2005. In the last ten years 'long haul' holidays have become more popular. Between 1996 and 2005, trips to Australia, the Middle East, South Africa and the Caribbean have more than doubled.

In 2005, 86.6 million holiday trips including at least one overnight stay, were made in the UK, including trips for pleasure and leisure, and visiting friends and relatives for a holiday. These trips made up nearly two-thirds (62 per cent) of all trips taken by UK residents. The remainder were business trips and other visits to friends and relatives. The most visited region in Great Britain by UK residents taking a holiday was the South West, with 18 per cent of all holidays of one night or more in Great Britain taken there (Map 13.7). The second most popular destination was the South East (12 per cent), followed by the North West and Scotland (both 11 per cent). Nearly two-thirds (65 per cent) of holidays were of one to three nights duration.

The UK has almost 6,500 visitor attractions, including country parks and farms, historic properties, theme parks, zoos, gardens, museums and galleries, and places of worship. The top three visitor attractions that charged admission in England in 2005 were the British Airways London Eye, Xscape Castleford (an attraction that combines extreme sports such as ice and rock climbing with other leisure activities such as cinemas and restaurants), both having 3.3 million visitors, and the Tower of London, with 1.9 million visitors. The top visitor attractions that charged admission in Scotland in 2005 were Edinburgh Castle, with 1.2 million visitors, and Edinburgh Zoo, 614,000 visitors, while in Wales the top paid attractions were Oakwood theme park, with 267,000 visitors and Portmeirion, an Italianate resort village with 252,000 visitors. The top attractions in Northern Ireland that charged admission were Belfast Zoological Gardens, with 211,000 visitors and W5 interactive discovery centre (205,000 visitors).

In 2005 most visitors to attractions in England (including those which charge admission and those which are free) were adults, less than four in ten visitors were children (Figure 13.8). When visitors to different types of attractions were divided between adults and those who were defined as children by the individual attractions, the most visited attractions by children were farms, where 48 per cent of visitors were children, and leisure and theme parks, where 43 per cent of visitors were children. The attractions with the smallest proportions of child visitors were

Figure **13.8**

Adult and child[1] visits to visitor attractions, 2005

England

Percentages

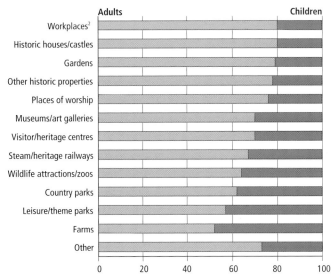

1 Child admission varies and is defined by the individual attraction.
2 Workplaces include operating industrial or craft attractions, vineyards etc.

Source: Survey of Visits to Visitor Attractions England 2005, VisitBritain

workplaces and historic houses or castles, where two in ten visitors were children. In Northern Ireland the most visited attractions by children were wildlife attractions and zoos where 56 per cent of visitors were children. The attractions with the smallest proportions of child visitors were gardens and places of worship (15 per cent and 18 per cent respectively). Visits to historic houses or castles by schoolchildren in England however, were the second most common type of school trip, visited by 17 per cent of all schoolchildren. The most common type of school trip was visits to museums or art galleries, visited by 37 per cent of all schoolchildren.

The number of attendances to plays in London's West End was 12.3 million in 2005, the highest on record. London's West End is the largest theatre district in the world and is the centre of UK commercial theatre, and home to many of the larger grant-aided theatres. There are, in total, around 50 large theatres in Central London. Theatre in London has long been an attraction for people who live across the UK and for visitors from overseas, as well as for people who live in London. In 2003/04, two in five people who lived outside London who visited a London theatre stated that the theatre was their main reason for visiting the Capital. Theatregoers in London's West End made on average around six visits to the theatre in London in the 12 months before interview in 2003/04, with London residents visiting around nine times and others living elsewhere in the UK around five times. Musical theatre was the most visited form of theatre in London for both male and female theatregoers (Figure 13.9), 66 per cent of men and 69 per cent of women had seen a musical production in the 12 months before interview. The second most attended productions were plays, visited by 50 per cent of men and 49 per cent of women. Some commercial productions show enduring popularity with theatregoers: in 2006 the longest running productions in the West End were *The Mousetrap* (54 years), *Les Misérables* (21 years) and *The Phantom of the Opera* (20 years).

The London region also had the most cinema admissions in 2005 (41.3 million), while across the UK there were 165 million admissions. According to the Cinema Advertising Association, 72 per cent of the UK population went to the cinema at least once a year in 2005, with 25 per cent going once a month or more. Cinema audiences in the UK reached their peak in 1946 when there were 1.6 billion admissions, but this figure decreased nearly every year to reach a low in 1984 with 54 million admissions. Young people aged 15 to 24 in Great Britain were the most likely of all age groups to go to the cinema (Figure 13.10). Just under half (46 per cent) of this age group reported attending the cinema once a month or more in Great Britain in 2005 compared with 16 per cent of those aged 35 and over. In 2005, 36 per cent of children aged 7 to 14 went to the cinema once a month or

Figure **13.9**

Types of theatre performance attended:[1] by sex, 2003/04

London[2]
Percentages

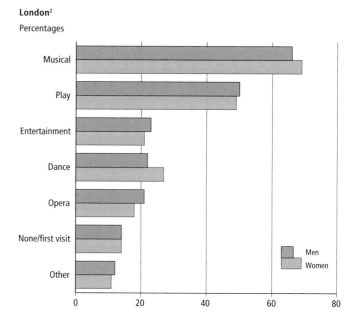

1 Theatregoers aged 15 and over were asked 'Which, if any, of the following types of performance have you been to in London during the last 12 months?' The survey was carried out at 45 London theatre performances between 13 March 2003 and 9 February 2004.
2 See Appendix, Part 13: London theatre district.

Source: The Society of London Theatre

more. Almost all children (96 per cent) aged 4 to 9 who visit the cinema are accompanied by an adult. Children generally start to go to the cinema with friends from the age of 10, with over six in ten children aged 10 to 14 doing so in 2005. In the same

Figure **13.10**

Cinema attendance:[1] by age

Great Britain
Percentages

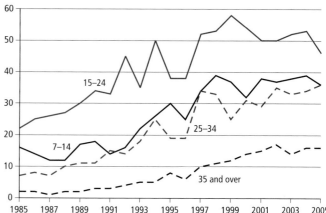

1 Respondents who said that they attend the cinema once a month or more.

Source: Cinema Advertising Association/Cinema and Video Industry Audience Research

year, four of the top five grossing films in the UK specifically targeted a young audience. The highest grossing film was *Harry Potter and the Goblet of Fire*, followed by *Star Wars: Episode 3: Revenge of the Sith*, *Charlie and the Chocolate Factory*, *The Chronicles of Narnia: The Lion, the Witch and the Wardrobe*, and *Wallace & Gromit: The Curse of the Were-Rabbit*. Three of these films have also been best-selling books.

A number of films that attract young cinemagoers are based on original fiction. Even with other distractions such as computer games and television, reading is still a popular pastime for many children. According to the National Literacy Trust, just over half (51 per cent) of children and young people aged 5 to 17 in England who were surveyed in 2005 enjoyed reading 'very much' or 'quite a lot'. Seven in ten read every day, almost every day or once or twice a week outside of school. The most popular reading materials outside of school were magazines, read by 76 per cent of children and young people, and websites (64 per cent). Females enjoy reading more than males, over half (57 per cent) of females stated that they enjoyed reading very much or quite a lot compared with 46 per cent of males. A further 14 per cent of males stated that they found no enjoyment in reading compared with 7 per cent of females. Adventure stories were the most popular genre for both males and females aged 5 to 17 that read fiction, with over six in ten including this in their list of preferences (Figure 13.11). Comedy and horror/ghost stories were also popular with both sexes. However, a greater percentage of males than females preferred fiction that was war and spy-related (48 per cent compared with 19 per cent) and sports-related (40 per cent compared with 20 per cent). Females preferred reading fiction about romance and relationships (39 per cent of females compared with 9 per cent of males) and realistic teen fiction (49 per cent compared with 22 per cent).

Between July 2004 and June 2005 the most borrowed fiction title by children from public libraries in the UK was *Harry Potter and the Order of the Phoenix* by JK Rowling according to Public Lending Right. Books by Jacqueline Wilson were also very popular; 16 of her books were in the top 20 borrowed books with *Lizzie Zipmouth* and *Best Friends* the second and third most borrowed children's fiction titles. Roald Dahl is the most popular children's classic author, of which *The BFG* and *The Witches* were the most popular. For adults the most borrowed fiction titles were *Blow Fly* by Patricia Cornwell and *Lovers and Liars* by Josephine Cox. The most popular classic title borrowed was *Catcher in the Rye* by JD Salinger.

People go to the library for many reasons. Borrowing, returning or renewing books was the main reason for 55 per cent of adults living in England aged 16 and over who used a library during the twelve months prior to interview in 2005/06 (Figure 13.12). Of those visiting the library for this reason,

Figure **13.11**

Types of fiction preferred by young people aged 5 to 17: by sex, 2005

England
Percentages

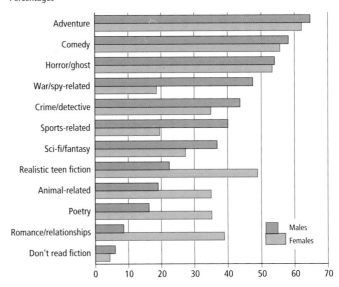

Souce: National Literacy Trust

Figure **13.12**

Main reasons why adults[1] visit a public library,[2] 2005/06

England
Percentages

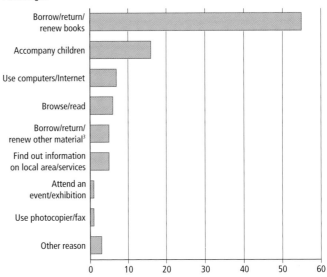

1 Aged 16 and over.
2 The estimates are based on interviews conducted over a nine month period (mid-July 2005 to mid-April 2006). See Appendix, Part 13: Taking Part survey.
3 Includes DVDs, CDs, videos, and CD roms.

Source: Taking Part: The National Survey of Culture, Leisure and Sport, Department for Culture, Media and Sport

66 per cent were aged 65 and over. A further 16 per cent stated their main reason was accompanying children, which was particularly evident among people aged 25 to 44 (25 per cent). Using the computers and Internet situated in the library was the main reason for visiting for 7 per cent of library users. Young people aged 16 to 24 were more likely than older age groups to use the library mainly for this reason (20 per cent). People aged 65 and over were more likely than younger library users to go to the library to find out information on the local area or services (11 per cent). Of the people who did not go to a library in the 12 months before interview, 38 per cent stated that their main reason for not going was that they had no need to go or were not really interested; of these nearly half were aged 16 to 24. A further 14 per cent said that it was difficult to find the time and 10 per cent preferred to buy their own books.

Sporting activities

According to the Department for Culture, Media and Sport's Taking Part Survey, 68 per cent of adults over the age of 16 in England in 2005/06 participated in at least one type of active sport in the 12 months before interview. Over seven in ten men (73 per cent) stated they had taken part in an active sport compared with over six in ten women (63 per cent). Participation varied with age. Over 80 per cent of people aged 16 to 44 had participated in a sporting activity compared with just over 33 per cent of those aged 65 and over. The main reasons for sports

participation were to keep fit, but not just to lose weight (32 per cent) and for enjoyment (31 per cent). Other reasons were meeting with friends (10 per cent) and taking their children (9 per cent). There are many factors that would encourage people who already take part in active sports perhaps only occasionally (at least once a year) to do so more often. The most common reasons include the participant being less busy, (24 per cent), cheaper admission prices at sports venues (17 per cent) or having someone to go with (12 per cent).

The most popular sporting activity (excluding walking), according to 15 per cent of all adults aged 16 and over who participate in sports, was indoor swimming or diving (Table 13.13). This was the most popular sporting activity for women (18 per cent) and especially among those aged 16 and 44 where around one-quarter of women participated. The second most popular category of sporting activity was health, fitness, gym, or conditioning activities such as abdominal and thigh exercises (13 per cent). Although there was very little difference in the proportion of men and women participating in this activity, it was the joint most popular activity favoured by men (13 per cent) and again especially for those aged 16 to 24 (22 per cent) and 25 to 44 (18 per cent). The sporting activities that had the largest difference in levels of participation between men and women were outdoor football, 12 per cent of men had played during the previous 12 months compared with 1 per cent of women; and

Table **13.13**

Top ten sports, games and physical activities[1] among adults: by sex and age, 2005/06

England   Percentages

	Men					Women				
	16–24	25–44	45–64	65 and over	All aged 16 and over	16–24	25–44	45–64	65 and over	All aged 16 and over
Indoor swimming or diving	16	18	10	5	13	23	24	16	6	18
Health, fitness, gym or conditioning activities	22	18	9	4	13	19	16	13	3	13
Recreational cycling	16	16	11	4	12	8	9	6	1	6
Snooker, pool, billiards	34	13	7	4	13	12	3	1	-	3
Keep-fit, aerobics, dance exercise	4	4	4	3	4	13	12	10	5	10
Outdoor football	43	14	3	-	12	5	1	1	-	1
Golf, pitch and putt, putting	10	9	9	9	9	1	1	2	1	1
Jogging, cross-country, road running	11	10	4	-	7	6	5	2	-	3
Tenpin bowling	9	4	3	1	4	8	4	2	-	3
Darts	16	6	3	1	6	4	2	1	1	2

1 The estimates are based on interviews conducted over a nine month period (mid-July 2005 to mid-April 2006). See Appendix, Part 13: Taking Part survey.

Source: Taking Part: The National Survey of Culture, Leisure and Sport, Department for Culture, Media and Sport

Figure **13.14**

Pupils who participate in PE and out-of-hours sport[1] at school:[2] by year group[3] and type of school, 2005/06

England
Percentages

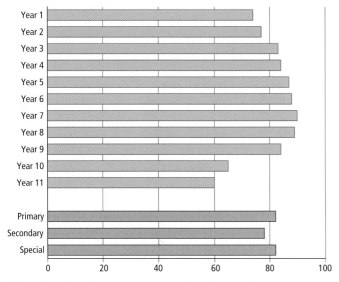

1 For at least two hours in a typical week. Includes high quality physical education (PE).
2 Schools that are part of a School Sports Partnership (SSP), which are groups of schools working together to develop physical education and sport opportunities. When the 2005/06 survey was conducted, 80 per cent of schools in England belonged to a SSP. As of the end of 2006 all schools in England belonged to a SSP.
3 See Appendix, Part 3: Stages of education.

Source: School Sport Survey, Department for Culture, Media and Sport, and Department for Education and Skills

snooker, 13 per cent of men and 3 per cent of women. Conversely women participated in keep-fit, aerobics and dance exercise more than men, 10 per cent compared with 4 per cent.

According to the Continuous Household Survey in Northern Ireland the top two sports, games or physical activities that men participated in the 12 months before interview in 2005/06, apart from walking and excluding cycling were swimming (20 per cent) and golf/putting (19 per cent). While swimming was popular with women in Northern Ireland (21 per cent), keep-fit, aerobics, yoga dance or exercise was the most popular category of physical activity with nearly one-quarter (24 per cent) participating. According to the Adults Sports Participation and Club Membership Survey in Wales the top two physical activities for men in 2004/05 apart from walking were multi-gym/weight training for fitness (10 per cent) and indoor swimming (9 per cent). Indoor swimming was the top physical activity apart from walking for women (15 per cent) followed by multi-gym/weight training for fitness (6 per cent).

Getting children of school age interested in sport and keeping them involved is seen as an important step in reducing obesity

and improving fitness levels, concentration and self-esteem. School Sports Partnerships (SSPs) are groups of schools working together to develop physical education and sport opportunities for all young people. In 2005/06 there were 411 live SSPs incorporating 80 per cent (or 17,122) of schools in England. An average partnership is made up of a sports college, acting as the hub with eight secondary schools and 45 primary or special schools clustered around it. According to the 2005/06 School Sport Survey, 80 per cent of pupils in SSP schools in England take part in two or more hours of high quality physical education (PE) and school sport each week, an increase of 11 percentage points since 2004/05. Just over eight in ten (82 per cent) primary and special school pupils in SSPs are participating in at least two hours of PE and sport, with just under eight in ten (78 per cent) of secondary school pupils doing so (Figure 13.14). The proportion of primary school pupils participating in sports and PE has risen by 18 percentage points since 2004/05. Across all years pupils spend on average 1 hour 51 minutes each week on curriculum PE. Over nine in ten schools offered football, dance, gymnastics and athletics during an academic year in 2005/06 and over eight in ten schools offered cricket, rounders, swimming and netball.

Social participation

Some organisations provide leisure time activities for young people. The Scout movement which has a combined membership of 360,000 children and young people aged between 6 and 25, celebrates its centenary in 2007 (Table 13.15 overleaf). The Guide movement, which will be celebrating its centenary in 2010 has a combined membership of 477,000 for those aged 6 to 25. Both the scout and guide movements promote a wide range of activities which include creativity, service projects, making friends, learning new skills to gain badges, and residential events such as indoor holidays and outdoor camps. The Boys' Brigade and Girls' Brigade are Christian youth organisations that cater for children and young people aged 5 to 19 and have memberships of 57,000 and 26,000 respectively. Activities include games, crafts, sports, Christian teaching, music and holidays. Some of these organisations are affiliated to and supported by the armed forces, such as the Air Training Corps and Army Cadet Force. The Clubs for Young People (CYP) organisation which was formed in 1925 has a membership of around 400,000 young people with 3,500 clubs and projects around the UK. CYP engages young people through arts, adventure and activities, and provides opportunities to get involved and achieve in their communities. The National Federation of Young Farmers' Clubs is the head of a nationwide body of more than 700 Young Farmers' Clubs located throughout England and Wales, dedicated to supporting young people in agriculture and the

Table **13.15**

Membership of selected organisations for young people, 2005

United Kingdom	Thousands
Beaver Scouts	97
Cub Scouts	134
Scouts	99
Explorer Scouts	26
Scout Network	4
Rainbow Guides	82
Brownie Guides	249
Guides	126
Senior Section (Ranger Guides, etc)	20
Boys Brigade[1]	57
Girls Brigade	26
Sea Cadets	13
Air Cadets	33
Army Cadets	45
Combined Cadet Force	42
Clubs for young people	400
National Federation of Young Farmers	21
Young Men's Christian Association[2]	85

1 Data are for 2005/06.
2 Data include both men and women, and are for 2004.

Source: Scout Association, Guide Association, Boys Brigade UK, Girls Brigade, Army Cadets, Clubs for Young People, National Federation of Young Farmers Clubs, Young Men's Christian Association

countryside. Their memberships comprise 21,000 young people aged between 10 and 26 years. The YMCA Movement in England is one of the largest youth development charities in the country, whose central purpose is to meet the needs of young people, particularly at times of need and regardless of their sex, race, or faith. In 2004 the YMCA had a membership of 85,000.

The Duke of Edinburgh's Award is also aimed at young people. This is not an organisation, but a programme of activities for 14 to 25-year-olds. Activities include helping people in the community, physical recreation and expeditions (training for, planning and completing a journey on foot or horseback, by boat or cycle). Begun in 1956, there have been around 3 million entrants with over 138,000 new entrants in 2004/05.

One of the ways that individuals contribute to their community is through volunteering, from formal volunteering activities such as running a scout or brownie group or the improvement of public open spaces, to informal activities such as giving advice, looking after a property or pet or providing childcare.

Figure **13.16**

Participation in voluntary activities at least once a month:[1] by age, 2005

England

Percentages

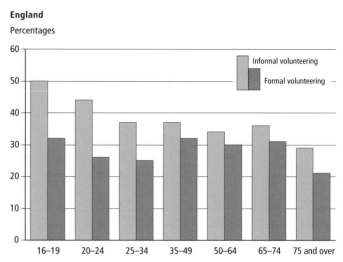

1 In the 12 months before interview.

Source: Citizenship Survey, Communities and Local Government

According to the Citizenship Survey, more than two-thirds (68 per cent) of adults aged 16 and over in England had participated in some form of informal voluntary activity in 2005. A lower proportion, 37 per cent, had done so at least once a month in the previous 12 months. Overall, 44 per cent of people had participated in formal voluntary activities in the 12 months before interview, with 29 per cent having done so at least once a month.

Informal volunteering at least once a month was highest among young people aged 16 to 19 where half (50 per cent) had performed an informal voluntary activity at least once a month in the year before interview (Figure 13.16). Participation was lowest among people aged 75 and over where nearly three in ten (29 per cent) had done so at least once a month. Women were more likely than men to volunteer informally at least once a month, 41 per cent compared with 32 per cent. Formal participation at least once a month during the year before interview was similar between most age groups at around 31 per cent, apart from those aged 20 to 24 and 25 to 34 (around 25 per cent) and those aged 75 and over (21 per cent). Women were again more likely than men to volunteer formally at least once a month, 31 per cent compared with 27 per cent.

The most common types of help given by those who participated in informal voluntary activities at least once a month included giving advice (52 per cent), transporting or escorting someone (38 per cent), keeping in touch with someone who had difficulty getting about (38 per cent) and looking after property (37 per cent). The most common types of formal activity participated in

Figure **13.17**

Voting turnout in the 2005 General Election:[1] by age

Great Britain

Percentages

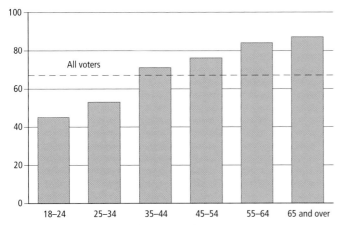

1 See Appendix, Part 13: Parliamentary elections.

Source: British Election Study

at least once a month included organising or helping run an activity or event (54 per cent) and raising or handling money or taking part in a sponsored event (52 per cent).

Participating in the political process in the UK includes voting for local and national governments. In the General Election held in May 2005 (reported in detail in *Social Trends 36*) there were evident age differences in the turnout. People aged between 18 and 34 were less likely to vote than those in the older age groups. According to the British Election Study, under half of young people aged 18 to 24 (45 per cent) and just over half (53 per cent) of those aged 25 to 34 voted in the 2005 General Election in Great Britain, compared with over 70 per cent in each of the age groups over 34 (Figure 13.17). Nearly nine in ten (87 per cent) people aged 65 and over voted.

The electoral turnout is becoming progressively older. In 1964, 11 per cent of young people aged 18 to 24 and 19 per cent of those aged 25 to 34 were non-voters. Overall electoral turnout in 1964 was 77 per cent. During the 1970s and 1980s an average of around 25 per cent of those aged 18 to 24 and 19 per cent of those aged 25 to 34 were non-voters. Turnout in these two decades varied from 72 per cent to 79 per cent. In 2005 the proportion of people in these two age groups who did not vote had risen to 55 per cent and 47 per cent respectively. Electoral turnout in 2005 was 61 per cent. This was above the 59 per cent turnout at the 2001 elections which was the lowest turnout since the Second World War.

There is little to suggest that young people are interested in politics before they reach the age at which they become entitled to vote. According to the British Social Attitudes survey and the

Young People's Social Attitude Survey in 2003, children and young people aged 12 to 19 are less interested in politics than adults. A 'great deal' or 'quite a lot' of interest in politics was shown by 30 per cent of adults in 2003 compared with 8 per cent of those aged 12 to 19. Over one-third (36 per cent) of those aged 12 to 19 said that they had no interest in politics at all.

During the campaign in the run up to the 2005 general election people had many ways to learn about and possibly interact with, the political parties running for parliamentary seats. In 2005 according to the British Social Attitudes survey, the most common way was reading a leaflet or other printed material or watching a Party Election Broadcast or film produced by a party or candidate (both 56 per cent). Men were more likely than women to watch a television programme or listen to a radio show specifically about the election (58 per cent of men compared with 44 per cent of women) and read articles in a newspaper specifically about the election (53 per cent of men compared with 41 per cent of women).

Religion

In 2005, 60 per cent of the population in Great Britain were estimated to belong to a specific religion. Of these 54 per cent were estimated to be Christian and the majority, 27 per cent, belonged to the Church of England (Table 13.18). After Christians,

Table **13.18**

Belonging to a religion,[1,2] 2005

Great Britain

	Percentages
Christian	
Church of England/Anglican	*26.6*
Christian – no denomination	*9.6*
Roman Catholic	*9.2*
Presbyterian/Free-Presbyterian/Church of Scotland	*3.3*
Baptist/Methodist	*3.3*
United Reform Church (URC)/Congregational	*0.4*
Other Protestant/other Christian	*1.5*
Non-Christian	
Islam/Muslim	*2.6*
Hindu	*1.2*
Jewish	*0.8*
Sikh	*0.8*
Buddhist	*0.3*
Other non-Christian	*0.6*
No religion	*39.9*

1 Respondents were asked 'Do you regard yourself as belonging to any particular religion?' and those who said yes were asked which religion. Excludes those who answered 'Don't know' or did not answer.
2 See Appendix, Part 13: Measurement of religion.

Source: British Social Attitudes Survey, National Centre for Social Research

the largest religious group in Great Britain were Muslims (3 per cent). When asked how often people attended services or meetings connected with their religion apart from such special occasions as weddings, funerals and baptisms, over half (52 per cent) stated that they never or practically never attended.

In 2005, 3.2 million people in England attended church on a Sunday according to the English Church Census. This had fallen by 2.2 million since 1979 when 5.4 million people attended. The average age of people who go to church has increased from age 37 in 1979 to age 45 in 2005. Nearly three in ten (29 per cent) churchgoers were aged 65 and over, of which 12 per cent were aged 75 and over.

Church attendance has fallen for all age groups since 1979 (Figure 13.19). The largest percentage decrease was for young people aged 15 to 19 where the number of churchgoers fell by 69 per cent between 1979 and 2005 and for those aged 20 to 29, the numbers fell by 61 per cent. In 2005 one in ten (10 per cent) churchgoers in England were Black.

Since 1998 more than 1,000 new Christian churches have been created. All the major denominations opened new churches but about half of these were Black Pentecostal churches. However, during this period more churches closed than opened, with the

Figure **13.19**

Attendance at church services: by age

England

Thousands

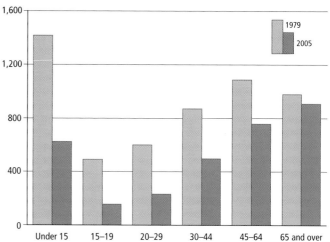

Source: English Church Census, Christian Research

Methodists closing the most. The Methodist Church suffered a net loss of about 300 churches, and the Church of England, a net loss of more than 100.

Websites and contacts

Chapter 1: Population

Websites

Eurostat
www.europa.eu.int/comm/eurostat

General Register Office for Scotland
www.gro-scotland.gov.uk

Government Actuary's Department
www.gad.gov.uk

Home Office Immigration and Asylum Statistics
www.homeoffice.gov.uk/rds/immigration1.html

Northern Ireland Statistics Research Agency
www.nisra.gov.uk

Scottish Executive
www.scotland.gov.uk

Statistics Estonia
www.stat.ee

United Nations Population Division
www.un.org/esa/population/unpop.htm

Welsh Assembly Government
http://new.wales.gov.uk/

Contacts

Office for National Statistics

Internal Migration
01329 813872

International Migration
01329 813255

Population Estimates
01329 813318

Population Projections
020 7533 5222

Other organisations

Eurostat
00 352 4301 33408

General Register Office for Scotland
0131 314 4254

Home Office
020 8760 8274

Northern Ireland Statistics and Research Agency, General Register Office
028 9034 8160

Welsh Assembly Government
029 2082 5058

Chapter 2: Households and families

Websites

Communities and Local Government
www.communities.gov.uk

Department of Health
www.dh.gov.uk

ESRC Research Centre for Analysis of Social Exclusion
http://sticerd.lse.ac.uk/case

Eurostat
www.europa.eu.int/comm/eurostat

General Register Office for Northern Ireland
www.groni.gov.uk

General Register Office for Scotland
www.gro-scotland.gov.uk

Home Office
www.homeoffice.gov.uk

Institute for Social and Economic Research
www.iser.essex.ac.uk

Northern Ireland Statistics and Research Agency
www.nisra.gov.uk

Scottish Executive
www.scotland.gov.uk

Teenage Pregnancy Unit
www.teenagepregnancyunit.gov.uk

Welsh Assembly Government
http://new.wales.gov.uk/

Contacts

Office for National Statistics

Fertility and Birth Statistics
01329 813758

General Household Survey
01633 655740

Labour Market Statistics Helpline
020 7533 6094

Marriages and Divorces
01329 813758

Other organisations

Communities and Local Government
020 7944 3303

Department of Health, Abortion statistics
020 7972 5533

ESRC Research Centre for Analysis of Social Exclusion
020 7955 6679

Eurostat
00 352 4301 35336

General Register Office for Scotland
0131 314 4243

Home Office, Family Policy Unit
020 7217 8393

Institute for Social and Economic Research
01206 872957

Northern Ireland Statistics and Research Agency, Customer Services
028 9034 8160

Welsh Assembly Government
029 2082 5058

Chapter 3: Education and training

Websites

Department for Education and Skills
www.dfes.gov.uk

Department for Education and Skills, Research and Statistics Gateway
www.dfes.gov.uk/rsgateway

Department for Education and Skills, Trends in Education and Skills
www.dfes.gov.uk/trends

Higher Education Statistics Agency
www.hesa.ac.uk

Learning and Skills Council
www.lsc.gov.uk

National Centre for Social Research
www.natcen.ac.uk

National Foundation for Educational Research
www.nfer.ac.uk

Northern Ireland Department of Education
www.deni.gov.uk

Northern Ireland Department for Employment and Learning
www.delni.gov.uk

Office for Standards in Education
www.ofsted.gov.uk

Organisation for Economic Co-operation and Development
www.oecd.org

Scottish Executive
www.scotland.gov.uk

Welsh Assembly Government
http://new.wales.gov.uk/

Contacts

Department for Education and Skills
01325 392754

Learning and Skills Council
0870 900 6800

National Centre for Social Research
020 7250 1866

Northern Ireland Department of Education
028 9127 9279

Northern Ireland Department for Employment and Learning
028 9025 7400

Scottish Executive
0131 244 0325

Welsh Assembly Government
029 2082 3507

Chapter 4: Labour market

Websites

Department of Trade and Industry
www.dti.gov.uk

Department for Work and Pensions
www.dwp.gov.uk

Eurostat
www.europa.eu.int/comm/eurostat

Jobcentre Plus
www.jobcentreplus.gov.uk

Learning and Skills Council
www.lsc.gov.uk

Nomis
www.nomisweb.co.uk

Contacts

Office for National Statistics

Labour Force Survey Data Service
020 7533 5614

Labour Market Statistics Helpline
020 7533 6094

Other organisations

Eurostat
00 352 4301 33209

Learning and Skills Council
0870 900 6800

Chapter 5: Income and wealth

Websites

Department for Education and Skills
www.dfes.gov.uk

Department for Work and Pensions
www.dwp.gov.uk

Eurostat
www.europa.eu.int/comm/eurostat

HM Revenue and Customs
www.hmrc.gov.uk

HM Treasury
www.hm-treasury.gov.uk

Institute for Fiscal Studies
www.ifs.org.uk

Institute for Social and Economic Research
www.iser.essex.ac.uk

National Centre for Social Research
www.natcen.ac.uk

Women and Equality Unit
www.womenandequalityunit.gov.uk

Contacts

Office for National Statistics

Annual Survey of Hours and Earnings
01633 819024

Effects of taxes and benefits
020 7533 5770

National Accounts
020 7533 5938

Department for Work and Pensions

Families and Children Study
020 7712 2090

Family Resources Survey
020 7962 8092

Households Below Average Income
020 7962 8232

Individual Income
020 7712 2781

Pensioners' Incomes
020 7962 8975

Pensions
020 7712 2721

Other organisations

Department for Education and Skills, Student Income and Expenditure Survey
020 7925 6248

HM Revenue and Customs, Strategy and Personal Tax
020 7147 3026

Institute for Fiscal Studies
020 7291 4800

Institute for Social and Economic Research
01206 872957

National Centre for Social Research
020 7250 1866

Chapter 6: Expenditure

Websites

Association for Payment Clearing Services
www.apacs.org.uk

Bank of England
www.bankofengland.co.uk

Department for Education and Skills
www.dfes.gov.uk

Department of Trade and Industry
www.dti.gov.uk

Eurostat
www.europa.eu.int/comm/eurostat

Insolvency Service
www.insolvency.gov.uk

Contacts

Office for National Statistics

Comparative price levels
020 7533 5840

Expenditure and Food Survey
020 7533 5752

Harmonised index of consumer prices
020 7533 5840

Household expenditure
020 7533 6058

Retail Prices Index
020 7533 5840

Volume of retail sales/retail sales index
01633 812713

Other organisations

Association for Payment Clearing Services
020 7711 6223

Bank of England
020 7601 5353

Department for Education and Skills, Student Income and Expenditure Survey
020 7925 6248

Insolvency Service
020 7215 3286

Chapter 7: Health

Websites

Department for Environment, Food and Rural Affairs
www.defra.gov.uk

Department of Health
www.dh.gov.uk/publicationsAndStatistics/statistics

Department of Health, Social Services and Public Safety, Northern Ireland
www.dhsspsni.gov.uk/stats&research/index.asp

Eurostat
www.europa.eu.int/comm/eurostat

General Register Office for Scotland
www.gro-scotland.gov.uk

Government Actuary's Department
www.gad.gov.uk

Health Protection Agency
www.hpa.org.uk

Home Office Research, Development and Statistics
www.homeoffice.gsi.gov.uk/rds

Information Centre for health and social care
www.ic.nhs.uk

ISD Scotland
www.isdscotland.org

Northern Ireland Cancer Registry
www.qub.ac.uk/nicr

Northern Ireland Statistics and Research Agency
www.nisra.gov.uk

Northern Ireland Statistics and Research Agency, General Register Office for Northern Ireland
www.groni.gov.uk

Scottish Executive
www.scotland.gov.uk

Welsh Assembly Government
http://new.wales.gov.uk/

Welsh Cancer Intelligence and Surveillance Unit
www.velindre-tr.wales.nhs.uk/wcisu

Contacts

Office for National Statistics

Cancer statistics
020 7533 5230

Condom use
01633 655703

General Household Survey
01633 813441

General Practice Research Database
020 7533 5240

Healthy life expectancy
020 7533 5768

Life expectancy
020 7533 5222

Mortality statistics
01329 813758

Psychiatric Morbidity Survey
020 7533 5305

Sudden Infant Death Syndrome
020 7533 5198

Department of Health

Key health indicators
020 7972 1036/3734

Prescription Cost Analysis
020 7972 5515

Information Centre for health and social care

Health Survey for England
0845 300 6016

Immunisation and Cancer Screening
0845 300 6016

Smoking, Misuse of Alcohol and Drugs
0845 300 6016

Northern Ireland Statistics and Research Agency

Continuous Household Survey
028 9034 8246

General Register Office for Northern Ireland
028 9025 2031

Other organisations

Department for Environment, Food and Rural Affairs, Expenditure and Food Survey (Family Food Report)
01904 455067

Department of Health, Social Services and Public Safety, Northern Ireland
028 9052 2800

Eurostat
00 352 4301 32056

General Register Office for Scotland
0131 314 4227

Health Protection Agency
020 8200 6868

National Centre for Social Research
020 7250 1866

NHS National Services Scotland, Information Services Division
0131 275 7777

Northern Ireland Cancer Registry
028 9026 3136

Welsh Assembly Government, Health Statistics and Analysis Unit
029 2082 5080

Welsh Cancer Intelligence and Surveillance Unit
029 2037 3500

Chapter 8: Social protection

Websites

Charities Aid Foundation
www.cafonline.org/research

Department for Education and Skills
www.dfes.gov.uk

Department of Health
www.doh.gov.uk/public/stats1.htm

Department of Health, Social Services and Public Safety, Northern Ireland
www.dhsspsni.gov.uk/stats_research.html

Department for Social Development, Northern Ireland
www.dsdni.gov.uk

Department for Work and Pensions
www.dwp.gov.uk

Economic and Social Research Council
www.esrc.ac.uk

Eurostat
www.europa.eu.int/comm/eurostat

Information Centre for health and social care
www.ic.nhs.uk/pubs/Allmonthspast

ISD Scotland
www.isdscotland.org

Local Government Data Unit – Wales
www.dataunitwales.gov.uk

National Centre for Social Research
www.natcen.ac.uk

Northern Ireland Statistics and Research Agency
www.nisra.gov.uk

Scottish Executive
www.scotland.gov.uk

Welsh Assembly Government
http://new.wales.gov.uk/

Contacts

Office for National Statistics

General Household Survey
01633 655740

Labour Market Statistics Helpline
020 7533 6094

Department for Education and Skills

Children's services
020 7925 7482

Day care for children
01325 392827

Department of Health

Acute services activity
0113 254 5522

Community and cross-sector services
020 7972 5524

Mental illness/handicap
020 7972 5546

NHS expenditure
0113 254 6012

Non-psychiatric hospital activity
020 7972 5529

Department of Health, Social Services and Public Safety, Northern Ireland

Community health and personal social services activity
028 9052 2960

Health and personal social services manpower
028 9052 2468

Department for Work and Pensions

Families and Children Study
020 7962 8648

Family Resources Survey
020 7962 8092

Number of benefit recipients
0191 225 7373

Information Centre for health and social care

Adults' social services
0113 254 7254

General dental and community dental service
0845 300 6016

General medical services statistics
0845 300 6016

NHS medical staff
0845 300 6016

NHS non-medical manpower
0845 300 6016

Personal social services expenditure
0113 254 7254

Residential care and home help
0113 254 7254

Social services staffing and finance data
0113 254 7254

Scottish Executive

Adult community care
0131 244 3777

Children's social services
0131 244 0313

Social work staffing
0131 244 0311

Other organisations

Charities Aid Foundation, Research Department
01732 520125

Department for Social Development, Northern Ireland
028 9052 2280

Eurostat
00 352 4301 34122

National Centre for Social Research
020 7250 1866

NHS National Services Scotland, Information Services Division
0131 275 6000

Northern Ireland Statistics and Research Agency
028 9034 8243

Welsh Assembly Government
029 2082 5080

Chapter 9: Crime and justice

Websites

Court Service
www.hmcourts-service.gov.uk

Crime Statistics for England and Wales
www.crimestatistics.org.uk

Criminal Justice System
www.cjsonline.org

Crown Office and Procurator Fiscal Services
www.crownoffice.gov.uk

Crown Prosecution Service
www.cps.gov.uk

Department of Constitutional Affairs
www.dca.gov.uk

Home Office
www.homeoffice.gov.uk

Northern Ireland Court Service
www.courtsni.gov.uk

Northern Ireland Office
www.nio.gov.uk

Northern Ireland Prison Service
www.niprisonservice.gov.uk

Prison Service for England and Wales
www.hmprisonservice.gov.uk

Police Service of Northern Ireland
www.psni.police.uk

Scottish Executive
www.scotland.gov.uk

Scottish Prison Service
www.sps.gov.uk

Welsh Assembly Government
http://new.wales.gov.uk/

Contacts

Department of Constitutional Affairs
020 7210 8500

Home Office
0870 000 1585

Northern Ireland Office
028 9052 7538

Northern Ireland Statistics and Research Agency, Continuous Household Survey
028 9034 8243

Police Service of Northern Ireland
028 9065 0222 ext. 24865

Scottish Executive, Justice Department
0131 244 2228

Welsh Assembly Government
029 2080 1388

Chapter 10: Housing

Websites

Communities and Local Government
www.communities.gov.uk

Council of Mortgage Lenders
www.cml.org.uk

Department for Social Development, Northern Ireland
www.dsdni.gov.uk

Department for Work and Pensions
www.dwp.gov.uk

Eurostat
www.europa.eu.int/comm/eurostat

HM Courts Service
www.hmcourts-service.gov.uk

Land Registry
www.landreg.gov.uk

Northern Ireland Statistics and Research Agency
www.nisra.gov.uk

Scottish Executive
www.scotland.gov.uk

Social Exclusion Unit
www.socialexclusionunit.gov.uk

Welsh Assembly Government
http://new.wales.gov.uk/

Contacts

Office for National Statistics

Expenditure and Food Survey
020 7533 5752

General Household Survey
01633 655740

Communities and Local Government

Housing Data and Statistics
020 7944 3317

Planning and Land Use Statistics
020 7944 5533

Other organisations

Council of Mortgage Lenders
020 7440 2251

Court Service
020 7210 1773

Department for Social Development, Northern Ireland, Statistics and Research Branch
028 9081 9953

Eurostat
00 352 4301 32056

Land Registry
0151 473 6008

Northern Ireland Statistics and Research Agency
028 9034 8209

Scottish Executive
0131 244 7236

Welsh Assembly Government
029 2082 5063

Chapter 11: Environment

Websites

Centre for Ecology and Hydrology
www.ceh-nerc.ac.uk

Communities and Local Government
www.communities.gov.uk

Department for Environment, Food and Rural Affairs
www.defra.gov.uk

Department of the Environment Northern Ireland
www.doeni.gov.uk

Department of Trade and Industry
www.dti.gov.uk/energy/index.html

Environment Agency
www.environment-agency.gov.uk

Environment and Heritage Service
www.ehsni.gov.uk

European Environment Agency
www.eea.eu.int

Eurostat
www.europa.eu.int/comm/eurostat

Forestry Commission
www.forestry.gov.uk/statistics

Joint Nature Conservation Committee
www.jncc.gov.uk

Northern Ireland Statistics and Research Agency
www.nisra.gov.uk

Scottish Environment Protection Agency
www.sepa.org.uk

Scottish Executive
www.scotland.gov.uk

Welsh Assembly Government
http://new.wales.gov.uk/

Contacts

Centre for Ecology and Hydrology
01491 838800

Communities and Local Government
020 7944 5534

Department for Environment, Food and Rural Affairs
020 7082 8608

Department of the Environment Northern Ireland
028 9054 0540

Department of the Environment Northern Ireland, Environment and Heritage Service
028 9023 5000

Department of Trade and Industry
020 7215 2697

Environment Agency
0845 9333 111

European Environment Agency
00 45 3336 7100

Eurostat
00 352 4301 33023

Forestry Commission
0131 314 6337

Joint Nature Conservation Committee
01733 562626

Scottish Environment Protection Agency
01786 457700

Scottish Executive
0131 244 0445

Welsh Assembly Government
029 2082 5111

Chapter 12: Transport

Websites

Civil Aviation Authority, Economic Regulation Group
www.caaerg.co.uk

Department of the Environment Northern Ireland
www.doeni.gov.uk

Department of Trade and Industry
www.dti.gov.uk

Department for Transport
www.dft.gov.uk/transtat

European Commission Directorate-General Energy and Transport
http://ec.europa.eu/dgs/energy_transport/index_en.html

National Centre for Social Research
www.natcen.ac.uk

Office of Rail Regulation
www.rail-reg.gov.uk

Passenger Focus
www.passengerfocus.org.uk

Scottish Executive
www.scotland.gov.uk

Contacts

Office for National Statistics

Census Customer Services
01329 813800

Expenditure and Food Survey
020 7533 5752

Household Expenditure
020 7533 6001

International Passenger Survey
020 7533 5765

Retail Prices Index
020 7533 5874

Department for Transport

General Enquiries
020 7944 8300

National Travel Survey
020 7944 3097

Other organisations

Civil Aviation Authority, Economic Regulation Group
020 7453 6258

Department of the Environment Northern Ireland
028 9054 0540

Department of Trade and Industry
020 7215 5000

Driving Standards Agency
0115 901 2852

National Centre for Social Research
020 7250 1866

Office of Rail Regulation
020 7282 2192

Passenger Focus
0870 336 6037

Police Service of Northern Ireland
028 9065 0222 ext. 24135

Scottish Executive
0131 244 7255/7256

Chapter 13: Lifestyles and social participation

Websites

Christian Research
www.christian-research.org.uk

Communities and Local Government
www.communities.gov.uk

Department for Culture, Media and Sport
www.culture.gov.uk

Department for Education and Skills
www.dfes.gov.uk

enjoyEngland
www.enjoyengland.com

National Centre for Social Research
www.natcen.ac.uk

National Literacy Trust
www.literacytrust.org.uk

Ofcom
www.ofcom.org.uk

Pearl and Dean
www.pearlanddean.com

Public Lending Right
www.plr.uk.com

Radio Joint Audience Research Ltd
www.rajar.co.uk

The Electoral Commission
www.electoralcommission.org.uk

The Society of London Theatre
www.OfficialLondonTheatre.co.uk

The UK Film Council
www.info@ukfilmcouncil.org.uk

VisitBritain
www.visitbritain.com

VisitScotland
www.visitscotland.com

VisitWales
www.visitwales.com

Contacts

Office for National Statistics

Expenditure and Food Survey
020 7533 5752

International Passenger Survey
020 7533 5765

Omnibus Survey (Internet access module)
01633 813116

Other organisations

Christian Research
020 8294 1989

Communities and Local Government
020 7944 0557

Department for Culture, Media and Sport
020 7211 6200

National Centre for Social Research
020 7250 1866

National Literacy Trust
020 7828 2435

Northern Ireland Tourist Board
028 9023 1221

Ofcom
020 7981 3000

Pearl and Dean
020 7882 1113

Radio Joint Audience Research Ltd
020 7292 9040

The Electoral Commission
020 7271 0612

The Society of London Theatre
020 7557 6700

The UK Film Council
020 7861 7861

VisitBritain
020 8846 9000

VisitScotland
0131 472 2384

VisitWales
0870 830 0306

References and further reading

From January 2005 Office for National Statistics (ONS) products published by TSO are now available from Palgrave Macmillan. Many can also be found on the National Statistics website: www.statistics.gov.uk

General

Regional Trends, ONS, Palgrave Macmillan, available at:
www.statistics.gov.uk/statbase/product.asp?vlnk=836

Focus on Ethnicity and Identity, Internet only publication, ONS, available at:
www.statistics.gov.uk/focuson/ethnicity

Focus on Families, Internet only publication, ONS, available at:
www.statistics.gov.uk/focuson/families

Focus on Gender, Internet only publication, ONS, available at:
www.statistics.gov.uk/focuson/gender

Focus on Health, Internet only publication, ONS, available at:
www.statistics.gov.uk/focuson/health

Focus on London, Internet only publication, ONS, available at:
www.statistics.gov.uk/focuson/london

Focus on Older People, Internet only publication, ONS, available at:
www.statistics.gov.uk/focuson/olderpeople

Focus on People and Migration, Internet only publication, ONS, available at:
www.statistics.gov.uk/focuson/migration

Focus on Religion, Internet only publication, ONS, available at:
www.statistics.gov.uk/focuson/religion

Focus on Social Inequalities, ONS, TSO, available at:
www.statistics.gov.uk/focuson/socialinequalities

Focus on Wales: Its People, Internet only publication, ONS, available at:
www.statistics.gov.uk/focuson/wales

Ffocws ar Gymru: Ei Phobl, Internet only publication, ONS, available at:
www.statistics.gov.uk/focuson/cymru

UK 2005: The Official Yearbook of the United Kingdom of Great Britain and Northern Ireland, ONS, Palgrave Macmillan

Chapter 1: Population

Annual Report of the Registrar General for Northern Ireland, Northern Ireland Statistics and Research Agency, available at:
www.nisra.gov.uk/demography/default.asp?cmsid=20_45_100&cms=demography_Publications_Registrar+General+Annual+Reports&release

Annual Report of the Registrar General for Scotland, General Register Office for Scotland, available at:
www.gro-scotland.gov.uk/statistics/library/annrep/index.html

Asylum Statistics – United Kingdom, Home Office, available at:
www.homeoffice.gov.uk/rds/immigration1.html

Birth Statistics, England and Wales (Series FM1), Internet only publication, ONS, available at:
www.statistics.gov.uk/statbase/Product.asp?vlnk=5768

Bradford B (2006) *Who are the 'Mixed' ethnic group?*, Internet only publication, ONS, available at:
www.statistics.gov.uk/CCI/article.asp?ID=1580

Census 2001: First results on population for England and Wales, ONS, TSO

Control of Immigration: Statistics, United Kingdom, Home Office, TSO

European Social Statistics – Population, Eurostat

Health Statistics Quarterly, ONS, Palgrave Macmillan, available at:
www.statistics.gov.uk/statbase/Product.asp?vlnk=6725

International Migration Statistics (Series MN), Internet only publication, ONS, available at: www.statistics.gov.uk/statbase/Product.asp?vlnk=507

Key Population and Vital Statistics (Series VS/PP1), ONS, Palgrave Macmillan, available at: www.statistics.gov.uk/statbase/Product.asp?vlnk=539

Mid-year Population Estimates, Northern Ireland, Northern Ireland Statistics and Research Agency, available at: www.nisra.gov.uk/demography/default.asp?cmsid=20_21_24&cms=demography_population%20statistics_Mid%2Dyear+population+estimates&release

Mid-year Population Estimates, Scotland, General Register Office for Scotland, available at: www.gro-scotland.gov.uk/statistics/library/mid-2005-population-estimates/index.html

Mid-year Population Estimates for England and Wales, Internet only publication, ONS, available at:
www.statistics.gov.uk/statbase/product.asp?vlnk=601

Migration Statistics, Eurostat

Mortality Statistics for England and Wales (Series DH1, 2,3,4), Internet only publications, ONS, available at:
www.statistics.gov.uk/statbase/Product.asp?vlnk=620
www.statistics.gov.uk/statbase/Product.asp?vlnk=618
www.statistics.gov.uk/statbase/Product.asp?vlnk=6305
www.statistics.gov.uk/statbase/Product.asp?vlnk=621

National Population Projections, UK, GB and constituent countries (Series PP2), Palgrave Macmillan, available at:
www.gad.gov.uk/Publications/Demography_and_statistics.htm

Patterns and Trends in International Migration in Western Europe, Eurostat

Persons Granted British Citizenship – United Kingdom, Home Office

Population and Projections for areas within Northern Ireland, Northern Ireland Statistics and Research Agency, available at:
www.nisra.gov.uk/ demography/default.asp?cmsid=20_21_25&cms=demography_population%20statistics_Population+projections&release

Population Projections, Scotland (for Administrative Areas), General Register Office for Scotland, available at: www.gro-scotland.gov.uk/statistics/library/popproj/04population-projections/index.html

Population Projections for Wales (sub-national), Welsh Assembly Government/Welsh Office Statistical Directorate, available at http://new.wales.gov.uk/topics/statistics/

Population Trends, ONS, Palgrave Macmillan, available at:
www.statistics.gov.uk/statbase/Product.asp?vlnk=6303

Chapter 2: Households and families

Abortion Statistics (Series AB), TSO (to 2001)

Abortion Statistics Statistical Bulletin, Department of Health (from 2002)

Annual Report of the Registrar General for Northern Ireland, Northern Ireland Statistics and Research Agency, available at:
www.nisra.gov.uk/demography/default.asp?cmsid=20_45_100&cms=demography_Publications_Registrar+General+Annual+Reports&release

Annual Report of the Registrar General for Scotland, General Register Office for Scotland, available at:
www.gro-scotland.gov.uk/statistics/library/annrep/index.html

Birth Statistics, England and Wales, (Series FM1), Internet only publication, ONS, available at:
www.statistics.gov.uk/statbase/Product.asp?vlnk=5768

Birth Statistics: Historical Series, – FM1 datasets, ONS, available at:
www.statistics.gov.uk/statbase/Product.asp?vlnk=8972

Choosing Childlessness, Family Policy Studies Centre

European Social Statistics – Population, Eurostat

General Household Survey 2005, Internet only publication, ONS, available at: www.statistics.gov.uk/ghs/

Health Statistics Quarterly, ONS, Palgrave Macmillan, available at: www.statistics.gov.uk/statbase/Product.asp?vlnk=6725

Household and population estimates and projections, Communities and Local Government, available at: www.communities.gov.uk/index.asp?id=1156093

Key Population and Vital Statistics (Series VS/PP1), ONS, Palgrave Macmillan, available at: www.statistics.gov.uk/statbase/Product.asp?vlnk=539

Marriage, Divorce and Adoption Statistics 1837–1983 (Series FM2), ONS, TSO

Marriage, Divorce and Adoption Statistics, England and Wales, (Series FM2), Internet only publication, ONS, available at: www.statistics.gov.uk/statbase/Product.asp?vlnk=581

Penn R and Lambert P (2002) *Attitudes towards ideal family size of different ethnic/nationality groups in Great Britain, France and Germany*, Population Trends, no 108, pp 49-58, Palgrave Macmillan, also available at: www.statistics.gov.uk/statbase/Product.asp?vlnk=6303

Population Trends, ONS, Palgrave Macmillan, available at: www.statistics.gov.uk/statbase/Product.asp?vlnk=6303

Projections of Households in England to 2021, Office of the Deputy Prime Minister

Recent Demographic Developments in Europe, Council of Europe

Housing in England: Survey of English Housing, Communities and Local Government, TSO, available at: www.communities.gov.uk/index.asp?id=1503868

Teenage Pregnancy, Report by the Social Exclusion Unit, TSO

The British Population, Oxford University Press

Chapter 3: Education and training

British Social Attitudes – The 23rd Report, National Centre for Social Research, Sage publications

Clemens S, Ullman A and Kinnaird R (2006) *2005 Childcare and Early Years Providers Survey Overview Report*, BMRB Social Research for the Department for Education and Skills, available at: www.dfes.gov.uk/ research/data/uploadfiles/RR764.pdf

Education at a Glance, OECD Indicators 2006, Organisation for Economic Co-operation and Development, available at: www.oecd.org/document/ 52/0,2340,en_2649_34515_37328564_1_1_1,00.html

Kitchen S, Mackenzie H, Butt S and Finch S (2006) *Evaluation of Curriculum Online Report of the third survey of schools*, BECTA ICT Research for the Department for Education and Skills, available at: http://publications.becta.org.uk/display.cfm?resID=25949&page=1835

Longitudinal Study of Young People in England, Department for Education and Skills, available at: www.esds.ac.uk/longitudinal/access/lsype

National Employers Skills Survey 2005, Learning and Skills Council, available at: http://research.lsc.gov.uk/LSC+Research/published/ness/ness2005.htm

Statistical Volume: Education and Training Statistics for the United Kingdom (2006), Internet only publication, Department for Education and Skills, available at: www.dfes.gov.uk/rsgateway/DB/VOL/v000696/index.shtml

Student Income and Expenditure Survey 2004/05, DfES Research Report 725, National Centre for Social Research and Institute for Employment Studies, available at: www.dfes.gov.uk/research/data/uploadfiles/RR725.pdf

Chapter 4: Labour market

Grainger H (2006) *Trade Union Membership 2005*, Department of Trade and Industry, available at: www.dti.gov.uk/employment/research-evaluation/ trade-union-statistics/index.html

Guide to Labour Market Statistics, ONS, available at: www.statistics.gov.uk/about/data/guides/LabourMarket

Holt H and Grainger H (2005) *Results of the second flexible working employee survey*, Department of Trade and Industry, available at: www.dti.gov.uk/files/file11441.pdf

How Exactly is Unemployment Measured?, ONS, available at: www.statistics.gov.uk/statbase/Product.asp?vlnk=2054

Humphrey A, Costigan P, Pickering K, Stratford N and Barnes M (2003) *Factors affecting the labour market participation of older workers*, Department for Work and Pensions, available at: www.dwp.gov.uk/asd/asd5/rports2003-2004/rrep200.asp

Kersley B, Alpin C, Forth J, Bryson A, Bewley H, Dix G and Oxenbridge S *Inside the Workplace. First findings from the 2004 Workplace Employment Relations Survey*, Department of Trade and Industry, available at: www.dti.gov.uk/employment/research-evaluation/ wers-2004/index.html

Labour Force Survey Historical Supplement, ONS, available at: www.statistics.gov.uk/statbase/Product.asp?vlnk=11771

Labour Market Review 2006, ONS, Palgrave Macmillan, available at: www.statistics.gov.uk/labourmarketreview/

Labour Market Trends, ONS, Palgrave Macmillan, available at: www.statistics.gov.uk/statbase/Product.asp?vlnk=550

Local area labour markets: statistical indicators July 2006, ONS, available at: www.statistics.gov.uk/statbase/Product.asp?vlnk=14160

Northern Ireland Labour Force Survey, Department of Enterprise, Trade and Investment, Northern Ireland, available at: www.statistics.detini.gov.uk

What exactly is the Labour Force Survey?,ONS, available at: www.statistics.gov.uk/statbase/Product.asp?vlnk= 4756

Chapter 5: Income and wealth

Annual Survey of Hours and Earnings, Internet only publication, ONS, available at: www.statistics.gov.uk/statbase/Product.asp?vlnk=13101

Attitudes to inheritance, Joseph Rowntree Foundation

Berthoud R, Bryan M and Bardasi E (2004) *The dynamics of deprivation: the relationship between income and material deprivation over time*, DWP Research Report 219

Brewer M, Goodman A, Myck M, Shaw J and Shephard A (2004) *Poverty and Inequality in Britain: 2004*, Commentary no. 96, Institute for Fiscal Studies

British Social Attitudes – The 23rd Report, National Centre for Social Research, Sage publications

Changing Households: The British Household Panel Survey, Institute for Social and Economic Research

Clark T and Leicester A (2004) *Inequality and two decades of British tax and benefit reforms* Fiscal Studies, vol. 25, pp 129-58

Economic Trends, ONS, Palgrave Macmillan, available at: www.statistics.gov.uk/statbase/Product.asp?vlnk=308

Eurostat National Accounts ESA, Eurostat

Family Resources Survey, Department for Work and Pensions

Fiscal Studies, Institute for Fiscal Studies

For Richer, For Poorer, Institute for Fiscal Studies

Households Below Average Income, 1994/95–2004/05, Department for Work and Pensions

Income and Wealth. The Latest Evidence, Joseph Rowntree Foundation

Individual Incomes 1996/97–2004/05, Women and Equality Unit

Labour Market Trends, ONS, Palgrave Macmillan

Lyon N, Barnes M and Sweiry D (2006) *Families with children in Britain: Findings from the 2004 Families and Children Study (FACS)*, Department for Work and Pensions, Corporate Document Services, available at: www.dwp.gov.uk/asd/asd5/rports2005-2006/rrep340.pdf

Monitoring Poverty and Social Exclusion, Joseph Rowntree Foundation

Opportunity for All Annual Report, Department for Work and Pensions

Pension Trends, ONS, Palgrave Macmillan, available at www.statistics.gov.uk/statbase/Product.asp?vlnk=14173

Royal Commission (1978) 'Distribution of Income and Wealth 1975'; in Atkinson A B and Harrison A J (eds), *Distribution of Personal Wealth in Britain*, Cambridge University Press, Table 6.1

Student Income and Expenditure Survey 2004/05, DfES Research Report 725, National Centre for Social Research and Institute for Employment Studies, available at: www.dfes.gov.uk/research/data/uploadfiles/RR725.pdf

The Pensioners' Incomes Series, Department for Work and Pensions

United Kingdom National Accounts (The Blue Book), ONS, Palgrave Macmillan, available at:
www.statistics.gov.uk/statbase/Product.asp?vlnk=1143

Chapter 6: Expenditure

C&E 2: Alcohol and Tobacco Duties, Internet only publication, HM Revenue and Customs, available at: www.hmrc.gov.uk/budget2001/ce2.htm

Consumer Trends, Internet only publication, ONS, available at:
www.statistics.gov.uk/consumertrends

Economic Trends, ONS, Palgrave Macmillan, available at:
www.statistics.gov.uk/statbase/Product.asp?vlnk=308

Family Spending, ONS, Palgrave Macmillan, available at:
www.statistics.gov.uk/statbase/Product.asp?vlnk=361

Financial Statistics, ONS, Palgrave Macmillan, available at:
www.statistics.gov.uk/statbase/Product.asp?vlnk=376

Focus on Consumer Price Indices (Formerly the Business Monitor MM23), ONS, Palgrave Macmillan, available at:
www.statistics.gov.uk/statbase/Product.asp?vlnk=867

Leicester A (2005), *Fuel taxation*, Briefing Note No. 55, The Institute for Fiscal Studies, available at: www.ifs.org.uk/bns/bn55.pdf

Retail Sales Business Monitor (SDM28), Internet only publication, ONS, available at: www.statistics.gov.uk/rsi

Student Income and Expenditure Survey 2004/05, DfES Research Report 725, National Centre for Social Research and Institute for Employment Studies, available at: www.dfes.gov.uk/research/data/uploadfiles/RR725.pdf

United Kingdom National Accounts (The Blue Book), ONS, Palgrave Macmillan, available at:
www.statistics.gov.uk/statbase/Product.asp?vlnk=1143

Chapter 7: Health

A Complex Picture HIV and other Sexually Transmitted Infections in the United Kingdom: 2006, Health Protection Agency Centre for Infections, available at:
www.hpa.org.uk/publications/2006/hiv_sti_2006/default.htm

Alcohol Harm Reduction Strategy for England, The Cabinet Office, available at: www.cabinetoffice.gov.uk/strategy/downloads/su/alcohol/pdf/CabOffce%20AlcoholHar.pdf

Annual Report of the Registrar General for Northern Ireland, Northern Ireland Statistics and Research Agency, available at: www.nisra.gov.uk/demography/default.asp?cmsid=20_45_100&cms=demography_Publications_Registrar+General+Annual+Reports&release

Annual Report of the Registrar General for Scotland, General Register Office for Scotland, available at:
www.gro-scotland.gov.uk/statistics/library/annrep/index.html

At Least Five a Week – Evidence on the Impact of Physical Activity and its Relationship to Health, A Report from the Chief Medical Officer, Department of Health, available at: www.dh.gov.uk/PublicationsAndStatistics/Publications/PublicationsPolicyAndGuidance/PublicationsPolicyAndGuidanceArticle/fs/en?CONTENT_ID=4080994&chk=1Ft1Of

Babb P and Quinn M (2000) *Cancer Trends in England and Wales, 1950–1999*, Health Statistics Quarterly, no 9, pp 5-19, available at:
www.statistics.gov.uk/CCI/article.asp?ID=1493

Choosing Health – Making Healthy Choices Easier, Cm6374, TSO, available at: www.dh.gov.uk/PublicationsAndStatistics/Publications/PublicationsPolicyAndGuidance/PublicationsPolicyAndGuidanceArticle/fs/en?CONTENT_ID=4094550&chk=aN5Cor

Community Statistics, Department of Health, Social Services and Public Safety, Northern Ireland

Contraception and Sexual Health, 2005/06, ONS, Palgrave Macmillan, available at: www.statistics.gov.uk/statbase/Product.asp?vlnk=6988

Drug Misuse Declared: Findings from the 2005/06 British Crime Survey, Home Office, available at: www.homeoffice.gov.uk/rds/pdfs06/hosb1506.pdf

Family Food – Report on the Expenditure and Food Survey, Department for Environment, Food and Rural Affairs, available at:
http://statistics.defra.gov.uk/esg/publications/efs/default.asp

General Household Survey 2005, Internet only publication, ONS, available at: www.statistics.gov.uk/ghs

Geographic Variations in Health, ONS, Palgrave Macmillan, available at:
www.statistics.gov.uk/statbase/Product.asp?vlnk=6638

Health in Scotland. The Annual Report of the Chief Medical Officer on the State of Scotland's Health, Scottish Executive, available at:
www.scotland.gov.uk/Publications/Recent

Health Statistics Quarterly, particularly Results of the ICD-10 bridge coding study, England and Wales, 1999, Health Statistics Quarterly, no 14, pp 75-83, available at: www.statistics.gov.uk/statbase/Product.asp?vlnk=6725

Health Survey for England, Information Centre for health and social care, available at: www.ic.nhs.uk/pubs/hseupdate05

Key Health Statistics from General Practice 1998, ONS, Palgrave Macmillan, available at: www.statistics.gov.uk/statbase/Product.asp?vlnk=4863

Mapping the Issues HIV and other Sexually Transmitted Infections in the United Kingdom: 2005, Health Protection Agency Centre for Infections, available at:
www.hpa.org.uk/publications/2005/hiv_sti_2005/default.htm

Mental health of Children and Young People in Great Britain 2004, ONS, Palgrave Macmillan, available at:
www.statistics.gov.uk/statbase/Product.asp?vlnk=14116

Mortality Statistics for England and Wales (Series DH1,2,3,4), Internet only publications ONS, available at:
www.statistics.gov.uk/statbase/Product.asp?vlnk=620
www.statistics.gov.uk/statbase/Product.asp?vlnk=618
www.statistics.gov.uk/statbase/Product.asp?vlnk=6305
www.statistics.gov.uk/statbase/Product.asp?vlnk=621

New Frontiers – National Chlamydia Screening Programme Annual Report 2005/6, Health Protection Agency Centre for Infections, available at:
www.hpa.org.uk/publications/2006/ncsp

On the State of the Public Health – The Annual Report of the Chief Medical Officer of the Department of Health, Department of Health, available at:
www.dh.gov.uk/AboutUs/MinistersAndDepartmentLeaders/ChiefMedicalOfficer/CMOPublications/CMOAnnualReports/fs/en

Population Trends, ONS, Palgrave Macmillan, available at:
www.statistics.gov.uk/statbase/Product.asp?vlnk=6303

Psychiatric Morbidity Survey Among Adults Living in Private Households 2000, ONS, TSO, available at:
www.statistics.gov.uk/downloads/theme_health/psychmorb.pdf

Quinn M, Wood H, Cooper N and Rowan S (2005) *Cancer Atlas of the United Kingdom and Ireland 1991–2000*, ONS, Palgrave Macmillan, available at: www.statistics.gov.uk/statbase/Product.asp?vlnk=14059

Report of the Chief Medical Officer, Department of Health, Social Services and Public Safety, Northern Ireland, available at:
www.dhsspsni.gov.uk/ph_cmo_annual_report_2005.pdf

Scottish Health Statistics, Information Services Division, NHS Scotland, available at: www.isdscotland.org

Smoking, Drinking and Drug Use among Young People in England in 2005, Information Centre for health and social care, available at:
www.ic.nhs.uk/pubs/youngpeopledruguse-smoking-drinking2005

Smoking Kills – A White Paper on Tobacco, Presented to Parliament by the Secretary of State for Health and the Secretaries of State for Scotland, Wales and Northern Ireland in 1998, TSO

Smoking-related Behaviour and Attitudes, 2005, ONS, available at:
www.statistics.gov.uk/statbase/Product.asp?vlnk=1638

Statistical Publications on Aspects of Health and Personal Social Services Activity in England (various), Department of Health, available at:
www.dh.gov.uk/PublicationsAndStatistics/Statistics

Tackling Health Inequalities: Status Report on the Programme for Action, Department of Health, available at:
www.dh.gov.uk/assetRoot/04/11/76/97/04117697.pdf

Trew V (2003-2006) *Health Statistics Wales*, Welsh Assembly Government, available at: http://new.wales.gov.uk/topics/statistics/

Welsh Health: Annual Report of the Chief Medical Officer, Welsh Assembly Government

World Health Statistics, World Health Organisation, available at: www.who.int/whosis/en/

Chapter 8: Social protection

Anderson K *Community Care Statistics 2004–05, Referrals, assessments and packages of care for adults, England*, Information Centre for health and social care, available at: www.ic.nhs.uk/pubs/commcare05adultengsum

Anderson K *Community Care Statistics 2005, Home care services for adults, England*, Information Centre for health and social care, available at: www.ic.nhs.uk/pubs/commcare2005homehelpadulteng

Annual Statistical Publication Notices (various including 'Childrens's Social Work Statistics 2004-05), Scottish Executive, available at: www.scotland.gov.uk/statistics/

Benefit expenditure and caseload information, Department for Work and Pensions, available at: www.dwp.gov.uk/asd/asd4/expenditure.asp

British Social Attitudes – The 23rd Report, National Centre for Social Research, Sage publications

Charity Trends 2006, Charities Aid Foundation, available at: www.cafonline.org/research

Clarke A *Referrals, assessments and children and young people on child protection registers, England (First Release)*, Department for Education and Skills, available at: www.dfes.gov.uk/rsgateway/DB/SFR/s000692/index.shtml

Corke N *Children looked after in England (First Release)*, Department for Education and Skills, available at: www.dfes.gov.uk/rsgateway/DB/SFR/s000691/index.shtml

ESSPROSS Manual 1996, Eurostat

Family Resources Survey, Department for Work and Pensions, available at: www.dwp.gov.uk/asd/frs

General Household Survey 2005, Internet only publication, ONS, available at: www.statistics.gov.uk/ghs

Health and Personal Social Services Statistics (various), Information Centre for health and social care, available at: www.ic.nhs.uk/pubs

Hospital Statistics for Northern Ireland, Department of Health, Social Services and Public Safety, Northern Ireland, available at: www.dhsspsni.gov.uk/stats-cib-children_order_bulletin

Lyon N, Barnes M and Sweiry D (2006) *Families with children in Britain: Findings from the 2004 Families and Children Study (FACS)*, Department for Work and Pensions, Corporate Document Services, available at: www.dwp.gov.uk/asd/asd5/rports2005-2006/rrep340.pdf

Mooney E, Fitzpatrick M, Orr J and Hewitt R (2006) *Children Order Statistical Bulletin*, Department of Health, Social Services and Public Safety, Northern Ireland, available at: www.dhsspsni.gov.uk/stats-cib-children_order_bulletin

Social Services Statistics Wales, Local Government Data Unit, available at: www.dataunitwales.gov.uk

Chapter 9: Crime and justice

A Commentary on Northern Ireland Crime Statistics (2005), Northern Ireland Office, TSO, available at: www.nio.gov.uk/a_commentary_on_northern_ireland_crime_statistics_2004.pdf

Civil Judicial Statistics Scotland 2002, TSO, available at: www.scotland.gov.uk/Publications/2004/02/18897/33081

Costs, Sentencing Profiles and the Scottish Criminal Justice System 2002 (2004) Scottish Executive, available at: www.scotland.gov.uk/Publications/2004/06/19562/39571

Crime in England and Wales 2005/06, Home Office, available at: www.homeoffice.gov.uk/rds/pdfs06/hosb1206.pdf

Criminal Justice Series, Scottish Executive, available at: www.scotland.gov.uk/Publications/Recent

Criminal Statistics, England and Wales 2004, TSO, available at: www.homeoffice.gov.uk/rds/crimstats04.html

Crown Prosecution Service, Annual Report 2004/05, TSO, available at: www.cps.gov.uk/publications/reports/index.html

Digest 4: Information on the Criminal Justice System in England and Wales (1999), Home Office, available at: www.homeoffice.gov.uk/rds/digest41.html

Digest of Information on the Northern Ireland Criminal Justice System 4, TSO, available at: www.nio.gov.uk/digest_information_on_the_ni_criminal_justice_system_4.pdf

Experiences of Crime in Scotland, Scottish Executive

HM Prison Service Annual Report and Accounts, TSO, available at: www.official-documents.gov.uk/document/hc0506/hc01/0193/0193.asp

Home Office Departmental Report 2005, TSO, available at: www.official-documents.gov.uk/document/cm65/6528/6528.asp

Home Office Research Findings, Home Office, available at: www.homeoffice.gov.uk/rds/pubsintro1.html

Home Office Statistical Bulletins, Home Office, available at: www.homeoffice.gov.uk/rds/hosbpubs1.html

Judicial Statistics, England and Wales, TSO, available at: www.official-documents.gov.uk/document/cm67/6799/6799.asp

Northern Ireland Judicial Statistics, Northern Ireland Court Service, available at: www.courtsni.gov.uk/en-GB/Publications/Targets_and_Performance/

Offender Management Caseload Statistics, Home Office, available at: www.homeoffice.gov.uk/rds/omcs.html

Police Service of Northern Ireland Statistical Report, 2003/2004, 2004/2005 & 2005/2006, Police Service of Northern Ireland, available at: www.psni.police.uk/index/statistics_branch.htm

Perceptions of crime: Findings from the 2005 Northern Ireland Crime Survey, Northern Ireland Office available at: www.nio.gov.uk/media-detail.htm?newsID=13868

Police Statistics, England and Wales, CIPFA

Prison Statistics, England and Wales 2002, TSO

Prison Statistics Scotland 2005/06, Scottish Executive, available at: www.scotland.gov.uk/Publications/2006/08/18103613/0

Prisons in Scotland Report, TSO

Race and the Criminal Justice System, Home Office, available at: www.homeoffice.gov.uk/rds/pdfs06/s95overview0405.pdf

Recorded crime in Scotland 2005/06, Scottish Executive, available at: www.scotland.gov.uk/Publications/2006/08/30140700/0

Report of the Parole Board for England and Wales, TSO, available at: www.official-documents.gov.uk/document/hc0506/hc16/1661/1661.asp

Report on the work of the Northern Ireland Prison Service, TSO, available at: www.official-documents.gov.uk/document/hc0304/hc08/0804/0804.asp

Review of Crime Statistics: a Discussion Document, Home Office, available at: www.homeoffice.gov.uk/rds/pdfs04/review.pdf

Review of Police Forces' Crime Recording Practices, Home Office

Scottish Crime Survey, Scottish Executive

Shepherd A and Whiting E (2006) *Re-offending of adults: results from the 2003 cohort*, Home Office Statistical Bulletin 20/06, available at: www.homeoffice.gov.uk/rds/pdfs06/hosb2006.pdf

Statistics on Women and the Criminal Justice System, Home Office

The Criminal Justice System in England and Wales, Home Office

The Work of the Prison Service, Home Office

Whiting E and Cuppleditch L (2006) *Re-offending of juveniles: results from the 2004 cohort*, Home Office Statistical Bulletin 10/06, available at: www.homeoffice.gov.uk/rds/pdfs06/hosb1006.pdf

Wilson D, Sharp C and Patterson A (2006) *Young People and Crime: findings from the 2005 Offending, Crime and Justice Survey*, Home Office, available at: www.homeoffice.gov.uk/rds/pdfs06/hosb1706.pdf

Chapter 10: Housing

Bate R, Best R and Holmans A (Eds) (2000) *On the Move: The Housing Consequences of Migration*, Joseph Rowntree Foundation, YPS, available at: www.jrf.org.uk/knowledge/findings/housing/820.asp

Böheim R and Taylor M P (2000) *My Home Was My Castle: Evictions and Repossessions in Britain*, ESRC Institute for Social and Economic Research and Institute for Labour Research, available at: www.essex.ac.uk/ilr/discussion/ILRdps53.pdf

Bringing Britain Together: A National Strategy for Neighbourhood Renewal, Social Exclusion Unit (1998), Cabinet Office, available at: www.socialexclusionunit.gov.uk/publications.asp?did=113

Changing Households: The British Household Panel Survey, Institute for Social and Economic Research

Department for Communities and Local Government Annual Report, 2006, Communities and Local Government, TSO, available at: www.official-documents.co.uk/document/cm68/6816/6816.asp

Ermisch J and Halpin B (2000) *Becoming a Home-owner in Britain in the 1990s – The British Household Panel Survey*, ESRC Institute for Social and Economic Research, available at: www.iser.essex.ac.uk/pubs/workpaps/pdf/2000-21.pdf

English House Condition Survey 2004, Communities and Local Government, TSO, available at: www.communities.gov.uk/index.asp?id=1502421

Family Spending 2006, ONS, Palgrave Macmillan, available at: www.statistics.gov.uk/statbase/Product.asp?vlnk=361

General Household Survey 2005, Internet only publication, ONS, available at: www.statistics.gov.uk/ghs

Holmans A E *Divorce, Remarriage and Housing: The Effects of Divorce, Remarriage, Separation and the Formation of New Couple Households on the Number of Separate Households and Housing Demand Conditions*, Department of the Environment, Transport and the Regions, available at: www.communities.gov.uk/index.asp?id=1156484

Housing in England: Survey of English Housing, Communities and Local Government, TSO, available at: www.communities.gov.uk/index.asp?id=1503868

Living conditions in Europe – Statistical Pocketbook, Eurostat, available at: http://epp.eurostat.cec.eu.int/cache/ITY_OFFPUB/KS-53-03-831/EN/KS-53-03-831-EN.PDF

Local Housing Statistics, Internet only, Communities and Local Government, available at: www.communities.gov.uk/index.asp?id=1155991

Northern Ireland House Condition Survey, Northern Ireland Housing Executive, available at: www.nihe.gov.uk/HCS

Northern Ireland Housing Statistics, 2005/06, Department for Social Development, Northern Ireland, available at: www.dsdni.gov.uk/index/stats_and_research.htm

New Projections of households for England and the Regions to 2026 (2006), Office of the Deputy Prime Minister, TSO, available at: www.communities.gov.uk/index.asp?id=1002882&PressNoticeID=2097

Scottish House Condition Survey, Communities Scotland, available at: www.scotland.gov.uk/Topics/Statistics/SHCS

Smith S J, Munro M and Ford J with Davis R (2002) *A Review of Flexible Mortgages*, Council of Mortgage Lenders, CML Publications, available at: www.communities.gov.uk/index.asp?id=1155655

Statistical Bulletins on Housing, Scottish Executive, available at: www.scotland.gov.uk/Topics/Housing

Statistics on Housing in the European Community 2003, Eurostat, available at: www.ebst.dk/file/2256/housing_statistics_2003.pdf

The Social Situation in the European Union, Eurostat

UK Housing Review 2006/2007, Chartered Institute of Housing and Council of Mortgage Lenders

Welsh House Condition Survey 1998, Welsh Assembly Government, available at: http://new.wales.gov.uk/topics/statistics/publications/whcs98/

Welsh Housing Statistics, Welsh Assembly Government, available at: http://new.wales.gov.uk/legacy_en/keypubstatisticsforwalesheadline/content/housing/2004/hdw20040921-e.htm

Chapter 11: Environment

Accounting for Nature: Assessing Habitats in the UK Countryside, Department for Environment, Food and Rural Affairs, available at: www.defra.gov.uk/wildlife-countryside/cs2000/index.htm

Agriculture in the United Kingdom 2006, Department for Environment, Food and Rural Affairs, TSO, available at: http://statistics.defra.gov.uk/esg/publications/auk/default.asp

Air Quality Strategy for England, Scotland, Wales and Northern Ireland, Department for Environment, Food and Rural Affairs, TSO, available at: www.defra.gov.uk/corporate/consult/airqualstrat-review/consultation-vol1.pdf

Biodiversity: The UK Action Plan, Department for Environment, Food and Rural Affairs, TSO, available at: www.ukbap.org.uk/library/Reporting2005/UKBAPReport05.pdf

Digest of United Kingdom Energy Statistics 2006, Department of Trade and Industry, TSO, available at: www.dti.gov.uk/energy/statistics/publications/dukes/page29812.html

e-Digest of Environmental Statistics, Internet only publication, Department for Environment, Food and Rural Affairs, available at: www.defra.gov.uk/environment/statistics/index.htm

Energy Trends, Department of Trade and Industry, available at: www.dti.gov.uk/energy/statistics/publications/trends/index.html

Environmental Facts and Figures, Environment Agency, Internet only publication, available at: www.environment-agency.gov.uk/yourenv/eff/

Forestry Facts and Figures 2006, Forestry Commission, available at: www.forestry.gov.uk/pdf/fcfs206.pdf/$FILE/fcfs206.pdf

Forestry Statistics 2006, Forestry Commission, available at: www.forestry.gov.uk/website/ForestStats2006.nsf/byunique/index_main.html

GM Nation. The Findings of the Public Debate, Department for Environment, Food and Rural Affairs, available at: www.gmnation.org.uk/docs/gmnation_finalreport.pdf

General Quality Assessment, Environment Agency, available at: www.environment-agency.gov.uk/yourenv/eff/1190084/water/213902/river_qual/gqa2000/

Hydrological Summaries for the United Kingdom, Centre for Hydrology and British Geological Survey, available at: www.ceh.ac.uk/data/nrfa/publications.html

Land Use Change Statistics, Communities and Local Government, available at: www.communities.gov.uk/index.asp?id=1146601

Municipal Waste Statistics, Department for Environment, Food and Rural Affairs, available at: www.defra.gov.uk/environment/statistics/wastats/bulletin.htm

OECD Environmental Data Compendium, Organisation for Economic Co-operation and Development, available at: www.oecd.org/document/21/0,2340,en_2649_34303_2516565_1_1_1_1,00.html

Organic Statistics UK, Department for Environment, Food and Rural Affairs, available at: http://statistics.defra.gov.uk/esg/statnot/orguk.pdf

Quality of life counts 1999 – indicators for a strategy for sustainable development for the United Kingdom: a baseline assessment, Department of the Environment, Transport and the Regions, available at: www.sustainable-development.gov.uk/sustainable/quality99/index.htm

Quarterly Energy Prices, Department of Trade and Industry, available at: www.dti.gov.uk/energy/statistics/publications/prices/index.html

State of the Environment Report 2006, Scottish Environment Protection Agency, available at: www.sepa.org.uk/publications/state_of/index.htm

Securing the Future – UK Government sustainable development strategy (2005), Department for Environment, Food and Rural Affairs, TSO, available at: www.sustainable-development.gov.uk/publications/uk-strategy/index.htm

Survey of Public Attitudes to Quality of Life and to the Environment – 2001, Department for Environment, Food and Rural Affairs, available at: www.defra.gov.uk/environment/statistics/pubatt/index.htm

Sustainable Development Indicators in your Pocket 2006, Department for Environment, Food and Rural Affairs, available at: www.sustainable-development.gov.uk/progress/index.htm

State of the Environment 2005, Environment Agency, available at: www.environment-agency.gov.uk/yourenv/1088978/

The Environment in your Pocket, Department for Environment, Food and Rural Affairs, available at: www.defra.gov.uk/environment/statistics/eiyp/index.htm

Chapter 12: Transport

A New Deal for Transport: Better for Everyone (2005), Department for Transport, TSO, available at: www.dft.gov.uk/about/strategy/whitepapers/anewdealfortransportbetterfo5695

British Social Attitudes – The 23rd Report, National Centre for Social Research, Sage publications

Driving Standards Agency Annual Report and Accounts 2005/06, Driving Standards Agency, TSO, available at: www.official-documents.gov.uk/document/hc0506/hc11/1172/1172.asp

European Union Energy and Transport in Figures, 2005, European Commission

Focus on Freight: 2006 edition: Department for Transport, available at: www.dft.gov.uk/pgr/statistics/datatablespublications/freight/focusonfreight/pagefocusfreight06

Focus on Personal Travel: 2005 edition, Department for Transport, TSO, available at: www.dft.gov.uk/pgr/statistics/datatablespublications/personal/focuspt/2005/

National Passenger Survey Autumn 2006, Passenger Focus, available at: www.passengerfocus.org.uk/your-experiences/content.asp?dsid=496

National Rail Trends 2005–2006 Yearbook, Office of Rail Regulator, available at: www.rail-reg.gov.uk/server/show/nav.1528

National Travel Survey Bulletins, Department for Transport, available at: www.dft.gov.uk/pgr/statistics/recentforthcomingpublications/recentpublications

Northern Ireland Transport Statistics Annual 2005–2006, Department for Regional Development Northern Ireland, available at: www.drdni.gov.uk/DRDwww_Statistics/details.asp?publication_id=170

Office of Rail Regulation Annual report 2005–06, Office of Rail Regulation, available at: www.rail-reg.gov.uk/upload/pdf/290.pdf

Road Casualties Great Britain 2005 – Annual Report, Department for Transport, TSO, available at: www.dft.gov.uk/pgr/statistics/datatablespublications/accidents/casualtiesgbar/roadcasualtiesgreatbritain2005

Road Accidents Scotland 2005, Scottish Executive, available at: www.scotland.gov.uk/Publications/2006/11/22093058/0

Road Casualties: Wales 2005, Welsh Assembly Government, available at: http://new.wales.gov.uk/topics/statistics/publications/rcw2005/

Road Traffic Collision Statistics Annual Report 2005, Police Service of Northern Ireland, available at: www.psni.police.uk/rtc_report-4.pdf

Road Traffic Statistics Great Britain 2005, Department for Transport, available at: www.dft.gov.uk/pgr/statistics/datatablespublications/roadstraffic/traffic/rtstatistics/roadtrafficstatistics2005int5419

Scottish Transport Statistics: No 25 2006 Edition, Scottish Executive, available at: www.scotland.gov.uk/Publications/2006/12/15135954/0

Securing the Future – UK Government sustainable development strategy (2005), Department for Environment, Food and Rural Affairs, TSO, available at: www.sustainable-development.gov.uk/publications/uk-strategy/index.htm

Transport Statistics Bulletins and Reports, Department for Transport, available at: www.dft.gov.uk/pgr/statistics/recentforthcomingpublications/recentpublications

Transport Statistics for Great Britain 2006, Department for Transport, TSO, available at: www.dft.gov.uk/pgr/statistics/datatablespublications/tsgb/2006edition

Transport Trends 2006, Department for Transport, TSO, available at: www.dft.gov.uk/pgr/statistics/datatablespublications/trends/current/transporttrends2006

Travel Trends, A report on the 2005 International Passenger Survey (2006) ONS, Palgrave Macmillan, available at: www.statistics.gov.uk/statbase/Product.asp?vlnk=1391

Vehicle Licensing Statistics 2005, Department for Transport, available at: www.dft.gov.uk/pgr/statistics/datatablespublications/vehicles/licensing/vehiclelicensingstatistics2005b

Vehicle Speeds in Great Britain 2005, Department for Transport, available at: www.dft.gov.uk/pgr/statistics/datatablespublications/roadstraffic/speedscongestion/vehiclespeedsgb/vehiclespeedsingreatbritain2005a

Welsh Transport Statistics, Welsh Assembly Government, available at: http://new.wales.gov.uk/topics/statistics/publications/wts2006/

Chapter 13: Lifestyles and social participation

2005 Home Office Citizenship Survey, Communities and Local Government, available at: www.communities.gov.uk/index.asp?id=1503054

2005/06 School Sport Survey, Department for Education and Skills, available at: www.teachernet.gov.uk/docbank/index.cfm?id=10442

Andrews R (2005) *Annual Box Office Data Report*, The Society of London Theatre, available at: www.officiallondontheatre.co.uk/publications

Brierley P R*eligious Trends No 6, 2006/07*, Christian Research

Clark C and Foster A (2005) *Children's and young peoples's reading habits and preferences: The who, what, why, where and when*, National Literacy Trust, available at: www.literacytrust.org.uk/Research/readsurvey.html

Election 2005: Turnout, The Electoral Commission, available at: www.electoralcommission.org.uk/elections/generalelection2005.cfm

Media Literacy Audit: Report on media literacy amongst children, Ofcom, available at: www.ofcom.org.uk/advice/media_literacy/medlitpub/medlitpubrss/children/

RSU Statistical Yearbook, UK Film Council, available at: www.ukfilmcouncil.org.uk/information/statistics/yearbook/

The West End Theatre Audience, The Society of London Theatre

Travel Trends A report on the 2005 International Passenger Survey (2006), ONS, Palgrave Macmillan, available at: www.statistics.gov.uk/statbase/Product.asp?vlnk=1391

Geographical areas

The European Union,[1] 1 May 2004

EU-25 members

Non-EU-25 members

Sweden
Finland
Estonia
Latvia
Lithuania
Denmark
Netherlands
Ireland
United Kingdom
Germany
Poland
Belgium
Luxembourg
Czech Republic
Slovakia
Austria
Hungary
France
Slovenia
Italy
Portugal
Spain
Greece
Malta (not to scale)
Cyprus

Azores (Portugal)

Madeira Islands (Portugal)

1 Comprising the 25 states which were members of the European Union from 1st May 2004. Excludes Bulgaria and Romania, which became member states on 1st January 2007.

Canary Islands (Spain)

Government Office Regions

SCOTLAND

NORTHERN
IRELAND

NORTH
EAST

ENGLAND

―――― GOR boundary

YORKSHIRE
AND THE
HUMBER

NORTH
WEST

EAST
MIDLANDS

WEST
MIDLANDS

WALES

EAST OF
ENGLAND

LONDON

SOUTH WEST

SOUTH EAST

Police Force areas

Northern

Northern

Northern

Grampian

Tayside

Central

Fife

Strathclyde

GREAT BRITAIN

―――― Police Force area
boundary

Lothian and
Borders

NORTHERN
IRELAND

Dumfries
and Galloway

Northumbria

Cumbria

Durham

Cleveland

North Yorkshire

Lancashire

Humberside

W. Yorks.

Merseyside

G.M.P.

S. Yorks.

Lincolnshire

Cheshire

Derbys.

North Wales

Notts.

Staffs.

Leics.

Norfolk

Dyfed-Powys

West
Mercia

W. Mids.

Warks.

Northants

Cambs

Suffolk

Beds

Gwent

Gloucs.

Thames
Valley

Herts.

Essex

City

South Wales

Avon and
Somerset

Wiltshire

Met

Surrey

Kent

Devon and
Cornwall

Dorset

Hampshire

Sussex

Water and sewerage companies

SCOTLAND

ENGLAND and WALES

―――― Water and sewerage
company boundary

NORTHERN
IRELAND

NORTHUMBRIAN
WATER

UNITED
UTILITIES
WATER

YORKSHIRE
WATER

SEVERN TRENT
WATER

ANGLIAN
WATER

WELSH
DWR CYMRU
WATER

THAMES
WATER

WESSEX
WATER

SOUTHERN WATER

SOUTH
WEST
WATER

To obtain basic facts on the type of areas used in *Social Trends*,
as well as more specialist information on topics such as boundary
change visit the ONS Beginners' Guide to UK Geography at:
www.statistics.gov.uk/geography/beginners_guide.asp.

Major surveys

	Frequency	Sampling frame	Type of respondent	Coverage	Effective sample size[1] (most recent survey included in *Social Trends*)	Response rate (percentages)
Annual Population Survey	Continuous	Postcode Address File	All adults in household	UK	370,000 individuals	[2]
Annual Survey of Hours and Earnings	Annual	HM Revenue & Customs PAYE records	Employee	UK	255,000 employees	83
British Crime Survey	Annual	Postcode Address File	Adult in household	E&W	47,796 addresses	75
British Household Panel Survey	Annual	Postal addresses in 1991, members of initial wave households followed in subsequent waves	All adults in households	GB	5,502 households	88[3]
British Social Attitudes Survey	Annual	Postcode Address File	One adult per household	GB	7,778 addresses	55[4]
Census of Population	Decennial	Detailed local	Adult in household	UK	Full count	98
Citizenship Survey	Biennial	Postcode Address File	One adult per household	E&W	14,081 interviews	63[5]
Continuous Household Survey	Continuous	Valuation and Lands Agency Property	All adults in household	NI	3,882 addresses	67
e-Commerce Survey	Annual	Inter Departmental Business Register[6]	Employers	UK	9,000 employers	80
English House Condition Survey	Annual[7]	Postcode Address File	Any one householder	E	32,825 addresses	51[7]
Expenditure and Food Survey	Continuous	Postcode Address File in GB, Valuation and Lands Agency list in NI	All adults in households aged 16 or over[8]	UK	11,014 addresses[8]	57[8]
Families and Children Study	Annual	Child benefit records[9]	Recipients of child benefit (usually mothers)	GB	9,508 families[9]	82[9]
Family Resources Survey	Continuous	Postcode Address File	All members in household	UK	44,973 households	62
General Household Survey	Continuous	Postcode Address File	All adults in household	GB	12,802 households	72[10]
Health Survey for England	Continuous	Postcode Address File	All household members	E	6,367 households	71[10]
Infant Feeding Survey	Quinquennial	Birth registration records (August-October 2005)	Mother	UK	12,290	62
International Passenger Survey	Continuous	International passengers	Individual traveller	UK[11]	276,000 individuals	89
Labour Force Survey	Continuous	Postcode Address File	All adults in household	UK	52,000 households	71[12]
Longitudinal Study of Young People in England	Annual	School records	Young person and his/her parents/guardians	E	15,770 households	74[13]
Mental Health of Children and Young People, 2004	Ad hoc[14]	Child benefit records	Parents, children if aged 11–16, teachers	GB	7,977 families	76[14]
National Passenger Survey	Twice yearly	Passengers at 650 stations	Railway passengers	GB	50,000 individuals	37
National Travel Survey	Continuous	Postcode Address File	All household members	GB	13,582 households per year	62[15]

	Frequency	Sampling frame	Type of respondent	Coverage	Effective sample size[1] (most recent survey included in *Social Trends*)	Response rate (percentages)
Omnibus Survey	Continuous	Postcode Address File	Adults aged 16 or over living in private households	GB	Approximately 12,000[16]	66
Psychiatric Morbidity Survey	Ad hoc	Postcode Address File	Adults aged 16 to 74 years living in private households	GB	15,804 addresses	69
Retail Sales Inquiry	Continuous	Inter Departmental Business Register[17]	Retailers	GB	Approximately 5,000	64[17]
Smoking, Drinking and Drug Use Among Young People In England 2004	Annual	English schools[18]	Pupils in years 7 to 11	E	9,715 pupils	62[18]
Student Income and Expenditure Survey	Ad hoc	Institution records	Students	E&W	4,500 students	82
Survey of English Housing	Continuous	Postcode Address File	Household	E	27,342 households	67
Survey of Personal Incomes	Annual	HM Revenue & Customs PAYE, Claims and Self-assessment records	Individuals/taxpayers	UK	430,000 individuals	[19]
Taking Part Survey	Continuous	Postcode Address File	One adult aged 16 and over in private households and, where appropriate, one child aged between 11 and 15	E	18,190 adults aged 16 and over	[20]
Welsh Health Survey	Continuous	Postcode Address File	All household members (adults aged 16 and over, children under 16)	W	13,900 eligible households – 16,000 adult respondents and 4,100 child respondents	73
Work and Pensions Longitudinal Study	Quarterly	Benefit claimants	Benefit claimants/beneficiaries	GB	All benefit claimants	[19]

1 Effective sample size includes nonrespondents but excludes ineligible households.

2 The Annual Population Survey includes the English Local Labour Force Survey, Welsh Local Labour Force Survey, Scottish Labour Force Survey, Annual Population Survey 'Boost' and waves 1 and 5 of the Quarterly Labour Force Survey.

3 Wave on wave response rate at wave 12. Around 57 per cent of eligible wave 1 sample members were respondents in wave 12.

4 Response rate refers to 2005 survey.

5 In May 2006 the responsibility for the Citizenship Survey passed from the Home Office to Communities and Local Government. Response rate refers to the core sample of the 2005 survey.

6 UK businesses with employment of ten or more. Businesses with employment of less than ten were included in previous surveys and in the published results for 2002 and 2004.

7 Although the EHCS runs on a continuous basis, its reporting is based on a rolling two year sample. The EHCS response combines successful outcomes from two linked surveys where information is separately gathered about the household and the dwelling for each address.

8 There is an optional diary for children aged 7 to 15 in Great Britain. Basic sample for Great Britain only. Response rate refers to Great Britain.

9 For 2003 (wave 4) the panel sample was 7,901 cases and booster cases totalled 1,401. The overall response rate is given, which is the number of interviews as a proportion of the total initial sample.

10 Response rate for fully and partially responding households.

11 Includes UK and overseas residents.

12 Response rate to first wave interviews of the quarterly LFS over the period April to June 2006.

13 Response rate quoted refers to wave 1, which was conducted in 2004.

14 A similar survey was carried out in 1999. Response rate based on number of families approached for interview.

15 Sixty two per cent of eligible households were recorded as being 'fully productive'. However, a further 8 per cent co-operated partially with the survey, and the data from these households can be used on a limited basis.

16 Achieved sample size per Omnibus cycle. The Omnibus interviews at one household per sampled address and one adult per household. Data are weighted to account for the fact that respondents living in smaller households would have a greater chance of selection.

17 GB companies with 20 or more employment. Average response rate for 2005.

18 Excludes special schools. Based on overall response rate. The list of English schools comes from a database held by the National Foundation for Educational Research (NFER). In 2004, 70 per cent of schools and 89 per cent of selected pupils responded to the survey.

19 Response rate not applicable as data are drawn from administrative records.

20 A full year's data have not been collected so this cannot be provided.

Symbols and conventions

Geography	Where possible *Social Trends* uses data for the UK as a whole. When UK data are not available, or data from the constituent countries of the UK are not comparable, data for Great Britain or the constituent countries are used. Constituent countries can advise where data are available that are equivalent but not directly comparable with those of other constituent countries.
Reference years	Where, because of space constraints, a choice of years has to be made, the most recent year or a run of recent years is shown together with the past population census years (2001, 1991, 1981, etc) and sometimes the mid-points between census years (1996, 1986, etc). Other years may be added if they represent a peak or trough in the series.
Financial year	For example, 1 April 2004 to 31 March 2005 would be shown as 2004/05.
Academic year	For example, September 2004 to July 2005 would be shown as 2004/05.
Combined years	For example, 2002–05 shows data for more than one year that have been combined.
Units on tables	Where one unit predominates it is shown at the top of the table. All other units are shown against the relevant row or column. Figures are shown in italics when they represent percentages.
Rounding of figures	In tables where figures have been rounded to the nearest final digit, there may be an apparent discrepancy between the sum of the constituent items and the total as shown.
Provisional and estimated data	Some data for the latest year (and occasionally for earlier years) are provisional or estimated. To keep footnotes to a minimum, these have not been indicated; source departments will be able to advise if revised data are available.
Billion	This term is used to represent one thousand million.
Seasonal adjustment	Unless otherwise stated, unadjusted data have been used.
Dependent children	Those aged under 16, or single people aged 16 to 18 who have not married and are in full-time education unless otherwise indicated.
State pension age (SPA)	The age at which pensions are normally payable by the state pension scheme, currently age 65 for men and age 60 for women.
EU	Unless otherwise stated, data relate to the European Union of 25 countries (EU-25) as constituted since 1 May 2004. EU-15 refers to the 15 members of the EU before 1 May 2004.
Germany	Unless otherwise stated, data relate to Germany as constituted since 3 October 1990.
Ireland	Refers to the Republic of Ireland and does not include Northern Ireland.
Symbols	The following symbols have been used throughout *Social Trends:*

    .. not available

    . not applicable

    - negligible (less than half the final digit shown)

    * data have been suppressed to protect confidentiality

    0 nil

Appendix

Part 1: Population

Population estimates and projections

The estimated and projected populations are of the resident population of an area, that is, all those usually resident there, whatever their nationality. Members of HM Forces stationed outside the UK are excluded; members of foreign forces stationed in the UK are included. Students are taken to be resident at their term-time addresses. Figures for the UK do not include the population of the Channel Islands or the Isle of Man.

The population estimates for mid-2001 to mid-2005 are based on results from the 2001 Census, which have been updated to reflect subsequent births, deaths, net migration and other changes. The estimates used in this publication were released on 24 August 2006.

The most recent set of national population projections published for the UK are based on the populations of England, Wales, Scotland and Northern Ireland at mid-2004. These were released on 20 October 2005 and further details can be found on the Government Actuary's Department's website (**www.gad.gov.uk**).

Classification of ethnic groups

The recommended classification of ethnic groups for National Statistics data sources was changed in 2001 to bring it broadly in line with the 2001 Census.

There are two levels to this classification. Level 1 is a coarse classification into five main ethnic groups. Level 2 provides a finer classification of Level 1. The preference is for the Level 2 (detailed) categories to be adopted wherever possible. The two levels and the categories are in the box below.

Direct comparisons should not be made between the figures produced using this new classification and those based on the previous classification.

Further details can be found on the National Statistics website: **www.statistics.gov.uk/ about/classifications/downloads/ns_ ethnicity_statement.doc**

Internal migration estimates

Estimates for internal population movements in *Social Trends* are based on the movement of NHS doctors' patients between former Health Authority Areas (HAs) in England and Wales and Area Health Boards (AHBs) in Scotland and Northern Ireland. These transfers are recorded at the NHS Central Registers (NHSCRs) in Southport and Dumfries, and at the Central Services Agency in Belfast. The figures have been adjusted to take account of differences in recorded cross-border flows between England and Wales, Scotland and Northern Ireland.

The figures provide a detailed indicator of population movement within the UK. However, they should not be regarded as a perfect measure of migration as there is variation in the delay between a person moving and registering with a new doctor. Additionally, some moves may not result in a re-registration as individuals may migrate again before registering with a doctor. Conversely, others may move and re-register several times in a year.

It has been established that internal migration data under-report the migration of men aged between 16 and 36. Currently, however, there are no suitable sources of data available to enable adjustments or revisions to be made to the estimates. Further research is planned on this topic and new data sources may become available in the future.

International migration estimates

Using the UN recommendation, a long term international migrant is defined as someone who changes his or her country of usual residence for a period of at least a year, so that the country of destination becomes the country of usual residence. The richest source of information on international migrants comes from the International Passenger Survey (IPS), which is a sample survey of passengers arriving at, and departing from, the main UK air and sea ports and the Channel Tunnel. This survey provides migration estimates based on respondents' intended length of stay in the UK or abroad. The IPS does not cover all types of migration and therefore it is necessary to combine information from other sources to get a full picture of international migration to and from the UK.

The IPS is supplemented with the Irish Central Statistics Office (CSO) component that provides data on flows to and from the Republic of Ireland. Other data sources allow for the estimation of adjustments to the IPS and Irish flows. That is, broadly, an adjustment for asylum seekers and their dependants not counted by the IPS (using data from the Home Office) and an adjustment for switchers (people who change their intentions and their migratory status).

Refugees

The criteria for recognition as a refugee, and hence the granting of asylum, are set out in the 1951 United Nations Convention relating to the Status of Refugees, extended in its application by the 1967 Protocol relating to the Status of Refugees. The Convention defines a refugee as a person who 'owing to a well-founded fear of being persecuted for reasons of race, religion, nationality, membership of a particular social

---

Classification of ethnic groups

Level 1	Level 2
White	White
	British
	Irish
	Other White background
	All White groups
Mixed	White and Black Caribbean
	White and Black African
	White and Asian
	Other Mixed background
	All Mixed groups
Asian or Asian British	Indian
	Pakistani
	Bangladeshi
	Other Asian background
	All Asian groups
Black or Black British	Caribbean
	African
	Other Black background
	All Black groups
Chinese or Other ethnic group	Chinese
	Other ethnic group
	All Chinese or other groups
All ethnic groups	All ethnic groups
Not stated	Not stated

group or political opinion, is outside the country of his [or her] nationality and unable or, owing to such fear, is unwilling to avail himself [or herself] of the protection of that country; or who, not having a nationality and being outside the country of his [her] former habitual residence... is unable or, owing to such fear, is unwilling to return to it'.

Part 2: Households and families

Multi-sourced tables

Tables 2.1, 2.2, 2.4, 2.5 and 2.8 have multiple sources. In order to create long time series it is necessary to combine these sources even though they are not always directly comparable. Most of the multi-sourced tables include the General Household Survey (GHS), the Labour Force Survey (LFS) and the Census. For further information about the GHS see below and for the LFS see Appendix, Part 4: Labour Force Survey.

Households

Although definitions differ slightly across surveys and the Census, they are broadly similar.

A household is a person living alone or a group of people who have the address as their only or main residence and who either share one meal a day or share the living accommodation.

Students: those living in halls of residence are recorded under their parents' household and included in the parents' family type in the Labour Force Survey (LFS), although some surveys/projections include such students in the institutional population.

In the General Household Survey (GHS, see below), young people aged 16 or over who live away from home for purposes of either work or study and come home only for holidays are not included at the parental address.

Families

Children: are never-married people of any age who live with one or both parent(s). They include stepchildren and adopted children (but not foster children) and also grandchildren (where the parent(s) are absent).

Dependent children: in the 1971 and 1981 Census, dependent children were defined as never-married children in families who were either under 15 years of age, or aged 15 to 24 and in full-time education. In the 1991 Census, the Labour Force Survey (LFS) and the General Household Survey (GHS), dependent children are childless never-married children in families who are aged under 16, or aged 16 to 18 and in full-time education and living in the household and, in the 1991 Census, economically inactive (see Glossary in Chapter 4: Labour Market on page 43). In the 2001 Census a dependent child is a person aged under 16 in a household (whether or not in a family) or aged 16 to 18, in full-time education and living in a family with their parent(s).

A family: is a married or cohabiting couple, either with or without their never-married child or children (of any age), including couples with no children or a lone parent together with his or her never-married child or children provided they have no children of their own. A family could also consist of a grandparent(s) with their

grandchild or grandchildren if the parents of the grandchild or grandchildren are not usually resident in the household. In the LFS, a family unit can also comprise a single person. LFS family units include non-dependent children (who can in fact be adult) those aged 16 or over and not in full-time education provided they are never married and have no children of their own in the household.

One family and no others: A household comprises one family and no others if there is only one family in the household and there are no non-family people.

Multi-family household: A household containing two or more people who cannot be allocated to a single family as defined in 'a family' above. This includes households with two or more unrelated adults and can also include a grandparent(s) with their child or children and grandchild or grandchildren in one household.

A lone-parent family: in the Census is a father or mother together with his or her never-married child or children. A lone-parent family in the LFS consists of a lone parent, living with his or her never-married child or children, provided these children have no children of their own living with them. A lone-parent family in the GHS consists of a lone parent, living with his or her never-married dependent child or children, provided these children have no children of their own. Married lone mothers whose husbands are not defined as resident in the household are not classified as lone parents. Evidence suggests the majority are separated from their husband either because he usually works away from home or for some other reason that does not imply the breakdown of the marriage.

General Household Survey

The General Household Survey (GHS) is an interdepartmental multi-purpose continuous survey carried out by ONS collecting information on a range of topics from people living in private households in Great Britain. The survey has run continuously since 1971, except for breaks in 1997/78 (when the survey was reviewed) and 1999/2000 when the survey was redeveloped.

In 2005, the GHS adopted a new sample design in line with European requirements, changing from a cross-sectional to a longitudinal design. This will help monitor European social policy by comparing poverty indicators and changes over time across the European Community. The GHS was identified as the best vehicle for this work over other ONS social surveys because there were many overlaps in the topics covered. The GHS design has changed to a four-yearly rotation, with increased sample size, and additional core questions.

Between April 1994 and April 2005, the GHS was conducted on a financial year basis, with fieldwork spread evenly across the year April-March. However, in 2005 the survey period reverted to a calendar year and the whole of the annual sample (which has been increased to 16,560) was dealt with in the nine months April to December 2005. Future surveys will run from January to December each year.

Since the 2005 survey does not cover the January-March quarter, this affects annual estimates for topics that are subject to seasonal

variation. To rectify this, where the questions were the same in 2005 as in 2004/05, the final quarter of the 2004/05 survey has been added (weighted in the correct proportion) to the nine months of the 2005 survey. A higher sampling fraction was applied to the nine months of the 2005 survey compared with the final quarter of the 2004/05 survey.

Further details of the methodological changes made during 2005 can be found in the appendices to the GHS at **www.statistics.gov.uk/ghs**

The GHS collects information on a range of topics from people living in private households in Great Britain. These are:

- smoking
- drinking
- households, families and people
- housing and consumer durables
- marriage and cohabitation
- occupational and personal pension schemes

The GHS provides authoritative estimates in the topics of smoking and drinking. A detailed summary and a longer report on these topics can be found at: **www.statistics.gov.uk/ghs**

True birth order

At registration, the question on previous live births is not asked where the birth occurred outside marriage. At the registration of births occurring within marriage, previous live births occurring outside marriage and where the woman had never been married to the father are not counted. The information collected on birth order, therefore, has been supplemented to give estimates of overall true birth order, which includes births both within and outside marriage. These estimates are obtained from details provided by the General Household Survey (see above).

Conceptions

Conception statistics used in Table 2.20 include pregnancies that result in either a maternity at which one or more live births or stillbirths occur, or a legal abortion under the *Abortion Act 1967.* Conception statistics do not include miscarriages or illegal abortions. Dates of conception are estimated using recorded gestation for abortions and stillbirths, and assuming 38 weeks gestation for live births.

Part 3: Education and training

Stages of education

Education takes place in several stages: early years, primary, secondary, further and higher education, and is compulsory for all children between the ages of 5 (4 in Northern Ireland) and 16. The non-compulsory fourth stage, further education, covers non-advanced education, which can be taken at further (including tertiary) education colleges, higher education institutions and increasingly in secondary schools. The fifth stage, higher education, is study beyond GCE A levels and their equivalent, which, for most full-time students, takes place in universities and other higher education institutions.

Organisation of compulsory school years

	Pupil ages	Year group
England and Wales		
Key Stage 1	5–7	1–2
Key Stage 2	7–11	3–6
Key Stage 3	11–14	7–9
Key Stage 4	14–16	10–11
Northern Ireland		
Key Stage 1	4/5–8	1–4
Key Stage 2	8–11	5–7
Key Stage 3	11–14	8–10
Key Stage 4	14–16	11–12
Scotland		
(Curriculum	5–7	P1–P3
following	7–8	P3–P4
national	8–10	P4–P6
guidelines from	10–11	P6–P7
ages 5 to 14)	11–13	P7–S2
NQ[1]	14–15	S3–S4

1 Standard Grades are part of the National Qualifications (NQ) framework in Scotland. They are broadly equivalent to GCSEs.

Early years education

In recent years there has been a major expansion of early years education. Many children under five attend state nursery schools or nursery classes within primary schools. Others may attend playgroups in the voluntary sector or in privately run nurseries. In England and Wales many primary schools also operate an early admissions policy where they admit children under five into what are called 'reception classes'. The *Education Act 2002* extended the National Curriculum for England to include the foundation stage. The foundation stage was introduced in September 2000 and covers children's education from the age of three to the end of the reception year, when most are just five and some almost six years old. The 'Curriculum guidance for the foundation stage' supports practitioners in their delivery of the foundation stage.

Figure 3.1 covers children in early years education in maintained nursery and primary schools. Other provision also takes place in independent and special schools and in non-school education settings in the private and voluntary sector, such as nurseries (which usually provide care, education and play for children up to the age of five), playgroups and pre-schools (which provide childcare, play and early years education, usually for children aged between two and five), children's centres (for children under five) and through accredited childminders.

Primary education

The primary stage covers three age ranges: nursery (under 5), infant (5 to 7 or 8) and junior (8 or 9 to 11 or 12) but in Scotland and Northern Ireland there is generally no distinction between infant and junior schools. Most public sector primary schools take both boys and girls in mixed classes. It is usual to transfer straight to secondary school at age 11 (in England, Wales and Northern Ireland) or 12 (in Scotland), but in England some children make the transition through middle schools catering for various age ranges between 8 and 14. Depending on their individual age ranges middle schools are classified as either primary or secondary.

Secondary education

Public provision of secondary education in an area may consist of a combination of different types of school, the pattern reflecting historical circumstances and the policy adopted by the local authority. Comprehensive schools largely admit pupils without reference to ability or aptitude and cater for all the children in a neighbourhood, but in some areas they co-exist with grammar, secondary modern or technical schools. In Northern Ireland, post primary education is provided by grammar schools and non-selective secondary schools. In England, the Specialist Schools Programme helps schools, in partnership with private sector sponsors and supported by additional government funding, to establish distinctive identities through their chosen specialisms. Specialist schools have a focus on their chosen subject area but must meet the National Curriculum requirements and deliver a broad and balanced education to all pupils. Any maintained secondary school in England can apply to be designated as a specialist school in one of ten specialist areas: arts, business and enterprise, engineering, humanities, languages, mathematics and computing, music, science, sports, and technology. Schools can also combine any two specialisms.

Special schools

Special schools (day or boarding) provide education for children who require specialist support to complete their education, for example because they have physical or other difficulties. Many pupils with special educational needs are educated in mainstream schools. All children attending special schools are offered a curriculum designed to overcome their learning difficulties and to enable them to become self-reliant. Since December 2005, special schools have also been able to apply for the Special Educational Needs (SEN) specialism, under the Specialist Schools Programme (see secondary education above).

Pupil referral units

Pupil referral units (PRUs) are legally a type of school established and maintained by a local authority to provide education for children of compulsory school age who may otherwise not receive suitable education. The aim of such units is to provide suitable alternative education on a temporary basis for pupils who may not be able to attend a mainstream school. The focus of the units should be to get pupils back into a mainstream school. Pupils in the units may include: teenage mothers, pupils excluded from school, school phobics and pupils in the assessment phase of a statement of special educational needs (SEN).

Further education

The term further education may be used in a general sense to cover all non-advanced courses taken after the period of compulsory education, but more commonly it excludes those staying on at secondary school and those in higher education, that is doing courses in universities and colleges leading to qualifications above GCE A level, Higher Grade (in Scotland), General National Vocational Qualifications/National Vocational Qualifications (GNVQ/NVQ) level 3, and their equivalents. Since 1 April 1993 sixth form colleges in England and Wales have been included in the further education sector.

Higher education

Higher education (HE) is defined as courses that are of a standard that is higher than GCE A level, the Higher Grade of the Scottish Certificate of Education/National Qualification, GNVQ/NVQ level 3 or the Edexcel (formerly BTEC) or SQA National Certificate/Diploma. There are three main levels of HE courses:

- postgraduate courses leading to higher degrees, diplomas and certificates (including postgraduate certificates of education and professional qualifications) that usually require a first degree as entry qualification

- undergraduate courses, which include first degrees, first degrees with qualified teacher status, enhanced first degrees, first degrees obtained concurrently with a diploma, and intercalated first degrees (where first degree students, usually in medicine, dentistry or veterinary medicine, interrupt their studies to complete a one-year course of advanced studies in a related topic)

- other undergraduate courses, which include all other HE courses, for example Higher National Diplomas and Diplomas in HE.

As a result of the 1992 *Further and Higher Education Act*, former polytechnics and some other HE institutions were designated as universities in 1992/93. Students normally attend HE courses at HE institutions, but some attend at further education colleges. Some also attend institutions that do not receive public grants (such as the University of Buckingham) and these numbers are excluded from the tables.

Up to 2000/01, figures for HE students in Table 3.8 are annual snapshots taken around November or December each year, depending on the type of institution, except for Scotland further education colleges from 1998/99, for which counts are based on the whole year. From 2001/02, figures for HE institutions are based on the Higher Education Statistics Agency (HESA) 'standard registration' count, and are not directly comparable with previous years. The Open University is included in these estimates.

Main categories of educational establishments

Educational establishments in the UK are administered and financed in several ways. Most schools are controlled by local authorities (LAs), which are part of the structure of local government, but some are 'assisted', receiving grants direct from central government sources and being controlled by governing bodies that have a substantial degree of autonomy. Completely outside the public sector are non-maintained schools run by individuals, companies or charitable institutions.

Up to March 2001, further education (FE) courses in FE sector colleges in England and Wales were largely funded through grants from the respective Further Education Funding Councils (FEFCs). In April 2001, however, the Learning and Skills Council (LSC) took over the responsibility for funding the FE sector in England, and the National Council for Education and Training for Wales (part of Education and Learning Wales – ELWa) did so for Wales. The LSC in England is also responsible for funding provision for FE and some non-prescribed higher education in FE sector colleges; it also funds some FE provided by LA maintained and other institutions referred to as 'external institutions'. In Wales, the National Council – ELWa, funds FE provision made by FE institutions through a third party or sponsored arrangements. The Scottish FEFC (SFEFC) funds FE colleges in Scotland, while the Department for Employment and Learning funds FE colleges in Northern Ireland.

Higher education (HE) courses in HE establishments are largely publicly funded through block grants from the HE funding councils in England and Scotland, the Higher Education Council – ELWa in Wales, and the Department for Employment and Learning in Northern Ireland. In addition, some designated HE, mainly Higher National Diplomas (HND)/Higher National Certificates (HNC)) is also funded by these sources. The FE sources mentioned above fund the remainder.

Numbers of school pupils are shown in Table 3.3. Nursery school figures for Scotland before 1998/99 only include data for local authority pre-schools. Data from 1998/99 include partnership pre-schools. However, from 2005/06, figures refer to centres providing pre-school education as an LA centre or in partnership with the LA only. Secondary 'Other' schools largely consist of middle schools in England, and secondary intermediate schools in Northern Ireland. 'Special schools' include maintained and non-maintained sectors, while 'public sector schools' and 'non-maintained schools' totals exclude special schools. The 'All schools' total includes pupil referral units (see under 'Stages of education'), which accounted for around 16,000 pupils in 2005/06.

Special Educational Needs data

Information presented in Figure 3.5 is mainly drawn from two sources: the Schools' Census (SC) and the SEN2 Survey. Figures sourced from SC and the SEN2 Survey are not directly comparable.

The SC has collected information on pupils with special educational needs (SEN) on the census date in January from schools since 1985. It is completed by schools and records those pupils with and without statements who are educated at the school, regardless of which local authority (LA) is responsible. Figures for pupils with SEN without statements were collected from maintained primary and secondary schools for the first time in 1995.

The SEN2 Survey has collected information on children with statements on the census date in January and new statements made in the previous calendar year from LAs since 1984. SEN2 is completed by LAs and records those children for whom the LA is responsible (regardless of whether they are educated in the LA's own maintained schools, in schools in other LAs, in the non-maintained or independent sectors or educated other than at school).

In January 2002 the SC introduced a major change in that primary, secondary and special schools reported data at an individual pupil level for the first time. While the overall collection of pupil level data for these schools was successful, it is possible that some discontinuity in the time series data has resulted from this underlying change in data collection. For instance, the national trend in SEN pupils with statements between 2001 and 2002 in SC is different from that shown in the SEN2 survey. While there are valid reasons as to why the figures will be different between these surveys, it is unusual for the trends to differ to this degree.

Joint Academic Coding System

The Joint Academic Coding System (JACS) was introduced into the Higher Education Statistics Agency (HESA) data collection in 2002/03 and forms the basis of the data presented in Table 3.9. This subject-based classification measures subjects studied at UK higher education institutions and looks similar to that previously used by HESA (HESACODE), although it has been devised in a different way (therefore subject data between the two classifications are not comparable). The JACS system defines 159 principal subjects (as at 2004/05) studied at UK higher education institutions and aggregates them into 19 headline subject areas, as shown in Table 3.9. The subject areas do not overlap and cover the entire range of principal subjects. For more information on JACS, see the HESA website: **www.hesa.ac.uk**

Qualifications

England, Wales and Northern Ireland
In England, Wales and Northern Ireland the main examination for school pupils at the minimum school leaving age is the General Certificate of Secondary Education (GCSE), which can be taken in a wide range of subjects. This replaced the GCE O Level and Certificate of Secondary Education (CSE) examinations in 1987 (1988 in Northern Ireland). In England, Wales and Northern Ireland the GCSE is awarded in eight grades, A* to G, the highest four (A* to C) being regarded as equivalent to O level grades A to C or CSE grade 1.

GCE A level is usually taken after a further two years of study in a sixth form or equivalent, passes being graded from A (the highest) to E (the lowest).

For achievement at GCE A level shown in Figure 3.14, data are for pupils in schools and students in further education institutions aged 17 at the start of the academic year as a percentage of the 17-year-old population. Data before 1995/96, and for Wales and Northern Ireland from 2002/03, are for school pupils only.

In September 2000, following the Qualifying for Success consultation in 1997, a number of reforms were introduced to the qualifications structure for young people aged 16 to 19. Under these reforms, students were encouraged to follow a wide range of subjects in their first year of post-16 study, with students expected to study four Advanced Subsidiaries (AS) before progressing three of them on to full A levels in their second year. New specifications introduced in 2001 are in place and A levels now comprise units, normally six for a full A level and three for the AS level, which is half a full A level. The full A level is normally taken either over two years (modular)

or as a set of exams at the end of the two years (linear). In addition, students are encouraged to study a combination of both general and vocational advanced level examinations.

The AS qualification equates to the first year of study of a traditional A level, while the programmes of study in the second year of the full A level are called 'A2' and represent the harder elements of the traditional A level. The AS is a qualification in its own right, whereas A2 modules do not make up a qualification in their own right, but when taken together with the AS units they comprise a full A level.

Scotland
In Scotland, National Qualifications (NQs) are offered to students. These include Standard Grades, National Courses and National Units. The Standard Grade is awarded in seven grades, through three levels of study: Credit (1 or 2), General (3 or 4) and Foundation (5 or 6). Students who do not achieve grade 1 to 6, but do complete the course, are awarded a grade 7. Standard Grade courses are made up of different parts called 'elements', with an exam at the end. National Courses are available at Intermediate, Higher and Advanced Higher, and consist of National Units that are assessed by the school/college, plus an external assessment. Grades are awarded on the basis of how well a student does in the external assessment, having passed all of the National Units. Pass grades are awarded at A, B and C. Grade D is awarded to a student who just fails to get a grade C. Intermediate courses can be taken as an alternative to Standard Grade or as a stepping stone to Higher. Access units are assessed by the school/college, with no exam involved. Groups of units in a particular subject area can be built up at Access 2 and 3 to lead to 'Cluster Awards'. In Scotland pupils generally sit Highers one year earlier than the rest of the UK sit A levels.

Vocational qualifications
After leaving school, people can study towards higher academic qualifications such as degrees. However, a large number of people choose to study towards qualifications aimed at a particular occupation or group of occupations – these qualifications are called vocational qualifications.

Vocational qualifications can be split into three groups: National Vocational Qualifications (NVQs), General National Vocational Qualifications (GNVQs) and vocationally related qualifications.

- NVQs are based on an explicit statement of competence derived from an analysis of employment requirements. They are awarded at five levels. Scottish Vocational Qualifications (SVQs) are the Scottish equivalent.

- GNVQs are a vocational alternative to GCSEs and GCE A levels. General Scottish Vocational Qualifications (GSVQs) are the Scottish equivalent. They are awarded at three levels: Foundation, Intermediate and Advanced. Advanced GNVQs were redesigned and relaunched as Vocational A levels or, more formally, Advanced Vocational Certificates of Education (VCEs) and, as well as being available at AS level and full A level, there are also double awards (counting as 12 units).

- There are a large number of other vocational qualifications, which are not NVQs, SVQs,

GNVQs or GSVQs, for example: a Business and Technology Education Council (BTEC) Higher National Diploma (HND) or a City & Guilds craft award.

Other qualifications (including academic qualifications) are often expressed as being equivalent to a particular NVQ level so that comparisons can be easily made:

- An NVQ level 1 is equivalent to one or more GCSEs at grade G (but is lower than five GCSE grades A* to C), a BTEC general certificate, a Youth Training certificate, other Royal Society of Arts (RSA), or City & Guilds craft qualifications.

- An NVQ level 2 is equivalent to five GCSEs at grades A* to C, an Intermediate GNVQ, an RSA diploma, a City & Guilds craft or a BTEC first or general diploma.

- An NVQ level 3 is equivalent to two A levels, an advanced GNVQ, International Baccalaureate, an RSA advanced diploma, a City & Guilds advanced craft qualification, an Ordinary National Diploma (OND) or Ordinary National Certificate (ONC) or a BTEC National Diploma.

- An NVQ level 4 is equivalent to a first degree, a HND or HNC, a BTEC Higher Diploma, an RSA Higher Diploma, a nursing qualification or other Higher Education qualification.

- An NVQ level 5 is equivalent to a higher degree.

The National Curriculum

Under the *Education Reform Act 1988* a National Curriculum has been progressively introduced into primary and secondary schools in England and Wales. This consists of English (or the option of Welsh as a first language in Wales), mathematics and science. The second level of curriculum additionally comprises the so-called 'foundation' subjects, such as history, geography, art, music, information technology, design and technology, and physical education (and Welsh as a second language in Wales). The *Education Act 2002* extended the National Curriculum for England to include the foundation stage. It has six areas of learning:

- personal
- social and emotional development
- communication, language and literacy
- mathematical development
- knowledge and understanding of the world
- physical development and
- creative development.

Measurable targets have been defined for four key stages, corresponding to ages 7, 11, 14 and 16. Pupils are assessed formally at the ages of 7, 11 and 14 by a mixture of teacher assessments and by national tests (statutory testing at Key Stages 1 to 3 has been abolished in Wales with the last tests taking place in 2005 at Key Stage 3) in the core subjects of English, mathematics and science (and in Welsh speaking schools in Wales, Welsh as a first language), though the method varies between subjects and countries. Sixteen-year-olds are assessed by the GCSE examination. Statutory authorities have been set up for England and for Wales to advise the

Government on the National Curriculum and promote curriculum development generally.

Northern Ireland has its own common curriculum that is similar but not identical to the National Curriculum in England and Wales. Assessment arrangements in Northern Ireland became statutory from September 1996 and Key Stage 1 pupils are assessed at age eight.

Expected attainment levels in England

England	Attainment expected
Key Stage 1	Level 2 or above
Key Stage 2	Level 4 or above
Key Stage 3	Level 5/6 or above
Key Stage 4	GCSE

In Scotland there is no statutory national curriculum and responsibility for the management and delivery of the curriculum belongs to education authorities and head teachers. Pupils aged 5 to 14 study a broad curriculum based on national guidelines, which set out the aims of study, the ground to be covered and the way the pupils' learning should be assessed and reported. Progress is measured by attainment of six levels based on the expectation of the performance of the majority of pupils on completion of certain stages between the ages of 5 and 14: Primary 3 (age 7/8), Primary 4 (age 8 /9), Primary 7 (age 11/12) and Secondary 2 (age 13/14). It is recognised that pupils learn at different rates and some will reach the various levels before others.

The 5 to 14 curriculum areas in Scotland are:

- language
- mathematics
- environmental studies
- expressive arts
- religious and moral education with personal and social development and
- health education

In Secondary 3 and 4, it is recommended that the core curriculum of all pupils should include study within the following eight modes:

- language and communication
- mathematical studies and applications
- scientific studies and applications
- social and environmental studies
- technological activities and applications
- creative and aesthetic activities
- physical education and
- religious and moral education

For Secondary 5 and 6 these eight modes are important in structuring the curriculum, although it is not expected that each pupil will study under each mode but that the curriculum will be negotiated. At present the Scottish curriculum 3 to 18 is being reviewed under *A Curriculum for Excellence*.

Adult education

The establishment of the LSC (Learning and Skills Council) in March 2001 led to changes in the arrangements for planning and funding learning opportunities for adults in England as well as in data collection. Since 2003/04, adult and community learning data have been collected by the LSC and incorporated into the Individualised Learner Record (ILR). The ILR already covers learners in further education and on work based learning for young people. Data in Figure 3.20 are taken from the ILR.

Part 4: Labour market

Labour Force Survey

The Labour Force Survey (LFS) is the largest regular household survey in the UK and much of the labour market data published are measured by the LFS. The concepts and definitions used in the LFS are agreed by the International Labour Organisation (ILO), an agency of the United Nations. The definitions are used by EU member states and members of the Organisation for Economic Co-operation and Development.

On 20 October 2005 the Government Actuary's Department (GAD) published revised projections for 2005 and later years, based on the Office for National Statistics (ONS) population estimates published on 25 August 2005. These revised population estimates have been incorporated into LFS estimates used in the following tables and figures 4.1, 4.4, 4.10, 4.15, 4.17 and 4.18. The following tables and figures are based on population estimates published in spring 2003: 4.2, 4.3, 4.6, 4.7, 4.12, 4.13, 4.14, 4.19 and 4.20.

An EU requirement exists whereby all member states must have a Labour Force Survey (LFS) based on calendar quarters. The UK LFS complied with this from May 2006. The survey previously used seasonal quarters where, for example, the March-May months covered the spring quarter, June-August was summer and so forth. This has now changed to calendar quarters where micro data are available for January-March (Q1), April-June (Q2), July-September (Q3) and October-December (Q4). However some figures and tables using quarterly LFS data in the labour market chapter still use seasonal data (4.3, 4.13, 4.14, and 4.20).

ONS has produced a set of historical estimates covering the monthly period 1971–91, which are fully consistent with post-1992 LFS data. The data cover headline measures of employment, unemployment, economic activity, economic inactivity and hours worked. These estimates were published on an experimental basis in 2003, but following further user consultation and quality assurance, these estimates have now been made National Statistics. As such, they represent ONS's best estimate of the headline labour market series over this period. The labour market chapter uses data from these estimates only where headline data are reported (Figures 4.1, 4.4, 4.15 and 4.17) since the historical estimates are not yet available for subgroups of the population, other than by sex and for key age groups. Therefore, tables and figures showing further breakdowns of headline data are not fully consistent with the historical estimates.

205

Annual Population Survey

The Annual Population Survey (APS) was introduced in 2004. The APS included all the data of the annual local area Labour Force Survey (LFS), but also included a further sample boost aimed at achieving a minimum number of economically active respondents in the sample in each local authority district in England. The first APS covered the calendar year 2004, rather than the annual local area LFS period of March to February. Also, the annual local area LFS data were published only once a year, whereas the APS data are published quarterly, but with each publication including a year's data.

Like the local area LFS data set, the APS data is published by local authority area. However, it contains an enhanced range of variables providing a greater level of detail about the resident household population of an area. In particular, more variables are provided on ethnic group, health and sex. For more information, see: 'Local area labour markets statistical indicators incorporating the Annual Population Survey', pp 307–319, *Labour Market Trends*, September 2006. www.statistics.gov.uk/cci/article.asp?ID=1635

Standard Occupational Classification 2000 (SOC2000)

The Standard Occupational Classification (SOC2000) was first published in 1990 (SOC90) to replace both the Classification of Occupations 1980, and the Classification of Occupations and Dictionary of Occupational Titles. SOC90 was revised and updated in 2000 to produce SOC2000. There is no exact correspondence between SOC90 and SOC2000 at any level.

The two main concepts which SOC2000 is used to investigate are:

- kind of work performed and
- the competent performance of the tasks and duties.

The structure of SOC2000 is four-tier covering:

- major groups/numbers
- sub-major groups/numbers
- minor groups/numbers and
- unit groups/numbers (occupations)

For example, the group/number breakdown for the occupation of a chemist is as follows:

major group	2	Professional occupations
sub-major group	21	Science and technology professionals
minor group	211	Science professionals
unit group	2111	Chemists

SOC2000 comprises 9 major groups, 25 sub-major groups, 81 minor groups and 353 unit groups (occupations). The major groups are:

- managers and senior officials
- professional occupations
- associate professional and technical occupations
- administrative and secretarial occupations
- skilled trades occupations
- personal service occupations
- sales and customer service occupations
- process, plant and machine operatives
- elementary occupations

For more information on SOC2000 see: **www.statistics.gov.uk/methods_quality/ns_sec/soc2000.asp**

Public sector employment

Public sector employment comprises employment in central government, local government and public corporations as defined for the UK National Accounts. Data are collected from public sector organisations through the ONS Quarterly Public Sector Employees Survey and other sources. Employment estimates for the private sector are derived as the difference between Labour Force Survey employment estimates for the whole economy (not seasonally adjusted) and the public sector employment estimates.

The public sector employment estimates given in Figure 4.11 include a number of workers with a second job in the public sector whose main job is in the private sector or in a separate public sector organisation. The private sector estimate will thus tend to be correspondingly understated by a small percentage. The revised population estimates published on 25 August 2005 (as mentioned in Labour Force Survey section) have been incorporated into LFS estimates used in Figure 4.11.

Model-based estimates of unemployment

On 28 July 2006 ONS launched model-based estimates of unemployment for unitary and local authorities as National Statistics. These estimates are the best available for total unemployment in these areas. For local areas, even the annual local area Labour Force Survey (LFS) or Annual Population Survey (APS) have small samples. This means that estimates for these areas are likely to be less reliable than those for larger areas, since the sampling variability is high. In particular, this affects estimates of events that are uncommon, like unemployment. A statistical model was developed to provide reliable unemployment estimates for all local authorities. Unemployment rates by local area data in Figure 4.16 use these model-based estimates.

For more information, see: 'Local area labour markets statistical indicators incorporating the Annual Population Survey', *Labour Market Trends*, pp 307–19, September 2006. **www.statistics.gov.uk/cci/article.asp?ID=1635** and **www.statistics.gov.uk/StatBase/Product.asp?vlnk=13574**

Labour disputes

Statistics of stoppages of work caused by labour disputes in the UK relate to disputes connected with terms and conditions of employment. Small stoppages involving fewer than ten workers or lasting less than one day are excluded from the statistics unless the aggregate number of working days lost in the dispute is 100 or more. Disputes not resulting in a stoppage of work are not included in the statistics.

Workers involved and working days lost relate to persons both directly and indirectly involved (unable to work although not parties to the dispute) at the establishments where the disputes occurred. People laid off and working days lost at establishments not in dispute, due for example to resulting shortages of supplies, are excluded.

There are difficulties in ensuring complete recording of stoppages, in particular near the margins of the definition; for example short disputes lasting only a day or so, or involving only a few workers. Any under-recording would affect the total number of stoppages much more than the number of working days lost.

For more information, see 'Labour disputes in 2005', pp 174–190, *Labour Market Trends*, June 2006. **www.statistics.gov.uk/cci/article.asp?ID=1586**

Labour market statistics

For more information on labour market statistics, sources and analysis, including information about all aspects of ONS's labour market outputs, see the *Labour Market Review 2006* **www.statistics.gov.uk/labourmarketreview/** and the online *Guide to Labour Market Statistics* **www.statistics.gov.uk/about/data/guides/LabourMarket/**

Part 5: Income and wealth

Household income data sources

The data for the household sector as derived from the National Accounts have been compiled according to the definitions and conventions set out in the European System of Accounts 1995 (ESA95). Estimates for the household sector cannot be separated from the sector for non-profit institutions serving households and so the data in *Social Trends* cover both sectors. The most obvious example of a non-profit institution is a charity. This sector also includes many other organisations of which universities, trade unions, and clubs and societies are the most important. Non-profit making bodies receive income mainly in the form of property income (that is, investment income) and of other current receipts. The household sector differs from the personal sector, as defined in the National Accounts prior to the introduction of ESA95, in that it excludes unincorporated private businesses apart from sole traders. The household sector also includes people living in institutions such as nursing homes, as well as people living in private households. More information is given in *United Kingdom National Accounts Concepts, Sources and Methods* published by The Stationery Office and is available on the Office for National Statistics (ONS) website: **www.statistics.gov.uk/downloads/theme_economy/Concepts_Sources_&_Methods.pdf**

In ESA95, household income includes the value of national insurance contributions and pension contributions made by employers on behalf of their employees. It also shows property income (that is, income from investments) net of payments of interest on loans. In both these respects, national accounts' conventions diverge from those normally used when collecting data on household income from household surveys. Employees are usually unaware of the value of the national insurance contributions and pension contributions made on their behalf by their employer, and so such data are rarely collected. Payments of interest are usually regarded as items of expenditure rather than reductions of income. In Table 5.2, household income excludes employers' national insurance and pension contributions and includes property income gross of payment of interest on loans, to correspond more closely with the definition generally used in household surveys.

Survey sources differ from the National Accounts in a number of other important respects. They cover the population living in households and some cover certain parts of the population living in institutions such as nursing homes, but all exclude non-profit making institutions. Survey sources are also subject to under-reporting and non-response bias. In the case of household income surveys, investment income is commonly underestimated, as is income from self-employment. All these factors mean that the survey data on income used in most of this chapter are not entirely consistent with the National Accounts household sector data.

Individual income

Total individual income refers to the weekly gross personal income of women and men plus tax credits as reported in the Family Resources Survey. Income is from all sources received by an individual, including earnings, income from self-employment, investments and occupational pensions/annuities, benefit income, and tax credits. Income that accrues at household level, such as council tax benefit, is excluded. Income from couples' joint investment accounts is assumed to be received equally. Benefit income paid in respect of dependants, such as Child Benefit, is included in the individual income of the person nominated for the receipt of payments. Full details of the concepts and definitions used may be found in *Individual Income 1996/97 to 2004/05* available on the Women and Equality Unit website: www.womenandequalityunit.gov.uk/indiv_incomes

In 2002/03, the Family Resources Survey was extended to cover Northern Ireland. Now that three years of data are available, data presented from 2002/03 cover the UK rather than Great Britain. Estimates for the UK are very similar to those for Great Britain.

Pensioners' income

Information on the income of pensioners based on the Family Resources Survey is provided in the Department for Work and Pensions (DWP) publication *Pensioners' Income Series* the latest year of which is 2004/05 available both in hard copy and on the DWP website: www.dwp.gov.uk/asd/asd6/pensioners_income.asp. It contains estimates and interpretation of trends in the levels and sources of pensioners' incomes in Great Britain over time.

A pensioner benefit unit, or family, is one where the head is over state pension age. The head of the benefit unit is either the household reference person where he or she belongs to the benefit unit, otherwise it is the first person listed at interview in the benefit unit – for couples it is usually the man.

In 2002/03, the Family Resources Survey was extended to cover Northern Ireland. Now that three years of data are available, data presented for pensioners income from 2002/03 cover the UK rather than Great Britain. Estimates for the UK are very similar to those for Great Britain.

Earnings surveys

The Annual Survey of Hours and Earnings (ASHE) replaced the New Earnings Survey (NES) from October 2004. ASHE improves on NES by extending the coverage of the survey sample, introducing weighting and publishing estimates of quality for all survey outputs. The new survey methodology produces weighted estimates, using weights calculated by calibrating the survey responses to totals from the Labour Force Survey by occupation, sex, region and age. The survey sample has been increased to include employees changing jobs between the survey sample identification and the survey reference date. The new survey design also produces outputs that focus on median rather than mean levels of pay. Full details of the methodology of ASHE can be found on the ONS website at: www.statistics.gov.uk/articles/nojournal/ASHEMethod_article.pdf

Back series using ASHE methodology applied to NES data sets are available for 1997 to 2004 at: www.statistics.gov.uk/statbase/Product.asp?vlnk=13101. However, it is not possible to adjust NES data sets to allow for the supplementary information collected by ASHE. Thus 2004 data are available on two bases, with and without this information, whereas estimates from 2005 onwards only include the supplementary information.

Equivalisation scales

The Department for Work and Pensions (DWP), the Office for National Statistics (ONS), the Institute for Fiscal Studies (IFS) and the Institute for Social and Economic Research (ISER) all use McClements equivalence scales in their analysis of the income distribution, to take into account variations in the size and composition of households. This reflects the common sense notion that a household of five adults will need a higher income than will a single person living alone to enjoy a comparable standard of living. An overall equivalence value is calculated for each household by summing the appropriate scale values for each household member. Equivalised household income is then calculated by dividing household income by the household's equivalence value. The scales conventionally take a couple as the reference point with an equivalence value of one; equivalisation therefore tends to increase relatively the incomes of single person households (since their incomes are divided by a value of less than one) and to reduce incomes of households with three or more persons. For further information see *Households Below Average Income 1994/95–2004/05* available on the DWP website: www.dwp.gov.uk/asd/hbai.asp. There are two McClements equivalence scales, one for adjusting incomes before housing costs and one for adjusting income after housing costs, see table below.

The DWP and IFS both use different scales for adjustment of income before and after the deduction of housing costs.

Households Below Average Income (HBAI)

Information on the distribution of income based on the Family Resources Survey (FRS) is provided in the Department for Work and Pensions (DWP) publication *Households Below Average Income: 1994/95–2004/05*, available both in hard copy and on the DWP website: www.dwp.gov.uk/asd/hbai.asp. This publication provides estimates of patterns of personal disposable income in Great Britain, and of changes in income over time. It attempts to measure people's potential living standards as determined by disposable income. Although as the title would suggest, HBAI concentrates on the lower part of the income distribution, it also provides estimates covering the whole of the income distribution. See also Individual income for more information on the FRS.

Disposable household income includes all flows of income into the household, principally earnings, benefits, occupational and private pensions, and

McClements equivalence scales:

Household member	Before housing costs	After housing costs
First adult (head)	0.61	0.55
Spouse of head	0.39	0.45
Other second adult	0.46	0.45
Third adult	0.42	0.45
Subsequent adults	0.36	0.40
Each dependant aged:		
0–1	0.09	0.07
2–4	0.18	0.18
5–7	0.21	0.21
8–10	0.23	0.23
11–12	0.25	0.26
13–15	0.27	0.28
16 or over	0.36	0.38

investments. It is net of tax, employees' national insurance contributions, council tax, contributions to occupational pension schemes (including additional voluntary contributions), maintenance and child support payments, and parental contributions to students living away from home.

Two different measures of disposable income are used in HBAI: before and after housing costs are deducted. This is principally to take into account variations in housing costs that do not correspond to comparable variations in the quality of housing. Housing costs consist of rent, water rates, community charges, mortgage interest payments, structural insurance, ground rent and service charges.

Gini coefficient

The Gini coefficient is the most widely used summary measure of the degree of inequality in an income distribution. The first step is to rank the distribution in ascending order. The coefficient can then best be understood by considering a graph of the cumulative income share against the cumulative share of households – the Lorenz curve. This would take the form of a diagonal line for complete equality where all households had the same income, while complete inequality where one household received all the income and the remainder received none would be represented by a curve comprising the horizontal axis and the right-hand vertical axis. The area between the Lorenz curve and the diagonal line of complete equality and inequality gives the value of the Gini coefficient. As inequality increases (and the Lorenz curve bellies out) so does the Gini coefficient until it reaches its maximum value of 1 with complete inequality.

Material hardship

The Department for Work and Pensions (DWP) Families and Children Study (FACS) examines the living standards of families with children according to their material deprivation – measured as the ability to purchase essential goods and to participate in leisure activities. Families were asked whether they possessed or took part in each of 34 items or activities, and if not, whether this was because they could not afford to or because they did not want or need the item. To account for the importance of different items and activities, each of the 34 items is weighted according to the proportion of families that own it. A higher weight is given to an item that is widely owned, so that to go without this item implies more serious deprivation. The Relative Material Deprivation Score (RMDS) is then constructed to summarise deprivation. The score on the RMDS is the outcome of the number of items or activities a family 'does not have, would like, but cannot afford' and the specific prevalence weight assigned to each item according to its possession in the population of families with children. A higher score equals greater deprivation. This is a similar concept to the measure used to monitor the government's child poverty measure, but uses a different data source and different items as indicators of deprivation.

For more details see Berthoud R, Bryan M and Bardasi E (2003–04) *The dynamics of deprivation: the relationship between income and material deprivation over time.* DWP Research Report no. 219, www.dwp.gov.uk/asd/asd5/rports2003-2004/rrep219.asp

Model-based estimates of income

The Office for National Statistics (ONS) has produced a set of model-based income estimates for wards in England and Wales on boundaries consistent with the 2001 Census. Model-based estimates have been produced for four different income types:

- total weekly household income (unequivalised)

- net weekly household income (unequivalised)

- net weekly household income before housing costs (equivalised) and

- net weekly household income after housing costs (equivalised).

The methodology used to produce the model-based estimates is relatively new and as a result may be subject to consultation, modification and further development. In view of this ongoing work the current model-based estimates are published as Experimental Statistics. The modelling methodology enables survey data to be combined with census and administrative data to produce estimates at a lower geographical level than is possible with survey data alone. Since the estimates are model-based they are different to standard direct estimates obtained from surveys and from statistics provided by administrative sources. These estimates are dependent upon correctly specifying the relationship between weekly household income and the census/administrative information. The main limitation of estimates for small areas is that they are subject to variability. ONS has produced confidence intervals associated with the model-based estimates in order to make the accuracy of the estimates clear. These ward estimates are constrained to the published Family Resources Survey estimates for each Government Office Region within England and for Wales. Further information on the methodology may be found in www.neighbourhood.statistics.gov.uk/dissemination/

Net wealth of the household sector

Revised balance sheet estimates of the net wealth of the household (and non-profit institutions) sector were published in an article in *Economic Trends* November 1999 www.statistics.gov.uk/cci/article.asp?ID=41. These figures are based on the new international system of national accounting and incorporate data from new sources. Quarterly estimates of net financial wealth (excluding tangible and intangible assets) are published in *Financial Statistics*.

Distribution of personal wealth

Estimates of the distribution of individual marketable wealth relate to all adults in the UK. They are produced by combining HM Revenue and Customs (HMRC) estimates of the distribution of wealth identified by the estate multiplier method with independent estimates of total personal wealth derived from the Office for National Statistics (ONS) National Accounts balance sheets. Estimates for 1995 onwards have been compiled on the basis of the new System of National Accounts, but estimates for earlier years are on the old basis. The methods used were described in an article in *Economic Trends* October 1990 entitled 'Estimates of the Distribution of Personal Wealth'. Net wealth of

the personal sector differs from marketable wealth for the following reasons:

Difference in coverage: the ONS balance sheet of the personal sector includes the wealth of non-profit making bodies and unincorporated businesses, while HMRC estimates exclude non-profit making bodies and treat the bank deposits and debts of unincorporated businesses differently from ONS.

Differences in timing: the ONS balance sheet gives values at the end of the year, whereas HMRC figures are adjusted to mid-year.

HMRC figures: exclude the wealth of those under 18.

Funded pensions: are included in ONS figures (including personal pensions) but not in HMRC marketable wealth. Also the ONS balance sheet excludes consumer durables and includes non-marketable tenancy rights, whereas HMRC figures include consumer durables and exclude non-marketable tenancy rights.

Part 6: Expenditure

Household expenditure

The National Accounts definition of household expenditure, within household final consumption expenditure, consists of:

- personal expenditure on goods (durable, semi-durable and non-durable) and services, including the value of income in kind

- imputed rent for owner-occupied dwellings and

- the purchase of second-hand goods less the proceeds of sales of used goods.

Excluded are interest and other transfer payments, all business expenditure, and the purchase of land and buildings (and associated costs).

In principle, expenditure is measured at the time of acquisition rather than when money is actually paid. The categories of expenditure include that by UK resident households, which take place in either the UK or the rest of the world. Expenditure by non-residents in the UK is excluded.

Until September 2003 UK economic growth was calculated using 'fixed base aggregation'. Under this method the detailed estimates for growth for different parts of the economy were summed to a total by weighting each component according to its share of total expenditure in 1995. The year from which this information was drawn was updated at five-yearly intervals. Since September 2003 UK economic growth has been calculated by 'annual chain-linking'. This uses information updated every year to give each component the most relevant weight that can be estimated. This method has been used for estimating change in household expenditure since 1971. For further details see *Consumer Trends* at: www.statistics.gov.uk/consumertrends

In April 2001 the Family Expenditure Survey (FES) and the National Food Survey (NFS) were merged to form the Expenditure and Food Survey (EFS). The EFS definition of household expenditure represents current expenditure on goods and services. This excludes those recorded payments that are savings or investments (for example, life assurance premiums). Similarly, income tax payments, national insurance contributions, mortgage capital repayments and other payments for major additions to dwellings are excluded. For further details see *Family Spending* at: http://www.statistics.gov.uk/StatBase/Product.asp?vlnk=361

Classification Of Individual Consumption by Purpose

Since 2001–02 the Classification Of Individual Consumption by Purpose (COICOP) system has been used to classify expenditure on the EFS. COICOP is the internationally agreed standard classification for reporting household consumption expenditure within National Accounts. COICOP is also used on Household Budget Surveys (HBS) across the EU. These surveys collect information on household consumption expenditure, which is then used to update the weights in the basket of goods and services used in consumer price indices.

Twelve categories are used in this edition of *Social Trends*: food and non-alcoholic drink; alcoholic drink and tobacco; clothing and footwear; housing, water and fuel; household goods and services; health; transport; communication; recreation and culture; education; restaurants and hotels; and miscellaneous goods and services.

A major difference exists in the EFS treatment of rent and mortgages. These were included as part of 'housing' expenditure under the FES. The COICOP system does not include expenditure related to housing, such as mortgage interest payments, purchases or alterations of dwellings, and mortgages in the 'housing, water and fuel' category, so under the EFS these are recorded under 'other expenditure items'.

Retail sales index

The retail sales index (RSI) is a measurement of monthly movements in the average weekly retail turnover of retailers in Great Britain. All retailers selected for the retail sales inquiry are asked to provide estimates of total retail turnover, including sales from stores, e-commerce (including internet), mail order, stalls and markets, and door-to-door sales. Retail turnover is defined as the value of sales of goods to the general public for personal and household use.

The sample is addressed to approximately 5,000 retailers of all sizes every month. All of the largest 900 retailers are included in the sample together with a random sample of smaller retailers. Estimates are produced for each type of store by size-band. These detailed estimates are aggregated to produce estimates of weekly sales for 17 retail sectors, the main industry aggregates and retailing as a whole.

Headline data are presented in constant prices (volume) seasonally adjusted and at current prices (value) not seasonally adjusted. For further details see *Retail Sales* at www.statistics.gov.uk/rsi

Retail prices index

The retail prices index (RPI) is the most familiar general purpose measure of inflation in the UK. It measures the average change from month to month in the prices of goods and services purchased by most households in the UK. The spending pattern on which the index is based is revised each year, mainly using information from the Expenditure and Food Survey (EFS). The RPI comprises all private households (that is, not those living in institutions such as prisons, retirement homes or in student accommodation) excluding:

- high income households, defined as those households with a total income within the top 4 per cent of all households, as measured by the EFS; and

- pensioner households that derive at least three-quarters of their total income from state pensions and benefits.

These households are likely to have atypical spending patterns and including them in the scope of the RPI would distort the overall average. Expenditure patterns of one-person and two-person pensioner households differ from those of the households upon which the RPI is based. Separate indices have been compiled for such pensioner households since 1969, and quarterly averages are published on the National Statistics website, *Focus on Consumer Price Indices (formerly known as the Consumer Price Indices (CPI) Business Monitor MM23)* www.statistics.gov.uk/statbase/Product.asp?vlnk=867. They are chained indices constructed in the same way as the RPI. It should be noted that the pensioner indices exclude housing costs.

A guide to the RPI can be found on the National Statistics website: www.statistics.gov.uk/rpi

Harmonised index of consumer prices

The harmonised index of consumer prices (HICP) has been known as the consumer prices index (see below) in the UK since 10 December 2003. HICPs are calculated in each member state of the EU for the purposes of European comparisons, as required by the Maastricht Treaty. Since January 1999 the HICP has been used by the European Central Bank (ECB) as the measure for its definition of price stability across the euro area. Further details are contained in an ECB Press Notice released on 13 October 1998: '*A stability oriented monetary policy strategy for the ESCB*'. www.ecb.int/press/pr/date/1998/html/pr981013_1.en.html. A guide to the HICP can be found on the National Statistics website: www.statistics.gov.uk/hicp

Before 1996 the HICP had to be estimated using available data sources. For 1988 to 1995 inclusive, the HICP was estimated from archived retail prices index (RPI) price quotes and historical weights data, and aggregated up to the published Classification Of Individual Consumption by Purpose (COICOP) weights. The estimated HICP was therefore based on the RPI household population and not all private households, and did not account for all items included in the official HICP. Between 1975 and 1987 the estimated HICP was based on published RPI section indices and weights, and unpublished item indices and weights for items excluded from the HICP. This estimated HICP can only be considered as a broad indicator of the official HICP.

For more information about how the HICP was estimated see the 'Harmonised Index of Consumer Prices: Historical Estimates' paper in *Economic Trends*, no.541. www.statistics.gov.uk/CCI/article.asp?ID=31

Consumer prices index

The consumer prices index (CPI) is the main UK domestic measure of inflation for macro-economic purposes. Before 10 December 2003 this index was published in the UK as the harmonised index of consumer prices (see above) and the two remain one and the same index.

The methodology of the CPI is similar to that of the retail prices index (RPI) but differs in the following ways:

- in the CPI the geometric mean is used to aggregate the prices at the most basic level whereas the RPI uses arithmetic means

- a number of RPI series are excluded from the CPI, most particularly, those mainly relating to owner occupiers' housing costs (e.g. mortgage interest payments, house depreciation, council tax and buildings insurance)

- the coverage of the CPI indices is based on the international Classification Of Individual Consumption by Purpose (COICOP), whereas the RPI uses its own bespoke classification

- the CPI includes series for university accommodation fees, foreign students' university tuition fees, and unit trust and stockbrokers charges, none of which are included in the RPI

- the index for new car prices in the RPI is imputed from movements in second hand car prices, whereas the CPI uses a quality adjusted index based on published prices of new cars

- the CPI weights are based on expenditure by all private households, foreign visitors to the UK and residents of institutional households. In the RPI, weights are based on expenditure by private households only, excluding the highest income households and pensioner households mainly dependent on state benefits and

- in the construction of the RPI weights, expenditure on insurance is assigned to the relevant insurance heading. For the CPI weights, the amount paid out in insurance claims is distributed among the COICOP headings according to the nature of the claims expenditure, with the residual (that is, the service charge) being allocated to the relevant insurance heading

A guide to the CPI can be found on the National Statistics website: www.statistics.gov.uk/cpi

Purchasing power parities

The international spending power of sterling depends both on exchange rates and on the ratios of prices between the UK and other countries, which are measured by purchasing power parities. Spending power can be measured by comparative price levels, which are defined as the ratios of purchasing power parities to exchange rates. They provide a measure of the differences in price levels between countries, by indicating the number of units of a common currency needed to buy the same volume of goods and services in each country.

Part 7: Health

Expectation of life

The expectation of life is the average total number of years that a person of that age could be expected to live, if the rates of mortality at each age were those experienced in that year. The mortality rates that underlie the expectation of life figures are based, up to 2005, on total deaths occurring in each year for England and Wales and the total deaths registered in each year in Scotland and Northern Ireland.

Healthy life expectancy and disability-free life expectancy

Healthy life expectancy and disability-free life expectancy are summary measures of population health that combine mortality and ill-health. In contrast to life expectancy, these two indicators measure both the quality and length of life. Essentially they separate life expectancy into two components:

- years lived free from ill-health or disability and

- years lived in ill-health or with disability.

Life expectancy indicators are independent of the age structure of the population and represent the average health expectation of a birth cohort experiencing current rates of mortality and ill-health over their lifetime.

Healthy life expectancy (HLE) at birth is defined as the number of years that a newborn baby can expect to live in 'good' or 'fairly good' health if he or she experienced the current mortality rates and good or fairly good health rates, based on self-assessed general health for different age groups during their life span. The calculation of HLE uses Government Actuary's Department data on life expectancy, and General Household Survey (GHS) and census data on self-assessed health, specifically responses to the question 'Over the last 12 months would you say your health has on the whole been good, fairly good, or not good?' 'Good' and 'fairly good' responses are taken as a positive measure of health. The GHS was not conducted in either 1997 or 1999. The resulting modifications to the annual series of healthy life expectancy data are:

- no data points were calculated for the years 1996, 1998 and 2000

- the data points for 1997 and 1999 were each calculated using two years of GHS health data; 1997 on 1996 and 1998 data, and 1999 on 1998 and 2000 data.

Furthermore, HLE estimates for 2001 and 2002 were calculated using revised methodology to incorporate improved population estimates from the 2001 Census and changes in weighting methodology in the GHS. They are therefore not directly comparable with previous years. However, the level of change was small and the new series can be used to monitor trends over the longer term.

Disability-free life expectancy, defined as expected years lived without limiting long-standing illness, is calculated in exactly the same way as HLE, with the difference that it uses the GHS age-sex rates of 'without limiting long-standing illness' instead of the rates of 'good' or 'fairly good' health.

Self-reported illness

The General Household Survey includes two measures of self-reported illness:

- *Chronic illness.* Respondents aged 16 and over are asked whether they have any long-standing illness or disability that has troubled them for some time. Information about children is collected from a responsible adult, usually the mother. Those who report a long-standing condition, either on their own behalf or that of their children, are asked whether it limits their activities in any way (this is shown in Table 7.3 as 'limiting long-standing illness')

- *Acute sickness.* Respondents are asked whether they had to cut down on their normal activities in the two weeks before interview as a result of illness or injury (this is known as 'restricted activity')

Standardised rates

Directly age-standardised incidence rates enable comparisons to be made between geographical areas over time, and between the sexes, which are independent of changes in the age structure of the population. In each year, the crude rates in each five-year age group are multiplied by the European standard population for that age group (see below). These are then added up and divided by the total standard population for these age groups to give an overall standardised rate.

European standard population

The age distribution of the European standard population is presented in the table below:

Age	Population
Under 1	1,600
1–4	6,400
5–9	7,000
10–14	7,000
15–19	7,000
20–24	7,000
25–29	7,000
30–34	7,000
35–39	7,000
40–44	7,000
45–49	7,000
50–54	7,000
55–59	6,000
60–64	5,000
65–69	4,000
70–74	3,000
75–79	2,000
80–84	1,000
85 plus	1,000
Total	100,000

International Classification of Diseases

The International Classification of Diseases (ICD) is a coding scheme for diseases and causes of death. The Tenth Revision of the ICD (ICD10) was introduced for coding the underlying cause of death in Scotland from 2000 and in the rest of the UK from 2001. The causes of death included in Figure 7.4 correspond to the following ICD10 codes: circulatory diseases I00-I99; cancer C00–D48; and respiratory diseases J00–J99. Rates for 2000 are for England and Wales only.

The data presented in Figure 7.4 cover three different revisions of the ICD. Although they have been selected according to codes that are comparable, there may still be differences between years because of changes in the rules used to select the underlying cause of death. This can be seen in deaths from respiratory diseases where a different interpretation of these rules was used to code the underlying cause of death from 1983 to 1992, and from 2001 onwards in England and Wales, and 2000 onwards in Scotland.

The data presented in Figure 7.13, Figure 7.14 and Table 7.15 correspond to the following cancer specific ICD10 codes:

C16	Stomach
C18	Colon
C19–C20	Rectum
C18–C20	Colorectal
C34	Lung
C50	Breast
C54	Uterus
C56	Ovary
C61	Prostate
C67	Bladder

C00–C97 excluding C44 All malignant cancers excluding non-melanoma skin cancer.

National Statistics Socio-economic Classification (NS-SEC)

From 2001, the National Statistics Socio-economic Classification (NS-SEC) was adopted for all official surveys, in place of Social Class based on Occupation and Socio-economic Group. NS-SEC is itself based on the Standard Occupational Classification 2000 (SOC2000) and details of employment status (whether an employer, self-employed or employee). See also Appendix, Part 4: Standard Occupational Classification 2000.

The NS-SEC is an occupationally-based classification designed to provide coverage of the whole adult population. The version of the classification, which will be used for most analyses, has eight classes, the first of which can be subdivided. These are:

National Statistics Socio-economic Classification (NS-SEC)

1. Higher managerial and professional occupations, sub-divided into:
   1.1 Large employers and higher managerial occupations
   1.2 Higher professional occupations

2. Lower managerial and professional occupations
3. Intermediate occupations
4. Small employers and own account workers
5. Lower supervisory and technical occupations
6. Semi-routine occupations
7. Routine occupations
8. Never worked and long-term unemployed

The classes can be further grouped into:

i. Managerial and professional occupations	1, 2
ii. Intermediate occupations	3, 4
iii. Routine and manual occupations	5, 6, 7
Never worked and long-term unemployed	8

Users have the option to include these classes in the overall analysis or keep them separate. The long-term unemployed are defined as those unemployed and seeking work for 12 months or more. Members of HM Forces, who were shown separately in tables of social class, are included within the NS-SEC classification. Residual groups that remain unclassified include students and those with inadequately described occupations.

Further details can be found on the National Statistics website: www.statistics.gov.uk/methods_quality/ns_sec/default.asp

Body mass index

The body mass index (BMI) shown in Figure 7.9, is the most widely used index of weight among adults aged 16 and over. The BMI standardises weight for height and is calculated as weight (kg)/height (m)^2. Underweight is defined as a BMI of 18.5 or under, desirable over 18.5 to 25, overweight over 25 to 30 and obese over 30.

Alcohol consumption

A unit of alcohol is 8 grams by weight or 1 cl (10 ml) by volume of pure alcohol. This is the amount contained in half a pint of ordinary strength beer or lager, a single pub measure of spirits (25 ml), a small glass of ordinary strength wine (9 per cent alcohol by volume), or a small pub measure of sherry or fortified wine. Sensible Drinking, the 1995 report of an interdepartmental review of the scientific and medical evidence of the effects of drinking alcohol, concluded that daily benchmarks were more appropriate than the previously recommended weekly levels since they could help individuals decide how much to drink on single occasions and to avoid episodes of intoxication with their attendant health and social risks. The report concluded that regular consumption of between three to four units a day for men and two to three units for women does not carry a significant health risk. However, consistently drinking more than four units a day for men, or more than three for women, is not advised as a sensible drinking level because of the progressive health risk it carries. The Government's advice on sensible drinking is now based on these daily benchmarks.

Relative survival rates

Crude survival is the proportion of the original group of patients, in this case cancer patients, diagnosed in a particular period who are still alive at the specified time after diagnosis; this takes into account deaths from all causes. Relative survival takes into account that some cancer patients will die from causes other than their cancer. Relative survival is given by the ratio of the crude survival to the expected survival in a corresponding (age and sex) group in the general population. Expected survival is obtained from a life expectancy table.

Mental disorders

The data presented in Figure 7.16 were coded using the term 'mental disorder' as defined by the tenth revision of the International Classification of Diseases (ICD10, see above) to imply a clinically recognisable set of symptoms or behaviours associated in most cases with considerable distress and substantial interference with personal functions.

Part 8: Social protection

Expenditure on social protection benefits

Cash benefits
Income support: periodic payments to people with insufficient resources. Conditions for entitlement may be related to personal resources and to nationality, residence, age, availability for work and family status. The benefit may be paid for a limited or an unlimited period. It may be paid to the individual or to the family, and be provided by central or local government.

Other cash benefit: support for destitute or vulnerable people to help alleviate poverty or assist in difficult situations. These benefits may be paid by private non-profit organisations.

Benefits in kind
Accommodation: shelter and board provided to destitute or vulnerable people, where these services cannot be classified under another function. This may be short term in reception centres, shelters and others or on a more regular basis in special institutions, boarding houses, reception families, and others.

Rehabilitation of alcohol and drug abusers: treatment of alcohol and drug dependency aimed at reconstructing the social life of the abusers, making them able to live an independent life. The treatment is usually provided in reception centres or special institutions.

Other benefits in kind: basic services and goods to help vulnerable people, such as counselling, day shelter, help with carrying out daily tasks, food, clothing and fuel. Means-tested legal aid is also included.

In-patient activity

In Table 8.12 in-patient data for England are based on finished consultant episodes (FCEs). Data for Wales, Scotland and Northern Ireland are based on deaths and discharges and transfers between specialities (between hospitals in Northern Ireland). An FCE is a completed period of care of a patient using a bed, under one consultant, in a particular NHS Trust or directly managed unit. If a patient is transferred from one consultant to another within the same hospital, this counts as an FCE but not a hospital discharge. If a patient is transferred from one hospital to another provider, this counts as an FCE and a hospital discharge.

Data for England, Wales and Northern Ireland exclude NHS beds and activity in joint-user and contractual hospitals. For Scotland, data for joint-user and contractual hospitals are included.

Pension schemes

A pension scheme is a plan offering benefits to members upon retirement. Schemes are provided by the state, employers and insurance firms, and are differentiated by a wide range of rules governing membership eligibility, contributions, benefits and taxation.

Occupational pension scheme: An arrangement (other than accident or permanent health insurance) organised by an employer (or on behalf of a group of employers) to provide benefits for employees on their retirement and for their dependants on their death.

Personal pension scheme: A scheme where the contract to provide contributions in return for retirement benefits is between an individual and an insurance firm, rather than with an employer or the state. Such schemes may be joined by individuals under their own volition – for example, to provide a primary source of retirement income for the self-employed, or to provide a secondary income to employees who are members of occupational schemes – or they may be facilitated (but not provided) by an employer.

Stakeholder pension scheme: Available since 2001, a flexible, portable, defined-contribution personal pension arrangement (provided by insurance companies) with capped management charges, that must meet the conditions set out in the Welfare Reform and Pensions Act 1999 and be registered with the Pensions Regulator. They can be taken out by an individual or facilitated by an employer. Where an employer of five or more staff offers no occupational pension and an employee earns more than the Lower Earnings Limit (the entrance level for paying tax), the provision of access to a stakeholder scheme with contributions deducted from payroll is compulsory.

Benefit units

A benefit unit is a single adult or couple living as married and any dependent children, where the head is below state pension age (60 for women and 65 for men). A pensioner benefit unit is where the head is over state pension age, although couples where the woman is over state pension age but the man is under are excluded. The head of the benefit unit is either the household reference person, where he or she belongs to the benefit unit, or the first person listed at interview in the benefit unit – for couples this is usually the man.

Children looked after by local authorities

In Great Britain children's homes include homes, hostels (in Scotland these include children with learning and physical disability) and secure units. In Northern Ireland this category includes homes and secure units but excludes hostels, which are included in the 'other accommodation' category. Excludes children looked after under an agreed series of short-term placements.

In Scotland, 'with parents' and 'other accommodation' include children staying in the community with friends/relatives and 'other community' (for example, supported accommodation) and children staying in residential accommodation, which includes local authority (LA) and voluntary homes, residential schools, secure accommodation, women's refuge, LA or voluntary hostels for offenders or for drug/alcohol abuse. Excludes children looked after on a planned series of short term placements.

In Northern Ireland, data for the 'with parents' category used in Great Britain are collected as 'placed with family'. This refers to children for whom a Care Order exists and who are placed with their parents, a person who is not a parent but who has parental responsibility for the child or, where a child was in care and there was a Residence Order in force with respect to him/her immediately before the Care Order was made, a person in whose favour the Residence Order was made.

Part 9: Crime and justice

Types of offences in England and Wales

The figures are compiled from police returns to the Home Office or directly from court computer systems.

In England and Wales, indictable offences cover those offences that can only be tried at the Crown Court and include the more serious offences.

Summary offences are those for which a defendant would normally be tried at a magistrates' court and are generally less serious – the majority of motoring offences fall into this category. Triable-either-way offences are triable either on indictment or summarily.

Recorded crime statistics broadly cover the more serious offences. Up to March 1998 most indictable and triable-either-way offences were included, as well as some summary ones; from April 1998, all indictable and triable-either-way offences were included, plus a few closely related summary ones.

Recorded offences are the most readily available measures of the incidence of crime, but do not necessarily indicate the true level of crime. Many less serious offences are not reported to the police and cannot, therefore, be recorded. Moreover, the propensity of the public to report offences to the police is influenced by a number of factors and may change over time.

From 2000, some police forces have changed their systems to record the allegations of victims unless there is credible evidence that a crime has *not* taken place. In April 2002, the National Crime Recording Standard (NCRS, see below) formalised these changes across England and Wales.

There have been changes to the methodology of the British Crime Survey (BCS). Between 1982 and 2001 the survey was carried out every two years, and reported on victimisation in the previous calendar year. The 2002/03 and 2003/04 surveys cover the financial year of interviews and report on victimisation in the 12 months before the interview.

This change makes the BCS estimates more comparable with figures collected by the police. Because of these significant changes taking place in both measures of crime, direct comparisons with figures for previous years cannot be made.

Types of offences in Northern Ireland

In recording crime, the Police Service of Northern Ireland broadly follows the Home Office rules for counting crime. As from 1 April 1998 notifiable offences are recorded on the same basis as those in England and Wales. Before the revision of the rules, criminal damage offences in Northern Ireland excluded those where the value of the property damaged was less than £200.

National Crime Recording Standard

Changes in the counting rules for recorded crime on 1 April 1998 affected both the methods of counting and the coverage for recorded crime and had the effect of inflating the number of crimes recorded. For some offence groups – more serious violence against the person and burglary – there was little effect on numbers recorded. However the changes

have had more effect on figures for minor violence and criminal damage.

In April 2002 the National Crime Recording Standard (NCRS) was introduced in England and Wales with the aim of taking a more victim centred approach and providing more consistency between forces. Before 2002, police forces in England and Wales did not necessarily record a crime that was reported if there was no evidence to support the claim of the victim. Therefore crimes recorded from 1 April 2002 are not comparable with earlier years.

It is not possible to assess the effect of NCRS on recorded firearm crimes. NCRS inflated the overall number of violence against the person and criminal damage offences, but has had less effect on the number of robberies. Many firearm offences are among the less serious categories, and these types of offences are among those most affected by NCRS. The introduction of the NCRS may have had an effect on the recorded crime detection rate, but this is difficult to quantify.

Scottish Crime Recording Standard

In April 2004, the police implemented the Scottish Crime Recording Standard (SCRS), which means that no corroborative evidence is required initially to record a crime related incident as a crime, if so perceived by the victim. In consequence of this more victim oriented approach, the introduction of this new recording standard was expected to increase the numbers of minor crimes recorded by the police, such as minor crimes of vandalism and minor thefts. However, it was expected that the SCRS would not have much impact on the figures for the more serious crimes, such as serious assault, sexual assault, robbery or housebreaking.

Unfortunately it was not possible to estimate the exact impact of SCRS on the recorded crime figures. Around the time that the new standard was implemented police also introduced centralised call centres, which encouraged the reporting of incidents to the police. It had been hoped that the underlying trends in crime would be monitored through a new, much larger, Scottish Crime and Victimisation Survey (SCVS). Unfortunately, this has not proved possible.

Availability and comparability of data from constituent countries

Where possible *Social Trends* uses data for the UK as a whole. When UK data are not available, or data from the constituent countries of the UK are not comparable, data for Great Britain or the constituent countries are used. Constituent countries can advise where data that are not included in *Social Trends* are available that are equivalent but not directly comparable with those of other constituent countries.

Comparable crimes

Comparable crimes are a set of offences that are covered by both the British Crime Survey (BCS) and police recorded crime. Various adjustments are made to the recorded crime categories to maximise comparability with the BCS. Comparable crime is used to compare trends in police and BCS figures, and to identify the amount of crime that is not reported to the police and not recorded by them. The comparable subset includes common assaults (and assaults on a constable), and vehicle interference and tampering. Seventy-eight per cent of BCS offences reported through

interviews in the 2005/06 interview sample fall into categories that can be compared with crimes recorded under the new police coverage of offences adopted from 1 April 1998. With the introduction of new police counting rules in 1998/99, the 'old' comparable subset that was used in, up to and including the 1998 BCS was updated as it excluded common assaults, other household theft and other theft of personal property. Trends for 'old comparable' police recorded crime have been continued to the 2005/06 BCS by applying adjustments to take account of changes in police counting rules. Sixty-five per cent of offences reported through interviews in the 2005/06 interview sample fall into the old comparable subset.

Offences and crimes

There are a number of reasons why recorded crime statistics in England and Wales, Northern Ireland and Scotland cannot be directly compared:

Different legal systems: The legal system operating in Scotland differs from that in England and Wales and Northern Ireland. For example, in Scotland children aged under 16 are normally dealt with for offending by the Children's Hearings system rather than the courts.

Differences in classification: There are significant differences in the offences included within the recorded crime categories used in Scotland and the categories of notifiable offences used in England, Wales and Northern Ireland. Scottish figures of 'crime' have therefore been grouped in an attempt to approximate the classification of notifiable offences in England, Wales and Northern Ireland.

Counting rules: In all parts of the UK, only the main offence occurring within an incident is counted.

Burglary: This term is not applicable to Scotland where the term used is 'housebreaking'.

Theft from vehicles: In Scotland data have only been separately identified from January 1992. The figures include theft by opening lock fast places from a motor vehicle and other theft from a motor vehicle.

Urban and rural

The National Statistics rural and urban area classification 2004 has been used in this report. Rural areas are those classified as a small town and fringe, village, hamlet and isolated dwellings. More information is available through the National Statistics website at **www.statistics.gov.uk/geography/nrudp.asp**.

English Indices of Deprivation

Local area deprivation is measured in this report using the Indices of Deprivation 2004. There are seven domains of deprivation:

- income
- employment
- health and disability
- education, skills and training
- barriers to housing and services
- living environment and
- crime

There are a number of indicators of deprivation in each of these domains, such as level of unemployment and incapacity benefit claimants, which are combined into a single deprivation score for each local area on that domain. In order to examine how deprivation varies across the country the local areas are ranked according to their scores on a domain and divided into ten equally sized groups, called deciles; those areas in the first decile are the most deprived areas on the domain of interest, those in the tenth decile are the least deprived. An overall Index of Multiple Deprivation is also available, which combines all seven separate domains into one index. This has not been used here to examine the risk of being a victim of crime by the level of deprivation as it includes the crime domain; deprived areas using this index are, by definition, those areas which have higher levels of crime.

Anti-social behaviour indicators

The British Crime Survey (BCS) measures 'high' levels of perceived anti-social behaviour from responses to the seven individual anti-social behaviour strands list in Table 9.9.

Perceptions of anti-social behaviour are measured using a scale based on answers to the seven questions as follows:

- 'very big problem'   = 3
- 'fairly big problem'   = 2
- 'not a very big problem'   = 1 and
- 'not a problem at all'   = 0

The maximum score for the seven questions is 21. Those respondents with 'high' levels of perceived anti-social behaviour are those who score 11 or more on this scale.

Offenders cautioned for burglary

In England and Wales offenders cautioned for going equipped for stealing, and other similar offences, were counted against burglary offences until 1986 and against other offences from 1987. Historical data provided in Figure 9.11 have been amended to take account of this change. Drug offences were included under other offences for 1971.

Crime and Justice Survey core offences

The 2005 Crime and Justice Survey presents the key results on 20 core offences, including:

- *Property offences*
  Burglary (domestic, commercial)

  Vehicle related thefts (theft of vehicles, attempted theft of a vehicle, theft from outside a vehicle, theft from inside a vehicle, attempted thefts from a vehicle)

  Other thefts (from work, from school, shoplifting, thefts from person, other theft)

  Criminal damage (to a vehicle, to other property)

- *Violent offences*
  Robbery (of an individual, of a business)

  Assaults (with injury, without injury)

- *Drug offences*
  Selling drugs (Class A drugs, other drugs).

Sentences and orders

The following are the main sentences and orders that can be imposed upon people found guilty. Some types of sentence or order can only be given to offenders in England and Wales in certain age groups. Under the framework for sentencing contained in the *Criminal Justice Acts 1991, 1993* and the *Powers of Criminal Courts (Sentencing) Act 2000* the sentence must reflect the seriousness of the offence. The following sentences are available for adults aged 18 and over (a similar range of sentences is available to juveniles aged 10 to 17):

Absolute and conditional discharge: A court may make an order discharging a person absolutely or (except in Scotland) conditionally where it is inexpedient to inflict punishment and, before 1 October 1992, where a probation order was not appropriate. An order for conditional discharge runs for a period of not more than three years as the court specifies, the condition being that the offender does not commit another offence within the period so specified. In Scotland a court may also discharge a person with an admonition.

Community sentences
The term *'community sentence'* refers to attendance centre orders, reparation orders, action plan orders, drug treatment and testing orders, community rehabilitation orders, community punishment orders, community punishment and rehabilitation orders, supervision orders, curfew orders and referral orders. Under the *Criminal Justice and Courts Services Act 2000*, certain community orders current at 1 April 2001 were renamed. Probation orders were renamed community rehabilitation orders, community service orders were renamed community punishment orders and combination orders were renamed community punishment and rehabilitation orders.

Attendance centre order: Available in England, Wales and Northern Ireland for young offenders and involves deprivation of free time.

Reparation order: Introduced under the *Powers of Criminal Courts (Sentencing) Act 2000*. This requires the offender to make an apology to the victim or to apologise in person. Maximum duration of the order is 24 hours and is only available to juveniles aged 10 to 18 in England and Wales.

Action plan order: An order imposed for a maximum of three months in England, Wales and Northern Ireland to address certain behavioural problems. This is again available for the younger age groups and is considered as early intervention to stop serious offending.

Drug treatment and testing order: This is imposed as a treatment order to reduce the person's dependence on drugs and to test if the offender is complying with treatment. The length of order can run from six months to three years in England, Wales and Northern Ireland. This was introduced under the *Powers of Criminal Courts (Sentencing) Act 2000* for persons aged 16 and over. In Scotland, drug treatment and testing orders were introduced in phases on a court by court basis from 1999 onwards. They are now available in almost every Sheriff and High Court in Scotland.

Community rehabilitation order: An offender sentenced to a community rehabilitation order is under the supervision of a probation officer (social worker in Scotland) whose duty it is (in

England and Wales and Northern Ireland) to advise, assist and befriend him or her, but the court has the power to include any other requirement it considers appropriate. A cardinal feature of the order is that it relies on the co-operation of the offender. Community rehabilitation orders may be given for any period between six months and three years inclusive.

Punishment order: An offender who is convicted of an offence punishable with imprisonment may be sentenced to perform unpaid work for not more than 240 hours (300 hours in Scotland), and not less than 40 hours. Twenty hours minimum community service are given for persistent petty offending or fine default. In Scotland the *Law Reform (Miscellaneous Provisions) (Scotland) Act 1990* requires that community service can only be ordered where the court would otherwise have imposed imprisonment or detention. Probation and community service may be combined in a single order in Scotland. Community punishment orders came into effect under the *Powers of Criminal Courts (Sentencing) Act 2000* when they replaced supervision orders.

Community punishment and rehabilitation order: The *Criminal Justice Act 1991* introduced the combination order in England and Wales only, which combines elements of both probation supervision and community service. Meanwhile, Article 15 of the Criminal Justice (NI) Order 1996 introduced the combination order to Northern Ireland. The *Powers of Criminal Courts (Sentencing) Act 2000* brought into effect the community punishment and rehabilitation order, known as the combination order, which requires an offender to be under a probation officer and to take on unpaid work.

Detention and imprisonment
Detention and training order: This was introduced for juveniles aged 10 to 18 under the *Powers of Criminal Courts (Sentencing) Act*. It is for juveniles who have committed a serious crime. They can serve the sentence at a Young Offender Institution or at a Local Authority Establishment, or Local Authority Secure Training Centre. The sentence given is from 4 to 24 months, but sentences can run consecutively.

Imprisonment: Is the custodial sentence for adult offenders. Home Office or Scottish Executive consent is needed for release or transfer. In the case of mentally disordered offenders, hospital orders, which may include a restriction order, may be considered appropriate.

A new disposal, the 'hospital direction', was introduced in 1997. The court, when imposing a period of imprisonment, can direct that the offender be sent directly to hospital. On recovering from the mental disorder, the offender is returned to prison to serve the balance of their sentence.

The *Criminal Justice Act 1991* abolished remission and substantially changed the parole scheme in England and Wales. Those serving sentences of under four years, imposed on or after 1 October 1992, are subject to automatic conditional release and are released, subject to certain criteria, halfway through their sentence. Home detention curfews result in selected prisoners being released up to two months early with a tag that monitors their presence during curfew hours. Those serving sentences of four years or longer are considered for discretionary conditional release after having served half their sentence, but are automatically released at the two-thirds point of sentence.

The *Crime (Sentences) Act 1997*, implemented on 1 October 1997, included, for persons aged 18 or over, an automatic life sentence for a second serious violent or sexual offence unless there are exceptional circumstances. All offenders serving a sentence of 12 months or more are supervised in the community until the three-quarters point of sentence. A life sentence prisoner may be released on licence subject to supervision and is always liable to recall.

In Scotland the *Prisoners and Criminal Proceedings (Scotland) Act 1993* changed the system of remission and parole for prisoners sentenced on or after 1 October 1993. Those serving sentences of less than four years are released unconditionally after having served half of their sentence, unless the court specifically imposes a supervised release order that subjects them to social work supervision after release. Those serving sentences of four years or more are eligible for parole at half sentence. If parole is not granted then they will automatically be released on licence at the two-thirds point of sentence subject to days added for breaches of prison rules. All such prisoners are liable to be 'recalled on conviction' or for breach of conditions of licence, if between the date of release and the date on which the full sentence ends he/she commits another offence that is punishable by imprisonment, or breaches his/her licence conditions, then the offender may be returned to prison for the remainder of that sentence whether or not a sentence of imprisonment is also imposed for the new offence.

Custody probation order: An order unique to Northern Ireland reflecting the different regime there that applies in respect of remission and the general absence of release on licence. The custodial sentence is followed by a period of supervision for a period of between one and three years.

Fully suspended sentences: These may only be passed in exceptional circumstances. In England, Wales and Northern Ireland, sentences of imprisonment of two years or less may be fully suspended. A court should not pass a suspended sentence unless a sentence of imprisonment would be appropriate in the absence of a power to suspend. The result of suspending a sentence is that it will not take effect unless during the period specified the offender is convicted of another offence punishable with imprisonment. Suspended sentences are not available in Scotland.

Fines

The *Criminal Justice Act 1993* introduced new arrangements on 20 September 1993 whereby courts are required to fit an amount for the fine that reflects the seriousness of the offence and that takes account of an offender's means. This system replaced the more formal unit fines scheme included in the *Criminal Justice Act 1991*. The Act also introduced the power for courts to arrange deduction of fines from income benefit for those offenders receiving such benefits. The *Law Reform (Miscellaneous Provision) (Scotland) Act 1990* as amended by the *Criminal Procedure (Scotland) Act 1995* provides for the use of

supervised attendance orders by selected courts in Scotland. The *Criminal Procedure (Scotland) Act 1995* also makes it easier for courts to impose a supervised attendance order in the event of a default and enables the court to impose a supervised attendance order in the first instance for 16 and 17-year-olds.

Civil courts

England and Wales: The main civil courts are the High Court and the county courts. The High Court is divided into three divisions:

- the *Queen's Bench Division* deals with disputes relating to contracts, general commercial matters and breaches of duty – known as 'liability in tort' – covering claims of negligence, nuisance or defamation
- the *Chancery Division* deals with disputes relating to land, wills, companies and insolvency
- the *Family Division* deals with matrimonial matters, including divorce, and the welfare of children

Magistrates' courts also have some civil jurisdiction, mainly in family proceedings. Most appeals in civil cases go to the Court of Appeal (Civil Division) and may go from there to the House of Lords. Since July 1991, county courts have been able to deal with all contract and tort cases and actions for recovery of land, regardless of value. Cases are presided over by a judge who almost always sits without a jury. Jury trials are limited to specified cases, for example, actions for libel.

Northern Ireland: The High Court of Northern Ireland is, like the English equivalent, split into three divisions: the Queen's Bench Division, the Chancery Division and the Family Division. Below the High Court are county courts (including small claims courts, district judges' courts and family care centres), Crown Court for criminal cases, courts of summary jurisdiction (including domestic proceedings courts and family proceeding courts) and tribunals.

Scotland: The Court of Session is the supreme civil court. Any cause, apart from causes excluded by statute, may be initiated in, and any judgment of an inferior court may be appealed to, the Court of Session. The sheriff court is the principal local court of civil jurisdiction in Scotland. It also has jurisdiction in criminal proceedings. Apart from certain actions the civil jurisdiction of the sheriff court is generally similar to that of the Court of Session.

Part 10: Housing

Dwelling stock

The definition of a dwelling follows the census definition applicable at that time. Currently the 2001 Census is used, which defines a dwelling as 'structurally separate accommodation'. This was determined primarily by considering the type of accommodation, as well as separate and shared access to multi-occupied properties.

In all stock figures vacant dwellings are included but non-permanent dwellings are generally

excluded. For housebuilding statistics, only data on permanent dwellings are collected.

Estimates of the total dwelling stock, stock changes and the tenure distribution in the UK are made by Communities and Local Government for England, the Scottish Executive, the National Assembly for Wales, and the Northern Ireland Department for Social Development. These are primarily based on census output data for the number of dwellings (or households converted to dwellings) from the censuses of population for the UK. Adjustments are carried out if there are specific reasons to do so. Census year figures are based on outputs from the censuses. For years between censuses, the total figures are obtained by projecting the base census year's figure forward annually. The increment is based on the annual total number of completions plus the annual total net gain from other housing statistics, that is, conversions, demolitions and changes of use.

Estimates of dwelling stock by tenure category are based on other sources where it is considered that for some specific tenure information, these are more accurate than census output data. In this situation it is assumed that the other data sources also contain vacant dwellings, but it is not certain and it is not expected that these data are very precise. Thus the allocation of vacant dwellings to tenure categories may not be completely accurate and the margin of error for tenure categories is wider than for estimates of total stock.

For local authority stock, figures supplied by local authorities are more reliable than those in the 2001 Census. Similarly, it was found that the Housing Corporation's own data are more accurate than census output data for the registered social landlord (RSL) stock. Hence only the privately rented or with a job or business tenure data were taken directly from the census. The owner-occupied data were taken as the residual of the total from the census. For non-census years, the same approach was adopted except for the privately rented or with a job or business, for which Labour Force Survey results were used.

In the Survey of English Housing, data for privately rented unfurnished accommodation include accommodation that is partly furnished.

For further information on the methodology used to calculate stock by tenure and tenure definitions, see Appendix B Notes and Definitions in the Communities and Local Government annual volume *Housing Statistics* or the housing statistics page of the Communities and Local Government website at: **www.communities.gov.uk**

Dwellings completed

In principle a dwelling is regarded as completed when it becomes ready for occupation whether it is occupied or not. In practice there are instances where the timing could be delayed and some completions are missed, for example, because no completion certificates were requested by the owner.

Tenure definition for housebuilding is only slightly different from that used for dwelling stock figures (see above). For further information on the methodology used to calculate stock by tenure and tenure definitions, see Appendix B

Notes and Definitions in the Communities and Local Government annual volume Housing Statistics or the housing statistics page of the Communities and Local Government website.

Sustainable Communities Plan

The Sustainable Communities Plan (*Sustainable Communities: Building for the Future*), published in February 2003, set out a 15 to 20 year programme of action that included an investment of £22 billion to improve housing and communities in England. In July 2004 the Government announced a further £1.3 billion for the Plan during the period 2005/06 to 2007/08.

To meet the demand for affordable housing in the South East, the Plan identified four growth areas where land can be accessed relatively inexpensively and where large numbers of homes can be built. The areas are:

- Ashford, Kent
- Milton Keynes and the South Midlands
- the corridor from London to Stansted, and Cambridgeshire, and
- the Thames Gateway, a 64 kilometre strip of land covering parts of east London, south Essex and north Kent.

In July 2003, the Government committed £446 million over three years for projects in priority areas within the Thames Gateway. This is expected to generate additional funds and to help produce an extra 200,000 homes by 2016.

Sales and transfers of local authority dwellings

Right to buy was established by the *Housing Act 1980* and was introduced across Great Britain in October 1980. In England, large scale voluntary transfers (LSVTs) of stock have been principally to housing associations/registered social landlords. Figures include transfers supported by estate renewal challenge funding (ERCF). The figures for 1993 include 949 dwellings transferred under Tenants' Choice. In Scotland LSVTs to registered social landlords and the small number of transfers to housing associations are included.

Household reference person

From April 2000 the General Household Survey adopted the term 'household reference person' in place of 'head of household'. As of April 2001 the Survey of English Housing also adopted the term.

The household reference person is identified during the interview and is defined as the member of the household who:

- owns the household accommodation or
- is legally responsible for the rent of the accommodation or
- has the household accommodation as part of a jab or
- has the household accommodation by virtue of some relationship to the owner who is not a member of the household.

The household reference person must always be a householder, whereas the head of household was always the husband for a couple household, who might not be a householder. If there are joint householders, the household reference person will be the householder with the highest income.

Homeless at home

Homeless at home refers to any arrangement where a household for whom a duty has been accepted by the local authority (eligible for assistance, unintentionally homeless and in priority need) is able to remain in, or return to the accommodation from which they are being made homeless, or temporarily stay in other accommodation found by the household. Such schemes may locally be referred to as: Direct Rehousing, Prevention of Homelessness; Concealed Household Schemes; Prevention of Imminent Homelessness Schemes; Impending Homeless Schemes and Pre-eviction Schemes.

Decent home standard

Government targets set for 2010 are to bring all social housing in England into a decent condition and to increase the proportion of vulnerable households in private sector housing living in homes that are in decent condition. Vulnerable households are those in receipt of means tested or disability related benefits.

A decent home is one that:

- meets the current statutory minimum for housing (the 'fitness standard' for the reporting period of the data presented in Table 10.13)
- is in a reasonable state of repair
- has reasonably modern facilities and services and
- provides a reasonable degree of thermal comfort – it has efficient heating and effective insulation.

Poor quality environments

The identification of poor quality environments is based on surveyors' observed assessments of the severity of problems in the immediate environment of the home. The problems assessed fall into three groups:

- the upkeep, management or misuse of private and public buildings and space (scruffy or neglected buildings; poor condition housing; graffiti; scruffy gardens or landscaping; litter; rubbish or dumping; vandalism; dog or other excrement; nuisance from street parking)
- road traffic or other transport (presence of intrusive motorways and main roads; railway or aircraft noise; heavy traffic; ambient air quality)
- abandonment or non-residential use (vacant sites; vacant or boarded up buildings; intrusive industry; nonconforming use of domestic premises such as running car repair, scrap yard or haulage business).

A home is regarded as having a poor quality environment of a given type if it is assessed to have 'significant' or 'major' problems in respect of any of the specific environmental problems assessed and grouped under that type. The overall assessment of households with poor quality environments is based on whether the home has any of the three types of problems.

Standard Assessment Procedure

The Standard Assessment Procedure (SAP) is based on calculated annual space and water heating costs for a standard heating regime for a home and is expressed on a scale of 1 (highly energy inefficient) to 120 (highly energy efficient). Energy inefficient homes are those assessed with a SAP rating of 30 or below.

Property transactions

The figures are based on the number of particular delivered (PD) forms processed and stamp duty land tax certificates issued. They relate to the transfer or sale of any freehold interest in land or property, or the grant or transfer of a lease of at least 21 years and 1 day. In practice there is an average lag of about one month between the transaction and the date when the PD form is processed.

Mix adjusted prices

Information on dwelling prices at national and regional levels are collected and published by Communities and Local Government on a monthly basis. Up until August 2005 data came from a sample survey of mortgage completions, the Survey of Mortgage Lenders (SML). The SML covered about 50 banks and building societies that are members of the Council of Mortgage Lenders (CML). From September 2005 data come from the Regulated Mortgage Survey (RMS), which is conducted by BankSearch and the CML.

Data before the first quarter of 2002 were derived from a 5 per cent sample of completions data and were calculated on an old mix adjusted methodology. As a consequence of a significantly increased sample (to an average 25,000 cases per month), Communities and Local Government introduced a monthly series in 2003 and also provided this data back to February 2002. The mix adjusted methodology was also enhanced. The RMS collects 100 per cent of completions data from those mortgage lenders who take part (and as a result the sample size increased to around 50,000 from September 2005). Annual figures have been derived as an average of the monthly prices. The annual change in price is shown as the average percentage change over the year and is calculated from the house price index.

A simple average price will be influenced by changes in the mix of properties bought in each period. This effect is removed by applying fixed weights to the process at the start of each year, based on the average mix of properties purchased during the previous three years, and these weights are applied to prices during the year.

The mix adjusted average price excludes sitting tenant (right to buy) purchases, cash purchases, remortgages and further loans.

Housing expenditure

Housing expenditure data presented in Chapter 6, Expenditure, are based on the Classification Of Individual Consumption by Purpose (COICOP) definition (see Appendix, Part 6: Classification of Individual Consumption by Purpose). Housing costs that are included in the COICOP classification are:

- net rent for housing (gross rent less housing benefit, rebates and allowances received)
- second dwelling rent
- maintenance and repair of dwelling
- water supply and miscellaneous services relating to dwelling
- household insurances

Under the COICOP classification, expenditure on mortgage interest payments, mortgage protection premiums, council tax and Northern Ireland domestic rates are included in 'other expenditure items'.

Data presented in Table 10.20 are based on a comprehensive definition of housing costs. In addition to the housing costs included within the COICOP classifications of housing expenditure and other expenditure items outlined above, this also includes the following non-consumption expenditure on the purchase or alteration of dwellings and mortgages:

- outright purchase of dwelling including deposits
- capital repayment of mortgage
- central heating installation
- DIY improvements
- home improvements (contracted out)
- bathroom fittings
- purchase of materials for capital improvements
- purchase of second dwelling

Part 11: Environment

Global warming and climate change

Emissions estimates for the UK are updated annually to reflect revisions in methodology and the availability of new information. These adjustments are applied retrospectively to earlier years and hence there are differences from the data published in previous editions of Social Trends.

In Figure 11.2, the Kyoto reduction targets cover a basket of six gases: carbon dioxide (CO_2), methane (CH_4), nitrous oxide (N_2O), hydrofluorocarbons (HFCs), perfluorocarbons (PFCs) and sulphur hexafluoride (SF_6). For the latter three gases, signatories to the Protocol may choose to use 1995, rather than 1990, as the base year from which to calculate targets, since data for 1995 for these gases tend to be more widely available and more reliable than for 1990. The UK announced in its Climate Change Programme that it would use 1995 as the base year for the fluorinated gases – therefore the 'base year' emissions for the UK target differ slightly from UK emissions in 1990.

Emissions of the six greenhouse gases are presented based on their relative contribution to global warming. Limited allowance is given in the Protocol for the absorption of CO_2 by forests, which act as so-called carbon sinks.

Water supply

There are ten water service companies, supplying both water and sewerage services to premises across England and Wales. These companies supply the majority of water in England and Wales, and the boundaries can be seen in the Geographical Areas section on page 197. In addition there are 13 smaller water supply companies, which do not provide sewerage services. These are found mainly in the south east of England. They are: Bournemouth & West Hampshire; Bristol; Cambridge; Dee Valley; Folkestone & Dover; Mid Kent; Portsmouth;

South East; South Staffordshire; Cholderton; Sutton & East Surrey; Tendring Hundred; and Three Valleys. In 2004/05, they supplied a combined 2,800 megalitres of water a day, compared with 13,000 megalitres a day supplied by the ten water service companies.

Production of primary fuels

The indigenous production of primary fuels includes the extraction or capture of primary commodities and the generation or manufacture of secondary commodities. Production is always gross; that is, it includes the quantities used during the extraction or manufacturing process. Primary fuels are coal, natural gas (including colliery methane), oil, primary electricity (electricity generated by hydro, nuclear, wind and tide stations, and also electricity imported from France through the interconnector – four pairs of cables between Sellindge in England and Les Mandarins in France – and renewables, includes solid renewables such as wood, straw and waste, and gaseous renewables such as landfill gas and sewage gas).

Oil and gas reserves

UK reserves are based on data collected from operators during January to March 2006, but are sometimes presented as at the end of 2005. A total of 641 fields and potential developments or past discoveries, both offshore and onshore, were reviewed. Key terms are defined as follows:

Total recoverable reserves: Also known as ultimate recovery, the total recovery from a field, that is reserves plus past production.

Reserves: Discovered, remaining reserves which are recoverable and commercial. Can be proven, probable or possible depending on confidence level (as described below).

Proven: Reserves that on the available evidence are virtually certain to be technically and commercially producible, having a better than 90 per cent chance of being produced.

Probable: Reserves that are not yet proven, but that are estimated to have a better than 50 per cent chance of being technically and commercially producible.

Possible: Reserves that at present cannot be regarded as probable, but that are estimated to have a significant but less than 50 per cent chance of being technically and commercially producible.

Potential additional reserves: Discovered reserves that are not currently technically or economically producible.

Air pollutants

Volatile organic compounds (VOCs) comprise a wide range of chemical compounds including hydrocarbons, oxygenates and halogen-containing species. Methane (CH_4) is an important component of VOCs but its environmental impact derives principally from its contribution to global warming, see above.

Sources of air pollution

Three different classification systems can be used when measuring air pollution:

- a National Accounts basis

- the format required by the Inter-governmental Panel on Climate Change (IPCC) and
- the Co-operative Programme for Monitoring and Evaluation of the Long-range Transmission of Air pollutants in Europe (known as EMEP) format used by the United Nations Economic Commission for Europe (UNECE) used in Table 11.12.

The EMEP source categories are detailed below, together with details of the main sources of these emissions. In Table 11.12, 'Transport' consists of *road transport, other transport* and *military aircraft and shipping*; 'Agriculture' consists of agriculture and land-use change and forestry; 'Other' consists of waste treatment and disposal and all other sources not classified below:

Energy industries: Public electricity and heat production, petroleum refining, manufacture of solid fuels, and other energy industries

Manufacturing industries and construction: iron and steel, autogenerators, foundries, sinter production, other industrial fuel combustion including ammonia, fletton brick and cement production

Road transport: Passenger cars, light duty vehicles, buses, HGVs mopeds, motorcycles; gasoline evaporation from vehicles, tyre and brake wear

Other transport: Civil aviation (domestic cruise, take-off and landing cycles), railway locomotives, national navigation, fishing vessels, and other mobile sources including agricultural machinery; gardening, construction and aircraft support equipment and mobile industrial equipment powered by diesel or petrol engines

Military aircraft and shipping: Military road vehicles are included in road transport

Commercial and institutional: Public sector industrial and commercial combustion, and railways stationary combustion

Residential: Residential plant, household and gardening (mobile)

Agriculture and forestry fuel use: Stationary, off-road vehicles and other machinery

Fugitive emissions from fuels: Solid fuel transformation, exploration production, transport, venting and flaring

Industrial processes: Emissions from industrial processes other than fuel combustion

Solvent and other product use: Paint application, degreasing and dry cleaning, chemical products, manufacture and processing, wood impregnation and tyre manufacture

Agriculture: Culture with and without fertilisers; enteric fermentation and manure management of animals

Land-use change and forestry: Emissions from managed and unmanaged forests, and forest and grassland conversion

Waste treatment and disposal: Treatment of domestic, industrial and other waste, including landfill, but excluding incineration with energy recovery; and including accidental fires

Water pollution incidents

Data shown in Figure 11.13 relate to substantiated reports of pollution and correspond to categories 1 and 2 in the Environment Agency's pollution incidents classification scheme for England and Wales. For Scotland the term 'significant incidents' is used and compares broadly with all of category 1 and most of category 2 used by the Environment Agency. In Northern Ireland the terms 'high severity' and 'medium severity' are used; these compare broadly with all of categories 1 and 2 used by the Environment Agency.

The Environment Agency defines four categories of pollution incidents.

Category 1: The most severe, incidents that involve one or more of the following:

- potential or actual persistent effect on water quality or aquatic life
- closure of potable water, industrial or agricultural abstraction necessary
- major damage to aquatic ecosystems
- major damage to agriculture and/or commerce
- serious impact on man, or
- major effect on amenity value

Category 2: Severe incidents, which involve one or more of the following:

- notification to abstractors necessary
- significant damage to aquatic ecosystems
- significant effect on water quality
- damage to agriculture and/or commerce
- impact on man, or
- impact on amenity value to public, owners or users

Category 3: Minor incidents, involving one or more of the following:

- a minimal effect on water quality
- minor damage to aquatic ecosystems
- amenity value only marginally affected, or
- minimal impact on agriculture and/or commerce

Category 4: Incidents where no impact on the environment occurred.

Rivers and canals

The chemical quality of rivers and canal waters in the UK are monitored in a series of separate national surveys in England and Wales, Scotland and Northern Ireland. In England, Wales and Northern Ireland the General Quality Assessment (GQA) Scheme provides a rigorous and objective method for assessing the basic chemical quality of rivers and canals based on three determinands: dissolved oxygen, biochemical oxygen demand (BOD) and ammoniacal nitrogen. The GQA grades river stretches into six categories of chemical quality, from A (very good) to F (bad). Table 11.14 uses two broader groups – good (categories A and B) and fair (categories C and D). Classification of biological quality is based on the River Invertebrate Prediction and Classification System (RIVPACS).

The length of rivers chemically classified in Northern Ireland increased by more than 40 per cent between 1991 and 2001.

In Scotland water quality is based upon the Scottish River Classification Scheme of 20 June 1997, which combines chemical, biological, nutrient and aesthetic quality using the following classes: excellent (A1), good (A2), fair (B), poor (C) and seriously polluted (D). In 1999 a digitised river network was introduced to improve accurate measurement river lengths, automate the classification procedure and allow electronic reporting.

Noise complaints

Complaints about road traffic, aircraft and other noise, which fall outside the responsibilities of Environmental Health Officers (EHOs), are likely to be considerably understated in this data. Complaints about road traffic noise are more likely to be addressed to highway authorities or the Department for Transport (DfT) and complaints about aircraft noise would be more likely to be reported to aircraft operators, airports, DfT or the Civil Aviation Authority so would not be included in Figure 11.15. Consequently, the information reported to EHOs is considered to give an approximate indication of the trend in noise complaints from these sources.

Land use

Land use refers to the main activity taking place on an area of land, for example, farming, forestry or housing. Land cover refers specifically to the make up of the land surface, for example, whether it comprises arable crops, trees or buildings.

Other agricultural land includes set aside and other land on agricultural holdings, for example, farm roads, yards, buildings, gardens, ponds.

The figures for agricultural land use are derived from the Agricultural and Horticultural Censuses carried out by the Department for Environment, Food and Rural Affairs (Defra) and the other UK Agricultural Departments in June each year. Information on the area of forest and woodland in Great Britain is provided by the Forestry Commission (FC) and for Northern Ireland by the Forest Service, an agency of the Department of Agriculture and Rural Development (DARD). Data cover both private and state-owned land.

There is no comparable source of information on the amount of urban land in the UK, and the figures for the *Urban land and land not otherwise specified* category are derived by subtracting the area of land used for agriculture and forestry from the total land area. The figures include land under non-agricultural semi-natural environments, such as sand dunes, grouse moors and grassland that is not farmland. It also includes land used for transportation, recreation, residential and other urban uses.

Land use change

The uses of land given are as defined in *Land Use Change Statistics*, published by Communities and Local Government.

Land use change data have been obtained from Ordnance Survey (OS) since 1985. A land use change is recorded as part of OS's map revision process, when the current land use category of a parcel of land differs from that depicted on the existing OS map. A change is also recorded where there is no change in the appropriate land use category, but new features are added, such as a house being demolished and one or more built in its place, or an additional house being built within the grounds of an existing house. Change is not recorded if it does not affect the OS map, generally where there is no physical change. This would include, in particular, conversions within existing buildings.

The majority of changes are recorded within five years of the change occurring. However, changes involving physical development (for example, new houses or industrial buildings) tend to be recorded more quickly than changes between other uses (for example, between agriculture and forestry).

Part 12: Transport

Road traffic

Minor revisions have been made to the road traffic data for 2002 and 2003 because of some time delays in taking account of traffic on recently built major roads or re-classified roads, the inclusion of some tunnels (under the river Mersey, Liverpool and Aldwych, London) from 2002 onwards, and the resolution of some anomalies.

Improvements were made to the methodology used to estimate minor roads traffic in 2004. From 2000 to 2003, trends in traffic flow, derived from a relatively small number of automatic traffic counters, were used to update 1999 base-year estimates. For the 2004 and 2005 estimates, the trends were derived from a set of some 4,200 manual traffic counts instead.

For more details, see *How the National Road Traffic Estimates are made* from the Department For Transport, **www.dft.gov.uk/stellent/ groups/dft_transstats/documents/page/dft_ transstats_027415.hcsp**

Socio-economic Group

The Socio-economic Group (SEG) classification is derived from occupational unit group, employment status and size of establishment. The final version was based on the 1990 edition of the Standard Occupational Classification (see Appendix, Part 4: Standard Occupational Classification 2000). The classification aimed to bring together people with similar social and economic status into 17 groups, three of which were subdivided. For details of these groups, as well as how they relate to the separate and more recent NS-SEC classification described in Appendix, Part 7: National Statistics Socio-economic Classification (NS-SEC), see **www.statistics.gov.uk/methods_quality/ ns_sec/continuity.asp**

Figure 12.2 uses a collapsed version of the SEG classification, which is as follows:

Descriptive definition	Socio-economic Group numbers
Professional	3, 4
Employers and managers	1, 2, 13
Intermediate and junior non-manual	5, 6
Skilled manual	8, 9, 12, 14
Semi-skilled manual and personal service	7, 10, 15
Unskilled manual	11

National Travel Survey

The National Travel Survey (NTS) is designed to provide a databank of personal travel information for Great Britain. It has been conducted as a continuous survey since July 1988, following ad hoc surveys since the mid-1960s. The NTS is designed to identify long-term trends and is not suitable for monitoring short-term trends.

For the first time, the annual Statistical Bulletin *National Travel Survey: 2005* contained weighted data, and data from 1995 onwards have now been weighted. The weighting methodology adjusts for nonresponse bias and also adjusts for the drop-off in the number of trips recorded by respondents during the course of the travel week. All results now published for 1995 onwards are based on weighted data, and direct comparisons cannot be made to earlier years or previous publications.

During 2005, over 8,400 households provided details of their personal travel by filling in travel diaries over the course of a week. The drawn sample size from 2002 has nearly trebled compared with previous years following recommendations in a National Statistics Review of the NTS. This enables most results to be presented on a single year basis from 2002. Previously data was shown for a three year time period because of the smaller sample size.

Travel included in the NTS covers all trips by British residents within Great Britain for personal reasons, including travel in the course of work.

A trip is defined as a one-way course of travel having a single main purpose. It is the basic unit of personal travel defined in the survey. A round trip is split into two trips, with the first ending at a convenient point about half-way round as a notional stopping point for the outward destination and return origin. A stage is that portion of a trip defined by the use of a specific method of transport or of a specific ticket (a new stage being defined if either the mode or ticket changes).

Cars are regarded as household cars if they are either owned by a member of the household, or available for the private use of household members. Company cars provided by an employer for the use of a particular employee (or director) are included, but cars borrowed temporarily from a company pool are not.

The main driver of a household car is the household member that drives the furthest in that car in the course of a year.

The purpose of a trip is normally taken to be the activity at the destination, unless that destination is 'home', in which case the purpose is defined by the origin of the trip. The classification of trips to 'work' is also dependent on the origin of the trip. The following purposes are distinguished:

- *Commuting*: trips to a usual place of work from home, or from work to home.

- *Business*: personal trips in the course of work, including a trip in the course of work back to work. This includes all work trips by people with no usual place of work (for example, site workers) and those who work at or from home.

- *Education*: trips to school or college by full-time students, students on day-release and part-time students following vocational courses.

- *Escort*: used when the traveller has no purpose of his or her own, other than to escort or accompany another person, for example, taking a child to school. Escort commuting is escorting or accompanying someone from home to work or from work to home.

- *Shopping*: all trips to shops or from shops to home, even if there was no intention to buy.

- *Personal business*: visits to services, for example, hairdressers, launderettes, dry-cleaners, betting shops, solicitors, banks, estate agents, libraries, churches; or for medical consultations or treatment;or for eating and drinking, unless the main purpose was entertainment or social.

- *Social or entertainment*: visits to meet friends, relatives, or acquaintances, whether at someone's home or at a pub, restaurant, etc; all types of entertainment or sport, clubs, and voluntary work, non-vocational evening classes, political meetings, and others.

- *Holidays or day trips*: trips (within Great Britain) to or from any holiday (including stays of four nights or more with friends or relatives) or trips for pleasure (not otherwise classified as social or entertainment) within a single day.

- *Just walking*: walking for pleasure along public highways, including taking the dog for a walk and jogging.

Area type classification

In the National Travel Survey households in Great Britain are classified according to whether they are within an urban area of at least 3,000 population or in a rural area. Urban areas are subdivided for the purpose of this publication as follows:

- *London boroughs*: the whole of the Greater London Authority
- *Metropolitan built-up areas*: the built-up areas of former metropolitan counties of Greater Manchester, Merseyside, West Midlands, West Yorkshire, Tyne and Wear and Strathclyde (excludes South Yorkshire)
- *Large urban*: self-contained urban areas over 250,000 population
- *Medium urban*: self-contained urban areas over 25,000 but not over 250,000 population
- *Small/medium urban*: self-contained urban areas over 10,000 but not over 25,000 population
- *Small urban*: self-contained urban areas over 3,000 but not over 10,000 population
- *Rural*: all other areas including urban areas under 3,000 population

Freight commodity classification

The data in Table 12.7 were produced from a variety of sources. The Continuing Survey of Road Goods Transport (CSRGT) provides information on the activity of GB-registered goods vehicles over 3.5 tonnes gross vehicle weight in Great Britain. There were about 430,000 of these vehicles in 2005. Heavy goods vehicles over 3.5 tonnes gross vehicle weight account for around 95 per cent of all freight moved by road. The survey is based upon a sample of about 330 vehicles each week.

The Roll-on Roll-off enquiry is based on quarterly returns provided by roll-on/roll-off ferry operators, giving the number of powered vehicles and unaccompanied trailers carried on each route to mainland Europe, and upon monthly information supplied by Eurotunnel for the Channel Tunnel. The International Road Haulage Survey (IRHS) covers international work undertaken by GB-registered powered goods vehicles carrying goods on roll-on/roll-off ferries or through the Channel Tunnel. The CSRGT (Northern Ireland) is a separate survey of NI-registered vehicles. Respondents are asked to provide details of all journeys undertaken within a survey week.

Tonne kilometres is a measure of freight moved that takes account of the weight of the load and the distance it is hauled. For example, a load of 26 tonnes carried 100 kilometres represents 2,600 tonne kilometres.

The categories in the chart include the following commodities:

- *Agricultural products*: bulk cereals, potatoes, other fresh and frozen fruit and vegetables, sugar (including beet), live animals and animal foods
- *Beverages*: alcoholic and non-alcoholic (except tea, coffee and milk)
- *Other foodstuffs*: meat, fish, dairy products, fruit cereals, other foods (including tea and coffee), tobacco
- *Wood, timber and cork*: as specified
- *Fertiliser*: both natural and chemical
- *Sand, gravel and clay*: as specified
- *Other crude minerals*: stone, chalk and other minerals
- *Ores*: ferrous and non-ferrous ores, iron and steel waste
- *Crude materials*: wool, cotton, man-made fibres and other textile materials, hides, skins, rubber, paper (including pulp and waste)
- *Coal and coke*: including lignite and peat
- *Petrol and petroleum products*: includes crude oil
- *Chemicals*: as specified
- *Cements*: cement and lime
- *Other building materials*: bricks, concrete, glass, glassware and pottery
- *Iron and steel products*: pig iron, crude steel (sheets, bars etc), unwrought and non-ferrous alloys
- *Other metal products*: includes structural parts and similar manufactured goods
- *Machinery and transport equipment*: vehicles, tractors, electrical and non-electrical machines
- *Miscellaneous manufactures*: leather, textiles and clothing; other manufactured articles
- *Miscellaneous articles*: arms and ammunition, unknown commodities, packing containers, packaging, pallets, parcels, household waste

Car ownership

The figures for household ownership include four-wheeled and three-wheeled cars, off-road vehicles, minibuses, motorcaravans, dormobiles, and light vans. Company cars normally available for household use are also included.

Passenger death rates

Passenger fatality rates given in Table 12.18 can be interpreted as the risk a traveller runs of being killed, per billion kilometres travelled. The coverage varies for each mode of travel and care should be exercised in drawing comparisons between the rates for different modes.

The table provides information on passenger fatalities. Where possible, travel by drivers and other crew in the course of their work has been excluded. Exceptions are for private journeys and those in company owned cars and vans, where drivers are included.

Figures for all modes of transport exclude confirmed suicides and deaths through natural causes. Figures for air, rail and water exclude trespassers and rail excludes attempted suicides. Accidents occurring in airports, seaports and railway stations that do not directly involve the mode of transport concerned are also excluded, for example, deaths sustained on escalators or falling over packages on platforms.

The figures are compiled by the Department for Transport (DfT). Further information is available in the annual publications *Road Casualties Great Britain: Annual Report* and *Transport Statistics Great Britain*. Both are published by The Stationery Office and are available at: **www.dft.gov.uk/transtat**

The following definitions are used:

Air: accidents involving UK registered airline aircraft in UK and foreign airspace. Fixed wing and rotary wing aircraft are included but air taxis are excluded. Accidents cover UK airline aircraft around the world, not just in the UK.

Rail: train accidents and accidents occurring through movement of railway vehicles in Great Britain. As well as national rail, the figures include accidents on underground and tram systems, the Channel Tunnel, and minor railways.

Water: figures for travel by water include both domestic and international passenger-carrying services of UK registered merchant vessels.

Road: figures refer to Great Britain and include accidents occurring on the public highway (including footways) in which at least one road vehicle or a vehicle in collision with a pedestrian is involved and which becomes known to the police within 30 days of its occurrence. Figures include both public and private transport.

Bus or coach: figures for work buses are included. From 1 January 1994 the casualty definition was revised to include only those vehicles equipped to carry 17 or more passengers regardless of use. Before 1994 these vehicles were coded according to construction, whether or not they were being used for carrying passengers. Vehicles constructed as buses that were privately licensed were included under 'bus and coach' but Public Service Vehicle (PSV) licensed minibuses were included under cars.

Car: includes taxis, invalid tricycles, three-wheeled and four-wheeled cars and minibuses. Before 1999 motorcaravans were also included.

Van: vans mainly include vehicles of the van type constructed on a car chassis. From 1 January 1994 these are defined as those vehicles not over 3.5 tonnes maximum permissible gross vehicle weight. Before 1994 the weight definition was not over 1.524 tonnes unladen.

Two-wheeled motor vehicle: mopeds, motor scooters and motor cycles (including motor cycle combinations).

Pedal cycle: includes tandems, tricycles and toy cycles ridden on the carriageway.

Pedestrian: includes persons riding toy cycles on the footway, persons pushing bicycles, pushing or pulling other vehicles or operating pedestrian controlled vehicles, those leading or herding animals, occupants of prams or wheelchairs, and people who alight safely from vehicles and are subsequently injured.

Part 13: Lifestyles and social participation

Media Literacy Audit

A total of 1,335 'core' interviews were conducted in English with parents and children aged between 8 and 11 (672 interviews) and between 12 and 15 (664 interviews) along with a 'boost' interview of 201 children from ethnic minority groups. All interviews were conducted in the respondent's home, with certain questions asked of parents and the remaining questions asked of the child. Interviews conducted with the children aged between 8 and 11 took an average of 15 minutes to complete, and interviews with those aged between 12 and 15 took an average of 25 minutes to complete. Parents were allowed to stay with their child during the interview, although the interviewer explained that it would be preferable to interview the child alone in case the parent's presence altered the child's responses. In most cases a parent was present while their child was being interviewed: for 656 of the 772 interviews with those aged between 8 and 11 and for 508 of the 764 interviews with those aged between 12 and 15. Interviewers conducting the research recorded very few incidences of parents answering on behalf of their child or influencing the responses.

Internet connection

There are two types of Internet connection:

- *Narrowband:* The computer uses the telephone line to dial up an Internet connection. Because narrowband access uses normal telephone lines, the quality of the connection can vary and data rates are limited. A narrowband user cannot be online and use the telephone to make calls at the same time.

- *Broadband:* Broadband access to the Internet is many times faster than dial-up access, and is typically always on (so there is no need to dial up or 'connect' each time for access). There are several ways that a broadband connection can be delivered. The two most common methods are through cable or a digital subscriber line (DSL). Cable modems deliver an Internet connection through the same cables that deliver cable television, whereas a DSL line uses normal telephone lines.

London theatre district

The London theatre district consists mainly of commercial theatres but also is home to the larger grant-aided theatres: The National Theatre, The Barbican, The Royal Court, Sadler's Wells, The Royal Opera House and The London Coliseum. The majority of theatres in London are in the West End, which is traditionally defined by The Strand to the south, Oxford Street to the north, Regent Street to the west, and Kingsway to the east.

Taking Part survey

The aim of the Taking Part survey is to find out how people choose to spend their own time and their views on the leisure activities and facilities available to them. The main sectors for which data are gathered in the Taking Part survey are:

- the arts
- museums and galleries
- libraries
- archives
- heritage and
- sport

For each of these sectors data are collected regarding the frequency of participation/attendance and the reasons why people do and do not participate or attend.

The estimates in Figure 13.12 and Table 13.13 are based on interviews over a nine-month period (mid-July 2005 to mid-April 2006). The estimates are provisional as final weights will not be applied to the data until the full year's data have been gathered. For the nine-month period temporary weights have been applied. Given the timescale of the data and the nature of the activities, the estimates will be influenced by seasonality.

Parliamentary elections

A general election must be held at least every five years, or sooner if the Prime Minister of the day so decides. At the May 2005 election there were 646 constituencies, each of which returns one Member of Parliament to the House of Commons. Constituency boundaries are determined by the Boundary Commissions (one each for England, Scotland, Wales and Northern Ireland). These Commissions are required to undertake a general review every 8 to 12 years to ensure electoral equality – that is that the size of the electorate in each constituency is as similar as possible (currently about 70,000 electors, typically reflecting a total population of 90,000).

Measurement of religion

The BSA question *'Do you regard yourself as belonging to any particular religion?'* produces a much smaller proportion of Christians and a much larger proportion of people with no religion compared with the Census question, *'What is your religion?'* Part of the difference is because the two surveys cover different populations and a further difference is bought about by the different wording of the questions. The Census question may suggest an expectation that people would have a religion while the BSA question introduced the possibility that people might not have a religion. For more information see *Focus on Ethnicity and Religion 2006*, available on the ONS website:

www.statistics.gov.uk/downloads/theme_ compendia/foer2006/FoER_main.pdf

Index

The references in this index relate to chapters, to figure, table and map numbers. Analyses by sex will generally be found under their main entries.